Why and how has race become a central aspect of politics during this century? This book addresses this pressing question by comparing apartheid and resistance to it in South Africa, the Jim Crow laws and protests against them in the United States, and the myth of racial democracy in Brazil. Anthony Marx argues that these divergent experiences had roots in the history of slavery, colonialism, miscegenation, and culture, but were fundamentally shaped by efforts and elite bargains to build national unity. In South Africa and the United States, ethnic or regional conflicts among whites were gradually resolved by unifying whites as a race and excluding blacks, while Brazil's longer-established national unity required no such legal racist crutch. Race was thus central to projects of nation building, and nationalism shaped uses of race. Professor Marx extends this argument to explain popular protest and the current salience of issues of race, and to suggest how building national unity also builds upon and reinforces social divisions more generally.

Making Race and Nation

Cambridge Studies in Comparative Poliltics

General Editor
Peter Lange, *Duke University*

Associate Editors
Robert H. Bates, *Harvard University*
Ellen Comisso, *University of California, San Diego*
Peter Hall, *Harvard University*
Joel Migdal, *University of Washington*
Helen Milner, *Columbia University*
Ronald Rogowski, *University of California, Los Angeles*
Sidney Tarrow, *Cornell University*

Other Books in the Series

Making Race and Nation

A COMPARISON OF
SOUTH AFRICA,
THE UNITED STATES,
AND BRAZIL

ANTHONY W. MARX
Columbia University

CAMBRIDGE
UNIVERSITY PRESS

PUBLISHED BY THE PRESS SYNDICATE OF THE UNIVERSITY OF CAMBRIDGE
The Pitt Building, Trumpington Street, Cambridge, United Kingdom

CAMBRIDGE UNIVERSITY PRESS
The Edinburgh Building, Cambridge CB2 2RU, UK
40 West 20th Street, New York, NY 10011-4211, USA
477 Williamstown Road, Port Melbourne, VIC 3207, Australia
Ruiz de Alarcón 13, 28014 Madrid, Spain
Dock House, The Waterfront, Cape Town 8001, South Africa

http://www.cambridge.org

First published 1998
First paperback edition 1998
Reprinted 1999, 2002

Printed in the United States of America

Typeset in Janson

A catalog record for this book is available from the British Library

Library of Congress Cataloging in Publication data is available

ISBN 0 521 58455 8 hardback
ISBN 0 521 58590 2 paperback

For Karen

Contents

CONTENTS

Preface and Acknowledgments

This is not the book I intended to write. I have written previously on the emergence of race, national and class identity, and varying forms of mobilization in South Africa. In doing so, I became intrigued by the parallels with ideology and strategies of protest pursued by African-Americans. There seemed to be odd similarities, given the dramatic differences in context, not least demographic differences. I then became further intrigued by the case of Brazil. Given South African and American experiences, it seemed surprising that comparable racial inequalities in Brazil were not more fully challenged. So I added Brazil to what expected to be a comparative study of racial mobilization.

What then accounts for the divergences? The obvious answer was that South Africa and to a lesser extent the United States had imposed legal segregation, with nothing comparable having been enforced in post-abolition Brazil. If this helped to explain the corresponding difference in levels and forms of identity consolidation and mobilization, then I had to explain why Jim Crow segregation and apartheid developed, and such legal institutions did not in Brazil. A comparative study of black politics forced me into a related study of different forms of white supremacy, which themselves required explanation. And addressing this new concern forced me back in time, for surely such policies were grounded in the legacies of slavery, colonialism, culture, earlier solidarities, and economic development. Thus, to answer the initial question of what accounts for differences in black protest, I was propelled into a much bigger and broader comparative study of interacting institutional and identity formation.

The results of this study are here presented in the reverse order in which they emerged in my initial thinking. Logic and consistency suggest beginning with the historical contexts, particularly in regard to determinants of Brazil's "exceptionalism." I then incorporate past legacies into an explanation of "race making" as connected to the processes of nation-state consolidation, beginning with analysis of the most draconian case of South Africa. The state emerges as a major actor in explaining the imposition of official rules of racial exclusion and domination. But this obvious point does not account for why states, responding to both external pressures and internal divisions, did or did not establish such rules. Nor does it explain how race was so constructed and used in varying forms. It is this dependent outcome that this book seeks first to explain. I then argue that black identity and protest – building upon earlier emergent racial solidarity – were shaped by state policies, and those policies were later reversed in response to the protests they had provoked. Thus, "white" and "black" politics were inextricably connected in racial dynamics, though they have too often been studied in relative isolation. Analysis of race making requires examination of processes and assertions from both above and below.

To pursue this comparison, it is imperative not to reify what is meant by race. To do so would be to fall into the trap of essentialism. Assumptions of primordial difference and pervasive race prejudice did emerge, but from distinct histories, and informing varying practices. This study seeks to explain how such different meanings and uses of race emerged. Even the terms "black" and "white" remain unfortunate shorthand for socially constructed and varying identities. Indeed, the process by which who is signified by these terms was established remains a central concern, logically prior to the more conventional political question of who gets what, when, and how.

To explain how and whether prejudice was legally encoded, I put forward a theory of race making that acknowledges the intentionality of actors within and outside the state. I argue that amid contestation elites strike bargains and deploy state authority to unify a core constituency of whites within the nation-state by excluding blacks. Put simply, racial domination or the lack thereof did serve strategic purposes of coalition building by those in power. The nation-state and economy were thereby preserved and developed. But racial domination had unforeseen consequences, most notably in provoking "black–white" conflict.

Again, I am eager not to reify. The state is not a unitary actor, and policy outcomes cannot be explained by reducing all else to the state. The social science tendency to talk about what states "do" gives a false impression, for states are multifaceted and permeable to outside influences. States do act, for instance in codifying racial orders, but such policies emerge in fits and starts, shaped by different histories and state structures, trial and error, continued conflict and competition. State elites do pursue the goal of stability, and did effectively use racial domination toward that end. But what appears "functional" in retrospect was not, for "the system" was itself divided and fought over, rather than unitary in its impositions. Indeed, the very nature or form of states, and of nations, was shaped by such contestation. It is this process that I also hope to elucidate, suggesting a new approach to understanding nation-state building and related social cleavages.

The story that emerges here has one driving force. Those pursuing or in power in each country seek to gain or preserve that power by "whatever means necessary." Elites generally seek peace, among themselves and with subordinates, for stability preserves them in power and maintains the aura of legitimacy. Even when elites engage in war, they often do so to preserve or restore the status quo and stability. Peace is also essential for economic development, by which elites enrich themselves and fund the instrument of the state. Race making emerges from this combined political and economic imperative. That said, I hasten to add that who the elites are, their own divisions, how they understand and categorize themselves, are also fluid. Similarly, the historical challenges that elites face also change and mesh. History does not present "problems" or "solutions" in discrete stages. I will try to avoid implying the contrary in what follows, despite the temptations of periodization.

What I present here is an analytic essay on historical variation inside and across cases, with all the defects and virtues of this form. To account for important historical processes, I may be accused of selectivity, though I hope thereby to reveal key issues that are decisive and not otherwise clear. There are of course other stories and explanations, but as in all such attempts, I make wagers of willful distortion, as it is impossible to capture fully all complexity. Others will judge if these wagers pay off. Those committed to alternative explanations may not be convinced, but I hope they will be provoked to further consideration.

A note on methodology and research is important. This study is informed by historical studies and by sociological theory, but it remains an instance of comparative politics. I combine a focus on historical institutions, such as the state, with analysis of the social forces that built, impinged upon, and divided institutional actors and identities. The result is a rather eclectic approach, incorporating the histories of three countries, itself an impossible task to fulfill, relying on secondary sources checked for bias, archives, primary documents and interviews, and building narratives to solve problems that have long bedeviled analysis.

This study seeks to explain major developments in three countries, though I am cognizant that the experiences of each interacted and informed each other. Brazilians were eager to avoid the sort of conflict that had torn apart the United States in the Civil War. South Africans were aware of Jim Crow in the United States. Americans were eager to avoid the sort of conflict that came to engulf South Africa after the mid-twentieth century, and were inspired by the image of Brazil's "racial democracy." Afro-Brazilians and black South Africans were inspired by the American civil rights and Black Power movements. African-Americans were inspired by South Africa's anti-apartheid movement. The stories are interconnected, though they are presented here somewhat more discretely. Presenting this study in thematic sections, rather than by fully separating the cases, encourages consideration of both general patterns and historical interconnections.

The complexity and interconnectedness of the history of South Africa, the United States, and Brazil emerge in historical narrative, but were reinforced for me by my own research experiences. Informants were often fascinated by the comparison, as were earlier analysts and actors. The timing of my study surely reinforced my own engagement with the comparison. I found myself interviewing George Wallace in his Montgomery sickbed, and a month later attending Nelson Mandela's inauguration in Pretoria. The South African Defense Force saluted its new commander and former adversary with a dramatic fly-by of jets. Central state authority was passed to its former nemesis. Back in the United States, such central state authority was itself being newly challenged by an assertion of states' rights led by the Republican Party – the same party that had defended the Union under Lincoln. And then I found myself in Brazil talking to black activists just before a former scholar of Brazilian race relations was elected to the presidency. Under such circumstances and juxtaposition, comparison came alive.

Living in and studying contentious issues of race in three countries also reaffirmed for me the importance of getting the comparison right. In each country, historical interpretations and policy prescriptions often made reference to the other two cases. Such comparison was often ill informed and problematic in its implications. For instance, in 1991 Nelson Mandela traveled to Brazil, hailing that country's "racial democracy" as a model for South Africa, much as American liberals had hailed Brazil's tolerance during the 1960s. Afro-Brazilian activists were quick to correct Mandela's false impression and analogy, urging him not to accept Brazil's inequality as a model for his own country. Mandela's staff described to me his dismay in finding that the impression of Brazil's racial tolerance, so widely credited when he was jailed in 1963, was no longer accepted after his release twenty-seven years later. Understandings of Brazilian reality had progressed, informed by comparison. I hope here to add to such analytic progress.

My research was made possible by a number of collections. In the United States, I benefited from the Martin Luther King Center Archive in Atlanta, the Oral History project at Columbia University and its libraries, the New York Public Library, and the archive of the Joint Center for Economic and Policy Studies in Washington; in Brazil from the archive of the Center for Afro-Asiatic Studies in Rio de Janeiro; and in South Africa from numerous archives of political organizations, unions, universities, and individuals.

I also drew heavily from several hundred interviews, conducted in English and Portuguese (often combined with Spanish). Of course, interviews were limited to those living and willing, and then had to be subjected to cross-checking to diminish retrospective or self-interested bias. I remain most grateful to all those who agreed to be subjected to my note pads and tape recorder.

This leads me directly to acknowledge all those who have been of help in this project. I cannot hope to be exhaustive in this happy endeavor.

My first note of thanks is to an institution, Columbia University, where I have pursued this study over the last six years. I am acutely conscious of the shoulders on which I stand here, going back at least to Boaz, Schermerhorn, and Tannenbaum. I have often been inspired and amused to find myself in rooms or buildings named after these predecessors, some of whose findings I here dispute.

Among the current scholars at Columbia and Barnard, my debts are many. I can only here list those to whom I am most grateful: Karen Barkey, Alan Brinkley, Douglas Chalmers, Jean Cohen, Barbara Fields, Herb Gans, Charles V. Hamilton, Patrick Heller, David Johnston, Mark Kesselman, Herbert Klein, Robert Lieberman, Manning Marable, Peter Marcuse, Kelly Moore, Robert Shapiro, Jack Snyder, Steve Solnick, Philip Thompson, and Harrison White. Eric Foner and Charles Tilly in particular provided invaluable comments on the entire manuscript. And Ira Katznelson has throughout generously provided extraordinary guidance, valuable suggestions, and warm encouragement. These acknowledgments demonstrate how lucky I have been to pursue this study at this place.

For my research in and on Brazil, and for comments on the manuscript or ideas, I am most grateful to Carlos Hasenbalg, Nelson do Valle Silva, Rebecca Reichmann, Anani Dzidzienyo, Anthony Pereira, and all the folks at the Center for Afro-Asiatic Studies in Rio who offered their hospitality and help. Working at the Center was a great inspiration, as was the view from my office window looking out onto Guanabarra Bay and the Ilha das Cobras, from which Brazil's last emperor set sail.

For study in and on South Africa, I continue to be indebted to John and Nora Samuel, Mark Orkin, Jenny Glennie, Francis and Lindy Wilson, Rupert Taylor, Dunbar Moodie, Tom Lodge, Stephen Ellman, Neville Alexander, and Tom Karis, who reviewed the entire manuscript. This help was all the more invaluable during the 1980s when the South African authorities sought unsuccessfully to prevent my research. An office I used at CASE in Johannesburg did not have the majestic scenic view I later enjoyed in Rio, but it did on occasion look out onto an impressive sea of protestors in the street.

I am also grateful for the advice offered by Benedict Anderson, Jeff Goodwin, David Laitin, Lloyd Rudolph, James Scott, Sidney Tarrow, Louise Tilly, and anonymous reviewers. William Julius Wilson and Jennifer Hochschild provided invaluable suggestions on the entire manuscript. Conversations with Mahmood Mamdani, Eric Hobsbawm, and the late Claude Ake were more helpful than they could imagine. Claude will now be much missed. Sheldon and Lucy Hackney have consistently offered warm encouragement and wisdom. And I continue to be guided by the inspiration of former teachers: Robert Lane, Robert Dahl, Henry Bienen, Albert O. Hirschman, and Theda Skocpol.

Opportunities to present summaries or sections of this study have been provided by the American Political Science Association, the African Studies Association, the Social Science History Association, the American Sociological Association, the Committee on Historical Studies at the New School for Social Research, the South Africa Study Group based at New York Law School, the Center for Afro-Asiatic Studies in Rio de Janeiro, the Faculty of Social Sciences of the Federal University of Rio de Janeiro, the Wilder House Workshop on Comparative Politics at the University of Chicago, Princeton University, and the Comparative Race Relations Initiative of the Southern Education Foundation. Similar opportunities were provided at Columbia, by the Institute for Latin American and Iberian Studies, the Identities Workshop of the Center for the Social Sciences, the Comparative Politics Workshop, and the Institute for Research in African-American Studies. I am also particularly grateful for the insights gained from my students, both at Columbia and at Yale. Logistical support has been provided by Columbia's Institute for African Studies, under the leadership of George Bond and Ron Kassimir.

Funding for this project has been provided by the United States Institute of Peace, the Social Science Research Council and American Council of Learned Societies' Joint Committee on Latin America, the National Endowment for the Humanities, the Tinker Foundation Fellowships of Columbia's Institute for Latin American and Iberian Studies, and the Harry Frank Guggenheim Foundation.

At Cambridge University Press, Alex Holzman has been a much-valued critic, editor, and ally. It has been a pleasure to work with him and his colleague Aura Lippincott-Daluz, and with copyeditor W. M. Havighurst – all authors should be so fortunate.

Finally, thanks to my parents, family and friends – Mom and Dad, Jak and Tuna, Henri and Ellen, Debby and Chip, Andrew and Kristen, David and Monica, Josh and Cathy, Paul and Marisol, Claire and Tasia. But most importantly I am grateful to Joshua and Karen. If Joshua had not cooperated, not least by sleeping through the night during his first two years, when this book was largely written, I surely would have collapsed. Throughout, he remained an inspiration and joy. The next book will be for him. And without Karen's love, support, ideas, and encouragement, I would not have made it to finish this project. She is my inspiration as teacher and scholar, and my life companion. I dedicate this book to her.

1

Introduction

W. E. B. Du Bois called "the problem of the color line" the pivotal question for the twentieth century.[1] In South Africa, the United States, and elsewhere, the century has brought both reinforcements of the color line and militant struggles against it. Momentous conflict has confounded expectations that racial domination and mobilization, supposedly archaic residues of another age, would simply wither away. Far from displacing race as an issue, industrialization, class conflict, rising nationalism, and state consolidation have actually spurred racially defined contention. As a result, struggle centers increasingly on state action or inaction. The end of Du Bois's fateful century challenges us to rethink the links between racial conflict and nation-state building and development.

The initial driving force of this study is a major puzzle of widespread concern: What accounts for twentieth-century race relations? This question can be broken down into more manageable parts, though each impinges on the others. How, and to what extent, were such relations prefigured by earlier history? How did political and economic processes during this century shape divergent racial orders? And how did challenges from below emerge, interact with, and force changes in racial domination from above? My approach to these issues is comparative, rejecting U.S. exceptionalism without diminishing the distinctiveness of that or other cases.

Discrimination according to race predates this century and became pervasive where Europeans sought to justify their rule. But modern, official policy did not always build upon prejudice to encode racial domination, or did so in varying forms of exclusion from citizenship rights. Similar early practices of discrimination did not consistently produce the same legal racial orders and outcomes. And whether the state was so deployed to enforce racial domination shaped all other aspects of race relations. Where authorities legally reinforced discrimination, the unintended result was major social conflict between those who ruled via exclusion and those demanding inclusion in the polity. In the absence of official racial domination, such conflict was muted.

States made race: amid pervasive discrimination, official actions enforced racial distinctions or did not, with profound consequences. This state-centered argument builds upon and incorporates previous explanations of modern race relations. But to argue simply that states can and do impose official racial domination – that states enact such state policies – is tautological. The key is to explain *why* states so act. Specific state policy is historically embedded, reflects ideology, is constrained by dominant political and economic claims, and responds to protests. Under what circumstances do each of these particular factors become salient, and with what results?

Political and economic elites have consistently been eager to ensure the stability of their societies by building institutions of coercion and coordination. By consolidating state power within varying structures, they sought to preserve their power, to bolster their legitimacy, and to provide the conditions for economic growth. But such stability was often undermined by major violent conflict, such as the British–Afrikaner ethnic conflict in South Africa and the North–South regional conflict in the United States, dividing prominent loyalties. To diminish these conflicts, elites acted strongly to strike bargains, selling out blacks and reinforcing prior racial distinctions and ideology in order to unify whites. The state instantiated "white nationalism," with the torque of this enforced racial identity proving powerful enough to integrate populations otherwise at war and engaged in ongoing competition. "To bind up the nation's wounds" among whites, blacks were bound down, and the wound of race was left to fester. Polities were shaped by this dynamic, with varying forms of official racial domination in South Africa and the American South persisting until black opposition replaced intrawhite conflict as the most pressing challenge to the nation-state. Brazil, by contrast, with relatively little intrawhite conflict, was less pressured to reconcile whites via racial domination, and the state instead embraced the ideology of "racial democracy," even amid continued discrimination.

Analysis of race making may then tell us something more generalizable about the processes and effects of nation-state building through either exclusion or inclusion. Not only have such institutional rules consolidated particular social cleavages, but manipulation of cleavages such as race or ethnicity has also shaped how dominant institutions and loyalty to them were built. Selective exclusion was not tangential to nation-state building, as liberals argue, but was instead central to how social order was maintained.[2] If constructions of race and of nation-states have been so linked as prominent developments of this century, focusing on the former will also reveal fundamental aspects of nation-state building not otherwise apparent.

Bounding the State and Institutionalizing Identities

Racial domination rests on a distinction of peoples according to categories of physical difference. Until at least the mid twentieth century, people of European ancestry generally assumed that such racial demarcations reflected natural white superiority. The color line was seen as having been drawn by God or biology. Slavery, proscriptions against miscegenation, colonialism, imperialism, manifest destiny, racially exclusive forms of citizenship or nationalism, and exploitation were all justified by whites as preordained in nature.[3] Such racism became "a mode of thought endemic in Western civilization,"[4] buttressed by eugenics, social Darwinism, and explicitly racist theories such as those of Count Gobineau.[5] Primordialism serving the interests of whites made the domination of darker peoples seem inescapable.

Assumptions of natural racial distinctions, as notably enforced by the Nazis, have been refuted. After the Second World War, the scientific community reached a consensus that race had no scientific basis.[6] Categorical distinctions of race were recognized to be artificial and inconsistent with the continuum of skin color evident in the world's increasingly mixed population. If biology did not draw the color line, then race had no basis in fact. Marx and Engels had earlier argued that "all fixed, fast-frozen relations, with their train of ancient and venerable prejudices and opinions, are swept away" by class conflict.[7] Following Weber and Durkheim, liberals also assumed that as mere myth such a distinction would fade with development or assimilation.[8] They were wrong.

Vicious discrimination has remained, even if particular forms of racial domination varied. "Modernity has not sealed off the pathway to this bottomless depth of sorrow and chaos," but rather reinforced aspersions of human difference.[9] Describing race as having no basis in science did not dispel its power as myth. Prejudice has continued to serve as a criterion of stratification, embedded in economic relations, political institutions, and ideology.[10] If the basis of such distinctions was not naturally ascriptive, then it had to be socially constructed. But seeing race as situational only begins the analysis of why and how such lines are drawn. Specifying where this process is centered can help in understanding it.

Domination has been officially encoded in racial terms, suggesting that the state plays a role in constructing and enforcing the institutional boundaries of race. And as social movements have developed against racial domination, such protest reflects the terms of that state rule. The state sets the focal point for analysis, providing clues about the interconnected processes of race making from above and below. Following Weber, if public policy by the state makes explicit the terms of domination or resistance,[11] then it should be possible to so specify these processes. And briefly adopting the shorthand of analyzing the state focuses the question of what states do, before turning to the question of why.[12]

States are compulsory and continuous associations claiming control of society within a territory. They differ over time and place in their capacity to rule, in their autonomous power, and in their particular forms. But all states seek to contain challenges or instability threatening order and growth. To do so, ruling elites structure relations between states and civil society, shaping norms and reinforcing social and political identities accordingly.[13] The central identity encouraged by states is that of the nation, defined as the popular loyalty of a population held together in being obliged to serve and be served by the state.[14] By encouraging allegiance to the nation, states enhance their claimed monopoly of legitimacy.[15] Accordingly, state elites and others have been inspired by the goal of the nation-state, a coincidence of institutional rule and allegiance to it that would diminish internal conflict. As John Stuart Mill argued, "the boundaries of governments should coincide in the main with those of nationalities" or "fellow-feelings."[16]

Benedict Anderson has suggested that the nation emerges as an "imagined community."[17] His argument discusses preconditions for the emergence of such nationalist solidarity. Economic development,

4

literacy, mass communication, education, and urbanization make possible the emergence of such expansive loyalty, but this implies a more spontaneous and inclusive process of nation building than was often the case. Official boundaries purposefully defined and enforced who was imagined as part of the nation and who was not.[18] Such imaginings were often not benign. Where states were formed before a nation emerged, the explicit efforts of the state to limit and encourage selective nationalism are particularly evident. Specified exclusion has provided a crucial referent demarcating those included.[19] In such instances, group formation, identities, ideas, and "social categories . . . are shaped, manifested and entrenched through the state."[20] Inclusion then solidifies loyalty among those officially incorporated. While such nationalism may erode certain group loyalties by their inclusion, it also reinforces solidarity among others purposefully excluded.[21]

Citizenship is a key institutional mechanism for establishing boundaries of inclusion or exclusion in the nation-state.[22] It selectively allocates distinct civil, political, and economic rights, reinforcing a sense of commonality and loyalty among those included.[23] But by specifying to whom citizenship applies, states also define those outside the community of citizens, who then live within the state as objects of domination. Even in formal democracies, some are not included nor have their interests served. Such imposed exclusion inadvertently may serve as a unifying issue, mobilizing the excluded group to seek inclusion in the polity as a central popular aspiration.[24] Gradual expansion of citizenship is then gained through protracted contestation.[25] The goal of gaining citizenship rights, which were not originally universal, thus has often served as a frame for mobilization.[26] Extending a provocative analogy, groups use their voice to overcome their enduring and forced exit from the polity.[27]

The process of defining the nation with rules of citizenship is of obvious relevance for how racial categories are established and reinforced. Coercive powers have been used to define citizenship according to race – states bind the nation they claim to represent by institutionalizing identities of racial inclusion and exclusion. The extension of citizenship rights has been blocked by constructing racial boundaries. Barbara Fields has suggested that such official racial domination began at a particular historical moment, when the modern nation-state emerged.[28]

States then play a central role in imposing the terms of official

5

domination, with unintended consequences. Official exclusion, as by race, legitimates these categories as a form of social identity, building upon and reshaping historical and cultural solidarities. In the short run, such exclusion benefits those included and hurts others. But in the longer run, institutionalized exclusion may further consolidate subordinate identity and encourages self-interested mobilization and protest. State-sanctioned racial categories impose real costs on their subjects but also offer oppressed populations both legal grounds for redress and bases for political mobilization. The reverse reasoning would also hold. Where and when a state does not impose categorical exclusion, potential subordinates are not so directly disadvantaged. But in the longer run, the preferable absence of such exclusion also may deprive informally subordinated peoples of an unavoidable demarcation unifying them as a group. Ironically, the lack of official racial domination then becomes an obstacle to effective collective action forcing redress of real inequality. In either case, state rule and solidarity from below continually interact.

Arguing that states have the capacity to establish racial boundaries of citizenship, provoking resistance accordingly, does not explain why a state does or does not enforce a racial cleavage. Such an explanation must be cognizant that the state is itself not unitary, but reflects divisions of the society in which it is imbedded, and is itself often torn by competing global, national, and local pressures. For instance, does the state construct and use race because of international pressures, to preserve itself, to ensure revenues, to meet specific interests, to avoid class conflict, or to reflect popular racist beliefs? To proceed further, it is useful to turn to comparative historical analysis, looking both inside the state and outside to its social context. How autonomous was the state? How consequential were different state structures? The analytic category of "the state," though suggestive, must be broken down to explain the motives for particular forms of nation building and for specific official policies and outcomes.

Comparing and Excavating Historical Foundations

South Africa, the United States, and Brazil are the three most prominent cases in which European settlers dominated indigenous populations or slaves of African origin. In all three of these major regional powers, modern social and economic indicators demonstrate significant disparities between black and white. The legacies of slavery and of conquest established a common pattern of discrimination.[29] Indeed, there has been a rich tradition of comparison between two or three of these "big three" cases, the histories of which have often interacted.[30]

The common history of racial dynamics, so understood, makes the comparison of South Africa, the United States, and Brazil obvious. Their differences make comparison fruitful. Given earlier economic development in the United States and other significant variations of history, culture, state structures, and demography, the similarities in South African and U.S. rhetoric and practices of racial domination are striking, particularly in regard to segregation policies between the world wars.[31] There has also been remarkable comparability in the ideology and strategy of resistance challenging racial domination.[32] Yet a dichotomy of racial domination and conflict in South Africa and the United States, contrasted with Brazil's so-called racial democracy and relatively mild black protest, is too simple. Despite the commonality of early discrimination and maintained inequality, post abolition state policies encoded differing racial orders, with varying results. South African apartheid was more centrally imposed and pervasive than was Jim Crow segregation and exclusion in the more decentralized post-Reconstruction United States. And if South African race relations bark most loudly and the United States a bit more softly, why was Brazil the dog that didn't bark? These divergent outcomes present a useful puzzle.

Including Brazil is pivotal, reminding us that legal racial domination was not inevitable. While South Africa and the United States used earlier discrimination as the base for constructing continued racial domination, the connection between past and present in Brazil is more problematic. There, early prejudice and large-scale slavery seem oddly inconsistent with the later absence of legal segregation. This apparent disconnect between the foundation of historical discrimination and modern policies might be reconciled by rejecting the rosy Brazilian self-image of post-abolition racial democracy. But while discrimination and inequality are evident in modern Brazil, the lack of any official policy comparable to either apartheid or Jim Crow remains remarkable. Alternatively, Brazil's past may have been particularly tolerant, prefiguring its present, as argued by Gilberto Freyre.[33] But Brazil had imported an African population widely denigrated as "forever constituting one of the causes of our inferiority as a people."[34] If the historical record contradicts the thesis of early tolerance, Brazil's later racial order was not so preordained. Instead, the past was reconceived into a benign image, unlike elsewhere. Belief in racial tolerance was thereby reinforced, the legacy of inequality was camouflaged, and quiescence among Afro-Brazilians was encouraged. Brazil's distinctiveness did not then rest upon less historical discrimination, but rather in the country's purposeful denial of that legacy. What accounts for this divergence?

The most obvious difference of conditions across the three cases here compared is demographic. There is an indigenous African majority in South Africa, a roughly equal mix of African and European ancestry in Brazil, and an African-descendant minority in the United States (though some Southern states had close to a majority black population by the mid-nineteenth century).[35] This demographic difference was consequential, but does not coincide with the continuum of outcomes. A black majority in South Africa and a black minority in the United States were subject to more or less strict forms of post-abolition legal exclusion by race, while in the intermediate case, Afro-Brazilians were not.

Differences of early labor coercion also do not correspond with later outcomes. To meet labor needs not met by indigenous populations, the Southern United States and Brazil engaged in massive importation of slaves from Africa, becoming the two largest slaveholder societies in modern history.[36] But out of these legacies of extensive bondage, the United States later enacted legal segregation and Brazil did not. Tannenbaum argued that Brazil's post-abolition racial democracy was the result of a more humanitarian form of slavery, influenced by Catholic doctrines of natural equality, and the historical record does suggest that Brazilian slavery permitted some greater rights for slaves and a higher level of manumission than elsewhere.[37] But the overriding fact remains that Brazilian slavery was one of the most extensive forms in history, particularly brutal and deadly. Even the Church itself owned slaves and was long unable to force abolition.[38] Though Brazilian slavery (and Catholic influences over it) certainly took different forms than elsewhere, to call it "humanitarian" is absurd.

Slavery established heinous patterns of discrimination in both Brazil and the United States, and so differences in their common systems of extensive slavery cannot directly explain their later divergence of racial orders. Indeed, if a softening of slavery in itself predetermined later tolerance, then South Africa's greater dependence on free indigenous labor and British-imposed abolition as early as 1833 should have produced the most tolerant racial order of the three cases. But South Africa, with its more limited legacy of slavery, enacted the most pernicious form of institutionalized racism.

Analysts have also suggested that Brazil's post-abolition racial democracy was a bequest of early patterns of Portuguese colonialism. But was such colonialism more racially tolerant than that imposed by the British or Dutch in South Africa and the United States? Again, the historical record suggests not. Portuguese colonialism was distinctive in the greater extent and longevity of direct, centralized state involvement, but the Portuguese state used its power to maintain slavery, to impose its own color bar, and to establish discrimination against blacks in Brazil as in its African colonies.[39] Such early state practices cannot then be credited for having imported early racial tolerance.

A final historical explanation for Brazil's relative tolerance is that the high level of miscegenation made it impossible to draw strict racial boundaries. The mobility of mulattoes purportedly made strict segregation and discrimination unworkable. According to Carl Degler, "the mulatto escape hatch" of advancement vitiated any efforts at imposing a harsh racial order.[40] High levels of miscegenation practiced by outnumbered and disproportionately male Portuguese are a historical fact. And free mulattoes did serve intermediary functions of control over slaves. But few mulattoes advanced very far and most were and remained subject to discrimination comparable to that suffered by blacks.[41] The image of mulatto mobility is largely a myth.

Comparison further suggests that the existence of a large number of mulattoes is not in itself sufficient to produce or explain later tolerance. In both South Africa and the United States there was a substantial intermediate population, but this did not prevent authorities from eventually grouping these mixed peoples with blacks as common victims of racial domination. The higher proportion of mulattoes in Brazil would have made comparable segregation more difficult, but not impossible. That Brazil did not attempt to go down this road cannot be explained by the history of miscegenation, but rather by how this fact was interpreted and how categories were constructed.

None of this is to deny the importance of early historical legacies, but rather to demonstrate that the past did not directly prefigure later outcomes of legal racial orders. Instead, nationalists would shape historical interpretations and omissions to legitimate the present, with such uses of history and culture subject to contestation.[42]

Constructing Racial Domination

Legacies of prior relations, slavery, and ideology laid a foundation for later and varying social constructions, specifying race as a salient issue. But as Brazil most notably demonstrates, the past may be affirmed or reinvented, according to particular biases, as history is brought forward. The modern house of race in each country was built on similar foundations of prejudice, but constructed according to varying circumstances. Like a Roman church built on top of an older basilica covered by the debris of time, the modern structures of racial order settled on top of the older constructions of discrimination. But they were built according to modern specifications, with architects and their critics disputing renovations. The result was a conjuncture of old and new. Why and how was the past carried forward or denied?

The import of inherited conditions and ideas in shaping state policy may be most evident at key turning points, when lengthy processes are crystallized. In the aftermath of abolition and state consolidation during the late nineteenth or early twentieth century, South Africa, the United States, and Brazil all faced extended moments of relative indeterminacy and an unhappy repertoire of alternative possible configurations of race relations. With the formation of South Africa after Britain's Boer War victory, with abolition and the U.S. North's Civil War victory, and abolition and republic in Brazil, the issue of whether and how to include free blacks in the polity could not be avoided. Focusing on such pivotal historical moments may help to explain why forms of racial domination were enacted or not.[43] At the same time, such turning points can only be understood in the broader historical context in which they developed.[44]

The dilemma of whether and how to incorporate an African descendant population had long divided whites, undermining whites' potential loyalty to the state. The more contentious the issue had been, the greater the degree of resolution required. Ruling elites had to manage conflict and design race relations anew, to resolve or avoid division among whites that could threaten central rule, stability, and development. Without a solution, instability would disrupt political consolidation of the nation-state and economic growth. Particularly in South Africa and the United States, ruling elites faced problems of white disunity exacerbated by disputes over the future treatment of blacks.[45] Their overriding interest in order and security required building a unifying racial order, to which ideals of equality, freedom, and justice were subordinated.[46] Their solutions built upon ideologies of racism that had emerged to defend exploitation or slavery against liberal reform factions.

Was there something similar about transitional moments in South Africa and the United States, but different for Brazil, that can account for the pattern of outcomes? One possible answer stands out immediately. Abolition and/or state consolidation in South Africa and the United States emerged out of the bloodiest conflicts in the histories of those countries, while Brazil suffered nothing remotely comparable to the Boer War or Civil War.[47] This divergence fits the general pattern of outcomes. But why would imperial conquest or internal wars and their aftereffects have produced apartheid and Jim Crow? Indeed, just the opposite might seem logical. It was the more liberal abolitionist British and Northerners who won those wars, yet later policies toward blacks were closer to those advocated by the defeated Afrikaners and Southerners. Something more than who won was at work. Furthermore, why would the lack of major internal war result in the absence of official racial domination in Brazil? Again this result is counterintuitive. The more peaceful process of abolition and state consolidation in Brazil left the earlier racial order and social hierarchy relatively undisturbed, yet in Brazil earlier racial discrimination was not codified in later state institutions.

Looking just at pivotal moments cannot fully account for the divergence in racial orders. Outcomes even ran counter to the victors' possible advantage. If the British had aligned themselves with and protected black South Africans, they could have forged a majority coalition to outvote Afrikaners. With the hubris of victory, the U.S. North assumed they could indeed forge such a coalition with blacks and impose reforms under Reconstruction, but this project was abandoned. Instead, the British and the North sought a coalition with the Afrikaners and the white South, respectively, because those defeated whites had earned a reputation in the prior conflict as being capable of violent disruption. Afrikaners and Southerners posed a viable threat of continuing disruption after the Boer War and during Reconstruction. Liberal interest in blacks was overshadowed by the stronger imperative to unify whites within the nation-state, in part because blacks themselves, divided by ethnicity in South Africa and outnumbered in the United States, were not seen as a comparably violent threat.[48] Earlier images of racial inferiority, shared by whites across ethnic or regional lines, reinforced the idea that blacks were not capable of organized and united disruption, and so could and should be subordinated. The strategic and ideological imperatives for a white coalition then set the terms of official racial domination. During the "moments of madness"[49] capping cataclysmic and violent change, official policies established the trajectory of racial order for close to a century.

South African and U.S. nation-state consolidation followed a similar logic. "Liberal" and industrializing forces defeated agrarian powers tied to coercive labor practices, with the victors then facing the challenge of reconciling divided loyalties reinforced by conflict. Ethnic tensions and sectionalism had to be diminished, even if they could not be altogether vanquished.[50] Afrikaners and Southerners demanding that citizenship not be extended to blacks were appeased. Intrawhite conflict was diminished by projecting white racial unity and domination. Blacks were sacrificed on the altar of white unity. In this sense, in the aftermath of the Civil and Boer Wars, further open conflict was contained by inscribing inequalities on which whites generally agreed into social institutions.[51] As Stinchcombe concludes, "the tragedy of social life is that every extension of solidarity . . . to nation, presents also the opportunity of organizing hatred at a larger scale."[52] Institutionalizing common prejudice against blacks reinforced white nationalism.[53] Both countries followed a "golden law . . . that every white bargain must be sealed by an African sacrifice."[54] The pragmatic goal of conflict resolution and nation-state building consistently eclipsed liberal calls for racial justice.

Why did intrawhite conflict trigger the particular use of racial cleavage for domination and nation building? In South Africa and the United States, issues of race and the treatment of Africans were embedded in emerging ethnic or regional conflict, reinforcing existent racist ideologies. Issues of race exacerbating intrawhite conflict were then turned into an instrument for encouraging unity. And as elites victorious in war were more concerned with winning over their white rivals than blacks, constructing a racial order of white supremacy could and did diminish intrawhite conflict. Racial domination was embraced or allowed because it was potentially powerful enough to gradually integrate white populations in violent conflict with each other. Continuing ethnic or section conflicts would have exacerbated disruption. Neither capital nor labor could be so excluded because prosperity required the inclusion of both business and workers. And national unity could not be built on the exclusion of foreigners, who were needed as immigrant labor.

There remains a danger of exaggerating the similarity between the cases of South Africa and the United States. South Africa's newly forged state authority had either to exclude or include blacks, and to unify whites it pursued exclusion imposed from the center. The potential threat from the African majority impelled such strong intervention, which was matched by increasingly strong central state capacity, reinforced by the strength of the British Empire and encoded in a nonfederal political system of concentrated power.[55] Unlike South Africa, in the United States reforms were attempted, but the central state was too weak to persist in Reconstruction in the South, or even to impose a uniform racial order against the black minority. Much as the federalist compromise had allowed for state building a century earlier, a decentralized state of limited capacity was held together by allowing for local variation. Rather than exert its authority, the central state acted by withdrawal, consolidating its authority as best it could by avoiding further conflict. African-Americans were abandoned anew, with Lincoln's earlier rhetoric of national reconciliation applied only to whites. A generation after the Civil War, Jim Crow was gradually imposed as law in the South and informally maintained in the North, serving both to diminish regional conflict and to unify white Southerners. Segregation was enforced by mob rule, to which the federal government turned a blind eye. Guarantees of equality were unenforced, whereas in South Africa no such guarantees existed and the state acted with force and impunity.

The pattern of racial domination used to diminish intrawhite conflict in South Africa and the United States should also not be misunderstood as having been reified at one point in time. What appears neatly functional after the fact was instead messy, refined by the feedback of ongoing political party competition among whites maneuvering to find varying solutions to real problems.[56] Even the identifications of racial, ethnic, or regional actors remained fluid, shaped by ongoing conflict and policy. Increasingly consolidated as a group, Afrikaner nationalists were not easily appeased. Throughout much of the first half of this century their party representatives sought to trump the racial segregation policies of the English-speakers. But the overriding policy of black exclusion helped to contain English–Afrikaner conflict within a single polity. This ongoing competition finally led to an Afrikaner-controlled state in 1948, with segregation reinforced under apartheid. And in the United States, Southern distinctiveness and antagonism against the North were used to reinforce the Democratic Party there after Reconstruction. Regional antagonism and competition did not disappear, but again were successfully contained within a single polity, albeit a loosely controlled one. The original "deal" of a white coalition was made and remade, with outcomes varying to limit ongoing conflict. Indeed, such continued tensions kept alive the intrawhite dynamic refining racial domination in an ongoing process. A racial strategy aimed at preserving nation-state unity was repeatedly and purposefully invoked by selective democratic competition, with both some success and unforeseen consequences.

The other major or potential conflict that continued to shape racial orders was economic. Functionalist arguments have suggested that Jim Crow and apartheid were implemented to protect native or immigrant whites from black competition amid industrialization and urbanization, slower to develop in Brazil.[57] But in the United States, Jim Crow was enforced more fully in the less industrialized South, and racial domination was not encoded in Brazil amid urbanization and later job competition in the more industrialized Southeast. South African and U.S. segregation did serve the interests of capital in supplying cheap black labor, and the interests of privileged white labor by ensuring reserved jobs or higher wages.[58] But to reduce racial orders to an expression of such white class interests ignores major divisions within and between capital and labor, and the extent to which states maintained racial policies despite economic costs and pressures for reform.[59] Capital's demands were not always met. Instead, racial orders emerged to diminish or avoid inter- and intraclass conflict, all the more potentially disruptive in overlapping with "ranked" ethnic or regional tensions.[60] To hold together the nation-state, preserving stability needed for growth, whites were unified across class by race in South Africa and the United States. Economic interests were subordinated to white racial unity, with this class compromise made explicit and enforced by state policy varying in response to ongoing class tensions. Race trumped class.[61]

Brazilian nation-state making and race making followed an altogether different linked trajectory. There was no competing European fragment akin to the Afrikaners in South Africa, so that the Portuguese were unchallenged in establishing central colonial authority.[62] In general, slavery was countrywide, producing little regional conflict over abolition, nor the elaboration of a programmatic racist ideology to defend slavery against such challenges.[63] A relative lack of early conflict was further preserved by Brazil's slow economic growth, contrasted with faster development producing more class conflict earlier among whites in South Africa and the United States. Brazilian unity had been preserved by compromise, and the continued rule of Portugal and Portuguese-descendant emperors ensured the persistence of an established order and religious-social hierarchy, with slaves at its bottom.[64] Brazil then modernized and peacefully transformed itself from colony to empire and to republic, and from slaveholding to free.[65] A "prefabricated" central state was in place when the winds of modernity hit. Abolition did raise the question of whether and how to incorporate blacks, but in the relative absence of major intrawhite conflict, there was little impetus to unify whites through racial exclusion. Whites were already relatively united; the nation was already bound up, at least among elites.

Brazilian elites found that they could maintain their long-established social order of white privilege without enforcing racial domination. Having experienced larger slave revolts, the Brazilian ruling class was more fearful of blacks than their U.S. or South African counterparts. They were eager to submerge potential racial conflict. Policies were debated and discrimination was evident in preferences for European immigrants and bars on Africans entering the country.[66] Racial categories were even encoded, but Brazil did not use these categories as a basis for domination. Inherited and continued racial inequality was denied or explained as reflecting unavoidable but fluid class distinctions. Some Afro-Brazilians were able to advance themselves, encouraging accommodation. Further miscegenation was promoted to "whiten" and unite the population. Seeking "the best of both worlds, such racial democracy maintains the structure of white privilege and non-white subordination, [and] avoids the constitution of race into a principle of collective identity and political action."[67] That prejudice was not legally instantiated had significant consequences. With no official segregation requiring strong state intervention, the republic decentralized power with little conflict or dissent.[68]

This analysis suggests a schematic pattern. For all three countries, racial discrimination was historically embedded, distinguishing blacks as blacks. But elites sharing this prejudice acted differently in response to the particular conflicts they faced or feared. In the United States and South Africa, nineteenth-century builders of the nation-state faced the threat of a potential triadic tension between two white groups and blacks. A coalition among whites was encouraged by enforcing an ideology and practice of racial domination, shifting the conflict to a more manageable dyadic form of white over black. Intrawhite conflict required reconciliation, and racial domination was imposed to unify white nationalism and allow for state centralization. In Brazil, with no comparably violent ethnic and less regional conflict standing in the way of unity, no reconciliation by exclusion was pursued. A more inclusive nationalism developed in place of a biracial divide. The earlier consolidated Brazilian state required no dyadic racial crutch to preserve the polity even as the form of rule repeatedly shifted. Thus, racial domination was constructed selectively and strategically as a tool for pursuing the goal of the nation-state, a twentieth-century preoccupation.

This divergence of South Africa and the United States from Brazil follows a pattern similar to one found in Europe, as described by Rogers Brubaker. Divisions within the potential German nation were purposefully overcome by state policies of ethnically exclusive citizenship aimed at unifying those included. By contrast, an earlier unified French state adopted formal rules of "civic," inclusive citizenship. Already achieved French unity did not require reinforcement with official "ethnic" exclusion, though informal discrimination is increasingly evident.[69] In South Africa, the United States, and Brazil, colonialism, slavery, and geography had left a substantial and historically differentiated black population. "Bounded citizenship"[70] according to race was constructed in South Africa and to a lesser extent in the United States to bolster nation building, much as German unity was reinforced by excluding ethnic groups defined as not German. In the relative absence of regional or any ethnic division, race was not so used in Brazil, akin to the French example of long avoiding official ethnic exclusion.

For all their variation, racial orders helped to achieve stability and development. In South Africa and the United States, ethnic or regional and class conflict were contained by encouraging white racial unity. In South Africa after 1948, Afrikaner political power over a strong state gradually satisfied and enriched its constituency, dampening animosity with the English-speakers. In the United States, allowing for Jim Crow served to help reconcile North and South and to unify whites as whites, thereby reducing the divisive pressures that had once and could again tear apart the Union. Continued regional and party competition reinforced the post-Reconstruction deal of white unity encouraged by racial domination. The central state subsequently grew in capacity as the South was gradually Americanized.[71] With the greater resolution of intrawhite conflict in the United States, as in South Africa, economic growth and structural change proceeded. In Brazil, racial democracy in its own way helped to preserve the polity and growth, with class and racial conflict contained within a corporatist order. But if these racial orders did gradually diminish internal conflict, how then do we account for the abandonment of apartheid and Jim Crow, and rising challenges to Brazil's racial order?

Challenging the Racial Order

Whites had the political, economic, and military power to take the lead in defining themselves as a race and in establishing racial order. But this domination also consolidated mobilization by blacks, building upon their own historical solidarity of shared culture, experience, and fate.[72] Using race to reinforce national unity created new conflicts, challenging that unity.[73] Refinements of racial domination toward greater repression or reform and the eventual abandonment of official segregation all came in response to real or perceived challenges posed by blacks. To complete an analysis of these dynamics of race making, "a history from above . . . is thus no less essential than a history from below,"[74] with either incomplete on its own. Previously concerned with explaining why states do or do not impose racial domination, we must reverse the terms of analysis to explore the consequences of state policy. How did enactment of racial domination or the ideology of racial democracy contribute to resistance that challenged those orders? In other words, if state institutions were constructed to encourage exclusive or inclusive national identities, how did these same institutions shape identities[75] and action among blacks, and with what results?

Analysis of pressures from below should avoid any artificially neat state determinism. Intrablack distinctions of color or origin remained, but emergent racial identity among blacks was evident in political, religious, and other associations before racial domination was codified. And such identity has remained after the legal demise of apartheid or Jim Crow, and even in the absence of such policies in Brazil. Nor have protests always been tightly linked to state policy. Activists have applied varying strategies, learning the strengths and weaknesses of each and refining their efforts accordingly.[76] Often more than one form of protest was pursued at a time, and often the same people participated in different movements. And blacks have often pursued their own interests by migrating, as from the U.S. South to the North. Indeed, racial identity, movement, and protest cannot be understood simply as a response to actions from above. Blacks have pursued their own ideas and actions, often forcing a reconfiguration of rule imposed upon them.

To the extent that those dominated retain their own agency, their actions must be explained in terms of structural and cultural forces.[77] What specifically accounts for the formation of a self-consciously identified racial group capable of protest? Even when race is so reinforced as a salient identity, why does it only sometimes lead to mobilization? And where or when such mobilization emerges, why do its ideology, strategy, and goals vary? When and if protest does emerge in varying forms, what accounts for its timing and effectiveness? If race making from above and below are interconnected processes, then any explanation of changing rules of official domination should also help explain actions by those so dominated. Such patterns would be most evident in South Africa and the United States, where post-abolition race policy and repression have been explicit and protests massive. Yet even in Brazil, where racial identity has grown and the reality of racial democracy has been challenged, more limited forms of protest may accord with similar patterns.

Attempts to answer why and how mobilization against racial domination develops have remained incomplete. Black protest (with or without white allies) has been explained as a result of relative deprivation, though deprivation has not consistently provoked mobilization.[78] If relatively constant deprivation cannot explain outbursts and variations in the form of protest, then such outcomes may be dependent on the availability of resources, including allies, financing, and internal organization.[79] But again, such resources have been available without protest resulting, and when it does result, its form varies.[80] Finally, mobilization has been explained as the response to political opportunities, which encourage people to pursue specific means of collective action.[81] Both reforms and repression may provide such opportunities for protest, but neither have always been acted upon.[82]

Identity formation is a prerequisite for mobilization. In the absence of a self-conscious group, there is no collectivity that can interpret and act upon its situation. The fact that relative deprivation can inspire mobilization does not explain why such deprivation is perceived and acted upon by a group defined by race. That resources and political opportunities are seized as a basis of mobilization also does not explain why such openings are interpreted and acted upon according to race.

It is not sufficient to argue that certain social factors polarize racial identity, for this essentializes race as preexisting and cannot account for different ways in which race has been socially constructed, interpreted, and used. Analysis must explain why social distinctions and conflict come to be projected in terms of physical differences or purported race in the first place, rather than alternative cleavages. Social movement theorists seeking to explain black protest have generally failed to make this shift from using race to analyze events rather than making race the object of analysis.[83] Instead, like theorists of racial domination, they have tended to assume as a given the salient identity around which mobilization (or domination) builds. Activists have also tended to essentialize their race. The question remains, Why does race become salient at all, with blacks singled out? Why and how any such identity becomes politicized must be specified.[84]

The defining identity of those provoked to mobilization may or may not be shaped by official policies of exclusion and enforced deprivation. A state-led process of identity formation is not necessarily applicable to all forms of protest. Some new social movements have been demarcated precisely by their autonomous process of identity consolidation.[85] But state action to impose race has built upon and reinforced historical and cultural foundations of black solidarity, helping to provoke collective response.

The Faustian bargain of officially encouraging white unity at the expense of blacks had a later cost. Racial domination had the unintended consequence of consolidating and legitimating subordinated racial identity into a potential basis for resistance. Extending Karl Marx's argument about class solidarity, a group must self-consciously exist "in itself" before it can act "for itself."[86] Rules enforced according to physical differences helped reinforce such group self-consciousness among blacks, who then interpreted and responded to structural conditions accordingly. Blacks emerging from history with greater solidarity as a group were then provoked to action for themselves as that group. Internal divisions often remain unresolved, but as domination and conflict proceed, those experiences may submerge conflicts within the subordinated group. As state power was consolidated and increasingly penetrated civil society, it also deepened imposed identities and expanded the potential for group mobilization.[87]

In the United States and South Africa, white racial identity was enforced by state institutions and apparatuses diminishing intrawhite conflict.[88] But the consolidation of segregation after the Boer War and American Reconstruction also provoked further efforts at black racial unity, such as those spearheaded by the African National Congress (ANC) or by Du Bois. Dominant institutions thus reinforced and shaped dominated identity, which then asserted itself and pressed for change in those institutions. By contrast, Brazil's absence of an official race order provided no explicit target of state policy against which racial identity could be consolidated.[89]

Racial identity can be expressed or channeled into varying strategies of mobilization. Subordinated blacks may seek to enter white society to achieve voice and material benefits, but may also withdraw to avoid prejudice and develop self-worth.[90] Protest can then be aimed at integration and/or separatism, both of which can and have been pursued with more or less militancy. These alternatives are not mutually exclusive and have been pursued simultaneously by different people, often interacting, reinforcing and enriching each other.[91] Both approaches are "always going on . . . [but] there is always a dominant form."[92]

The timing of protest and preferences for integration or separatism, militancy or accommodation, are connected to shifts in state policy presenting distinct resources and opportunities. State building not only creates opportunities for collective action, but the form of such action also reflects the form of the state.[93] No less a figure than Nelson Mandela subscribes to this reasoning, arguing that

> A freedom fighter learns the hard way that it is the oppressor who defines the nature of the struggle, and the oppressed is often left no recourse but to use methods that mirror those of the oppressor. At a certain point, one can only fight fire with fire. . . . [For instance,] If the oppressor uses violence, the oppressed have no alternative but to respond violently.[94]

If this reasoning is correct, we should see the timing and forms of mobilization influenced by shifts between greater state repression or reform.

Interaction between state policy and black protest can be specified, though unifying whites through heightened racial domination may not immediately produce mass protest. During the first half of this century in South Africa and the United States, blacks generally engaged in migration or limited peaceful petitioning, remaining hopeful for redress and eager to escape or avoid repression. (The Garvey movement was a notable exception, advocating return to Africa rather than redress.) Throughout, identity was being consolidated and organizations were being built, though relatively stable state policy and repression provided little opportunity or resources for protest. Even in the 1960s, South Africa was able to impose relative quiet.

Transitions and crises in state rule provided openings for mobilization. When whites had unified enough to allow for relaxing segregation, reforms tended to encourage more moderate, often integrationist forms of protest.[95] The ANC Youth League and later the United Democratic Front in South Africa, the U.S. civil rights movement, and the Frente Negra in Brazil emerged during such periods of relative reform. These protest responses to reform strengthened white hard-liners who wanted to reverse reforms. Resulting black disillusionment then encouraged more militant, often separatist or nationalist movements, such as the Pan Africanist Congress and Black Consciousness in South Africa, Black Power in the United States, and the Movimento Negro Unificado in Brazil.[96] When whites turn away from blacks, blacks tend to follow suit.

Finally, state structure and policy also shape the aim of protest. In South Africa, no constitutional guarantees of equal rights existed for blacks to appeal to, and central authority was stronger earlier and had been used to reinforce racial domination. Rather than look for reform from the center, protest eventually focused on forcing an end to the state as it existed. Such protest built to the equivalent of internal war; racial domination could only be ended through a fundamental political transition.

The situation in the United States was dramatically different. After Reconstruction, constitutional amendments had guaranteed equal rights, suggesting that later protest might force federal authorities to fulfill those abandoned obligations. The civil rights movement in the South purposefully attempted to engage federal intervention against Jim Crow.[97] By contrast, discrimination in the North was de facto rather than de jure, with federal intervention both less likely and less effective than in the South, where laws could be and were changed. Northern mobilization was thus less successful at gaining federal intervention, provoking greater frustration, militancy, and violence. But amid such regional distinctions, most African-Americans supported greater state centralization, expecting that such authority would then enforce constitutional guarantees locally resisted.

As a crucial part of this dynamic, analysis of mobilization helps to complete analysis of race making in accounting for the pressures that forced an end to legal racial domination where it had been enacted. Unlike in Brazil, this was the aim of those social movements provoked by apartheid and Jim Crow. But such protest had been long-standing in South Africa and the United States, even while apartheid and Jim Crow were maintained. State strength and coercion remained. What changed?

The interaction of racial domination and mobilization eventually produced a new dynamic leading to greater inclusion. Preservation of the nation-state no longer depended upon racial domination by whites, who had become more unified on this basis. And the preservation of the nation-state, stability, and growth came to be challenged by black agency and protest consolidated by subordination. To head off this new challenge, apartheid and Jim Crow were abandoned. Such reform also reflected international conditions and economic structural changes, which had altered the quality and nature of interactions. But the undermining of racial domination brought about by industrialization, migration, urbanization, and reliance on black labor and consumption was also made possible by prior racial orders preserving polities and economies.

This dynamic, bringing together the two parts of my analysis, suggests considerable analytical leverage, but the reality was much less neat. The end of legal racial domination was protracted. And the legal demise of apartheid and Jim Crow has not ended discrimination or the salience of race. Identities have persisted even after enforcing institutions were reformed. The dynamics of race making remain.

What Is at Stake?

That states constructed legal racial orders prompts the questions of why, how, and with what consequences. As David Laitin has argued, such a "pattern of political cleavages . . . are best explained by a focus on the actions of a hegemonic state. . . . [Even] the political organizations that make demands on the state are themselves partly a function of state actions."[98] But left unspecified, this argument does not account for particular cleavages and their consequences. In general terms, how did particular situations shape race making? Or more directly, why did state-building elites respond to varying pressures and seek to consolidate their support by using race to achieve a specified nationalism?[99]

Race was not chosen randomly as a bulwark for nationalism. Issues of race had been long imbedded in practices of slavery, exploitation, and discrimination. These practices were justified with images of white racial superiority, which were widely believed. This ideological foundation could be and was built upon. Elites' use of race to solidify white support for the nation-state could piggyback on this powerful "symbolic repertoire."[100] Indeed, elites generally shared this belief structure with the white popular sector. State structures, boundaries of democratic inclusion, and citizenship rules were shaped by such essentialist beliefs.[101] These outcomes were also rational within the historical context in which they occurred. The same issue of race that previously had exacerbated division among whites in South Africa and the United States could now be used to heal that division. But neither such rationality nor ideology can fully account for the persistence of these relationships.[102] Indeed, racial domination was maintained even when it was costly and challenged.

In Part One, this book takes up the question of how the enactment or not of legal racial domination during the twentieth century was shaped by earlier experiences. More specifically, how did colonialism, slavery, and miscegenation influence what would become apartheid in South Africa, Jim Crow in the United States, and racial democracy in Brazil? If these legacies cannot directly explain why Brazil did not encode legal racial domination, or the varying forms of such policies in South Africa and the United States, then the past is not so constraining. Cultural and historical inheritances play a role in policy formulation, but state actions may also shape how such legacies are interpreted to legitimate that action. At stake is why and how aspects of history are brought forward.

Part Two addresses the circumstances that shaped the particular racial orders that were enacted and how the past was used accordingly. Why were certain policies encoded? Why was race used in particular ways? What accounts for changes over time? To answer these questions, we must trace the interests and actions of real actors. It is not sufficient to talk abstractly about the state, as if this were a unitary or intentional actor establishing unchanging policy. We know the policy outcomes, but to account for these we must explore the actual and ongoing pressures, deliberations, debates, and consequences. At stake is why institutional rules codify particular identities and relations.

Part Three takes a different perspective, focusing on how state policy shaped and was shaped by black protest. Such mobilization, or the threat of it, played a central role in motivating racial domination and then in undermining it. But to make this argument, I challenge the prevailing tendency to take for granted the identity around which protest forms. I argue instead that it was shifting state policy that reinforced prior black solidarity, providing the basis and the target against which protest emerged. At stake is how codified identity shapes mobilization and forces institutional change.

Finally, in the Conclusion, the threads of the argument are brought together. If the prior analysis holds, it should then also help to explain why racial domination was officially abandoned and what the implications are of continued informal racial discrimination. In the process, I argue that the impetus for resolving conflict by means of nation-state building was integral to race making and to the unmaking of legal racial domination. But I also suggest the reverse, that within the three cases examined here issues of race have been integral to nation-state building. Nationhood was institutionalized on the basis of race; the political production of race and the political production of nationhood were linked. Even changing structures of the state, whether more or less centralized or corporatist, were shaped by the deals elites made about race in pursuit of nation-state consolidation.

There is also a more far-reaching potential payoff. In contrast to the image of the nation-state as an inclusive "imagined community," a distinctive and divisive route to nation-state building is suggested. State-imposed exclusion of a specified internal group, used to reinforce the allegiance and unity of a core constituency, may be a more pervasive pattern. Indeed, nation-states have often been based on such exclusion, not only according to race, but also ethnicity, class, and other cleavages. Even in supposedly inclusive nations and democracies, assimilation often rested on informal distinctions and hierarchy. Such selective nation-state building would then explain why particular cleavages become institutionalized. And such manipulation of cleavages may be central to how and in what form the nation-state was built and later challenged. If so, the dynamics explored here may be suggestive of a more widespread historical pattern of nation-state building through exclusion, reinforcing cleavages and thereby exacerbating conflicts that continue to bedevil us.

PART ONE

Historical and Cultural Legacies

P RIOR PRACTICES AND BELIEFS set the context in which post-abolition and post-colonial racial order was constructed. Analysts of Brazil's "exceptional" lack of legal racial domination and conflict have argued that Portuguese colonialism, Catholicism, more "humanitarian" slavery, and a greater physical mixing of populations preordained a later, more tolerant racial order. By implication, racial domination and conflict in South Africa and the United States (for all their differences) can then be explained by their alternative legacies of British or Dutch colonialism, Protestantism, harsh slavery, and lesser extent of miscegenation. In Part One, I assess these arguments, using trilateral comparisons to demonstrate that prior historical trajectories were not so fully determinant in their own right.

To simply refute the explanatory power of early history and culture as uncertain, and thereby to dismiss consideration of them, would be a serious mistake, inviting simple-minded, ahistorical conclusions. Instead, I will argue that colonialism, religious tradition, slavery, and miscegenation were later interpreted in particular ways to fit the political situations in each of the three cases under consideration. These interpretations were widespread in each culture, shaping perceptions of what and how post-abolition racial order could be and was constructed. And after that construction was refined, selective interpretations of past legacies justified the racial order that would come to prevail in each country. The point is that it was not historical facts per se that predetermined subsequent racial orderings, but purposeful interpretations of those facts.

The past impinged but did not bind. Societies were not as locked into past patterns as Louis Hartz suggested,[1] but instead developed their own dynamics building on past divisions and practices. History presented "problems" that actors sought to address in varying ways, with each such "solution" rationalized as historically necessary. But interpretations of cultural legacies and values change over time, and the point is to explain such change. Early historical bequests thus remain relevant. To explicate this argument, it is necessary first to assess the prior historical record, before we can appreciate how interpretations of this record twisted, forgot, or embraced the past to fit emerging projects of race making.

2

Trajectories from Colonialism

How did differing experiences of colonialism and its aftereffects shape later racial orders? I begin with an examination of Brazil, where arguments for such historical determinacy have been employed to explain the later lack of racial domination. To check such arguments, I then turn to comparisons with the colonies that would become South Africa and the United States.

Portuguese Brazil

The image of a Portuguese colonial legacy of racial tolerance is tantamount to an official ideology, at least within the former colonial power. Modern Portuguese officials have claimed that among Europeans, their predecessors "alone practiced the principle of multi-racialism, which all now consider the most perfect and daring expression of human brotherhood . . . in which men are limited only by their ability."[1] As early as 1923, the usually astute W. E. B. Du Bois agreed that "between the Portuguese and the African and the near-African there is naturally no racial antipathy – no accumulated historical hatreds, dislikes and despisings."[2] According to Gilberto Freyre, the leading advocate of this thesis, "the absence of violent rancors due to race constitutes one of the peculiarities of the feudal system in the tropics," characteristic of Portuguese rule. In their colonies, the Portuguese supposedly pursued policies of incorporation more than imposition, consistent with a "plasticity of the national character, of its classes and institutions, which are never indurated or definitely stratified."[3]

Colonial racial tolerance has been described as the result of Portugal's geographic proximity and contact with Africa. Freyre argued that the early experience of domination by the Moors, "a dark-skinned race but one that was superior to the white race in various aspects of moral and material culture," had helped to prepare the Portuguese for respectful and friendly interaction with Africans.[4] The purported result was "an ancient element of racial cosmopolitanism here, which facilitated the absorption of the non-European into the feudal structure."[5] However, their North African rulers "were no darker than the Portuguese,"[6] and even Freyre notes that the Portuguese were united in their "hatred for the Moor."[7] Such foreign rule may have made it difficult for the Portuguese to "nourish preconceptions of racial superiority," but "the long warfare between Portuguese and Moors [did not] result in a spirit of racial toleration."[8] Moorish rule more likely encouraged racial antagonism, camouflaged by the Portuguese as racial tolerance and respect in order to preserve their pride.

After the withdrawal of the Moors, Portugal was the first European power to project itself into Africa during the sixteenth century. The image of racial tolerance was later extended to this experience. Because "the Portuguese in the mother country had for centuries been acquainted with people of darker skins," they were supposedly predisposed to "essentially harmonious" race relations in Africa.[9] But just as it is unlikely that the Portuguese thought of their relations with Moorish conquerors as harmonious, it is at least as difficult to imagine that the victims of later Portuguese incursions into Africa would have described their slave and colonial masters in such friendly terms. Instead, Portuguese colonialism in Africa was highly discriminatory and produced "the absolute, literal nadir of African misery."[10] Freyre's efforts to find a consistent pattern of Portuguese racial tolerance led him to misrepresent the reality of Portuguese colonial practice in Africa. Of course, other colonial powers were similarly and falsely self-laudatory.

The general argument for a tolerant Portuguese colonial legacy is unfounded, and as applied to Brazil is best assessed separately. Financial pressures on the Portuguese crown impelled early conquests, including that of Brazil, where the land was initially divided among captaincies tied to the crown. In the sixteenth and seventeenth centuries, the crown saw Brazil as a source of goods to be extracted, with the geography allowing for only coastal settlement, limiting colonization.[11] As a dominant European empire already in decline, Portugual was threatened and injured in its pride by the invasion of northern Brazil in 1624 by the rising Dutch empire.[12] By 1654, free and enslaved blacks fighting with the Portuguese had repelled the Dutch, leaving in their wake a country more unified by its "struggle against a common enemy."[13] However, the complete withdrawal of the Dutch left no remnant of this common enemy against which national unity might otherwise have continued to be refined. "No great sense of national identity" remained in Brazil.[14] Slavery and subordination of blacks did remain.

Portugal's persistence against the Dutch paid off handsomely. Within forty years after their victory in the "War of Divine Liberty," gold was discovered in Brazil, sparking two centuries of economic growth and trade. The gold find proved a boon to the Portuguese crown, which used resulting revenues to pay for imports, largely from Britain.[15] A royal monopoly and tax on the gold trade was imposed, with gold production encouraging a rapid expansion in the importation of slave labor to work the mines.[16] Mining and the rising threat of British and French competition further impelled Portuguese penetration inland. And as the flow of gold ebbed, sugar, diamonds, and coffee took its place. Global demand for Brazilian sugar exploded when French production fell in the wake of the slave revolt in St. Dominique.[17] The good fortune of diminished international competition, sequential mineral finds, increased agricultural production, and cheap slave labor combined to make Brazil into what the Portuguese king called the "milk cow" of his empire.[18]

Profits from Brazil flowed directly to the Portuguese king, reinforcing state consolidation and centralized rule. The Dutch and the British would later develop their colonies by relying on strong private companies. By contrast, the Portuguese crown invested for itself, eclipsing any merchant class at home, while developing Brazil as "the king's plantation" under a strong bureaucracy. But by the eighteenth and early nineteenth centuries, Portuguese centralization and profit-taking fed growing Brazilian nationalist resentment. In 1709, a Paulista revolt against Portuguese control and taxation of the gold trade was crushed, providing a further impetus for the crown to exert its authority.[19] With reduced gold production, local resistance rose gradually toward crisis. In Minas Gerais, where debt to Portugal soared despite the mineral wealth taken, a plot for sovereignty in 1789 was inspired by U.S. independence, and crushed. The crown then sought compromise, for instance in reducing its "royal fifth" of profits by half, in order to avoid further confrontations and to retain its lucrative colonial rule.[20] But despite such efforts at appeasement or repression to retain colonial rule, by the end of the eighteenth century analysts concluded that "Portugal without Brazil is an insignificant power," and that "so heavy a branch cannot long remain on so rotten a trunk."[21]

Economically inspired Brazilian independence seemed to loom, but geopolitics conspired against a dramatic break. In November 1807, Napoleon's army advanced toward Lisbon. The British, concerned about Portuguese assets falling into French hands, threatened to destroy the fleet of its ally. The threat was credible – the British had earlier bombarded Copenhagen. With only four days to spare before the French took Lisbon, Dom João IV acceded to British demands that they escort him, his court, fleet, treasury, and even a printing press, into exile in Brazil. Joáo's arrival in Bahia in 1808 marked the first time a reigning European monarch had set foot in the Americas.[22] A royal exile began, made palatable by the greater wealth and development of the colony than of the home country. Even more astonishingly, the monarch and his family settled and established strong roots in the tropical soil, turning the table of domination from Europe to colonial rule from a colony. Heirs of the Portuguese crown remained in situ and in command of Brazil until 1889.

The unique historical development of a European power ruling from a colonial seat had a profound impact. With its royal presence, emergent Brazilian nationalism shifted from being anti-Portuguese to embracing a localized monarchy. The Brazilian Empire was consolidated around the symbolism of the "moderating power" of the crown. The result was a remarkable degree of unity and stability, reinforced by state-controlled exports and British support for its trading partner.[23]

When serious conflict did emerge, it was consistently defused by compromise and rearrangements in the distribution of central power, which did not seriously disrupt the basic order. A troop rebellion in 1821 gained the support of the regent Pedro, who simply declared independence and named himself emperor of Brazil the next year, after his father the king had reluctantly decided to leave Brazil and return to Lisbon. Formal independence was achieved out of "continuity" more than "rupture," without a shot being fired.[24] Another outburst of protest in 1831 led Pedro I to abdicate in favor of his son, Pedro II, who then ruled Brazil for fifty-eight years of relative tranquillity, punctured by serious revolts in the 1830s and 1840s and a war with Paraguay from 1865 to 1870.[25] Despite such occasional instability, loyalty to the Emperor largely endured. Astonishingly, though he was a descendant of the Portuguese royal house, Pedro II was embraced by Brazilians as "like us," even in skin color.[26]

The Brazilian Empire was remarkable for the persistence of Portuguese rule of an independent country. Amid conflict, the center held; "there was no Brazilian civil war."[27] This relative stability also provided the opportunity for a dramatic further consolidation of state power. The Portuguese colonial tradition of a strong crown and weak private sector provided a strong base on which the two emperors could build. Provincial governments, the judiciary, Church, army, mines, the business community, locally powerful and wealthy coffee and sugar barons, all remained under the control of the crown, whose rule has been described as a form of "tropical feudalism," albeit centralized.[28] The result was an occasionally clogged but still highly effective royal authority, able to circumvent or withstand challenges while the same elite remained in power.[29] According to Stein Rokkan, this centralization was reinforced by the unifying influence of the state-supported Catholic Church, as contrasted with the sect divisions and exclusiveness of Protestantism.[30] Thus, the Brazilian tradition of prebendal clientalist or patrimonial rule was firmly established by Catholic Portuguese colonialism and maintained through the peaceful transition to independent empire.

Did Brazil's early political consolidation come with an imported tradition of racial tolerance? The Portuguese "royal family set the example of social acceptance of the darker Brazilians," with the emperor liberating his own slaves in 1840 and freeing some 6,000 slaves who fought in the Paraguay War of 1865–70.[31] More generally, Freyre argued that the recurrent tendency to head off revolts and challenges through compromise also encouraged "no absolute ideals, with no unyielding prejudice."[32] But most importantly, stability was also preserved by an informal religious and "racial hierarchy."[33] For instance, remarkably low state investment in education, indicated by the lack of any university and high rates of illiteracy, reinforced the low status of Afro-Brazilians.[34] Whites went from Brazil to Coimbra for university study. Blacks did not. The resulting hierarchy enabled the state to "divide and rule" by fragmentation, using a nonconfrontational strategy that effectively enforced the racial order at little cost.

State authorities also enacted formal discrimination, contradicting claims of official racial tolerance. For instance, already in 1755 Portugal had limited "mixed marriages," religious distinctions were consistently used to enforce discrimination, and only Portuguese served as ministers of the empire.[35] As Boxer concludes, "the oft-made claim that the Portuguese had no colour-bar cannot be substantiated," for there remained few "darker skinned" officials either in Portugal or its colony.[36] Exceptions were notable. If anything, racial *in*tolerance was a strong part of Portuguese tradition, consistent with its history of Catholic fundamentalism defeating the Moors, the Inquisition, and its status as the largest slave-trading nation in history. Despite its universalistic doctrines, the Catholic Church itself reinforced status distinctions by race, with Africans at the bottom of the formally inclusive hierarchy.

Arguments that Portuguese colonialism brought a legacy of racial tolerance have purposefully misrepresented the facts. The image of a tolerant tradition emerges as "a romantic myth (at best), or an invidious lie (at worst), used to obscure the realities of Portuguese colonialism," which was highly extractive and racially discriminatory.[37] The mythology of racial tolerance was consciously fashioned "to abolish . . . differences within a single, mystic unity" that simply did not exist. What did exist was a high level of Portuguese "economic and social retardation,"[38] in contrast to the more advanced form of decentralized development established elsewhere by British and Dutch colonialism. Rather than face this fact, Lusophiles "turned the country's inferiority complex inside out and converted Brazil's multiracial past from a liability into an asset," in part to impress liberal foreigners.[39] If the Portuguese could not claim comparable success at development, they would at least claim success in establishing tolerance. Archaic feudal hierarchy imposed on a colonial setting was projected as an advanced form of liberalism, with history later misrepresented accordingly.

Portuguese colonial and imperial rule over Brazil is distinguished by the dramatic extent to which state authority was imposed and preserved. State-led colonialism, which developed under the Portuguese before a strong private sector emerged (if it ever did), left a legacy of patrimonial rule. The Portuguese crown, its descendants, and related elites established firm control over the colony and its economy, proving themselves astonishingly resilient. Power was distributed among the elite, but that elite remained dependent on the center. Most notably, the unique happenstance of the Portuguese court being forcibly transferred to Brazil reinforced colonial rule and diminished separatist nationalism. The resulting lack of major violent conflict compared to elsewhere, notably the absence of any war of independence, is startling. Even after the economy of the former colony had outpaced that of its "mother country," the same Portuguese elites remained in control of Brazil, finessing pressures for greater separatism through accommodation and reform. But they were only "racially tolerant" by accommodating blacks at the bottom of their well-entrenched hierarchy.

Dutch and British Colonial Legacies

Early Portuguese explorers of South Africa's Cape of Good Hope did not firmly established their claims. A century after Vasco da Gama anchored near Table Bay in 1499, Portugal was already in relative decline and Dutch power on the rise. The Dutch East India Company was founded and began to replace Portuguese traders and claims.[40] By 1652, the company had established a small station on the Cape to provide provisions to ships making their way around Africa to India. With little fresh water and few perceived opportunities for trade or industry in the Cape, and with Holland having no population surplus seeking migration, the Dutch initially saw little interest in establishing a major settlement. But to encourage greater productivity, the Dutch East India Company did permit private landholding by burghers after 1657. Only in 1700 did the Dutch begin to actively encourage greater settlement by offering free passage to the Cape.[41]

While Brazil was enjoying a golden economic boom across the Atlantic, the Dutch Cape colonials in South Africa spent the eighteenth century developing slowly. The Dutch settlers, or Afrikaners, farmed for their own sustenance and to trade with in-transit sailors. They initially distinguished themselves from the indigenous population not so much on the basis of race, but as Christians rather than heathens, with some Africans incorporated by baptism.[42] Afrikaner

Calvinist beliefs were unadulterated by the European Enlightenment, from which they were largely cut off.[43] The natives were more densely settled and more needed for labor than in the Americas. Africans were forced to trade or work, pushed off their land, defeated in small wars, and decimated by disease, such as smallpox.[44] Meanwhile, Europe seemed to disappear for a time far over the horizon.

By the end of the eighteenth century, South Africa's relative isolation was broken. The aftermath of the French Revolution sent shockwaves not only west to Brazil but also south to the Cape. Though they were initially uninterested in colonizing the region, the British were eager to keep the strategically located Cape from falling into Napoleon's hands, much as they were concerned about the fate of the Portuguese fleet. Lacking a surrogate ally to protect their interests akin to the Portuguese king, the British acted for themselves. By 1795, a year after the Dutch East India Company had declared bankruptcy, the rising British Empire moved to displace formal Dutch rule on the Cape.[45] To "stabilize the frontier" of their new possession and to export excess domestic labor, the British sent 5,000 settlers to the Eastern Cape in 1820.

British colonial policies toward the African population were inconsistent. Missionary education was extended to Africans. British subjects were not permitted to own slaves, and liberals such as Dr. John Philip successfully pressed for further reforms, consistent with the extensions of citizenship in Great Britain. In 1828 "statutory discrimination" was formally abolished, overturning requirements that coloureds (people of mixed African and European – and later East Asian – ancestry) carry passes or avoid vagrancy, and ending prohibitions against blacks owning land, the chief mechanisms by which the Afrikaners had previously forced coloureds to labor for them.[46] In 1833 emancipation was mandated, with little or no compensation to slave owners. By the latter part of the century a minority of Africans had been granted the franchise in the Cape, though property qualifications were raised to ensure white dominance as more blacks were incorporated into the territory.[47] A tradition of tolerance was apparently established that would later be as proudly hailed by the British as it was by the Portuguese. But during the same period, in the rural areas the British purposefully pitted one "tribe" against another or forced "removals," and when that was not sufficient to establish control, used direct military force. Most notably, after suffering a major defeat at the hands of the Zulus at Isandhlwana in 1879, the British moved to crush the Zulu kingdom and adopted rhetoric "dehumanizing" Africans.[48] Coloured students were expelled from Cape schools, and urban segregation was pioneered in Durban under British rule after 1843.[49] By 1894, the Glenn Grey Act formally established segregation in the Eastern Cape, ostensibly under the guise of reforming land tenure. Shepstone pursued a similar policy in Natal, where "native reserves" had been established in 1864.[50] All told, racial segregation was pioneered by the British, sometimes despite official colonial policy, long before formal apartheid was enacted.

Liberal aspects of British policies toward the Africans adversely affected the empire's relations with the Afrikaners, who represented the greatest threat to colonial rule. Unlike Brazil, where the Portuguese repelled the Dutch and remained then as unchallenged European rulers, in South Africa the late-arriving British encountered the Dutch descendants who had taken root. The British incursion was not welcomed by the fiercely independent Afrikaners, who particularly resented policies anglicizing their education. Early British reforms in the treatment of Africans, who had by then been long subordinated under Dutch rule, further aggravated relations, provoking a series of rebellions by Afrikaners in 1795, 1799, and 1815.[51] They deeply resented, as an early Afrikaner put it,

> the shameful and unjust proceedings with reference to the freedom of our slaves . . . as their being placed on an equal footing with Christians, contrary to the laws of God, and the natural distinctions of race and colour, so that it was intolerable for any decent Christian to bow down beneath such a yoke, wherefore we rather withdrew in order thus to preserve our doctrines in purity.[52]

In the less generous interpretation of a British official, the Afrikaners were united and mobilized by their insistence on being able "to wollop their own niggers."[53] In either case, the Afrikaners resisted the extension of citizenship rights to Africans.

Determined "to preserve proper relations between masters and servant" and with little hope of defeating the British Empire, thousands of Afrikaners opted for flight rather than to fight, trekking north. Eager to avoid an "irresolvable conflict," Britain let them go.[54] But the seeds of British–Afrikaner animosity had been planted, with British and Afrikaner loyalties solidifying in opposition to each other.

Despite much agreement on white superiority, treatment of Africans had been established as a focal point of the emerging conflict for power. Afrikaner racist ideology was consolidated by resistance to British impositions of reform.

The trek north relieved pressure between Afrikaners and British, for a time. Afrikaners still resisted state rule, even their own, breaking up into separate republics in the Transvaal and the Orange River Sovereignty. To mollify the Boer trekkers, in 1852 and 1854 the British grudgingly ceded independence to these republics, concluding that imperial interests were not threatened by such ramshackle, inland states often in conflict with each other.[55] In kind, Paul Kruger's South African Republic in the Transvaal ostensibly sought to be inclusive toward its English inhabitants, while limiting their franchise in order to maintain an Afrikaner majority.[56] The republics were less accommodating toward Africans. The 1858 constitution of the Transvaal Republic declared that "there shall be no equality between white and black in church or state."[57] By 1893–5, job "colour bars" and a mandatory "pass system" were in place.[58] British protest was muted and the republics remained with their racial policies intact.

The uneasy peace between Britain and the Afrikaner republics was broken by the destabilizing effects of major mineral finds. After their discovery in 1867, South Africa produced half of the world's diamonds. The British responded initially with some uncertainty. With the excuse of offering protection for the Zulus, the British annexed the Transvaal and its diamond fields by 1877. Transvaal self-rule was then reestablished in 1881.[59] But in 1886 gold was discovered there, which would come to make up one-quarter of global supply. Thereafter "the story of South Africa is the story of gold."[60]

The form, scale, and timing of the gold discoveries were crucial, exacerbating intrawhite conflict. Afrikaner Calvinists were concerned about the "pernicious moral influence on our national character" of such material "temptation."[61] Kruger resisted private claims and investment and blocked the extension of railroads to carry the gold. But the ore was of poor quality and far from ports, requiring substantial investment in refining and railroads, which the British were eager to provide and to protect under their rule.[62] The British were then suffering a domestic economic crisis and facing increased global competition in their efforts to achieve dominance. Britain needed the riches that had fallen into the laps of the more ambivalent and isolated

Afrikaners. Establishing rule in South Africa beyond "the mother colony" of the Cape, both to assert British supremacy and to turn "the richest spot on earth" into a treasury for the empire, was too great a temptation to resist.[63] If the British state still hesitated, its subjects did not. Cecil Rhodes launched a raid on the Transvaal in 1895–6, and after that failed British colonials continued to push for state intervention. Afrikaner resistance and British agitation grew apace in the years that followed.

Long-standing conflicts over power were coming to a head, spurred on by the prospect of great wealth. South Africa seemed to advance "politically by disasters and economically by windfalls."[64] Fortune brought misfortune. The discovery of gold just when the British Empire was reaching its height and needed further resources brought the full force of the world's greatest power down on the heads of the Afrikaners.

What then is the implication of this overview of South African colonial history in terms of race relations? The Afrikaners were committed to labor coercion and racial domination, and were even willing to give up land in the Cape to preserve such domination and to avoid their being dominated in turn by the British. Their views on race reflected their own interests and religion, rather than official Dutch colonial policies or eugenics, from which Afrikaners were relatively isolated. British policies toward the Africans were somewhat more ambivalent, with reforms and abolition enforced from London but segregation and conquest pursued by local officials. With British and Afrikaners in control of different parts of what was to become South Africa, policies on race relations were officially recognized as "diverse."[65] But a common early pattern of discrimination and exploitation was established, whether by British liberalism or Afrikaner conservatism.

Describing the treatment of Africans in this way highlights the overriding influence of the conflict between British and Afrikaners. This conflict was the major legacy of the colonial period in South Africa. By the end of the nineteenth century, with imperial aims and mineral riches drawing British north from the Cape, the contest for control between the British and Afrikaners could no longer be finessed. Relations with Africans were of secondary importance, shaped by the more pressing competition between European descendants. The contrast of this situation with that of Brazil is marked, for there no such intra-European conflict emerged, nor did a fully fledged ideology of racism develop to counter externally imposed reforms. Relations with African descendants in Brazil developed more unilaterally. Thus, while Brazil's resulting colonial legacy was one of relative stability and unity, that of South Africa was instability and growing conflict.

Whereas colonial (or imperial) rule lasted in Brazil and parts of South Africa for most of the nineteenth century, it lasted in the United States only until the end of the eighteenth. Unlike the Portuguese monarchy, the British crown was effectively challenged at home by Parliamentary opposition and abroad by Spanish and French competition. The Seven Years' War (1756–63) consolidated British control of its American colonies but also shattered the image of British invincibility and raised the self-esteem of colonialists who had fought for Britain. The crown remained unable or unwilling to engage itself in direct colonial investment. Instead, Britain relied on the private investment of large firms or individuals granted territory.[66]

Domestic political power was decentralized among the thirteen American colonies, including those in the more agrarian and rural South, and what would become a more rapidly industrializing North. Native Americans were pushed aside, establishing a pattern of racial exclusion. Within the South, particularly Virginia, early rebellions had raised the fear of insurrection uniting black slaves and white indentured servants. "Resentment of an alien race" was gradually encouraged by white planters in order to unify whites "in common contempt for persons of darker complexion."[67] Benefits for poorer whites were offered to head off insurrection, solidifying cross-class white support for the enslavement of black labor.

The South's commitment to labor-coercive slavery helped to unify whites within those colonies, but also exacerbated later division between the regions. For instance, when independence was declared, the South rejected Northern efforts to condemn the slave trade. Such division would emerge as more similar to South Africa than to the unified colonial rule of Brazil, though in the United States later tensions tended to focus on regional interests and slavery, in contrast to South Africa's conflict over ethnic self-determination and the treatment of free Africans. But as in South Africa and Brazil, U.S. whites generally agreed, in the words of Jefferson, that "blacks, whether originally a distinct race, or made distinct by time and circumstances, are inferior to whites in body and mind."[68]

American independence was won by military victory, again in contrast to the peaceful transition to empire in Brazil. The United States was born out of violent conflict akin to that which would give birth to a unified South Africa more than a century later. But unlike South Africa, the British were defeated in the United States by a cross-regional effort unifying whites.

In the aftermath of the War of Independence, the thirteen colonies formed a united state. As a leading force in the independence movement, the South resisted any threats to its autonomy, while assuming that it would control the central authority. Constitutional negotiations among the former colonies left purposefully unresolved the issue of the future of Southern slavery. This compromise allowed for a degree of unity, but also reinforced the potential for a regional divide. Despite Northern opposition, the South remained committed to "ride the tiger" of slavery, particularly when the Napoleonic Wars led to increased demand for slave-harvested cotton, made all the more profitable by the cotton gin after 1794.[69]

The ambivalence of this arrangement was reflected in the U.S. Constitution. Federal authority and a veneer of coordination were established, but decentralized states' rights maintained. Guarantees of equal rights were set forth, but without mention of race or the effective exclusion of blacks. Governance was established, but "who were these people to be governed" was not finally resolved.[70] This delicate arrangement allowed for the formation of the United States. But the balance of state and federal power and the extension of rights remained unresolved issues that would fuel later conflict.

Maintaining black slavery served not only Southerners' economic interests, but also provided the basis for political order within the region. As in Virginia even before independence, racial antagonism was used to encourage cross-class white unity, especially where blacks outnumbered whites.[71] Nonslaveholding whites, socially tied to planters, joined in supporting slavery, enjoying "the privilege of whipping someone else."[72] Southerners rallied around regional "solidarity at the price of provincial status," with that solidarity defined by the commitment "that the South shall remain a white man's country."[73] When slavery was further challenged from the North, more explicitly racial justifications of it and of the cross-class white coalition emerged, further consolidating Southern white solidarity on the basis of race. As V. O. Key concluded later, "there is one, and only one, real basis for Southern unity: the Negro."[74]

While the North opposed slavery, it also used race as a basis for unity across class. With few blacks and with slavery abolished in the North by the mid-nineteenth century, labor was drawn from native whites and later European immigrants.[75] To protect the interests of white workers from potential black competition, Northern states enacted early forms of Jim Crow. Indeed, segregation was pioneered in the North, as contrasted with the use of slavery, religious distinctions, and lack of segregation in the more rural South. New York levied a special tax of $250 on black voters, after 1803 newly admitted Northwestern states prohibited blacks from entering and from voting, and only five Northern states "allowed the black man equal suffrage, and even there he was confined to menial occupations and subjected to constant discrimination."[76] Early racial prejudice was not then peculiar to the South. Indeed, Tocqueville noted that racial prejudice was nowhere "more intolerant than in those states where slavery was never known" or abolished.[77]

While the North and South were not divided on the issue of race, sectional tensions over the fate of slavery remained, requiring constant adjustment. Disagreements over the future and extension of slavery were finessed by a series of concessions to Southern interests, for instance with the Missouri Compromise of 1820 balancing the admission of a slave and a free state to the Union. The Dred Scott decision of 1857 denied blacks citizenship even in free territory. As long as such arrangements held, the union remained intact, reinforced by common economic interests. The South continued to draw its capital from the North, which in turn earned profits by processing and trading the crops grown in the South. The ideology of "manifest destiny" reinforced common racial assumptions of white superiority over blacks and Indians, the latter being "removed," "scattered," and "exterminated."[78] And the South's concern about Northern domination was further assuaged by the high proportion of central government positions filled by Southerners.[79] As much as these unifying pressures eased the tension, they did not erase the fundamental regional divide and potential for conflict.

Comparative Overview

The early histories of South Africa, colonial North America, and Brazil reflected the competition of imperial powers based in Europe. The Iberian powers were first to emerge on the world scene, primarily as traders rather than as settlers or colonialists. Such early expansion brought Portugal to the fore with all of the strengths and weaknesses of a global power just emerging from feudalism. As such, the Portuguese crown depended heavily on coercion at home, and projected itself without an independent capital sector. This left "Lisbon and its king relatively independent of powerholders elsewhere in Portugal, but dependent on frequently corrupt officials. Such a monarchy could only prosper when gold and goods flowed freely from the colonies."[80] Diminished production left Portugal relatively marginalized after 1640. Already by the 1620s the Dutch Empire had become predominant, relying on a high level of independent capital concentration. Increased competition for power within the emerging burgher class and between the major trading companies then contributed to a rapid decline.[81] By 1763, the British Empire had become dominant, relying on strong independent capital pursuing profits globally under the protection of a well-funded navy.

The rise and fall of European empires had direct consequences for the colonies of Brazil, in North America, and in South Africa. The Portuguese "discovered" Brazil in 1500, began the importation of slaves by 1538, and after repelling Dutch incursions, remained the rulers of Brazil, with the later acquiescence of Britain. In North America, the British, French, and Dutch established early settlements and then separate colonies, with the British emerging as triumphant until their defeat in the American War of Independence. South Africa was "discovered" by the Portuguese, but effectively abandoned to the Dutch traders and settlers who came in 1652. By the start of the nineteenth century, British incursions produced an ethnic conflict between European fragments of Dutch and British ancestry, which came to a head a century later, when the British established dominance. South African colonial history thus recapitulated the evolution of imperial power and competition.

Running through this interconnected history of colonialism is a vein of gold. Its discovery in Brazil in 1695 "revived the Portuguese colonial economy, but failed to restore anything like Portugal's seventeenth century hegemony."[82] Already by 1712, gold production had peaked, though it remained sufficient to pay for goods imported from Britain, with the English not yet powerful enough to exert direct control.[83] History's largest cache of gold was discovered in South Africa in 1886, preceded by diamonds two decades earlier. These riches whetted the appetite of an ascendant Britain. Finally, the discovery of gold in California in 1848 came too late to draw European powers back into the United States. But the ensuing gold rush did add fuel to the rising North–South conflict over the extension of slavery into the West.

If one figure looms over a major turning point in this history, it is not a Dutch, British, or Portuguese, but instead a French emperor. Napoleon's incursion into Portugal in 1807 brought pressure from Britain on the Portuguese king to flee and take up residence in Brazil. The Portuguese thereby solidified their rule in Brazil, muting Brazilian nationalist urges. And Napoleon's costly war with Britain forced the French sale of the Louisiana Purchase to the United States, further exacerbating conflict over the extension of slavery into Western U.S. territories. Napoleon's defeat then freed the British to extend their control over South Africa. Before that, Napoleon's primary concern with war in Europe contributed to the success of the slave revolt in Haiti in 1791–1803. The resulting disruption of sugar production in Haiti bolstered Brazil's sugar trade. Britain's war with France also cut European cotton production, which was replaced by the U.S. South. The result was increased dependence on slave labor in the American South and Brazil, with the Haitian revolt sending shivers of fear through the slaveholders in both countries. Masters then proceeded to reinforce legal controls over slaves.

Competition between colonial powers produced or exacerbated conflicts within South Africa and the United States more than in Brazil. Relatively late British incursions into South Africa and the discovery of gold there brought conflict between them and Dutch descendants. While the United States rebuffed such potential European incursions after the War of Independence, European wars and the slave revolt in Haiti exacerbated conflict between the North and South over the future of slavery. In contrast, the early consolidation and consistent maintenance of Portuguese rule in Brazil helped leave that country relatively free of comparable internal conflict.

The most significant conclusion that thus emerges from an overview of comparative colonial history is the legacy of greater unity, stability, and state centralization inherited by Brazil than by South Africa or the United States. In Brazil, the crown ruled supreme, with regional captaincies and other elites dependent on the crown for their monopolies. Such greater state centralization brought relative stability, with the Portuguese rulers in situ peacefully able to finesse the transition from colony to independent empire. Portuguese Catholicism further reinforced such hierarchical unity and stability, in contrast to the Protestant divisions that accompanied British and Dutch colonialism.

South Africa and the United States enjoyed no solidified rule comparable to that of Brazil. During the nineteenth century what would become South Africa was divided between British colonies and Afrikaner republics in constant conflict with each other. The United States was also born with in-built potential divisions among colonies, states, and regions, though these were long contained and did not take the ethnic form they did in South Africa. The unifying federal authority in Washington remained weak, forced to compromise between conflicting interests for as long as possible. As a result, when elites in all three countries would seek to consolidate nation-state authority and unity in the late eighteenth and early nineteenth centuries, they confronted significant divisions and impediments in the United States and South Africa that were not equally present in Brazil.

In terms of early understandings and constructions of race, the contrast between the three cases emerges as less clear-cut. Indeed, in all three there is evidence of early racial prejudice among European descendants and in colonial policy. Analysts of Brazil have claimed exception to this trend, describing the Portuguese in Brazil as more moderate than the English in their prejudice.[84] Like other Latin American societies (even those that suffered other forms of major internal conflict), Brazil did apparently enforce and "experience comparatively low levels of overt racial strife," but this was accompanied by racial discrimination.[85] Economic underdevelopment further dampened incentives for racial provocation, together with an entrenched hierarchy that established a clear social order with blacks at the bottom. But in South Africa and the United States, British and Northern "liberalism" provoked more explicit racist ideologies among Afrikaners and Southerners, respectively. In the relative absence of such early conflict, racism was somewhat more muted in Brazil, though discriminatory practices were clearly evident.

For all its difference then, Brazil did inherit a colonial legacy of racial distinction and discrimination that might have been extended into modern forms of explicit racial domination. That this did not occur, contrary to the experiences of the United States and South Africa, cannot be adequately explained by colonial practices. Instead, Brazil's greater degree of unity and stability appears likely to be more significant in explaining later racial constructions.

3

Lessons from Slavery

Premodern slaveholding was justified as a form of national domination over "foreigners" or as property. By the nineteenth century slaveholding was increasingly defended by claims that slaves were naturally inferior.[1] Bondage encouraged racial distinctions and reinforced discrimination, whether or not it preordained specific post-abolition racial orders. The legacy of slavery was consequential.

South Africa has not figured prominently in comparative analyses of slavery, for slavery was there both somewhat limited and abolished relatively early. The Dutch East India Company, blocked from trading with West Africa by the Dutch West India Company, instead imported slaves from East Asia to supplement their labor needs after the indigenous population diminished.[2] By the end of the eighteenth century, slavery was a major fact of life, with Europeans in the wine-growing Cape outnumbered by and dependent on their 26,000 slaves.[3] By 1821, slaves formed 35 percent of the population of Cape Town.[4] Despite widespread manumission during the seventeenth century, decreasing thereafter, slaves were deprived of "the right to marry, had no rights of potestas over their children, and were unable to make legal contracts, acquire property or leave wills."[5] Such harsh treatment, provoking a minor slave revolt in 1808, was reinforced by rules against conversion and religious justifications for the exploitation of heathens.[6] British abolitionists condemned slavery, successfully pushing Britain to impose an end of the slave trade in 1807 and legal abolition in 1833 (leading to emancipation by 1838), several generations before the end of colonialism. This foreign-imposed, early abolition arguably diminished the relevance of slavery for later race relations. That many of South Africa's slaves were drawn from Asia further suggests that their treatment did not predetermine subsequent relations with Africans. And that early abolition did not lead to later racial tolerance in itself suggests that legacies of slavery are not straightforward. For all its significance in South Africa, the later implications of slavery are better assessed through those instances in which slavery was maintained longer, carrying its legacy more directly forward.

European powers engaged in transporting slaves out of Africa from 1500 on, bringing more than ten million African captives to the New World. Between one and two million died en route, succumbing to disease and exposure proportional to the length of the middle passage.[7] Upon their arrival in the colonies, African slaves were indispensable to the production of various products, including cotton, "the chief raw material for the industrial revolution."[8] Modernization was thus dependent on slavery, nowhere more so than in Brazil and the British colonies in North America, "the two largest slave societies of modern times."[9]

Analyses of the legacy of slavery have often focused on comparison of Brazil and North America. According to Frank Tannenbaum, Brazil accepted "the doctrine of the moral personality of the slave . . . [producing] a friendly, an elastic milieu . . . [making] possible the gradual achievement of freedom" and less conflictual post-abolition race relations. In North America, by contrast, "the slave was denied recognition as a moral person and was therefore considered incapable of freedom . . . the law and the mores hardened and became stratified, and their historical outcome proved to be violence and revolution."[10] But was Brazilian slavery any less harsh than that in the British colonies that later became the United States?

The Myth of Brazil's "Humanitarian" Slavery

Portugal had a relatively small home population, was reluctant to send settlers overseas, and was initially wary of the expense of transporting Africans to its colonies. Enslaving the indigenous population appeared to be the most promising available means to ensure a labor force for the Brazilian colony. But experience found these people to be "reluctant" laborers.[11] As Freyre describes them,

> the Indian, ill adapted to the needs of the new form of agrarian labor, became enveloped in the sadness of the introvert, and it was

necessary that his place be taken by the Negro, who with his youth-fulness, tense, vigorous energy, his extroversion and vivacity, stood in marked contrast to the American savage.[12]

Freyre characteristically overlooks the violence of this process. The native population was in large numbers exterminated, decimated by diseases and intermixture. An Indian population of 800,000 in 1570 was reduced to 360,000 by 1825.[13] Given the Portuguese propensity for finding positive interpretations of damaging fact, marginalization of the Brazilian Indians was instead hailed as a "replacement" with less "reluctant" Africans.

Portuguese importation of slaves from Africa to Brazil began in 1549. This trade peaked at 1.6 million during the nineteenth century, and by the end of the slave trade 3.5 million people had been forcibly brought to Brazil. Because slaves in Brazil were overworked and sub-ject to tropical desease, they did not reproduce their numbers as they did in North America. Massive continued importation was necessary to maintain sufficient slave labor. Portugal's dominance over the slave trade, and the relative proximity of Brazil to Portugal's African col-onies, diminished masters' incentive to encourage slave reproduction and ensured a ready supply of replacements.[14] By 1798 Brazil's pop-ulation of 3.25 million included a majority of African descent, in-cluding 1.5 million slaves and 400,000 freed slaves. Slaves and ex-slaves were dispersed nationally, constituting no fewer than 27 per-cent of the population in any single region by 1819.[15] Each of Brazil's economic booms, based on the production of gold, diamonds, to-bacco, cotton, and sugar in the North and coffee in the South, de-pended on massive slave labor. For instance, by 1600 up to 40 percent of Brazil's slaves were working to produce sugar, feeding Europe's sweet tooth.[16] Black slaves labored furiously; "no one else seemed to labor at all."[17] Rio de Janeiro became the greatest slave city in history, comparable only to Rome at the height of its empire.

Colonial Portuguese policies regarding African slavery had the ap-pearance of ambivalence. Slaves were freed in 1761 in Portugal, where "the easy transferability" of slave property did not fit into "a feudal society, with its limits on place and tenure."[18] However, this abolition deliberately excepted the much greater number of slaves in Brazil, from which Portugal profited greatly. While the Portuguese crown issued early edicts against the mistreatment of slaves in Brazil, it also directly licensed the slave trade, with its high level of mortality en route.[19] But once the slaves arrived in Brazil, according to Tannenbaum, they were treated as though their bondage was the result of "misfortune" rather than inferiority, and therefore "carried no taint."[20] The image of the well-treated house slave, akin to "an ordinary Brazilian but for his bare feet – slaves were forbidden to wear shoes," pervades historical descriptions, even though such domestic bondsmen were a minority.[21] Even in urban areas, slaves were not subject to legal segregation. According to Roberto da Matta, "in Brazil there can be intimacy between masters and slaves, superiors and inferiors, because the world is ordered according to a hierarchy."[22]

The image of a benign form of Brazilian slavery rests, in part, on an assumption that "the Catholic doctrine of the equality of all men in the sight of God" encouraged a more humanitarian treatment of slaves in Brazil.[23] The hierarchy of the universalistic Catholic Church also purportedly militated against an exclusive biracial divide. Consistent with this argument, the Church did condemn the slave trade, "insisted on the baptism of slaves, favored manumission, [and] encouraged marriage of slaves."[24] Such religious incorporation had the side effect of encouraging obedience.

Historical fact mitigates the argument about the effects of Catholicism, cutting against the doctrine of inclusion. The Church's insistence on fair treatment did imply acceptance of the institution of slavery; the Church raised no objections to how slaves were treated before 1822, and saw no contradiction in allowing slaves to be baptized at the same time they were branded.[25] The Catholic "unity of faith" and strict hierarchy served to reinforce the inferiority of heathen Africans, with religious intolerance used early on as a substitute for racism, as a justification of slavery.[26] More concretely, the Church itself practiced discrimination in appointments, held slaves, and condemned miscegenation.[27] Such practice was consistent with the Church's earlier role in the Crusades, the Inquisition, and support of colonialism. Even if these historical contradictions are ignored, it is unlikely that the Church could have enforced better treatment or an end to slavery even had it so desired. The Church remained subordinate to the Brazilian colonial state, for which it relied on funding, and it aligned itself with large landholders. Even Tannenbaum is forced to acknowledge that the Church was not effective in pressing for reforms.[28] Of course, questioning the intent or ability of the

Church to push for better treatment of slaves leaves unresolved the actual nature of such treatment.

Brazil's purportedly comfortable arrangement between slave and master was inscribed in officially "humanitarian" policies, though the reality of social practice contradicts such an interpretation. Slaves were permitted to marry each other or a free person, "even against the will of their master," though in reality slave marriage was rare.[29] Until 1869, masters could forcibly separate slave families.[30] The one or two days per week slaves were permitted to grow their own food provided barely enough for their subsistence without depleting the reserves of the master. Slaves were often trained in a wide variety of skills and gained some benefit from their work, but the result was to enable and motivate slaves to work throughout the economy to profit their masters.[31] Bans on masters' killing or injuring their slaves were largely ignored, and laws against the pervasive whipping of slaves were enacted only two years before abolition, after two slaves died upon receiving 300 lashes.[32] To prevent escape, slaves were locked in at night. To free their parents for work, some children of slaves were buried up to their necks during the day.[33]

Given the harsh treatment of slaves, the most important argument for a more humanitarian practice of bondage was the prospect of manumission. According to policy, "slaves in Brazil, by reimbursing the original purchase price, could compel their masters to free them."[34] As early as 1639, slaves banded together in "Black Brotherhoods" to save collectively to buy their freedom.[35] Though official guarantees of slaves' right to buy their freedom were enacted only in the 1880s, by the time of abolition in 1888 "there were three times as many free Negroes as slaves," including a disproportionate number of mulattoes.[36] Such large-scale manumission certainly eased the process of abolition. And Tannenbaum argues that such manumission indicates that Brazilian slavery was effectively "contractural," rather than being based on images of innate and inescapable inferiority.[37] As further evidence of the greater significance of legal status rather than race, freed blacks (and Indians) were often used as slave catchers. Some even came to own their own slaves.[38]

The significance of Brazilian manumission has been contested, not only because of its belated guarantee. Until 1871, savings with which slaves might buy their freedom were subject to seizure, and freed slaves were often treated as though they remained in bondage.[39] Particularly in rural areas, slaves could not save enough to buy their freedom, and if freed remained subject to reenslavement if they could not prove manumission.[40] Most often, masters freed the "ill, the crippled, the aged, in order to escape caring for them," and demanded continued labor from former slaves, who were generally illiterate and unable to advance economically.[41] Under such conditions, and given the general hierarchical nature of Brazilian society, manumission did not threaten the social order and freed blacks were often left worse off than slaves.

A last piece of evidence used to defend the idea of slave rights in Brazil is the extent to which slaves were permitted to retain aspects of African culture. "Tribal units were not deliberately broken up, as in Jamaica and the United States, and the Negro was thereby able to preserve and to transmit to his children a considerable portion of his African heritage," including "religious and magical rights and beliefs."[42] Rather than indicating greater tolerance, this persistence of African culture was the result of Brazil's greater reliance on continued slave trade, with newly imported slaves replenishing collective memory and heritage. Once the slaves arrived, kinship and language groups were inevitably dispersed and subject to assimilation. But continued importation, high concentrations of slave populations, and persistent cultural practice gave the appearance of greater tolerance, which "cannot reasonably be attributed to a supposed benevolence . . . nor to [Brazilian] character and culture being any less racist."[43]

Arguments for and against Brazil having had a humanitarian form of slavery are inconsequential in light of the overriding fact that slavery in Brazil was astonishingly deadly. All told, Brazil imported ten times the number of slaves brought to North America; a steady supply of new African slaves was needed to compensate for high mortality rates.[44] Brazil's slave population lived under conditions that made reproduction of their numbers impossible. Brazilian slaveholders unable to keep their slaves alive benefited from Portugal's dominance of the slave trade to import new slaves cheaply in large numbers.[45]

Disease, affecting whites as well, decimated the slaves. Masters accepted this attrition as the price of doing business, working their slaves even harder to gain a return on their investment before losing it to death. Slaves in the mines lived for an average of only seven to twelve years.[46] "Mortality among slave children was at least eighty percent . . . Labor . . . was so cheap that no one cared what became of the offspring."[47] Only after the forced end to the slave trade in 1850 led to a trebling of slave prices in 1855–75, did slave owners attempt to protect their investments by improving slave living conditions enough to encourage reproduction.[48] Given the role of disease, continued high slave mortality cannot be fully attributed to harsh treatment. But under such circumstances, importation was itself harsh. And to ignore high mortality requiring continued slave importation, instead projecting an image of early tolerance, can only be described as cynical at best.

Brazil's slaves, watching their fellows and children dying off from disease and overwork, were themselves not fooled by any claims of humanitarianism. Inspired by the energy and rebellious spirit of the recently imported and their large numbers in urban areas, slaves responded to their conditions with an unequaled history of revolts.[49] As early as the seventeenth century, slaves seeking to escape both bondage and their use as cannon fodder in the war against the Dutch fled inland to form runaway communities, or *quilombos*. Most notably, Palmares included 20,000 runaways and was strong enough to force a peace treaty with the Portuguese in 1678 before being destroyed by an army of 6,000 by 1695.[50] News of the massive slave rebellion begun in 1791 in Haiti fed well-founded white fears of further unrest.[51] In Bahia, mulattoes rebelled in 1798 and slaves revolted at least eight times between 1807 and 1844, with the largest such revolt in 1835 "close to becoming another Haiti," leaving seventy Muslim slaves dead.[52]

Brazil's slave revolts not only are indicative of the harsh treatment slaves suffered, but also contributed to the pressure for abolition. Brazil's elites feared that "racial assertiveness . . . seemed to have the potential to destroy society all together."[53] By 1837 and especially after the U.S. Civil War, elites were increasingly debating how to avoid conflict and reduce revolts, including the possibility of expelling all blacks from the country.[54] Indeed, masters came to see slavery as a costly diversion of capital and as a constraint on attracting immigrant laborers wary of slave competition; resulting conflict was regarded as an impediment to further economic growth or to attracting foreign investment.[55] Poorer regions in the North gradually pushed for abolition as their slaves were sold South, while Southern coffee planters gradually supported abolition of slavery with the arrival of cheap immigrant replacement labor.[56] Elites came to believe that continued slavery would produce further conflict, thereby threatening the basic social hierarchy, the preservation of which was judged to be more important and achievable only through gradual, orderly abolition and socialization of blacks. Brazil's "leaders preferred abolition to social revolution."[57] Immigration further eased the transition. And as slavery had been nationwide, abolition was not regional in impact. Its prospect provoked little regional conflict, nor an extensive racist ideological defense of slavery.

International influences also contributed to the pressure for abolition. Most notably, the British were eager to end the slave trade, due to both commitments at the Congress of Vienna and concern that cheap slave labor elsewhere diminished the competitiveness of British industry. The British used their significant influence with the emperor, quietly negotiating treaties calling for the end of the slave trade. Nonetheless, the trade continued illegally from 1831 to 1848, during which up to half a million more slaves entered Brazil. Exasperated with such violations, in 1850 the British navy seized slaving ships entering Brazil, finally ending the largest slave trade in history.[58] As reduced importation was not replaced by domestic reproduction, the viability of continued bondage decreased.[59] Then the Paraguay War in 1865–70 added further pressure. Not only were 20,000 slaves freed in return for their military service, but that service led the Brazilian army thereafter to favor abolition and reform, and to refuse to hunt runaways.[60] These pressures, together with the awkwardness of being the last major slave power in the hemisphere, had a cumulative effect.

Growing fears of revolt, economic interests, immigration, and international influences all contributed to an emerging consensus for abandoning slavery, much more than did pressure from a distinct abolitionist movement. Brazil's abolitionists were notably moderate in tone, careful to take cognizance more of the interests of slaveholders than of those of former slaves, and eager to align their cause with the nation's prosperity. They advocated gradual abolition and the replacement of blacks with white immigrant labor, condemning slave revolts and largely ignoring the post-abolition fate of blacks.[61] Despite such moderation and pandering to white racism, the relatively small number of abolitionists were still marginalized as "anti-Brazil," and remained significantly less influential than their U.S. counterparts.[62] Brazilian abolitionists managed to organize mass meetings and to declare the northeastern state of Ceará free of slavery only four years before total abolition was enacted, and long after Brazil was already committed to a gradual end to slavery.[63] The abolitionists in effect were swimming with a rising tide of liberalism that favored free labor and immigration over slavery.[64]

The actual process of legal abolition was gradual and orderly. Indicative of the typical slaveholder's interest only in bondsmen at the peak of their labor capacity, slave children were freed in 1871. But these children remained obligated to work for their former masters during their most productive years, until the age of twenty-one. In 1885 slaves over sixty, by then too old to work, were liberated.[65] With the final "Golden Law" of abolition in 1888, Princess Isabel "issued a law that ended an institution that was already dead," freeing 600,000 remaining slaves.[66] This "gift" of abolition was celebrated with music and street festivals, but in retrospect, blacks would find little to celebrate, for the 1888 law included no discussion of the transition to freedom nor any allowance for ex-slaves' welfare.[67] For whites, however, there was much to celebrate. Slavery had run its profitable course despite significant slave revolts. Abolition had been achieved gradually and with no violent conflict among whites, and in the end with almost no opposition. Final "emancipation was thus an act of continuity rather than of revolution."[68] This feat of peaceful abolition demonstrated the continued unity and stability of a ruling elite and social order able to finesse even a dramatic transition elsewhere achieved only with massive bloodshed.

Two conclusions emerge from this history of Brazilian slavery. The image of a "humanitarian" form of slavery in Brazil is largely fiction. The "myth of the friendly master" was just that, a myth. The use of slaves throughout the economy reflected their large numbers more than tolerance. Official rights for slaves were late in coming and often ignored in practice. Enslavement was "severe, barbarous . . . coercive" and deadly, provoking significant revolts.[69] If Tannenbaum was correct in arguing that post-abolition race relations were determined by the form of slavery, then Brazilian slavery was certainly harsh enough to have prefigured formal racial domination and to have fomented significant subsequent conflict. The relative lack of such domination and conflict, as discussed later, suggests that Tannenbaum's thesis of direct historical determinacy was overdrawn.

What remains is that the tragedy of Brazilian slavery was ended without additional tragedy for whites. Brazil's colonial inheritance of a strongly unified state provided an institutional center capable of managing a potentially explosive transition. The center held, and moved. The slave trade was abolished and then slavery itself was phased out without significant opposition or open conflict, though with the legacy of inequality firmly entrenched in society. Afro-Brazilians emerged greatly damaged; the Brazilian state and its ruling elite were not. By surrendering an archaic form of labor coercion, it maintained a larger social order that it continued to control. In accord with a popular aphorism, Brazilians concluded it was "better to give up the ring to save the hand," celebrating peaceful abolition with a wave of flower and song.

Slavery and Abolitionism in the United States

Slavery in North America was infamously brutal. Later U.S. racial segregation was also brutal, and so there is little debate about slavery's legacy for the subsequent racial order, unlike the case in Brazil. Still, assessing slavery in North America helps to specify its implications for abolition, subsequent race relations, and nation-state building.

As in Brazil, North American colonists found the indigenous population did not meet labor needs. The Indians were too sparse, vulnerable to disease, knew the territory well enough to escape, and could use their "tribal" loyalties for resistance. To provide a pool of labor to replace an also insufficient supply of white indentured servants, the colonists turned to the importation of slaves.[70] Africans were first brought to the North American colonies in 1619, almost a century later than in Brazil. Unlike Brazil, slavery in North America would become regionally concentrated. By the late eighteenth century, slavery was concentrated in the upper South, with two-thirds of all slaves held in Virginia and Maryland. Relatively few blacks lived in the North, where they were subject to discrimination as slavery there diminished.

Slavery proved highly profitable for cotton production concentrated in the deep South, where the slave population then exploded beyond that of the upper Southern states. By the mid-nineteenth century, one-quarter of white Southern families owned slaves, though the majority of slaves were held by a smaller minority of whites. On the basis of slavery, those Southern planters with available land developed a large plantation economy producing cotton, tobacco, sugar and rice. Per capita income for all Southern whites rose steadily, at levels only slightly lower than those in the more industrial North.[71] As a result, most nonslaveholding whites came to support slavery as the basis of growth. Bondage thus also encouraged white regional unity, with the nonslaveholding white majority proud to be "associated . . . with the masters."[72]

Slavery in the United States was distinguished from that in Brazil not only by its regional concentration, but also by less reliance on continual imports. Throughout most of the eighteenth century, "approximately one third of the British merchant fleet was engaged in transporting fifty thousand negroes a year to the New World."[73] However, the higher price of importing slaves the greater distance from Africa to North America rather than to Brazil, with high mortality en route, discouraged reliance on the trade. Domestic mortality rates roughly half that of Brazil (for whites as well as blacks) reduced the need for imports, so that though North America imported a fraction of the number of slaves brought to Brazil, the total slave populations in the two locales remained comparable.[74] The proportion of foreign-born slaves fell steadily, while the descendants of native-born slaves remained in bondage for generations.

Reproduction fed a pervasive image of Southern paternalism toward its slaves. As in Brazil, the experience of better-treated house slaves was held up as an example of white generosity and intimacy, ignoring the more prevalent experience of field hands. Where Freyre had spread the myth of the friendly master for Brazil with his writings in the 1930s, Ulrich Phillips spread the same myth applied to North America. Masters were not Simon Legrees, but simply took "the place of the accustomed chiefs" of Africa. Slaves were purportedly made content by the granting of rewards, gifts, fields to cultivate, and animals.[75] The 10 percent of slaves who lived in urban areas were often provided with skills and hired out, and during these periods lived away from their masters and sometimes were even given a share of their wages.[76]

The image of American paternalism and tolerance toward slaves was a lie, as it was in Brazil. While North American slaves were less subject to disease, lived longer, and reproduced more than their Brazilian counterparts, official policies denying slaves' rights were particularly harsh. As described by Du Bois:

slaves were not considered men. They had no right of petition. They were divisible like any other chattel. They could own nothing; they could make no contracts; they could hold no property, nor traffic in property; . . . they could not control their children; they could not appeal from their masters; they could be punished at will.[77]

Rape of a slave was not a crime. Slaves were legally forbidden to learn to read and write, and at the same time their ancestral traditions and languages were eroded by suppression, fading memories, and the relative lack of newly imported Africans.[78]

Most significantly, possibilities of manumission were steadily foreclosed through the early 1800s, and in South Carolina voided altogether in 1841.[79] Even freed blacks were continually under threat of heartbreaking reenslavement, or at least expulsion from the South.[80] Limiting manumission was consistent with masters' interest in reproducing the slave population and in avoiding unrest by those slaves hoping for or having gained freedom. Slave owners were eager to keep their slaves alive and in bondage, "confirming the blacks in perpetual slavery . . . making it possible for them to accept their fate."[81]

North American slaves did not simply accept their bondage. They prayed for abolition and often resorted to subtle forms of everyday resistance such as "malingering at their work," arson and theft.[82] On occasion, their anger exploded. Up to one hundred South Carolina slaves revolted in Stono in 1739. Inspired by the slave revolt in St. Dominique, up to five hundred New Orleans slaves revolted in 1811, and seventy joined Nat Turner's rebellion in 1831.[83] These episodes raised white fears of another Haiti, though in North America there were few such revolts and few comparable in size to those in Brazil. This difference has generally been ascribed to the lower influx of more rebellious Africans, for the loss of "African mental furnishings" and ties over time did diminish the prospect of collective action.[84] The lower proportion of slaves in urban areas also lessened chances of revolt, as compared with Brazil where urban concentrations allowed for conspiracies. Those slaves in Southern cities were under tight control, for instance needing passes to go out at night.[85] And because North American slavery was regional rather than national, some slaves did manage with great difficulty to flee to the North rather than fight or form local *quilombos*.

Unlike in Brazil, regional tensions over slavery were exacerbated by a much more vibrant abolitionist movement. In 1831, William Lloyd Garrison first published his *Liberator*, launching "a crusade almost quasi-religious in its liturgy." By 1852, with the abolitionists strongly organized, the unprecedented sale of 300,000 copies of *Uncle Tom's Cabin* demonstrated and expanded the breadth of the movement's appeal.[86] With few blacks and no slaves in the region, Northern abolitionists could afford to demand racial justice, pressing the Republican Party toward this goal and even advocating the end of segregation in the North.[87]

Alongside of and often opposed by the abolitionists, there emerged a more moderate movement in favor of returning slaves to Africa.[88] The American Colonization Society, founded in 1817, used federal government and other support to found Liberia and to transport 13,000 blacks there.[89] Lincoln himself advocated this approach, convinced that the "physical difference between the white and black race . . . will forever forbid the two races living together upon terms of social and political equality," and that the necessarily inferior position of blacks was inconsistent with American values.[90] Better they should leave. Lincoln even used the term "nigger," which would come into even greater usage after emancipation.[91]

In response to abolitionism, explicitly racist imagery and ideology forcefully emerged in the United States in the mid-nineteenth century as further justifications for continued slavery. By contrast, in Brazil abolition was more consensual and racist ideology to defend slavery less developed. According to Fredrickson, in the United States, "prior to the 1830s . . . open assertions of permanent inferiority were exceedingly rare. It took the assault of the abolitionists . . . to force the practitioners of racial oppression to develop a theory that accorded with their behavior." Black inferiority was projected as a rationale for subordination as "the destiny of the blacks."[92] Publication of Gobineau's racist theory in 1856, and interpretations of Darwin as suggesting that "blacks were a degenerate race with no future," would add scientific legitimacy to rising racism.[93] Full-blown racist ideology, however, would develop even further after emancipation, when continued domination of blacks without the institution of slavery required further justification. And only then would further formal rules of segregation be encoded. Such a "mechanism for maintaining social distance and control, was for the most part unnecessary and almost meaningless in the period when most Negroes were slaves, for slavery was very effective segregation – at least in the mind, where it counted."[94]

While racism was emerging, the regional divide of slavery shaped the American process of abolition, much as it had shaped state structures. The framers of the American Constitution had postponed the end of the slave trade to after 1808; American involvement in the slave trade to Brazil and elsewhere was outlawed in 1800. But because of reproduction – birth rate at least equal to the death rate – the end of the slave trade did not threaten slavery itself, as it did in Brazil. Meanwhile, power was carefully distributed between central authority and the states, appeasing Southern states, which used their power to protect the institution of slavery. Alexander Hamilton's calls for more centralized power had been rejected in part because Southerners viewed such a construction as threatening to slavery.

America's great invention of federalism was an offspring – or at least a stepchild – of America's great tragedy of slavery. And the issue of the federal balance of power continued to be calibrated according to the ongoing dispute over slavery. The South insisted upon and used "states' rights" to protect slavery, and in 1850 gained a federal commitment that fugitive slaves anywhere would be returned to their masters. Abolitionists in the North sought to turn federal power away from support of slavery. They eventually "abandoned their commitment to states rights and adopted an unqualified unionism, once it became apparent that this would further the anti-slavery cause."[95]

The emerging conflict between Northern abolitionist supporters of federal power and Southern proslavery states' righters became the fundamental political issue in the nation. On this score, the United States were not all that united. Henry Clay and Daniel Webster had to use all of their powerful rhetoric and political skill to preserve the Union with compromises on slavery. With westward expansion, "the exclusion of slavery in the territories offered [to the North] a constitutional, perhaps peaceful, strategy for taking control step by step of the federal apparatus."[96] The South resisted, asserting its interests in Washington. In the attempt to preserve the constitutional balance and slavery, compromises allowed for the extension of slavery within the Louisiana Purchase, across the Mississippi, and into Texas.

With the nomination of Abraham Lincoln for the presidency in 1860, this regional conflict was solidified into party politics. Southerners vilified Lincoln's faction as "the Black Republican Party."[97] Lincoln himself was steadfastly committed to preserving the Union, reinforcing common practices within "a nation, not a league of sovereign states," and ending slavery, albeit gradually.[98] Lincoln's electoral victory, based on Northern support, made it evident that the fundamental regional conflict could no longer be deferred by compromise.[99] The South saw the federal apparatus as having been captured by Northern interests, and this loss of balance rapidly eroded Southern willingness to remain in the Union.

The implications of this overview of American slavery and abolitionism can be briefly summarized. The treatment of slaves was harsh, evident in their absolute lack of rights and the virtual foreclosure of manumission. This treatment was somewhat offset by slaveholders' interest in keeping their human property alive, productive, and reproducing, so as to avoid costly purchase of replacements. The relatively small number of slave revolts is similarly inconclusive. But arguing that the lack of revolts demonstrates acceptance by slaves ignores the important role of repression. What is not ambiguous is the degree to which slavery and its defense encouraged images of black racial distinctiveness and inferiority, providing the foundation on which the post-abolition racial order would be built.

American slavery was shaped and most distinguished by its regional focus. The North's insistence on ending the slave trade pushed up the price of slaves, resulting in greater interest within the South in slave reproduction and in precluding manumission and flight so as to avoid purchasing replacements. Regional conflict was further exacerbated by debates over the westward extension of slavery. By the mid-nineteenth century, the fate of slavery became fully enmeshed in a regional conflict between Southerners seeking to reinforce states' rights to protect slavery, and Northerners pushed by abolitionists to use federal power to end it. The form, and even the survival, of the Union came to be inextricably tied to the future of slavery. This conflict gave rise to explicitly racist rhetoric and ideology used by the South to defend its institution under threat and then later to justify post-abolition racial domination.

Comparing Slavery and Its Implications

Brazilian slavery was not "humanitarian," nullifying such an explanation for the later lack of official racial domination there. The Catholic Church was itself ambivalent on the issue of slavery and, regardless of its predilections and practices, had only limited influence over Brazilian slave codes. Those codes did include some rights to own property, marry, and to buy freedom, which created a large group of freed blacks accepted by whites as such, easing the transition to abolition. But all of these rights were encoded only very late in the history of Brazilian slavery, by which time the entire edifice was crumbling, and they were often ignored in practice. By then racial discrimination and inequality had spread with extensive slavery.

Brazil's particular slave practices were part and parcel with slaveholders' replenishing their human stock via cheap new imports. Allowing slaves to buy their freedom after their peak years of labor freed the masters to buy new, more vigorous slaves and to enjoy being paid by their victims for the privilege. More importantly, most slaves did not live to take advantage of this official possibility, for slave owners could not keep their slaves alive and had little incentive to try. By contrast, manumission was less likely in North America but slaves were less subject to disease and more likely to survive. Slave stocks were replenished through reproduction rather than by replacement. Brazil's continued reliance on the slave trade to counter the astonishingly high mortality rate for slaves suggests that in its most fundamental sense, Brazilian slavery was at least as heinous as its counterpart to the north.

The different forms of reproduction of slave labor in Brazil and North America relate to the legacies of Portuguese and British colonialism. Tannenbaum argued the case for a Portuguese legacy of tolerance and humanitarianism, but its chief legacy was Brazil's access to a cheaper and extended slave trade to offset high mortality in the tropics. Alternatively, Tannenbaum argues that the British colonial legacy was one of harsh treatment. But Britain's opposition to the slave trade, which eventually forced its end even in Brazil, encouraged better treatment for slaves in the United States and later in Brazil. Britain's early expulsion from its American colonies actually reinforced slavery; "separation from England . . . liberated a plantation slave regime in the South. With the threat of British interference removed and a relatively weak central government to contend with, the road to regional power lay open before the slaveholders."[100] The more liberal influence of Britain is further indicated by its earlier role in abolishing slavery in South Africa.

Brazilian slavery, with its reliance on constant replenishment, was doomed by the British-enforced end to the slave trade. Abolition was also furthered by the dramatic history of revolts by slaves who faced the prospect of likely death, found themselves concentrated in large numbers, and had no chance to escape to a free region. Eventually, believing themselves faced with a choice between slave revolution and abolition, the Brazilian elite opted for the latter, thereby hoping to preserve the basic social order and hierarchy.

What then can we conclude about the direct legacy of slavery? Bondage took different forms in Brazil and North America, though plantations made much use of slaves in both. Myths of paternalism were embraced by defenders of slavery in both countries, but this commonality would not lead to comparable later treatment. And the realities of slavery in Brazil and North America were comparably harsh. Post-abolition racial orders, whether explicitly segregationist as in the United States (and South Africa) or not, as in Brazil, would develop in this context. Slavery reinforced the pattern of discrimination, even if it did not directly determine specific post-abolition racial orders. And arguably, if slavery did determine later outcomes, it did so in the opposite manner to that generally argued. More extensive slavery in Brazil entrenched inequality and discrimination, the legacy of which helped to preserve the racial order without later legal action or racial labor restriction. By contrast, less extensive slavery and earlier abolition in South Africa may have given further impetus to legally entrench later segregation and apartheid. The United States would fall between the two extremes.

What does emerge is the centrality of regional conflict, or lack thereof, in shaping the North American and Brazilian slave systems. In the United States, slaveholders were isolated in the South and deprived of continued slave imports by the North. In Brazil, where Portuguese rule had imposed a stronger unified state and spread slavery throughout the country, much less regional distinction in slavery emerged. Nor was there comparable regionalized pressure to help force an end to the slave trade.

The regional or national spread of slavery is also of fundamental importance in accounting for the different paths to abolition. In the United States, the fate of slavery was imbedded in an unresolved regional conflict over the distribution and use of federal and state power. In the end, compromise and negotiation failed, leading to the massive violence of the Civil War, during which emancipation was proclaimed by military edict. In Brazil, where slavery was widespread, the question of abolition and race relations "did not become the plaything of regional politics."[101] Slave-owning Brazil remained more united, facing no threat of regional secession and experiencing neither a significant abolitionist movement nor an opposing movement among slave owners to protect their property. As one American noted upon witnessing Brazil's flower-bedecked passage of an act toward gradual abolition in 1871, "I am going to send these flowers to my country to show how a law is passed in Brazil which caused the shedding of so much blood in the United States."[102]

Brazil's colonial legacy of a greater degree of unified control was distinguished from the legacy of decentralization in the United States. The resolution of slavery in the two countries was shaped by the same contrast. That earlier abolition had exacerbated ethnic conflict in South Africa suggests a greater similarity of this case with that of the United States, for in both resistance to abolition fed racist ideology. But the more limited and distant legacy of slavery in South Africa, and its later enactment of extensive segregation, further undermine the argument that more extensive slavery preordained more extensive racial domination. In Brazil, this connection between prior extensive slavery and later "legal treatment" was also indirect, if not reversed.

4

The Uncertain Legacy of Miscegenation

How were later race relations influenced by the extent to which blacks and whites mixed during colonialism and slavery, and the subsequent treatment of "mixed race" peoples? To answer, it is necessary to examine both the early historical record and debates, and how mulattoes were treated and categorized after slavery and colonialism were ended. If such practices varied over time in each country, then the determinacy of miscegenation will appear less certain.

How miscegenation shaped race relations has been most prominently explored in attempts to explain post-abolition Brazil's lack of racial domination and conflict. Analysts have suggested that this "exceptionalism" was the result of greater "cross-race" mixing in Brazil. Descendants of Africans and Europeans commingled in Brazil in extraordinarily high numbers. Their mulatto offspring were treated as an intermediary population both before and after abolition. This mixing and social fluidity supposedly made it impossible for Brazil to develop a strict biracial order, thereby also diminishing the prospect for racial conflict. I will address each of these arguments for Brazil, and in comparison with South Africa and the United States.

The high degree of miscegenation in Brazil was the result of historical circumstance, not cultural predilections. Though Freyre and others argued for a Portuguese Catholic tradition of racial tolerance dating back to contact with the Moors, no consistent Luso-tropical laxity toward miscegenation is evident. Portuguese settler colonials in Africa cohabited with blacks extremely rarely.[1] But the Portuguese came to Brazil initially for conquest and trade, rather than to settle, and few women were brought along.[2] Indeed, the Brazilian crown explicitly forbade Portuguese women from migrating to Brazil as early as 1732, so as to encourage growth of the small population at home.[3]

Reproduction and heterosexual pleasure for males depended upon their finding a female. As most women in Brazil were of darker skin than the Portuguese males, "cross-racial" sexual practices developed accordingly, disregarding official prohibition. Though the state and Church condemned miscegenation as against nature, the pope's power over nature proved as limited as that of the crown. Official, religious, and even early literary condemnations of miscegenation went unheeded, much to the dismay of the racist writer Count Gobineau, posted as a diplomat in Brazil in 1869–70.[4] Brazilians of African and European descent cohabited, with sexual preferences shaped by necessity, resulting in a "cult of the mulata" among Portuguese males. This desire was further inflamed by the relatively low proportion of imported slave women, making any woman highly prized.[5] Portuguese domination was extended even into the realm of sex – black women were "taken." And the simple demographic fact of close to equal proportions of people of European and African descent made miscegenation all the more likely than where Africans were a clear minority or majority.

The results of this mixing were dramatic. In 1818, Brazil's population of 3.5 million was categorized as 60 percent black and 10 percent mulatto. By 1890, the census showed 41 percent mulatto nationally, breaking down regionally to 24 percent mulatto in the Southeast and 48 percent in the rest of the country, with approximately 6 percent of officially registered marriages in Salvador being between whites and blacks.[6] The fourfold increase in the mulatto population during the empire indicates a high level of miscegenation. There was no "hypo-descent rule" that might have otherwise forced a biracial categorization of mulatto offspring simply as black, no matter how small the proportion of their African ancestry. Such biracial categorization was perhaps unlikely to be imposed by the Portuguese, whose own earlier mixing with the Moors had produced a darker self-image than elsewhere in Europe.[7]

Brazil's early lack of precise color lines allowed for the emergence of an intermediate category, reflecting physical mixing.[8] Many blacks welcomed the prospect of social advancement for their children by mixing with whites. Lighter-skinned offspring were more highly prized than darker, with those black women producing lighter chil-

dren praised for having "clean stomachs."[9] Reflecting these preferences, the black population diminished proportionately as the number
of mulattoes increased. Blacks and whites embraced miscegenation
and mulatto offspring, not seen as a diluting of the white race but as
"whitening" all Brazilians. The resulting mixture was widely celebrated as a social strength, as was true elsewhere in Latin America.[10]
The alternative interpretation argued by Count Gobineau – that such
mixing was a source of weakness – was clearly unattractive in the
Brazilian context.

Pre-independence Brazil did not recognize mulattoes idly, for doing so provided a population that could and did serve an economic
role between white masters and black slaves. The burgeoning population of mulattoes, often themselves recently freed from slavery,
worked as craftsmen, soldiers, overseers, and slave catchers. As such,
they filled vital functions that whites were too few and unwilling to
pursue.[11]

The emergence, social acceptance, and intermediate position of
numerous mulattoes in Brazil have been used to explain the lack of
formal discrimination in both the pre- and post-abolition eras. Carl
Degler argued that the possibility of blacks' social advancement
through miscegenation provided "an escape hatch" from subordination.[12] Given such fluidity, biracial segregation would have been difficult to construct. Mulattoes were supposedly too well off to be
discriminated against as blacks. And as mulattoes became more numerous, demarcating them into a common category with blacks
would have risked the construction of a larger antagonistic group and
potential conflict. Instead, mulattoes were absorbed, or at least encouraged in the belief that they could be "whitened."

Given tremendous racial mixing, Brazilians supposedly could not
devise a way of clearly distinguishing one group from another, which
prevented systematic discrimination.[13] Biology intruded on any attempts at biracial social engineering. Brazil's "consciousness of, and
concern for, physical appearance has thus paradoxically militated
against the drawing of precise color lines between distinct groups."[14]
With race defined as an identity associated with physical difference,
emphasizing such physicality of "color" where there was much mixing
undermined any artificially strict distinctions of race.

Analysts have concluded that there were no effective racial distinctions, but the historical record undermines such an inference.

Imperial Brazil recognized not a biracial but a three-way racial division, and discriminated accordingly, albeit often informally. The necessity for intermediaries was projected as the virtue of social fluidity, though the reality was not all that fluid. Mulattoes were stuck in a clearly demarcated intermediate position. As such, they were often better off than enslaved blacks, but still suffered from significant discrimination. They were marginalized with blacks, and distinguished from blacks only if freed.[15] For instance, after 1850, mulattoes could no longer serve as officers in the Guarda Nacional.[16] The mulattoes themselves well understood how they were circumscribed; they joined black revolts and movements, but at the same time reinforced their marginal superiority by avoiding marriages with blacks.[17] Whites also observed the racial stigma, steadfastly avoiding being reclassified as mulatto.[18]

Brazil's "mulatto found the door ajar." But focusing on the door of social advancement being partly open to mulattoes ignores the greater extent to which the door remained "not fully open."[19] To scholars from the United States, conditioned to believe that racial order must be bipolar, a tripartite order seemed to violate the precepts of racialism, and was described as prefiguring later tolerance. But such a three-way division of racial groups was consistent with Brazil's social structure, for "in a hierarchical society, it is easy to reflect intermediate categories."[20] And the resulting hierarchy did divide people according to color in a segmented continuum, with darker peoples worse off. As Degler acknowledged, "Brazilians are not color-blind," but simply recognize a somewhat greater "array of terms and gradations" than the white–black divide of the United States.[21]

Gradations of racial discrimination remain evident in Brazil. With a few notable exceptions, mulattoes are largely underprivileged. The "escape hatch" has either closed or never existed. Indeed, Degler himself did not provide any statistical evidence of black mobility beyond simply demonstrating the level of miscegenation. Brazilian culture remains inclusive. But recent scholarship has established that the difference in socioeconomic status between mulattoes and blacks is insignificant in comparison with the relative privilege of whites, whose average income was about twice that for nonwhites both in 1960 and in 1976.[22] Such evidence reaffirms that Brazil constructed an informal racial order that was highly discriminatory against blacks and browns. Earlier patterns of inequality were maintained, with just enough mulattoes advancing to encourage belief in mobility. But the small number of mulattoes in prominent positions during the empire all but disappeared thereafter. Continued popular belief in "the mulatto escape hatch" appears to be based less on material conditions than on an ideological project encouraging assimilation. Miscegenation did not produce mobility, but the myth of such mobility did dilute potential conflict.

The pre-abolition United States also faced the question of how to categorize mulattoes, although they existed in smaller proportion than in Brazil. With a larger settler population than Brazil and a more equal sex ratio among both blacks and whites, miscegenation occurred less frequently. Whites were not eager to encourage an increase in the mulatto population. In particular, white women purportedly protected their interests in the family structure by insisting on the exclusion of mulattoes from accepted white society.[23] By the mid-eighteenth century, six of the thirteen colonies outlawed interracial marriages, and after the mid-nineteenth century the offspring of interracial unions were generally categorized as blacks, even if they had only "one drop" of African blood.[24] Unlike in Brazil, few of the intermediate category of mulattoes filled the economic roles of craftsmen or overseers, with these functions jealously guarded by the larger number of nonslaveholding whites.[25] To protect whites' interests, manumission was rare and miscegenation discouraged precisely to avoid increasing the sort of intermediate population that emerged in Brazil.

Discouragement of miscegenation does not mean that there were no peoples of mixed ancestry in the United States. Prohibitions proved unable to curtail sexual practices, with offspring subject to categories that changed over time as the biracial order was refined. Between 1620 and 1850, approximately 7.7 percent of slaves were described as mulatto.[26] In 1850, 11.2 percent of the black population were categorized as mixed-race, rising to above 12 percent ten years later.[27] And during the last decade of slavery, the number of mulattoes in bondage reportedly increased by 67 percent.[28] Though the total number of mulattoes remained much smaller in the United States than in Brazil, the growing number of freed mulattoes provoked the larger number of poorer whites to push for a more rigid divide.

Only when abolition undermined slavery as the basis for social distinctions was a biracial order fully elaborated. As early as 1850, white Americans became increasingly concerned about the rising number of mulattoes as a threat to the racial order and to white privilege. The "one drop of blood" rule served to resolve this threat by defining and marginalizing the mulatto population together with blacks, subordinated by race rather than bondage. The resulting polar divide made it more difficult for light-skinned blacks than for later European immigrants to "pass" into a higher status, reinforcing both discrimination and black solidarity, extended even to so-called mulatto elites.[29] For instance, the Supreme Court's 1896 *Plessy* v. *Ferguson* decision upheld the extension of the black racial category even to a person seven-eighths white. Such extreme Jim Crow segregation forced Americans with any African ancestry together as fellow victims of racial domination. By the early twentieth century, most self-described mulattoes saw their fate as forcibly tied to the African-American community.

With segregation applied to anyone with the least African ancestry, the earlier distinct status of mulattoes was largely forgotten. Brown Americans disappeared as a separate category absorbed into black Americans. After the 1910 census recorded 21 percent of blacks as mulatto, the category of mulatto was excluded from the census.[30] Legal efforts to curtail race mixture remained on the books, for as late as 1967 sixteen states still had laws against miscegenation. Though the categories have been fluid, between 75 and 90 percent of African-Americans now are estimated to have some white ancestry, with those with "lighter skin" generally better off.[31] However, the biological fact of mixing became largely meaningless during most of this century, for social and legal practice enforced a biracial division, distinguished from Brazil's triracial order. Race was established and changed by official categories, not by nature.

The early history of South Africa also brought significant miscegenation. The original Dutch settlers on the Cape, few in numbers and even fewer in numbers of women, engaged in extensive mixing. "Marriages and extra-marital intercourse between Europeans and liberated full-blooded female slaves were forbidden."[32] Nevertheless, "during the first twenty years of settlement [on the Cape] three-quarters of the children born to the [Dutch East India] Company's slaves had white fathers." Between 1688 and 1807, about a quarter of "the founding marriages" of Afrikaners "involved one spouse, usually female, who had some known degree of nonwhite ancestry."[33] The offspring of such unions were accepted as and among whites, for instance with "dark-skinned" Simon van der Stel serving as governor from 1679 to 1699. Coloureds in South Africa were long able to advance socially, passing as whites and not as a distinct third category as in Brazil. In "an atmosphere of racial fluidity and public mixing," a traveler in the early nineteenth century, arriving in British-dominated Cape Town, might "wonder if he had taken the wrong ship and ended up in Brazil by mistake."[34]

A distinct "coloured" identity developed gradually in South Africa. The salience of this category was reinforced by varying official policies of relative privilege and of heightened discrimination, which from opposite directions demarcated coloureds as such. By 1861, coloured children in the Cape were "effectively banned from the public schools," though other forms of early official discrimination remained rare or uneven.[35] Natal and Cape coloureds could vote, while those in the Afrikaner republics "never had the vote at any stage."[36] After the Boer War, coloureds sought exemption from rising discrimination; a distinct coloured population was recognized as such for the first time in the 1904 census.[37] Eager to win over allies, the new Union government did provide the 10 percent of Cape voters designated coloured with representation by four senators, though these had to be white.[38]

The Union and later Republic of South Africa continued to distinguish coloureds with both greater privilege than blacks and less than whites, thereby hoping to encourage coloured loyalty and to discourage them from aligning with the African majority. In the 1920s Prime Minister J. B. M. Hertzog advocated better treatment for coloureds. In 1943, the Smuts government established a separate Coloured Affairs Department, with threatened discrimination provoking "coloured leaders in Cape Town to seek closer cooperation with Africans."[39] To head off such a realignment, in subsequent years some segregation laws were explicitly not applied to coloureds.[40] The National Party, after its 1948 victory, removed coloureds from the white voting role, but also sought to appease the coloureds with "labor preference" rights in the Cape after 1954.[41] In 1976, the government's Theron Commission advocated that coloureds be subject to reduced segregation and receive more equal wages, access to universities, and direct representation, but these recommendations were not immediately implemented.[42]

Despite some accommodation to coloureds as such, the logic of apartheid gradually led to increased discrimination of coloureds together with Africans, pushing these two groups toward a stronger alliance and convergence. Coloured per capita income remained much closer to that of blacks than to that of whites.[43] Recognizing increased discrimination against them, in 1955 the South African Coloured Peoples' Organization joined the Congress Alliance, reinforcing an emerging accord between coloureds and Africans as common victims of apartheid. Despite some reluctance, by the 1970s coloured students were joining Africans and Asians in the Black Consciousness movement, redefining themselves all as blacks and rejecting the divisive categories of Pretoria.[44] In the 1980s, the coloured population of close to three million was subject to continued discrimination, though still enjoying a higher average salary than Africans.[45] The discrimination proved salient, with most coloured organizations affiliating with the anti-apartheid United Democratic Front organizations in large numbers. The distinctive coloured identity inscribed in official regulations seemed to have all but faded into joint opposition. But while many coloureds remained committed to a joint black identity, their distinctiveness had not vanished, in part due to some continued privilege. In the landmark 1994 election, many Cape coloureds expressed their fear of African majority rule and the loss of their relative privilege by voting for the National Party, which had encouraged such fear.

Miscegenation produced "mixed race" populations in Brazil, the United States, and South Africa. But historian Carl Degler implied that particularly extensive "mixing" in Brazil vitiated strict racial categorization and discrimination. Marvin Harris suggests that in the absence of sharp distinctions, "systemic discrimination cannot be practiced," and conflict is thereby avoided.[46] This argument overlooks both Brazil's categorization of blacks, mulattoes, and whites as such, and the significant discrimination suffered jointly by blacks and the intermediate group. Contrary to Harris's reasoning, a particular form of discrimination was practiced in Brazil, with racial categories established accordingly. The lack of later racial conflict suggests that the myth of fluidity did take hold. It does not prove that there were no effective racial categories of discrimination applied to blacks and mulattoes.

Comparative analysis further undermines the argument that miscegenation in itself precludes categorical discrimination and domination. This argument implies that substantial mixing in South Africa and the United States should have militated against the imposition of strict segregation in those countries. But the large number of mulattoes in the United States and South Africa did not prevent construction of increasingly biracial categories. Instead, South African and U.S. authorities gradually resolved physical ambiguities by drawing strict racial boundaries. Mixing was a "problem" requiring "solution," as it was in Brazil. In South Africa, "the problem of how to tell where colored ended and white or African began"[47] was resolved by official edicts, which themselves varied over time and ultimately failed to "define explicitly who is coloured."[48] In the United States, the categorization of mulattoes was similarly fluid. Tocqueville assumed that, "it is the mulatto who forms the bridge between black and white; everywhere where there is a great number of mulattoes, the fusion of the two races is not impossible."[49] But this "Brazilian option" was not followed in the United States, where blacks and whites were not fused, but mulattoes and blacks were.

To some degree, the United States and South Africa pursued opposite "solutions" to the mulatto "problem." According to writer Gertrude Millin, "South Africa, in short, classes with the white any person who can conceivably pass as white, where America classes with the Negro any person who can conceivably pass as Negro."[50] The South African white minority bolstered its numbers with coloured allies, at least for a time. The American white majority was more confident of its ability to dominate a black minority. There was little interest in an alliance with mulattoes. But demographic proportions were not consistently determinant. The categories of such strategic calculations were themselves fluid, as were the calculations themselves. And in both South Africa and the United States, mulattoes were eventually excluded from most rights, though the interests of a white minority and majority intuitively should have produced opposite outcomes. Most startling is that even the white South African minority, pursuing racist ideology to its extreme, eventually discriminated against and alienated the coloureds. Being outnumbered did not preclude drawing lines of exclusion against former intermediaries.

Racial categories per se remained particularly fluid as long as slavery served as the primary social distinction. A person was either enslaved or free. The dividing line of bondage was firmly entrenched in law and social practice. As long as only and most Africans were slaves in the United States, racial categorization remained of secondary importance. The relatively "closed character of slavery in both South Africa and the United States" allowed for little manumission and produced less mixing, setting "the stage for a two-category pattern of race relations" that emerged once slavery was threatened and then abolished.[51] During the transition period, mulattoes were recognized as a distinct category, further demonstrating that shifting definitions followed historical developments rather than fixed distinctions. In Brazil, where slavery was less "closed" and miscegenation occurred to a greater extent, the mulatto population was larger and more widely recognized as a distinct group, serving necessary economic functions. After abolition, the mulatto category remained in place, though this population was subject to discrimination. The higher proportion of Brazilian mulattoes was significant but did not preclude categorization.

No doubt the higher level of miscegenation in Brazil would have made a biracial order more difficult to impose than elsewhere, though the Brazilian state was certainly capable of such an imposition, given its evident ability to manage social change. Biracialism would not have been impossible given sufficient will. Miscegenation by itself did not preclude an official racial order, which in the United States and South Africa was constructed biracially despite physical variation, and in Brazil was constructed as a more fluid triracial divide.

Degler argued not only that miscegenation in Brazil made strict racial categorization impossible, but that mixing also led to greater social fluidity vitiating racial segregation and domination. Yet even in Brazil, mobility was more celebrated than real, particularly in this century. Mulatto mobility was largely a myth aimed at appeasing the intermediate group, which was actually less privileged than implied by that term. And in South Africa and the United States, where post-abolition racial segregation and domination were imposed, there had been some early degree of mobility. Lighter-skinned American blacks and South African coloureds continued to enjoy somewhat higher economic status than blacks even after abolition. But by the early twentieth century, in both South Africa and the United States the relative privileges and distinction accorded to mulattoes were eroded by official racial domination. For instance, in the United States after

1850, the "one drop rule" defined mulattoes as blacks, subject to Jim Crow segregation as it emerged later in the century. Miscegenation was not determinant, but was instead purposefully ignored in order to preserve an emerging "collective racist fantasy" of a bipolar division of black and white.[52] South Africa never abandoned the intermediate category of mulattoes to the same extent as in the United States. But legal South African discrimination did increasingly subordinate coloureds together with Africans, provoking a gradual alliance of these victims of apartheid as blacks. Informal discrimination also affected mulattoes in Brazil, but in the absence of official biracial domination, the mulatto category remained more salient and a combined Afro-Brazilian identity was thereby discouraged.

If miscegenation in itself did not consistently determine the possibility or form of racial categories, nor determine the prospects for mobility, it cannot be said to have preordained the prospect for racial domination. Though people often believe and act as if race is physically determined, shifts of beliefs, categories, and practices demonstrate the contrary. Racists believe that physical distinctions are fixed, but racial orders are fluid and contingent. Biology itself draws no strict boundaries of racial categories, nor can it account for historical variations in how such boundaries were used. Mixing in itself is not determinant of where the lines of racial distinction are drawn by society. The real issue is how miscegenation was interpreted and offspring categorized. These outcomes were not preordained by mixing, but were instead the result of purposeful policies and changing predilections. Put simply, the common fact of miscegenation cannot account for the emergence of a biracial order in the United States and to a lesser extent in South Africa, as contrasted with the triracial order and image of "racial democracy" that emerged in Brazil. Demographics and the level of miscegenation did influence these outcomes, but not consistently. And differences of degree in miscegenation cannot account for differences in kind of later racial orders and conflict.

Physical differences in themselves do not explain social outcomes. Instead, socially constructed discrimination itself creates racial categories, varies, and reinforces solidarity accordingly. Such categorization and domination "had not much to do with objective economic and demographic factors, but rather, with subjective ones."[53] This critique lies at the heart of modern assumptions about race as situational and not primordial. We must look beyond the biological fact of miscegenation to why continuous physical variation was forced into strict biracial categories or an informal triracial order. The results of this difference were profound. Biracial categories were used for dyadic domination and inflamed antagonism. Informal triracialism was not.

Implications

Colonial and religious legacies, slavery, and miscegenation demonstrate that social constructions of race were evident in the early history of Brazil, South Africa, and the United States. These practices took different forms, but authorities consistently reinforced forms of discrimination, often justified by religious differentiation. Slavery itself may not have been initially associated with race per se, but its practice was racially distinguishing and defended accordingly. Rules about miscegenation and the treatment of "mixed race" peoples clearly referred to and encouraged ranked racial categorizations. In this sense, racial orders were evident by the nineteenth century, providing a foundation on which later social constructions could be and were built. Assumptions of primordial difference were prevalent, entrenched in institutions and culture, and given scientific credence.

This overview also demonstrates the fluidity of early images of race. As nature drew no sharp demarcations, distinctions understood as primordial took different shapes and meanings. Discriminatory practices and categories imposed according to physical differences varied by place and time, even within each of the three cases. Racism arose most explicitly when slavery was challenged or abolished, with the distinction on which domination rested shifting from that of being a slave to being black. The categorization and treatment of mulattoes also shifted within each country. In Brazil, and to a lesser extent in the United States and South Africa, mulattoes or coloureds were accorded distinct status by mid-nineteenth century when slavery was nearing extinction and whites were eager to find allies or intermediaries. This distinct category had either effectively been collapsed into a catch-all black identity in the United States or was gradually eroded in South Africa. The mulatto category was preserved within Brazil's "racial democratic" order, informally triracial rather than formally biracial. But even there mulattoes were increasingly subject to discrimination. Changing boundaries of races were not explicable by reference only to biological fact.

By comparing three major cases, it is difficult to see how most of the early historical experiences summarized here by themselves determined the divergent official racial orders that would emerge during the twentieth century. All three contained significant aspects of racial discrimination, but this commonality cannot in itself account for the difference in post-abolition legal racial orders as they emerged. Brazil's denial of such early discrimination as the basis for later tolerance cannot be sustained. The United States and South Africa, by contrast, constructed distinct social orders consistent with earlier racial discrimination. Prior experiences and legacies appear too similarly discriminatory to explain these dramatic differences in subsequent outcome. While it is always difficult to explicate counterfactuals, it is certainly possible to imagine Brazil having developed a racial order more similar to that of the United States or even apartheid South Africa. Yet this was not the case. Nor did comparable early discrimination produce identical racial orders in South Africa and the United States.

If early historical practices were not as different as later policies, can this later divergence be attributed to cultural differences? Portuguese Catholicism supposedly inspired more hierarchical inclusion (despite Church practices of exclusion), while British or Dutch Protestantism encouraged rigid exclusion of the "nonelect" from the liberal order. But the Portuguese were not always tolerant and inclusive, as indicated by their colonial practices in Africa. And both South Africa and the United States in particular periods included mulattoes as intermediaries in an effective racial hierarchy. Cultural distinctions were then not consistently evident, and changed over time. Nor were such distinctions uniform within religious traditions. Protestant Afrikaners and English in South Africa, or Southerners and Northerners in the United States, differed considerably in their "cultural" assumptions about race and treatment of Africans. Religious doctrines justified different views at different times and among different groups. Culture was itself variable.

The implication is that early history and culture did not automatically determine the future. Prior discrimination did establish pervasive social inequality. But it did not preordain the later legal order, which either reinforced such discrimination or hid it under a cloak of tolerance. Instead, early historical facts were interpreted in varying ways consistent with these distinct outcomes. As such, history was brought forward through the prism of later pressures. In the United States and South Africa, the dark light of past discrimination passed through this prism in a relatively straight line to racial domination, taking different forms. In Brazil, the line was refracted, so that looking back through the "Luso-tropical" prism gave the appearance of a more tolerant and "humanitarian" past than had been the case. Current practice was justified by historical myth. This difference was not due so much to the past as to the difference in those prisms through which it was seen. As we shall see in the next section, culturally informed historical interpretations were shaped by particular emerging political and economic pressures and experiences. Later we shall see that post-apartheid or post–Jim Crow race relations were also not fully determined by prior history. Paths from the past crucially depend on how that past is interpreted.

Post-abolition developments of a racial order did diverge, most notably with the relative lack of formal racial domination in Brazil. To explain that divergence, it is necessary to turn to an analysis of the dynamics of race making in the newly formed South Africa, the reunited United States, and the Republic of Brazil. Those dynamics in turned shaped interpretations and manipulations of the past to justify the new order. Only the legacy of greater colonial unity and stability in Brazil, contrasted with violent division in South Africa and the United States, proved persistently determinant. In the United States and South Africa, the issue of how to treat Africans exacerbated ethnic and regional conflicts among whites, and gave rise to racist ideology and practice. In Brazil, there had been a stronger and more centralized colonial state, no vying ethnic fragments, and less regional tension over slavery spread throughout the country. As a result, the social hierarchy was less shaken by peaceful abolition, the polity inherited less deeply entrenched major fault lines, and no explicit racist defense emerged against more liberal challenges. These differences, tied to the degree of internal conflict, shaped how the issues of race were later addressed. The level of such internal conflict presented distinctive political situations that could not be purposefully reinterpreted and instead proved decisive.

PART TWO

Racial Domination and the Nation-State

T HE STATES of South Africa, the United States, and Brazil were either formed or significantly reconfigured during the second half of the nineteenth and early twentieth century. But amid state consolidation, national loyalty remained largely divided or nascent. Primary political allegiance had been long given to the British Empire or Afrikaner republics in what was to become South Africa, given to each state and to regions in the United States, and diluted by loyalty to Portugal within Brazil. As political institutions were reconfigured in each case, elites were eager to unify national loyalty to central states – to turn Afrikaners and British-descendant settlers into South Africans, Virginians and New Yorkers into Americans, royalists and republicans into Brazilians. Official definitions of membership in a single nation-state did not immediately produce popular allegiances accordingly.

Symbolism developed and encouraged emergent loyalty to the central polity. Flags were emblems of such unified nationalism encouraged by the state. But in each case, the national flag also represented pictorially the process by which previous allegiances were formally incorporated. The flag of South Africa included a miniature British Union Jack and banners of the two Afrikaner republics on a backdrop of the colors of Holland, thus symbolizing the hybrid nature of an emerging nation built upon previously divided loyalties. Similarly, the flag of the United States included a stripe for each of the original thirteen colonies and a star added for each state, symbolizing the federal unity of localized authority and allegiance. By contrast, the Brazilian flag bore no such references to divided powers or loyalties. Instead, Brazil's banner projected the immutable unity of the post-

81

colonial nation, symbolized by the central motif of the constellation of southern stars at the moment of the founding of the republic. The Brazilian nation was thus projected not as an emerging political compromise, but as a fixed part of the natural order. The motto inscribed on the flag, "Order and Progress," reinforced an image of managed, coherent change. Flag imagery thus reflected a fundamental difference in nation-state building. Brazil emerged from a previously unified and preserved colony and empire. South Africa and the United States, for all their other differences, were constructed out of previously more independent units.

The issue of how to construct a racial order was central to the historical process of nation-state consolidation, as symbolized by the respective flags. In the United States, abolition of slavery came with the greater subordination of the states to federal power, forged in a bloody civil war and leaving the post-abolition racial order to be reconfigured. In South Africa, abolition came earlier. But the military establishment of central rule in South Africa implied a unified policy toward Africans to replace the varying approaches of the former colonies and republics. And the relatively peaceful process of abolition in Brazil ushered in the republic, which also faced the question of how to treat freed Afro-Brazilians.

All three countries reached climactic "moments" when political reconfiguration was tied to issues of race. The emergent nation-states would then each construct a legal racial order, building upon past experience, seeking to resolve prior or potential conflict. Unity had to be reinforced, for solidified subnational loyalties remained. Historical issues of race raised "problems" that had to be addressed to reduce or avoid embedded conflicts impinging upon efforts to reinforce the nation-state. These processes reached important turning points with abolition and/or state consolidation, when new or unified racial policies were debated and enacted. And these processes then played themselves out amid continued competition, uncertainty, and variations of policy. The outcomes of these processes differed. The conflicts and compromises inscribed in the history and even the flags of the United States and South Africa resulted in varying forms of legal racial domination. The stability inscribed in the Brazilian flag somehow gave rise to "racial democracy."

Divergent racial orders solidified after abolition and/or after the formation of a unified state. That all three countries had previously enacted or practiced forms of racial discrimination did not result in a common outcome of official racial domination. The tablet was not wiped clean, but these legacies were interpreted differently, carried forward to justify racial domination, or denied to justify purported racial democracy. Something happened on the way to nation-state consolidation that set each country off on its own trajectory of race making and corresponding reinterpretations of its past. In South Africa and less pervasively in the United States, segregation was legally imposed. Why blacks were so singled out in terms of race, to be so dominated, remains to be explained. Why the same result did not emerge in Brazil also requires explanation. To explicate what happened requires analysis of the historical processes of nation-state building in each case, with reference to the resulting racial orders and to interpretations of the past and of evolving political and economic interests.

5

"We for Thee, South Africa"

THE RACIAL STATE

The modern South African house of race began as two structures separately constructed. What was to become South Africa at the start of the twentieth century inherited from the previous century polities ruled by two fragments of European settlers, Dutch-descended Afrikaners and British-descended English-speakers (hereafter called "English); the two groups were themselves divided. Earlier-settled and isolated Afrikaners clung to images of racial distinction and order, amid the complicating fact of miscegenation. The British arrived later, bringing a post-Enlightenment "liberalism" that inspired the relatively early abolition of slavery. But such liberalism did not preclude the British from also imposing domination over "the natives," or later the Afrikaners. Political and economic tensions between these groups vying for power were aggravated by disagreements over the treatment of slaves, Africans, and coloureds. The distinct solidarity of the English and Afrikaners was reinforced by resulting conflict and antagonism, dividing them despite their shared sense of white superiority. After the turn the century, the British forcibly combined the houses of Afrikaner republics and crown colonies. The misaligned floors would have to be roughly joined until the more complete renovation of apartheid constructed a more uniform edifice of racial domination. To build a united nation for whites, shared racism would become the basis for gradual reconciliation amid continued competition.

White Conflict, Forced Unity, and Black Exclusion

The arrival of the British in South Africa had a dramatic effect upon the Afrikaners. The Boers had been a loose collection of fiercely in-

84

dependent and religious families seeking to avoid enforced coordination. But the Afrikaners found a common interest in antagonism against the British. The new English-speaking settlers and authority gradually provoked mobilization and forced unity, "shaping a nation" among the Afrikaners, who grudgingly came together to protect their interests and values.[1] Particular nationalist unity, as is often the case, was forged in adversity and resistance. By the mid-nineteenth century, the emerging Afrikaner nation sought expression in its own polities, but remained divided into separate republics. Formal disunity was thus simultaneous with a rising sentiment of Afrikaner nationalism that would only find unified expression in the crucible of war with the British Empire.

Violent conflict over who would rule South Africa came to a head at the turn of the century, exacerbated by British economic interests in gold and diamonds. The English mining magnates believed that a unified modern state was required to police labor, end internal tariffs, develop railroads to transport minerals, and reduce costly competition among the mining houses.[2] Division among separate crown colonies and republics stood in the way of coherent development. When Cecil Rhodes's own efforts to seize control of the Transvaal and force unification with the 1895–6 Jameson Raid failed, he and his fellow British capitalists used their control of the English-language media to push for direct imperial intervention. They decried the treatment of the English within the Afrikaner republics, "putting the heather a flame." Never mind that the English voluntarily working in the Transvaal for the mining houses were "helots in golden chains," that they mixed freely with Afrikaners, and that the English language was already becoming pervasive rather than needing to be "thrust . . . at the sword's point." There were enough isolated incidents of ill-treatment of English in the republics to inflame the imperialist-minded British public, despite the risks of waking "this demon of war in an entire nation" of Afrikaners.[3]

Mounting public pressure led an already eager, insatiable, and confident British Empire to use military force. The result was what the historian Hugh Seton-Watson calls the conflict "closest to the simple Marxist pattern of imperialist war."[4] But it was nationalist rhetoric and competing pressures for self-determination and imperial state consolidation that fed this conflict, rather than crass admissions of self-interest.

The emergence of two distinct nationalisms, Afrikaner and English-speaking South African, was an interactive process. The British-imposed reforms and their intervention "reinforced the aspirations of Afrikaner nationalism. In turn, Afrikaner nationalism stimulated British chauvinism, each movement drawing strength from its rival."[5] As the tension between these groups heightened with the mineral discoveries and competing claims for political control, each group was increasingly unified in antagonism with the other. As the more recent interlopers and an ascendant world power, the British took the lead in this dynamic. They were confident that their version of nationalism and a unified state could be imposed, even if such a conflictual process would further aggravate divided loyalties.

British military confidence was sorely shaken by what they called the Boer War and Afrikaners called the Second War of Freedom of 1899–1902. Imperial victory was far less easily achieved than had been expected. Britain retained a preponderance of force, putting an astonishing "448,000 men in the field, while the Boers could at no time call upon more than 70,000."[6] But the Afrikaners had the home advantage. They used their knowledge of the land to engage in a guerrilla campaign, waged effectively against a rigidly formal British military. Facing continued losses, Britain shifted its tactics. Victoria and her government were determined. The Queen's army inflicted "scorched earth" retribution, and sought to deprive its adversaries of domestic support by throwing Afrikaner women and children into concentration camps. As many as 28,000, including also many Africans, perished of famine and disease in those camps. Among the military, more than seven thousand British troops died and twenty thousand were injured. The Afrikaners lost more than four thousand, a remarkably high proportion of their male population.[7] A war expected by Britain to be won handily in a few months "proved to be the longest, the costliest, the bloodiest and the most humiliating war for Britain between 1815 and 1914."[8]

In May 1902, the leaders of the remaining Afrikaner forces gathered to discuss their prospects in a town that came to be named Vereeniging, meaning "union." The meeting transcript shows that while they tried to remain positive about the "splendid" Boer morale, the commanders acknowledged that their forces were severely depleted. At best, there remained 15,000 Afrikaner men facing an enemy of a quarter million troops.[9] The possibility of negotiating a conditional peace was discussed. Convinced that "gold was the cause of the war," some argued for an attempt to retain independence by giving to Britain what it wanted, Johannesburg and the mines. But it was too late for such appeasement. The British were judged unlikely to accept the mines, for doing so "would prove to the whole world that they only wanted the Gold Fields."[10] This would contradict the empire's rhetoric of more noble aims. Instead, the immense British war effort had convinced the commanders that Transvaal Republic president Paul Kruger had been correct in his earlier statement to the British that "it is our country that you want."[11] But to continue fighting, while honorable, seemed also suicidal. General Jan Smuts concluded that "we may not sacrifice the Afrikander [sic] people for independence."[12] Seeing no alternative, the commanders resigned themselves to surrender in the hope of preserving the Afrikaner nation as such, if not political independence.

For their part, the British were eager to end an embarrassingly protracted war and to reap the fruits of military victory. To consolidate their control over all of South Africa, they needed to make peace with the Afrikaners with whom they would have to live. The British high commissioner, Lord Milner, insisted on Afrikaner "capitulation," akin to that "of Lee at Appomattox."[13] London rejected the use of the word "surrender," thereby hoping "to heal the breach between the Boers and the British." The British government was eager to make of the Afrikaners "good British subjects, whom we desire to be loyal, against whom we do not wish to be obliged to keep an enormous garrison at an enormous expense."[14] Young Winston Churchill, a journalist covering the Boer War, agreed with London's view, employing a more positive American analogy: "I look forward to the day when we can take the Boers by the hand and say as Grant did to the Confederates at Appomattox, 'go back and plough your fields.' "[15] A unified state could be stabilized and economic development made viable only with such reconciliation of former combatants.

The terms of the final Treaty of Vereeniging demonstrate that the British had decided to forgo harsh retribution. Prosecutions of former adversaries were precluded, Afrikaner war debt was limited, Afrikaners were allowed to retain their arms, and use of "the Dutch language" was to be permitted in those schools "where parents and children desire it."[16] The British were confident that they could afford such magnanimity in victory to appease Afrikaners. In that spirit insisted upon by his superiors, Lord Milner concluded the signing of the treaty by "offering his hand, saying 'We are good friends now.' "[17]

Britain's extension of friendship to the Afrikaners was a rude shock to the African majority, coloureds, and Asians. These subordinates had taken the British at their word, expecting that a victorious empire would impose its will and implement long-advocated reforms. Hoping to reinforce this prospect, black South Africans had contributed to the British war effort. Despite official commitments by both Britain and the Afrikaners to exclude Africans from a "white man's war," both sides did use Africans as scouts, laborers, and servants, with the total so involved numbering up to fifty thousand.[18] The larger British force relied heavily on such African support, which was given in return for an expected share in the fruits of victory. Colonial Secretary Joseph Chamberlain himself "promised the British parliament that victory . . . would bring 'equal laws, equal liberty' to all, whilst Milner . . . presented discrimination against coloureds as a justification for intervention . . . Not surprisingly, coloureds . . . gave the British cause their enthusiastic support."[19] Africans looked to Britain and her queen as potential saviors, akin to American slaves' view of the Union and Lincoln. When British troops arrived in Pretoria in 1900, blacks publicly burned their passes, believing that a British victory meant the documents would no longer be required.[20] The Afrikaners feared what the Africans hoped for, that "all the Kaffirs which the enemy have on their side"[21] implied that a British victory would bring an end to black subordination and labor coercion.

Neither Afrikaner fears nor African expectations regarding "native" policies were substantiated in the final peace treaty ending the Boer War. Despite their own racism, the British ostensibly began the talks with a commitment to make good on the expectations of majority Africans. According to the negotiation transcript, the British draft treaty included the promising statement that "the franchise will not be given to natives until after the introduction of self-government." But the draft British proposals were edited in the handwriting of Boer Generals Smuts and Hertzog, with this clause struck out by a firm line and replaced with: "The question of the franchise to natives will not be decided until after the introduction of self-government."[22] The British authorities accepted this revision, with no noted objection. British rhetoric that they had waged war on behalf of the coloureds and Africans was revealed as pretense. The crown did not press the matter when it finally had the chance.[23] The imperial fist had taken its prize; its hand of liberal upliftment wavered and retreated to the regal posture, clasped behind.

Britain's compromising away its commitment to the native franchise revealed the overriding nation-state building imperative of the post–Boer War era. "Concessions . . . to Afrikaner sentiment" were expressly intended to placate the defeated adversary, to "denationalize" and incorporate them within a unified white nation.[24] The threat of British reforms, which had helped to mobilize and unify the Boers, was officially removed. This policy of conciliation reflected Britain's assessment that the Afrikaners had proved themselves in war a viable threat to stable rule. Eager to consolidate their hard-won control over all of South Africa and its wealth as "a linchpin of the Empire," the British sought as their primary goal to make peace with those who could most effectively challenge that control, the Afrikaners.[25] Achieving stable imperial rule and development "depended on the help of colonial collaborators, and [the British] believed that 'in South Africa collaboration had to be with the white communities,' including the Afrikaners, who constituted the majority among the whites."[26] As Britain's "Liberal Government was committed to unifying the white races so recently at war," concessions intended to appease the Afrikaners and to invite their support were consistent with the victor's objectives.[27] To the British, such conciliation toward the Afrikaners appeared liberal.

The imperative for postwar reconciliation was reinforced by the heightened antagonism generated by that war. Heroic resistance against the leading global power had the effect of unifying the Afrikaner nation across regions in their effort to expel English "uitlanders," or foreigners. The war had been interpreted both as divine intervention – "through this war He wishes to form us into a people" – and as comparable to the American War of Independence (rather than the Civil War analogies favored by the British).[28] By the end of the war, the long history of conflict had aggravated a strongly anti-British sentiment. Boer militants encouraged such animosity and Afrikaner solidarity, leaving "the reverberations of menace" to linger on. "Memory of the war, carefully nurtured as it was, did more to unite Afrikanerdom than Kruger had ever succeeded in doing."[29] The violent process by which institutional unity had been won exacerbated white divisions threatening that official unity.

Despite the militant objections of nationalists, among Afrikaner leaders there was considerable postwar receptivity to accepting Britain's "hand of friendship." They had been defeated and in the aftermath of war they saw little alternative to finding some modus vivendi for living together with the English and for making the best of the situation. British-educated Jan Smuts took the lead in arguing for such English–Afrikaner collaboration. In his view, these two people's "fates were bound up together and their welfare would depend on their capacity to co-operate . . . The imperatives [of both] were the same: bury the hatchet; promote the common interest; and build the future on trust and confidence."[30] General Botha joined Smuts in arguing that "white people in this land should be reconciled as "one nation . . . one solid, united and strong race."[31] Britain's agreement not to insist on the native franchise removed a major irritant that would otherwise have stood in the way of white unity. Of course, popular bitterness remaining from the prior conflict could not be so easily wished away by the strategic logic of elites. But while full-fledged popular reconciliation was not possible, a veneer of reconciliation could be and was constructed, based on British concessions.

The real losers in the peace were the coloureds, the Asians, and the African majority, whose expectations of British-imposed reforms were swept aside by the very terms of the Afrikaners' surrender. Though historical fact tends to obliterate counterfactual possibilities, this result was not foregone. Lord Balfour had argued for "segregation" of the Afrikaners after the Boer War, even if he did not go on to make the logical extension of arguing for an alliance with the "natives." In any case, Balfour's proposal was rejected by the British cabinet, for "the imperial project did not propose to usher in [such] a social revolution, the sentiments of the white community as a whole had to be taken into account."[32]

Describing the notion of an English alliance with blacks against Afrikaners as "revolutionary" and as violating "white sentiments" suggests a strong racial undertone to the debate. Certainly the history of earlier discrimination suggests that British and Afrikaner views of white superiority provided a point of commonality on which peace might be built. Britain's main objective was to take control of a unified South Africa, if need be by placating the Afrikaners. It was not primarily concerned with better treatment for the "natives," an aim long contradicted by Britain's own earlier practices. Indeed, the British were quite comfortable with the idea of white supremacy, and embraced such policies accordingly. Racism made an English–African alliance all but unthinkable, and a white alliance seem natural. Past discrimination was brought forward to justify the reinforcement of such a racial order and to diminish intrawhite conflict threatening state and economic consolidation.

That a post–Boer War alliance between English-speakers and Africans remains only as a fabulous historical fantasy further testifies to the strategic assessment that precluded it. Compared to the proven threat of Afrikaner resistance, the British perceived no equally viable threat from the majority. The Zulus had been defeated. Prior experience had demonstrated that "whites were able to exploit the cleavages in African society more successfully than Africans could exploit the cleavages in white society.... Africans [had] never created a united front and whites [had been] able to use African allies in every conflict."[33] Coloureds in particular preferred to try "passing for white," and blacks were forbidden to own arms, further undermining any united threat.[34] Believing their own racist rhetoric, the British belittled the prospect of black opposition, and this view was again confirmed by the decisive defeat of the Bambatha revolt by Zulus in 1906. The possibility that such revolts would grow in the future only further encouraged the idea of white unity as the surest way "to safeguard . . . the interests of the Europeans."[35]

After the peace treaty, racial prejudice came together with strategic advantage in encouraging an Afrikaner–English alliance and the further exclusion of "natives." The two policies were connected. Britain could only hope to rule its newly won territory by making peace with those "fellow whites" who had previously resisted and who insisted on the abandonment of Britain's promises of reform and the franchise. "The price of unity and conciliation was the institutionalization of white supremacy."[36] The former enemies had to be reconciled, and alliance between the whites was achieved at the expense of blacks and coloureds.[37] For Britain, breaking promises to blacks seemed a small price to pay for the sake of ensuring Afrikaner loyalty to the empire.[38] As Nelson Mandela would later describe these processes, "the white skinned peoples of South Africa patched up their differences and erected a system of racial domination against the dark-skinned peoples of their own land."[39] Often cynical and merely rhetorical prior commitments to liberal reforms were easily scuttled in favor of an alliance with Afrikaners deemed necessary for securing the prize.

This result had been anticipated. Upon his arrival in South Africa as high commissioner in 1897, Lord Milner wrote to Asquith regarding "the two great principles" that should guide his work: (1) the British rulers should seek to "restore the good relations between the Dutch [i.e., Afrikaners] and English," and (2) they should "secure for the Natives ... adequate and sufficient protection against oppression." But Milner went on to note

> that object No. 2 is the principal obstacle to the attainment of object No. 1 – is, and always has been ... I personally could win over the Dutch in the Colony and indeed in all of South African dominions ... You have only to sacrifice "the nigger" absolutely and the game is easy ... You have, therefore, this singular situation, that you might indeed unite Dutch and English by protecting the black man, but you would unite them against yourself, and your policy of protection. There is the whole crux of the South African position. . . . [Self-government], fearlessly and unflinchingly applied, would make South Africa as loyal as Canada – but what would be the price? The abandonment of the black races, to whom you have promised protection.[40]

This dilemma, presciently described before the Boer War, would be unavoidable by 1902. Nor was Milner alone in foreseeing this outcome. Writing in 1900, J. A. Hobson noted that "hitherto the two white races, however they might bicker amongst themselves, readily united to present a single front against the Kaffirs." Hobson foresaw that the "one inevitable effect of the present war will be to accentuate the race cleavage," for whites would unite against blacks to make their peace.[41]

The linkage between the strategic imperative of unifying the former white adversaries and the imposition of racial domination was evident already in the interregnum period between the peace and the formation of the Union of South Africa. Botha and other Afrikaner elites sought to reinforce racial segregation as a means of encouraging white unity and loyalty, much as the peace treaty had abandoned commitments to the native franchise. There was no escaping the "native question." How to shift "Bantu policy ... [from] its provincial character and assume a more uniform trend" had become an important matter to be resolved.[42] Already in the first two years after the Boer War, "colonies and ex-republics passed legislation compelling Africans to live in segregated compounds and locations." The lack of a unified state apparatus meant that such facilities had to be funded locally, as with a tax on beer.[43] Boer land seized during the war by Africans was forcibly returned to Afrikaner landlords.[44] By 1903–5, the South African Native Affairs Commission was discussing "restrictions upon the purchase of land by Natives" and the need to avoid mixing, "or weakening in any way the unchallenged supremacy and authority of the ruling race" of whites. The commission called for replacing "the diverse character of legislation . . . to arrive at uniform principles."[45] Without a formally unified state, it was impossible to coordinate and impose segregation.

In 1906, one of Milner's aides wrote what became known as the Shelborne memorandum. This text sets out British interests with astonishing clarity, advocating the formalization of a single state based on a union of English and Afrikaners. The division of South Africa among "separate governments" of colonies and defeated republics was decried, not least because these polities did not correspond with the "natural conditions . . . the division of race" unifying whites. Disunion was further decried for the resulting lack of coordination of railway development and fiscal policy, but it was "the native problem" that was most significant. Without a "federal union of some sort," whites would never be able to defend themselves from the majority. This problem prompted the obvious solution: "a fusion of thought, aim and blood between the British and Boer stock" and "political institutions" that would give expression to such unified "South African nationality" based on "the mutual respect begotten in the course of that arduous struggle" of the war. The memorandum concludes that union "is the only means whereby peace and prosperity can be attained in this country."[46] In subsequent years, Milner's "kindergarten" of young aides furthered the cause of union by publishing the fittingly titled monthly journal *The State*, envisioning a unity not yet achieved.

Pressure for union revealed a surprising consensus on this goal, albeit for different reasons. As Donald Denoon explains:

Imperialists . . . hoped that Union would bring prosperity, which would attract sufficient British migrants to swamp Afrikaner nationalism. Anti-imperialists hoped that Union would consolidate Afrikaner control. There was little disagreement over the immediate purposes of unification, and the catch-word "conciliation" served to stifle disputes over the long-term destiny of the region.[47]

Olive Schreiner and other Cape liberals well understood that such English–Afrikaner reconciliation implied greater racial animosity, domination and exploitation of the majority, drawing a "dark shadow" over the future. They sought to derail the movement to union.[48] But the coincidence of imperialist and Afrikaner interests in union was too strong. The train had already left the station with both former warring parties on board. Though Schreiner appealed to British sentiment for defending "the natives," this sentiment had already been forsaken in the peace treaty.

For Britain, as the victor in a war of imperial conquest, the imperative for consolidating control over its prize was worth much more than any moral commitments to blacks. With the record breaking 3,106-carat Cullinan diamond – given to King Edward VII by Botha in 1907 as proof of his loyalty – glimmering most brilliantly among the crown jewels, Britain yearned to reap the rewards from its richest new colonial possession. To do so, unity would have to be forged with the Afrikaners within a single state, at the price of turning a deaf ear to Schreiner's prophetic warning. The blood spilt in the Boer War brought the birth of a new state, but not a unified nation. As signaled by the treaty negotiations ending the war, racial domination would be used to encourage such national unity by means of a white-ruled state.

Ethnic Political Competition and Segregation

The conflict between English and Afrikaner would not simply disappear with the end of military belligerence. Appeasing Afrikaner nationalism proved less "easy" than Milner expected. The war would continue by the other means of protracted political competition. And efforts to resolve this ethnic conflict would continue to pursue the logic of 1902. Advocates of unified white "South African nationalism" would consistently fall back on the strategy of prioritizing the racial difference from blacks in order to submerge white ethnic difference. Afrikaner nationalists countered their competitors with calls for stronger racial domination. This ongoing dynamic would consistently result in refinements of segregationist policies.

With the British Parliament's passing of the Act of Union, in 1910 a single South African state came into existence. The form of that state was influenced both by the British model imported from London and by provision for an increasingly unified state reinforced by imperial power. The prior conflict had left little tolerance for a slow evolution of central state power, which might have encouraged even further conflict. The American model of federalism was also explicitly rejected as having "caused one of the greatest civil wars in history"; [49] South Africa had arguably just experienced a comparable watershed conflict and under British rule rather than federal union sought a political system that would avoid exacerbating tensions.[50] Instead, the South African state emerged almost full-blown on the imperial half-shell, as a "unitary state with parliamentary sovereignty. . . . The central government was legally supreme over all local institutions. Moreover, powers were not divided within the center."[51] As it would elsewhere in Africa, British colonialism forged a strong and unified state, assuming that such centralization of power would limit future conflict. This assumption would be proved fatally wrong, but in the meantime British interests were served.

The linkage between creating a strongly centralized state and forging Afrikaner–English unity on the basis of racial domination quickly became further evident with the formal extension of segregation. In accord with the findings of the South African Native Affairs Committee, land ownership was to be divided by "tribe" in order to reinforce divisions of blacks and thereby more easily suppress them.[52] The 1913 Native Land Act, limiting African residence to 7.3 percent of the land "reserved" for that purpose, reassured Afrikaners of the state's commitment to racial domination. This act thereby sought to unify whites, countering nascent support for Afrikaner nationalists under former General Hertzog.[53]

Franchise issues were addressed with somewhat greater cognizance of regional differences, with formal rules established by each province within a national framework.[54] But Afrikaner leaders insisted that the more liberal Cape franchise not be extended to the now-unified country, for to do so would "enable [natives] to out-vote Europeans . . . an intolerable situation."[55] Instead, Cape liberalism would be brought more into line with the other provinces. Franchise restrictions in the

Cape resulted in the 23 percent white population there having 85 percent of the vote by 1909.[56]

Racial domination not only encouraged white unity, thus allowing for state consolidation, but also reflected the pressures of dominant economic interests. Milner's objectives of postwar reconstruction under a unified state "depended on getting the gold mines back into full, profitable production."[57] Mining for abundant but low-grade ore, providing the engine of early development, required plentiful cheap labor, as would later industrial production.[58] Farmers also required cheap black labor. But self-sufficient Africans were officially decried for having an "absence of incentive to labor."[59] Before the war the British had begun to force such labor at low wages, but during the war they had been reluctant to proceed, fearing that doing so would have discouraged black support for the British cause. After the war and union, this threat dissolved, validating Hobson's prediction that "the first fruits of victory [in the Boer War] will be represented in a large, cheap, submissive supply of black and white labor."[60]

British capital's efforts to provoke the Boer War, forcing unification of the country, paid off handsomely. The newly founded South African state moved to reinforce earlier practices of racial domination and to encode uniform policies of labor control not previously possible. Poll or hut taxes, and the Native Lands Act of 1913 restricting the purchase of land by "natives," forced Africans off land where they could be self-sufficient, ensuring a large supply of cheap labor and avoiding the need to grant higher wage incentives to black labor, an option officially described as "out of place."[61] State policies serving the interests of capital transformed Africans into a proletariat, with labor-coercive policies specified by race helping to fuel economic expansion and state growth. It was certainly in the state's interest to bolster growth, suggesting a "pervasive convergence of interest between and within the state and capital."[62] White workers' interests were also served, for instance with a comprehensive "color bar" established in 1911 to ensure that forced black entry into the labor market would not displace those whites who were already advantaged by their skills. Such segregation and official job discrimination further reduced the price of labor by limiting blacks' options, and divided the working class into racial groups, diminishing its potential bargaining power. A trend of strong state intervention for economic gain was firmly established, with the imperial hand vigorously burnishing its new jewel.

Economic growth apparently reaffirmed English cultural chauvinism, asserted as "British race patriotism."[63] Despite formal commitments to the contrary, Lord Milner did not give up his interest in anglicizing South Africa, encouraging British immigration and countenancing the formation of Sons of England clubs. As early as 1903, school instruction in Afrikaans was limited to only three hours weekly.[64] But these efforts backfired, for instance with Afrikaners forming their own separate schools. Afrikaner nationalism grew, with the intrawhite tension of the war continuing after formal hostilities ceased. Ironically, had the British not tried to impose their cultural superiority, Afrikaners might have been assimilated and shifted to using English as the language of economic opportunity. But local British officials were not so patient, with unforeseen consequences. "To attempt to denationalize a people, and to fail, is to produce the very opposite result intended."[65]

Afrikaner nationalism found expression in the newly established political institution of the unified state. As a majority of whites, Afrikaners recognized their prospect of electoral control after the Boer War. The institutional resources of the centralized state could then be used to secure Afrikaner interests and defend Afrikaner culture. Confident in their own control over industry and finance, the English effectively ceded the political realm to the Afrikaners. In 1910, after a bitter election pitting Afrikaner against English, a former military leader of the defeated Afrikaner republics, Louis Botha, was elected prime minister, succeeded upon his death in 1919 by his ally, Jan Smuts.

The 1910 election outcome was ironic. Before the war, the Afrikaners had been disunited, protecting their interests by retreating into separate republics. The British had forced the Afrikaners together in a newly unified state, and then watched as that state became ruled by leaders of the defeated, who would use state power to further enforce segregation. Britain's victory had delivered to the Afrikaners what they had alone been unable to accomplish; it was as if a Southerner had been elected president of the United States after the Civil War and imposed Jim Crow nationally.

Botha's and Smuts's election did not signal triumphant Afrikaner nationalism, but the rise of realistic politicians who had accepted defeat and quickly turned to advocating reconciliation and the end of animosity between English-speaker and Afrikaner. Botha and Smuts sought to finesse the tension between white unity and Afrikaner nationalism, arguing that white "national unity is entirely consistent with the preservation of our language, our traditions, our cultural interests."[66]

Their rhetoric underplayed the extent to which Botha and Smuts sought to appease the British. In the eyes of many of their fellow Afrikaners, they "defected to the imperialist cause."[67] Smuts in particular was attacked by his fellow Boers for his support of English-language education in the schools and for his resistance to efforts at maintaining a separate Afrikaans culture. In the First World War Botha and Smuts sided with Britain against the Germans, who had supported the Afrikaners in the Boer War, provoking a small rebellion by more militant Afrikaners. Smuts was rewarded with the epithet of "handyman of the empire."[68] Nonetheless, he retained significant popularity as a hero of the Boer War, and thereby provided the British with the perfect vehicle for enacting their policies with impunity, appeasing the Afrikaners and unifying whites while pursuing imperial interest.

Sentimental attachment for former Boer commanders was not the only glue maintaining white unity in the early years of state building. The further enactment of racial domination served the same purpose, in accordance with the post–Boer War reasoning. Smuts generally preferred to leave the elaboration of race relations for the future, but when the issue could not be put off, he consistently upheld racial domination, on which Afrikaners and English could agree and unify. By 1917, Smuts was publicly committed to the exclusion of "non whites" from "common citizenship" and the armed forces, and to "keeping [blacks] apart as much as possible in our institutions."[69] Color bars were established on the mines and elsewhere. Influx control, limiting African urbanization, was proposed in 1922, followed the next year by the creation of separate Native Urban Areas.[70] This racial exclusion consolidated white support during the formative years of union, and received the blessing of the British Empire.

Changing geopolitical and economic conditions nevertheless destabilized the compromise arrangement of the South African Party government under Botha and then Smuts. During the First World

War, when many English workers went off to fight, the proportion of Afrikaners working in the mines increased. When gold profits later fell amid postwar inflation and a fall in the price of gold, the mining houses became eager to displace some of these whites with lower-paid blacks.[71] But the color bar protected white workers and thereby effectively restricted the minimization of labor costs. The Chamber of Mines consortium proposed to reduce the number of reserved jobs and to substitute "about 2000 semi-skilled whites by lower paid blacks."[72] White workers went on strike, provoking Smuts to use force to quell what had escalated into the Rand revolt. In March 1922, Smuts called in 7,000 troops and his air force, resulting in four days of conflict leaving up to 220 dead.

Defeated by force, Afrikaner workers sought to protect their interests by turning to political mobilization, fanning ethnic animosity against Smuts's policies. Having remained loyal to Smuts and his efforts at white unity, the Afrikaner majority now turned against him. Smuts had demonstrated that he favored the English mining capital's interests over the interests of Afrikaner workers. Unity was one thing; shooting Afrikaners was another. Though recent scholarship has questioned the direct causality, the Rand revolt did strengthen a 1924 alliance led by Barry Hertzog's Afrikaner Nationalists, which defeated Smuts in that year's election.[73] The reforms pursued by English capital had led to a reassertion of Afrikaner nationalism, which would push the state to act in favor of Afrikaner workers and against the interests of capital. As soon as the English and their Afrikaner allies had wavered from the post–Boer War "deal" of racial domination to unite whites, they found themselves pushed aside.

If the elections of Afrikaner Generals Botha and then Smuts were surprising in light of Britain's Boer War victory, then the 1924 election of the more militant Hertzog was all the more so. But Britain's ultimate commitment to democracy and unity among whites was steadfast, even to the point of empowering an Afrikaner nationalist. The British perhaps hoped that this outcome would itself again appease Afrikaners and promote white unity. Restoring that intrawhite peace was now seen to be more important than meeting the immediate demands of capital, for the Rand revolt had demonstrated that Afrikaner nationalism could still threaten stability and state unity, on which all profits depended. The newly forged, increasingly strong central state changed hands.

Trained in Holland rather than Britain, Hertzog had pragmatically agreed to union after the Boer War and argued that "all who gave their unconditional loyalty to South Africa were Afrikaners," even English.[74] But by 1912 his dismay at Botha's accommodation had grown, and his defense of Afrikaner cultural distinctiveness forced his resignation from Botha's cabinet. Thereafter, Hertzog argued for a "two stream" approach to white unity, with the Afrikaner and English peoples remaining distinct even as they flowed along parallel courses.[75] In particular, Hertzog pursued his advocacy of Afrikaans instruction to electoral advantage, "using language to throw his net very wide."[76] He delivered on his promise in 1925 by making Afrikaans an official language of the state.

Hertzog was eager to protect the interests of those who had elected him in the wake of the 1922 revolt. By then more than 30 percent of Afrikaner families were known as "poor whites," whose position was further eroded during the Depression.[77] The state-owned Iron and Steel Corporation and other growing state functions employed a high proportion of whites. The Afrikaner-dominated agriculture sector was also subsidized by the state.[78] With these practical policies of state support for poorer Afrikaners, together with his "two streams" rhetoric, Hertzog "played the nationalist banjo strongly."[79]

While Smuts had used racial segregation to unify whites, Hertzog pursued such policies even further for the alternative purpose of appealing to distinct Afrikaner nationalism and tradition. Smuts's racial policies were decried by Hertzog as overly liberal, and as not providing a "definite native policy" clarifying that South Africa was to be governed by the whites. Smuts himself was condemned by many Afrikaners as "a Kaffir lover."[80] The industrial color bar reserving certain jobs for whites, which Smuts had attempted to relax at his electoral peril, was reinforced in 1926. Unionization among blacks was banned, preventing blacks from gaining the bargaining power to raise their own wages and to compete more effectively.[81] The Native Land Bill called for the further separation of African reserves, helping to solve a crisis in agriculture by reinforcing farmers' control over black labor.[82] By 1929, Hertzog was using rhetorical warnings of a *swart gevaar* (black peril) to consolidate his electoral block.

Racial domination used earlier as the basis for encouraging white unity was pursued even further by an Afrikaner nationalist government. Hertzog used segregation to consolidate the Afrikaner voting majority and to distance it from English liberalism. Afrikaner nationalism sought to trump the competing tendency for white unity by even further developing the racial domination seen as advantageous by both camps.

These developments reveal the extent to which countertendencies within white politics ironically reinforced racial domination for opposing reasons. As useful as racial domination proved to be as a strategy for encouraging white unity and state building, English and Afrikaner tensions still did not disappear. Afrikaner nationalists remained suspicious of English liberalism and pushed for further segregation to protect Afrikaner interests and to prevent any return to English reforms. To counter this tendency, the English and their Afrikaner allies would advocate greater segregation to reassure and win over Afrikaner rank and file. In this way, Afrikaner nationalism reinforced the impetus for white unity via racial domination. The dynamic of intrawhite tension appeased by segregation continued to operate. Ongoing party competition among whites suggests that reconciliation was not achieved, but remained a goal requiring continued effort. No single, seamlessly functional agreement was reached. Instead, the pact of white unity and black domination was continually reforged, with party competition reflecting divided allegiance within a unified state.

While party competition provides an intervening explanation of deepening racial domination, it also kept intact the polity over which parties vied. For much of South Africa's first half century, official race policies continued to be driven by the competing tendencies either for white unity reinforced by racial exclusion or for distinct Afrikaner nationalism incorporating its own impetus for such exclusion. Both camps saw their interests as potentially being met within the polity. Whichever tendency proved predominant during a specific historical period, black South Africans suffered under tightening white rule.

By the 1930s, the two competing tendencies of white politics briefly converged. State intervention had effectively bolstered the relative economic standing and culture of Afrikaners. Hertzog concluded that "the two streams" could now flow together in a "spirit of complete equality between white men" and primary loyalty for South Africa.[83] Accordingly, in 1934 Smuts's South African Party and Hertzog's Nationalists fused into the United Party. As both had pursued policies of racial domination, this commonality helped to cement their merger. Hertzog and Smuts agreed that "to build up a white nation in South Africa it was essential that the principle of differentiation shall be the principle of native policy."[84] This principle justified the further exclusion of coloureds and Africans, including the separation of African voters in 1936, residential segregation applied to coloureds for the first time, and enactment of the Coloured Advisory Council's recommendations for the extension of a South African version of Jim Crow. Again, white unity was reinforced by racial domination. And that unity was perceived as then strong enough on its own to no longer require a special dispensation and alliance with coloureds.

As it had during the First World War, geopolitics again intruded on South Africa during the Second World War. Resulting tensions tore apart the alliance of the United Party. Smuts forced through a declaration of war to support Britain, overriding Hertzog's objections. In protest, Hertzog resigned from the government. While some Afrikaners supported the war effort, many did not, refusing to support British imperialism and preferring their former German allies from the Boer War.

The war exacerbated domestic ethnic tensions. The use of black service troops, though unarmed, was decried by racists. The anti-Nazi, antiracism rhetoric of the Allies' Atlantic Charter raised both blacks' expectations of reform and Afrikaner resentment at such intrusive moralism.[85] Many Afrikaners saw support of Britain as inconsistent with racial domination, against which the war was ostensibly being waged against Germany. On the home front, white workers gone to fight were replaced by blacks, with the prospects of such employment helping to create a 47 percent increase in the urban black population. Influx control effectively collapsed.[86] Afrikaner resentment grew and Afrikaner nationalism surged.

The resurgence of Afrikaner nationalism during the 1940s was not only the result of resentment at being dragged into "Britain's war." Suspicion of the English had lurked despite political alliances. There was a sense that "the Afrikaner was being exploited and his culture undermined. . . . Exclusive English clubs were closed to Afrikaners, mirroring the exclusiveness of high society in Britain."[87] Hardship during the Depression years exacerbated such resentment, which found combustible material among an increasingly urbanized poor Afrikaner population. This antipathy was reinforced by "fear of the

English using non-white votes to strengthen their position." United Party reforms of the color bar and increased African education fed concern among Afrikaners that the English intended to abandon the post–Boer War deal of white unity via segregation.[88] Such fears were heightened further by the unprecedented 1946 strike by 70,000 African miners, who expected Britain's war victory to result in better wages and treatment.[89] The perceived threat of being swamped by blacks fused with resentment at English cultural domination, inflaming Afrikaner nationalism.

Afrikaner nationalism had for decades been purposefully reconstructed and reinforced by militants. The leading vehicle for this project was the Broederbond, an originally secret society of Afrikaners founded in 1918 under the leadership of a then obscure D. F. Malan, among others. Dedicated to "the ideal of the eternal existence of a separate Afrikaner nation with its own language and culture," the Bond encouraged its large membership of teachers to advocate this ideal in the classroom and elsewhere.[90] But the Bond initially sought some moderation, seeking to incorporate or "Afrikanerize" the English within a single white nation and to avoid partisan political disputes that undermined "unity among the Afrikaners."[91]

After his alliance with Smuts, Hertzog rejected the Bond in 1935 as "a serious threat to the peace and order of the Union." The Bond subsequently took a more strident position. They turned to "obtaining and retaining political and economic power, especially political power, out of which would come economic."[92] Efforts to encourage *volkskapitalisme* continued, complemented by explicit acts of *volk* political mobilization. In 1938, the Broederbond celebrated the centennial of the Great Trek by sending replica ox wagons throughout the country, evoking an outpouring of Afrikaner nationalism among the rank and file. Anglo traditions were denied, for instance when the Afrikaans press purposefully ignored the royal visit of 1947.[93] And as early as 1935, the Bond advocated apartheid as a reinforcement of segregation, thereby seeking to trump again the United Party's policies and to identify racial domination with Afrikaner nationalism rather than with white unity.[94]

Within party politics, the Broederbond's Afrikaner nationalism was represented by the National Party. The party leader, D. F. Malan, provided an interlock with the Broederbond. Malan had earlier advocated a liberal form of nationalism according to which Afrikaners remained distinct but cooperative with the English. But Malan had moved to the right. In 1935 his National Party became the official opposition. Thereafter, the National Party firmly advocated ethnic solidarity, projecting themselves as "pro-Afrikaner, hostile even to the English."[95] The project of racial domination was not abandoned, but again redirected in its strategic purpose to reinforcing distinct Afrikaner solidarity. Historical resentment over English liberalism was reignited. Mindful of political advantage, the National Party combined Afrikaners' fears of the black majority with fears that the English would reverse their policies of segregation and embrace the majority. Some British-descendant South Africans shared this fear, and joined in supporting the National Party as a bulwark against "the torrent of blackness . . . and liberalism which a 'sickly West' had unloosed upon the world."[96] They agreed with many Afrikaners that the English–Afrikaner white unity via racial domination established after the Boer War could no longer be counted on. Preserving "European racial survival" could only be entrusted to the Afrikaner majority among whites, with their greater historical commitment to segregation.[97]

From 1910 to 1948, Afrikaner nationalists and an Afrikaner–English alliance advocating white unity had vied for power. This divide built upon earlier ethnic conflict, exacerbated by disputes over the treatment of Africans despite common assumptions of white supremacy. Political parties competed with each other for state power, with ethnic nationalists defending Afrikaner workers and a cross-ethnic alliance using race to unify whites. Their joint agreement on the use of central state power for such racial domination left them trying to outdo each other in segregation. This commonality kept the polity intact and the competition contained. Indeed, this party competition replicated and replayed the original deal of building the nation-state with racial domination. Only at mid-century did Afrikaner nationalists emerge victorious.

Apartheid and Greater White Unity

The post–Second World War realignment of white South African politics was consolidated with the unexpected victory in 1948 of the National Party. Malan became prime minister. Two generations of party competition culminated with the 1948 electoral victory of the

Afrikaner nationalists. The symbolism of this victory was reinforced with the dramatic construction of the Voortrekkers' Monument in Pretoria, wherein was inscribed (in Afrikaans) "We for Thee, South Africa." One Afrikaner in six attended the official dedication in 1949.[98] However, the party's victory had been narrow and Malan sought further consolidation and English support. Long-standing demands for a republic free of links to the United Kingdom were soft-pedaled. More extremist Afrikaner nationalists were initially excluded from the government.[99] Nor was the new government willing to risk interrupting tremendous economic growth. Between 1912 and 1952, with manufacturing's contribution to national income growing from 6.9 percent to 23.6 percent and mining down from 27.6 percent to 13.2 percent, real national income grew threefold.[100] With concomitantly increased revenues, the state grew apace, further empowering the Afrikaners who came to control it, but also raising concerns about any state efforts that might interrupt growth. But the constrained form of Afrikaner nationalism designed to appease English capital would not last; Malan and his brief-termed successor Johannes Strydom became transitional figures in a shift to strident Afrikaner ethnic domination.

Malan and Strydom did use the state to reinforce racial domination, de-linked from Anglo-Boer unity. The National Party's policy of apartheid envisioned eventually dividing the country into two states of blacks and whites. But Malan concluded that "for the foreseeable future, however, this is simply not practical."[101] Accordingly, plans for the establishment of viable separate black "homelands" proposed by the Tomlinson Commission were postponed because of the associated expense.[102] But the goal of total separation did inform policy measures that made significant strides toward that ideal. The 1950 Population Registration Act set the foundation for apartheid by establishing distinct racial categorization of the population according to subjective interpretations of reputation and "appearance."[103] Complementary acts forbade cross-racial marriage or sex, ignoring past Afrikaner indulgence. The Group Areas Act of the same year reinforced residential segregation, the pass system was "rationalized" in 1952, and in 1953 the Bantu Education and the Reservation of Separate Amenities Acts divided schools and most public facilities accordingly. Even the potential alliance with coloureds, formerly embraced by Afrikaner nationalists, was abandoned as inconsistent with racial domination. As most coloureds had supported the United Party, the Nationalists paid little cost in 1956 in depriving the coloureds of direct representation. They were placed on a separate voters' roll.

The linkage between racial domination and Afrikaner nationalism reached its apogee with the government of H. F. Verwoerd in 1958–65. Born in the Netherlands, Verwoerd embraced Afrikanerdom with the enthusiasm of the converted. In his view, the National Party represented "not an ordinary party. It is a nation on the move," in which the English could be absorbed only if they gave primacy to South Africa over the empire. Even the nation's key symbols had to conform to Afrikaner nationalism, with the remaining official status of the Union Jack and "God Save the Queen" already abandoned in 1957.[104] And once British influence had been curtailed by electoral victory and symbolic adjustment, Verwoerd focused on "the black threat." He saw *swaart gevaar* as more pressing than any remaining threat posed by the outvoted English, and more useful for mobilizing Afrikaner support. To address this issue systematically, Verwoerd dedicated all of his skills with the zeal of an ideological purist, expanding on the plans he had developed as minister of native affairs in the Malan government. According to Afrikaner nationalist stalwart Jaap Marais, "previously segregation was very loosely applied, fragmented, but Verwoerd forged this into a completely unified philosophy."[105] Total segregation, earlier advanced as an ideal but impractical form of social engineering, was pursued to its extreme.

The keystone to the policy of "separate development" was the idea of creating self-governing black "homelands," or bantustans, and formally excluding Africans from South African citizenship. Earlier concerns about the carrying capacity of overpopulated land and related costs were brushed aside.[106] From these homelands black labor could be selectively drawn without threatening white rule and interests. Business objected to the loss of black markets and argued that such protostates placed black labor out of reach. These objections were rebuffed, with the homelands purportedly intended to protect blacks from English capital's "exploitative propensities. . . . Verwoerd was perfectly willing to act against the interests of capitalists when he thought it in the larger interests of the nation."[107] In the process, Verwoerd expected to make allies of those black leaders who would benefit from state support for the bantustans. To implement this policy, the Transkei became the first "self-governing" homeland in 1963, with others following. Even the coloured community was subjected to the same logic of geographic separation. The Western Cape was reserved for whites and coloureds; over 20,000 Africans were forcibly removed from the region by 1961.[108]

Africans and coloureds did not appreciate Verwoerd's "largesse." When their protest erupted into violence in 1960, Verwoerd moved quickly to impose harsh repression, banning the major anti-apartheid organizations and forcing them into exile. Even they would be forced into formally "separate development" outside of South Africa.

The same logic of "separate development" was applied to whites. Even Verwoerd initially hesitated to fulfill the long-standing Afrikaner nationalist goal of declaring South Africa a republic outside the Commonwealth, thereby risking further antagonization of English speakers. But Britain itself provided a useful provocation. In February 1960, British Prime Minister Harold Macmillan came to Cape Town, and citing "the wind of change [that] is blowing through the continent," acknowledged emerging African nationalism.[109] Verwoerd shrewdly grabbed Macmillan's logic, arguing that South African whites' own nationalism justified their formal independence from an empire that no longer desired an association. Verwoerd also used the image of a Communist threat to unify whites against the Soviet backed African National Congress.

South Africa's departure from the Commonwealth marked another turning point in white politics. Verwoerd argued that Britain's liberalism left English speakers fearing black rule with little alternative but to abandon imperial loyalties and to rally round. Sensing such "new possibilities . . . the National Party became less focused on Afrikanerdom." Verwoerd shifted his rhetoric from Afrikaner nationalism to "white republicanism." To encourage white unity and a return to a fusion of Europeans "culturally and racially alien" to Bantus, he even hailed his former nemesis, Jan Smuts.[110] Earlier references to the Afrikaner *volk* shifted so as to include all South African whites in a common *volk*. "The wheel had come full circle," with Verwoerd sensing that Afrikaner nationalism had been sufficiently consolidated to allow for an extension of nationalism to include all whites.[111]

Much as Hertzog had prematurely concluded that the "two streams" of white South Africa could flow together, Verwoerd believed that the time was ripe for the same confluence. The gambit paid off, with English-speaker joining Afrikaner in supporting the 1961 formation of the Republic of South Africa. Verwoerd sought to strengthen English and Afrikaner support for the republic even further after 1961 by turning again to the well-rehearsed technique of heightening racial domination in order to unify a white nation. As the Tomlinson Commission had argued, "the creation of the European population" rested on "racial grounds," reinforced by discrimination and segregation.[112] This strategy appealed to Verwoerd's racist vision and to the popular white ideology of superiority. Ironically, achievement of the long-held Afrikaner goal of a separate republic now allowed for a relaxation of Afrikaner separatism.

By this circuitous route, South Africa emerged in the mid-1960s as a strong state and more unified white nation enriched by a booming economy. The state promoted both Afrikaner interests and white unity via a highly elaborated form of racial domination. All that Milner had foreseen had been achieved, except for British domination. All that the Afrikaner nationalists had sought had been won, despite earlier defeat. They had gained control of the state and built Afrikaner capital. State intervention to uphold racial domination also bolstered Afrikaner workers, ensuring their support. By 1969, white gold mine workers made on average twenty times the earnings of blacks, and in 1972 the average wage for all whites was close to seven times higher than for blacks.[113] A strong state imposing labor controls was able to override the rhetorical objections of "liberal" business. Leading industrialist Harry Oppenheimer decried Verwoerd as "a man prepared to slow down his nation's welfare on account of political theories. [We] are dealing with an impractical fanatic."[114] But such fanaticism further enriched Oppenheimer and his associates.

Not only did white workers benefit from the effects of apartheid's restraints on black advancement and wage differentials in the private sector. They also directly benefited from employment in the growing state apparatus enforcing these rules. According to Stephen Lewis, "the objective of South African governments since the 1920s, especially since the National Party came to power, has been to [advance] the class of poor whites."[115] State employment was the most direct way to address this problem. By 1972, "fully 43 percent of the white labor force was employed by the state sector," exploding in size to administer apartheid.[116] Loyalty was encouraged, if not directly bought, by such intervention. A more complete coincidence of white worker interests and state policies of racial domination is difficult to imagine. And state growth also served to unify whites by providing protection from the potential "black threat." The number of whites employed by the police and military grew rapidly. Thus, state growth served the multiple functions of developing the economy, promoting the cause of Afrikanerdom, encouraging white unity, and providing security from the excluded majority. The elaborately "impractical" construction of apartheid proved highly effective for nation-state building among whites.

Still, the impracticality of Verwoerd's apartheid could not be wished away by ideological vehemence. Even before the shock of disruptive protest and sanctions, the economic viability, if not the morality, of racial domination was subject to question. According to later Broederbond chairman P. J. de Lange, who by 1994 was inclined to be retrospectively realistic,

> the Broederbond warned against economic problems by the late fifties. We could not create a sufficiently large economy with the talent and resources of only four million out of twenty-five million. . . . [For instance,] work reservation was a mad policy. How do you build enough houses with white hands on the trowel and blacks only mixing the concrete? Influx control almost created a Broederbond revolt, in that it destroyed black family life. The Broederbond, being strongly Protestant, put a strong value on family life. In the early sixties, there was an argument within the Broederbond that the moral basis of apartheid was highly questionable.[117]

Even if this assessment overstates Afrikaner concern about apartheid, as is likely, it does suggest some early criticism and disquiet. Afrikaners had always been conscious of themselves as a minority within South Africa, as indicated by their various efforts to find allies among English-speakers, or coloureds. Even at the height of their dominance in the 1960s, Afrikaners were concerned about their own potential isolation, reaching out for allies among English capital even as they were vilifying "Hoggenheimer" capitalists for electoral advantage.[118] The National Party continually faced the challenge of how to maintain apartheid and Afrikaner dominance while seeking to make alliances seemingly inconsistent with these policies.

This challenge remained after Verwoerd was assassinated in 1966 by a crazed white messenger. B. J. Vorster, an Afrikaner nationalist who had been imprisoned for opposing South Africa's alliance with Britain during the Second World War, became prime minister. Nonetheless, Vorster now set out to win English support. By 1977, official publications noted that "Afrikaner nationalism has gradually broadened into a more comprehensive white South African nationalism. . . . Between those of British stock and their Afrikaner compatriots there has been a growing comradeship, a new identity of purpose."[119] While such white unity continued to be tied to racial domination, this linkage did not prevent Vorster from attempting also to find "nonwhite" allies, even as he reinforced apartheid. Embracing coloureds as part of the nation if not of the *volk*, Vorster's Theron Commission "made it clear that the present political solution cannot continue." Theron proposed the reinstatement of coloured voting, and in 1977 Vorster proposed a newly inclusive constitution.[120] But the contradiction with apartheid was too great, and these recommendations were not enacted, bitterly disappointing expectant coloureds. Vorster's failure to consolidate broader support was well demonstrated by the violent protests of the Soweto uprising during 1976 and 1977. A year later he fell from power amid a scandal over secret government funding of the media.

Vorster's fall did not disrupt National Party dominance, but brought to power P. W. Botha, an early advocate of apartheid and former minister of defense. In the wake of the 1976 revolt Botha committed his government to a combination of reluctant liberalization, an increasing centralization of power, and reinforced security.[121] Black protest had to be appeased or contained, given the economy's dependence on black labor. In 1978 Botha dramatically declared that South Africa must "adapt or die," and in 1979 one of his ministers, Piet Koornhof, declared that "apartheid is dead."[122] But eager not to lose his electoral base, Botha hedged on reforms. He simultaneously enacted a "total strategy" of heightened security. Citing the threat from black protest backed by international Communism, Botha exploited fear of a "total onslaught" to justify "the biggest use of state funding for the military."[123]

Botha's rhetoric of threat and bluster tended to overshadow his reforms. These were nevertheless dramatic, even if they left the underlying structure of apartheid intact. Education expenditures and other policies encouraged the growth of a small African middle class needed for skilled labor and intended as a form of "labor aristocracy" with an interest in stability. Botha's Wiehahn Commission proposed legalizing black unionization, assuming that registering "black trade unions as bargaining partners" would encourage orderly unionism.[124] In addition, Botha granted township residents ninety-nine-year leases in 1978, introduced a pilot program of compulsory education for African children in 1981, abolished most job color bars by 1983, and ended restrictions on Africans living in the Western Cape and university segregation in 1984. In 1985 he promised freehold rights and pledged to end both "forced removals" and bars on mixed marriages or miscegenation; in 1986 he repealed pass laws and allowed for the opening of central business districts.

Further reforms were discussed in cabinet. Gerrit Viljoen, then a minister, claims that by 1985 he had embraced the earlier findings of the Riekert Commission and "persuaded P.W. Botha to stop influx control and to cancel coloured labor priority in the Western Cape. [These policies] did not work and could not. They required martial law, injustice and enforced poverty and were inconsistent with economic development."[125] Botha himself claimed to have rejected "the antiquated, simplistic and racist approach. . . . This country is a multicultural society – a country of minorities. . . . The present system [of influx control] is outdated and too costly. . . . A solution will have to be found for [urbanized blacks'] legitimate rights."[126] He retained the homelands and official ethnic distinctions among blacks as a means of diluting the threat of African majority rule. His expectation was that a minority coalition government might emerge in which white power would be maintained.

The single most dramatic reform taken by Botha was his 1983 proposal for a new "tricameral" parliament, providing a separate chamber not only for whites, but also one for coloureds and one for Asians. Botha's proposal can be seen as an attempt "to phase out the polarity [of nonwhites opposed to whites]. He needed coloureds and Asians as part of the total strategy, and even Africans, if he could figure out which to trust."[127] Having been courted in a series of meetings with government beginning in 1979, English-dominated big business largely supported Botha's reforms. Two-thirds of whites, Afrikaner and English, voted in favor of the new constitution.[128]

Despite white support, the tricameral parliament did not produce the desired result among blacks. With Africans still excluded, the new constitution served to unify opposition within the newly formed United Democratic Front. Leaders of the Front voiced their skepticism that "you cannot expect Botha, who came to power on the apartheid ticket, to be the very person who dismantles apartheid."[129] Botha's reforms were described as "trying to find the secret of sharing power without losing control."[130] Bishop Desmond Tutu wrote to Botha, lamenting that eight years had been "wasted trying to beautify apartheid."[131] Such opposition and the protest it engendered demonstrated that Botha's efforts at appeasement had the reverse effect.

Rising popular protest was seen by Botha as rude ingratitude for his reforms, provoking him to swing toward the opposite pole of his ambivalent agenda. A 1985 speech demonstrated this reversal, for after claiming to have embraced reform, Botha concluded that "I am not prepared to lead white South Africans and other minority groups on a road of abdication and suicide."[132] Evoking Julius Caesar's return to Rome to crush insurrection, Botha claimed to have "crossed the Rubicon." That same year, Botha declared a state of emergency, which was interpreted by the black opposition as "an admission of defeat" for his purported reforms.[133] Oliver Tambo of the African National Congress (ANC) declared from exile that Botha had been "revealed as a military dictator, not a reformer."[134] But while the opposition decried his repression, whites rallied around Botha as their protector. His dramatic electoral victory by a two-thirds margin in 1987 led Botha to abandon fully the idea of sharing power with blacks. But still his ambivalence remained, for Botha continued to seek credit both for his use of repression to protect whites *and* for his reforms. As late as 1988, he still claimed that his "government has gone far to serve people, broaden democracy, remove hurtful and discriminatory legislation and social practices, provide for needs of all."[135] The regime appeared stuck between its two opposing aims.

By the late 1980s, mass protests had revived and reconfigured old splits among whites divided over how to restore stability. Afrikaners themselves divided between hard-liners advocating repression and soft-liners allied with English-speaking liberals pushing for further reforms. The "civil religion" of Afrikaner nationalism no longer united the *volk*, and by 1988, half claimed to have abandoned their support for "grand apartheid," favoring even more fundamental reforms of minority rule.[136] The Broederbond sided with these reformers, with its chairman beginning to "speak more publicly [that]

Afrikaner interests could not be promoted alone, for instance the vote needs to be extended to all," ostensibly raising the possibility of a black president.[137] But at the same time, one-third of the white electorate voted for representatives opposed to reform.[138] Seeking electoral advantage among these hard-liners, Andries Treurnicht argued against any "blurring of the Afrikaner consciousness into a kind of white unity." The right countered the Broederbond's reformism, provoking massive resignations by right-wing Broeders already during the 1970s.[139] In 1982, Treurnicht had formed the Conservative Party, gaining support from poorer Afrikaners and those who saw Botha as being the tool of the liberals.[140] Twenty-one members of Parliament abandoned the National Party to join the Conservative opposition.[141]

The white political block appeared to splinter: where once it had united, the maintenance of racial domination now divided. Afrikaners were again split along lines similar to those that had divided the United or South African Party. The National Party had repositioned itself on the reformist side of the divide despite its use of repression. It sought an alliance with English-speakers and claimed to represent all whites, maintaining the basic structures of racial domination even as it pursued reforms. The ambivalence of this agenda created divisions within the Afrikaner community. The ANC and other opponents of the regime did not agree with the conservatives in seeing Botha as a liberal, but they did find encouragement in the division within the ruling elite.[142]

But what appeared as a splintering of whites over the future of apartheid was actually also a fundamental realignment of white unity even more advantageous to the ANC and its allies. As the National Party shifted toward reform, it lost some Afrikaners but gained many English. In 1981, 85 percent of Afrikaners supported the National Party as compared to 20 percent of English. Eight years later, Afrikaner support for the Nationalists had fallen to 46 percent, demonstrating the new split. But English support had risen to 60 percent, creating a new coalition of white support for the Nationalists as they moved toward reform.[143] English capital was increasingly "going with the state while wringing their hands" over support of their former adversaries.[144] Whereas whites had earlier attempted unity on the basis of racial domination, they now moved toward unity for reform of the same policies. In 1986, 55 percent of Afrikaners and 82 percent of English supported the pace of reforms or an even faster pace, with the National Party enjoying a "voter base now almost equally English and Afrikaner."[145] By 1992, "a surprising 68.7 percent of South Africa's whites," Afrikaner and English, voted to support "negotiated abolition of their minority rule."[146]

English electoral support for reform had been reinforced by the economic transition of British-dominated big capital to a greater focus on manufacturing and less on mining, the latter having relied on forced, cheap, and unskilled black labor. The later-developing manufacturing sector was dependent on skilled and relatively permanent labor, which could then also add to the domestic market for goods produced.[147] Indeed, manufacturing helped attract Africans to the cities, with the proportion living in urban areas rising from 10.4 percent in 1904 to 27.1 percent by 1951.[148] Often within the same conglomerates, manufacturing firms pressed against the interests of mining capital to reduce the economic constraints of apartheid and to draw more skilled black labor into urban production. State policy shifted accordingly. By 1979, the Riekert Commission had agreed that influx control produced "lower productivity and restrictions on the mobility of labor. . . . [R]ecruitment and employment should not be restricted."[149] Thus, self-interested pressure for reform from English manufacturing capital later coincided with growing English-speaking electoral support for such reform.

That many English were prepared to support reforms is not surprising; what is more remarkable is the shift of Afrikaner support in that direction. In large part, many Afrikaners saw no alternative given the crisis of rising protest, economic dislocation, and informal and formal sanctions, as described by Robert Price.[150] The "black threat" had become ever more real in response to apartheid, threatening civil war. But Afrikaners were also increasingly ready to compromise because they had in effect accomplished what they had set out to gain through the exercise of state power and apartheid. They had used the state to support Afrikaner culture and to provide jobs. By 1977, the state and its parastatal corporations accounted for 20 percent of total economic activity, with the public sector representing more than 30 percent of GDP.[151] Large numbers of Afrikaners had been hired as civil servants to administer the burgeoning apartheid bureaucracy. Afrikaners benefiting from these policies achieved close to economic and social parity with the English, as the status of all whites was consolidated. In 1964, 75 percent of Afrikaners were "working class," but by the mid-1970s, after a decade of state-led embourgeoisement, 70 percent were "middle-class."[152] As a result, "Afrikaners had acquired more self confidence, with English and Afrikaners growing together."[153] Insecurity and separatism had diminished, as was further evident in high rates of intermarriage between English and Afrikaners.[154] Racial domination had served as a means of subordinating blacks, of achieving reconciliation of Afrikaners and English, and alternatively for advancing Afrikaner interests to greater parity with their former English adversaries. With these goals largely achieved, Afrikaner support for apartheid diminished, raising the possibility of and support for substantial reform.

That Afrikaners' interests were served by apartheid, gradually reducing the imperative for such policies, reveals a more general economic component of racial domination. In South Africa, economic interests were not unitary but long divided between and within white capital and labor. Such conflict posed "a threat to the survival of the white race"[155] and the state, for it exacerbated the historical conflict between Afrikaner and English that had torn the country at its birth. Class conflict aggravated ethnic tension, for most white workers were Afrikaner and capital was dominated by the English. Afrikaner economic advance also required that such competition not explode beyond control.

Racial domination emerged as a common vehicle for appeasing both British-dominated capital and the largely Afrikaner white working class. It served to unify whites across their contrary and divided class interests. Racial domination was thus reinforced not so much to serve one set of economic interests as to serve the interests of all whites. Capital growth spurted with early segregation, and continued to profit under apartheid. Fear of another Rand revolt kept employers from breaching the color bar despite the savings such action promised.[156] White workers benefited from black subordination, even as such subordination was later reformed. In the process, the overlapping class and ethnic conflict was contained, avoiding further disruption to the economic growth from which both capital and white labor profited. Loyalty to the minority regime was maintained by pandering to the white labor voting bloc, and economic viability was maintained by ensuring revenues for capital, with the two goals balanced against each other. "The principal function of segregationist ideology was to soften class and ethnic antagonisms among whites, subordinating internal conflicts to the unifying conception of race."[157] Racial domination diminished both class and ethnic conflict in an uneasy symbiosis.

The South African state's policies of racial domination appear in a certain sense autonomous – designed to preserve the social order, polity, and economy. Capital, itself divided, had to adjust, though at little financial sacrifice.[158] White workers also benefited, but did not achieve all their goals. Nevertheless, as much as this arrangement suggests state autonomy, it also reflects the degree to which the state was continually responding to varied interests. The state was pressed by sector-specific business demands, labor strikes, unrest, and electoral pressures, with competing parties representing vying interests. Varying forms of racial domination emerged from this mix of changing pressures upon the central state, reinforced by prevailing cultural traditions of racism. Rising competition did reinforce racial domination as means of containing potential conflict, but this dynamic emerged more from ongoing intrawhite than from black–white competition. The state compromised between competing white interests.

The powerful imperative for compromising between shifting and conflicting white economic interests is demonstrated by the tremendous costs of resulting policies. Policing and maintaining the pass laws alone cost more than R136 million per year by 1976; the total costs of inefficiencies imposed by apartheid were much higher.[159] But the larger cost of renewed intrawhite ethnic and class violence was avoided. Open conflict, as in the Boer War and Rand revolt, was not repeated.

The South African state's commitment to racial domination was thus reinforced by the need to head off challenges to the nation-state emerging from overlapping political and economic intrawhite tensions. In historical perspective, emerging white unity demonstrated that racial domination had served this strategic purpose, albeit fitfully. The Boer War had solidified antagonistic solidarities in a bloody mold, with English rallying to the empire and Afrikaners united by their resistance to foreign domination. The tensions exacerbated by war had to be resolved in peace. For the newly formed state to function, and not be torn by continued ethnic conflict, the groups solidified by the war would have to find a mode of cooperation. Treatment of Africans, one of the causes of earlier tensions and the war, was turned into a basis for encouraging unity. British liberal rhetoric aside, which is where it was placed, the common ground of white racist ideology and interests provided the foundation on which peace could be built. Exclusion of the Africans helped to unify the nation of whites, defined then as such in an effort to use race to heal the previous rift. South Africa thus emerged in its very formation as a "state of race," with newly enforced and unified segregation essential to state viability and growth.

White unity encouraged through racial domination became a recurring, if still unresolved, theme throughout the first half of the twentieth century. With every reemergence of the English–Afrikaner rift, the salve of racial domination was applied to keep the peace. What had worked in 1902 worked again and again; reconciliation was repeatedly encouraged at the expense of "nonwhites." Official segregation and discrimination categorized whites, Africans, coloureds, and Asians as such, as part of a race making process intended to heal the ethnic and class conflict between the English and Afrikaners. Racial groups were increasingly defined by the sharp knife of a state committed to carving up the population to achieve a stability in which growth could proceed. That process varied over time, but each variation served the strategic logic of forging an alliance for white nation-state consolidation.

A white coalition across ethnic lines proved long elusive. At times, Afrikaner nationalism was appeased by racial domination linked to white unity, as after the Boer War. But during other periods, unity governments threatened to abandon racial domination and the interests of poorer Afrikaners, as was the case under Smuts in the early 1920s and under the fusion government during the Second World War. Afrikaner nationalists used these opportunities to mobilize support by reaffirming their commitment to racial domination, thereby trumping advocates of white unity who wavered in this regard. This strategy helped to bring Hertzog to power in 1924 and Malan in 1948, with state intervention used after both these transitions to advance Afrikaners.

Racial domination became a political football used for advantage by both white and Afrikaner nationalists, serving the interests of both. Whichever tendency was predominant in any one period, the racial order was reinforced. Continued party and economic competition repeatedly reinvigorated the original "deal" of encouraging white unity and enforcing domination. This odd commonality explains the preservation of the union. The pressing issue of "the native question" served to unify whites within both camps, in that sense helping to hold the polity together. Union created a single prize, which Afrikaner and white South African nationalists sought to win by use of racial domination, despite some liberal objections and failed attempts at reform. In this sense, political and economic competition unintentionally served to stabilize the system, which retained its commitment to segregation and then apartheid. Growth proceeded, from which all whites benefited. Black South Africans suffered throughout.

The dynamic of intrawhite political competition was largely resolved after the National Party victory in 1948. The Afrikaner-controlled state dedicated itself to bolstering the social and economic status of its chief constituency. Apartheid profited the Boers while consolidating white privilege more generally. Afrikaners gradually moved toward parity with English-speaking whites, diminishing antagonism, resentment, and distrust. And as Afrikaner confidence in power grew, they became more magnanimous toward their former English adversaries. Verwoerd himself followed Hertzog's own earlier shift from a "two stream" approach toward white unity. Afrikaner nationalism was again diluted into white nationalism. The result was a greater degree of white unity, which eventually shifted toward reform of apartheid. Rising black protest played a major role in this shift, as will be discussed later.

South African racial domination was then closely tied to the gradual consolidation of a class compromise, a unified nation-state and political competition for control of that state. The racial order was not the result of natural or biological distinctions of physical differences alone, for such differences were interpreted in different ways at various times, as with the shifting treatment of coloureds. The British victors of the Boer War saw a pressing strategic advantage in aligning with the Afrikaners and imposing racial domination, not least because the Afrikaners represented a more viable, proven threat to the state than did the Africans. This strategic assessment importantly coincided with prior racial prejudice common to the English and the Afrikaners, despite policy differences. But prejudice in itself does not explain the outcome. There had been a significant English tendency for reform that was purposefully marginalized in order to make union possible.

As argued by Steve Biko, racial domination was "not a mistake on the part of whites but a deliberate act."[160] It served particular economic, political, and strategic interests of South African and Afrikaner nationalists alike. Indeed, racial domination was not the result of a unitary nation-state, but a product of vying efforts to forge such unity and the competition for state control. White supremacy was the glue that held South Africa together, inscribed in the very foundation of a polity born of historical conflict and exclusion. Only after that polity had matured for most of this century and its initial ethnic conflict had subsided would this glue begin to come unstuck.

6

**"To Bind Up the
Nation's Wounds"**

THE UNITED STATES AFTER
THE CIVIL WAR

The U.S. house of race was constructed on a foundation of prejudice. Native Americans were decimated. An elaborate ideology of racial inferiority was gradually applied to Africans, slave and freed, misceg-enation and the liberal tradition notwithstanding. This belief in black inferiority became a "self-fulfilling myth that prevented blacks from improving themselves and thereby disproving the image that whites had of them."[1] Though such discrimination was pervasive, the Amer-ican house of race was really two separate structures under one roof of a common Constitution. The agrarian South insisted on continued slavery, resisted by the North. To form a single republic, slavery concentrated in the South was allowed to continue, while the North took the lead in early segregation. Given continued regional tension over slavery, state unification was itself circumscribed. A weak central authority coordinated states retaining all powers not delegated to the center, including many of those regarding slavery. The genius of fed-eralism was that providing for the rights of states or regions to con-struct their own social order preserved a loose confederation of those states, avoiding conflict. These arrangements reinforced the fault line running along the Mason-Dixon line and accommodated in the Con-stitution's federalism.

The Nation Divided

The United States at mid-nineteenth century was torn by regional strife comparable to the ethnic conflict later culminating in the cre-ation of South Africa. The cataclysm of the Civil War eviscerated all previous compromise. No war was "more devastating to our economy or more threatening to our national survival."[2] Disputes over political control crystallized around the issue of slavery and the treatment of blacks, despite pervasive racism. Only gradually, in the aftermath of war, would this same issue be turned into a basis for holding the nation-state together.

The Civil War was not the result of liberal pressures for racial equality. The image of Negro inferiority was widespread among whites, with slavery defended as beneficial to both the slave and the master, and even liberals were careful to resist the charge of being pro-Negro.[3] Few seriously challenged the assumption of the 1857 Dred Scott decision that the African race, "separated from the white by indelible marks . . . [was] not intended to be included" in full citizenship.[4] Even Lincoln, in his 1858 debates with Stephen Douglas, was unequivocal: "I am not nor ever have been in favor of bringing about in any way, the social and political equality of the white and black races. . . . Blacks must remain inferior" and in his view should have been returned to Africa.[5] Only radical abolitionists questioned black inferiority, further inflaming racist ideological defense. Frederick Douglass concluded that the issue of race was "at the bottom of the whole controversy."[6] But there was not enough disagreement among whites on this issue to explain the outbreak of America's most violent internal conflict.

The future of "the peculiar institution" of slavery was a source of inescapable tension, but it was not the only cause of war nor the basis for its resolution. The Union had long stood divided on this issue. Compared with Brazil, slaves were reproducing without new imports and manumission was rare. There was little prospect of profitable slavery fading through attrition. With few blacks, the North had little to lose from abolition, and much to gain from the spread of free labor. Jefferson earlier had foreseen that slavery was "the rock upon which the old union would split," Lincoln saw it as "an apple of discord," and Du Bois later described it as "the symbol, but also the real basis of sectional conflict."[7] But disagreement over slavery cannot in itself explain why the previous compromise arrangements broke down. There was not enough new about this basic conflict to explain the sudden break with the past practice of compromise and mutual enrichment. Indeed, the Union acted against slavery with some hesitation. The Emancipation Proclamation came only in 1863, and was criticized by abolitionists for applying only to territories outside of

Union control in hopes of destabilizing the South, depriving it of slave labor supporting its war effort, and encouraging black Union volunteers. The proclamation invoked neither civic authority nor moralism, further suggesting that ending slavery was not *the* cause of war and more a consequence of that war.[8]

Tension over slavery was exacerbated in mid-nineteenth century by a growing economic divide, which raised difficult issues about the political control and economic intervention of central authority. The South's relative economic retardation had been of long standing, as observed by Tocqueville, without leading to conflict.[9] But as economic development proceeded in the North, it faced a number of bottlenecks that required centralized intervention. Industrialists increasingly looked to Washington for "tariff protection, aid in setting up a transportation network, sound money, and a central banking system. . . . [They] wanted to be able to do business without bothering about state and regional frontiers."[10] As in South Africa, economic development required central state coordination, threatening autonomous interests. Though eager for more federal investment, the South resisted any expansion of federal economic intervention or centralized authority that might threaten the institution of slavery.[11]

Economic differences had been long-standing, though a regional division of labor had been mutually beneficial. But as economic development increasingly raised issues about central authority, these issues did become disruptive. Regional economic interests did not tear apart the Union, but they did provoke a dispute about "whether the machinery of the federal government should be used to support one society or the other."[12] The "panic of 1857" exacerbated this dispute, for declining fortunes inspired greater calls from the North for federal intervention.

The Civil War was determined by such multiple and reinforcing pressures emerging from regional competition. The South sought to preserve and extend slavery, resisting any increase of centralized federal authority that might be used by the North to challenge or contain bondage. The North sought to increase centralized authority, thus challenging regional autonomy and slavery, and to support or regulate the North's own industrial development, at the expense of Southern agrarianism. The two issues, slavery and economic intervention, converged and reinforced each other and regional antagonism. North and South lined up on opposite sides of both issues. Neither region could be appeased without sacrificing the aims of the other. The polity reached an unavoidable crossroad, much as South Africa later reached a crisis of conflict between Afrikaners seeking to preserve their regional autonomy and the English seeking state consolidation.

Slavery, economic demands, and political realignment all came together in exerting unprecedented strain on the point of the polity's greatest vulnerability, the federal compromise between states' rights and central power. As a result, the preservation and consolidation of the Union and its power of local intervention emerged as the decisive issue over which no compromise could be found, as described by the rhetoric of the time. In 1858, Lincoln argued that the government could not long endure "divided"; Stephen Douglas responded that "the doctrine of uniformity" was inconsistent with "the sovereign right of each state."[13] Once the war had begun, Lincoln argued that "my paramount objective in this struggle is to save the Union and is not either to save or to destroy slavery."[14] Confederate President Jefferson Davis argued in 1881 that the war was "the offspring of sectional rivalry and political ambition." With some exaggeration, Davis added that the conflict "would have manifested itself just as certainly if slavery had existed in all the states, or if there had been no negro in America."[15] Slavery and economic intervention were the particular disputes revealing a more fundamental issue of Southern resistance to national unity and central state building.

The institutional structures of government, which had previously encouraged compromise, failed.[16] Until the 1850s, the admission of new states had carefully balanced slave and free territories so as to preserve the balance of power of North and South, with the latter retaining an effective veto within the Senate. Overconfident of their continued power and eager for new slave territory, the Southern-dominated Democratic Party agreed in 1850 to let new states decide for themselves whether to allow slavery or not. Their gamble was crucially miscalculated in abandoning the institutional arrangement that had protected their interests and preserved the federal compromise. The balance of regional power tilted perilously to the North's advantage, with political parties aligned according to sectional interests. The Northern-dominated Republicans replaced the Whigs as the party advocating central power, and in 1860 their candidate Lincoln was narrowly elected as president. The North had captured control of the central authority, leaving the South with no assurance that this authority would autonomously balance regional interests. Fearing intervention, and with few protections remaining, the Southern states saw no alternative but to secede. The nation-state fissured.

The power of the center could only be established by defeating the secessionists. As in South Africa, central state unity would either be enforced or not. According to the earlier observation of John Quincy Adams, the competing claims of federal and states' rights "can be settled only at the cannon's mouth."[17] The flame of regional tension had long been contained within a federalist fireplace, providing carefully controlled heat. But the flame outgrew its confines, engulfing the surrounding structure. The institutional balance between center and states that had long preserved the Union now became the basis for a conflict threatening to destroy the entire edifice. The result was a war in which at least 623,000 soldiers would die, more than those lost in all other wars the country has fought added together, world wars included.[18]

What Lincoln fought for, he won, but at terrible cost. The Union established militarily the formal sovereignty of the center. And in the very process of war mobilization and its aftermath, the central state authority increased its capacity to dominate local state structures. War making fed state building. Conscription boosted the Union army from 16,000 troops to more than one million, requiring greatly expanded administration and funding.[19] Newly enacted income taxes rapidly increased the tax burden in order to fund the war effort. A national banking system and currency were established to organize finances, while a huge federal debt was incurred.[20] By 1865, the federal budget had grown to over $1 billion from $63 million in 1860. And in the decades that followed, the federal government consolidated this increased size and power: the federal payroll grew from 53,000 to 256,000 between 1871 and 1901. A national pension system was created to meet the needs of veterans and their families, and land-grant colleges were founded to educate agricultural and mechanical laborers.[21] A modern centralized state was born out of its bloodiest conflict. Symbolizing this transition, the dome atop the Capitol in Washington was built even as the guns of war boomed.

Greater assertion of centralized state authority did not ensure equally consolidated popular loyalty to a united nation. Mobilization and victory by the Union forces created a modern state, but also further deepened sectional differences. The conflict and its aftermath reinforced solidarity on opposing sides, much as was true after South Africa's Boer War. Southern nationalism had emerged in the decade leading up to the war, been institutionalized by the Confederacy, and been forged in battle.[22] According to Wilbur Cash, the war "had left Southerners . . . far more aware of . . . the line which divided what was Southern and what was not."[23] In defeat, Southern "white men of upper and lower classes closed ranks in spite of antagonistic economic interests and submerged their differences in the cause of Redemption."[24] Similarly, the South's opening attack on Fort Sumter unified the North (other than the Copperheads). The conflict had then solidified the popular Northern view of the country, according to a leading newspaper, as "not one people. We are two people. We are a people for freedom and a people for slavery."[25]

Lincoln well understood that the prize of formally centralized rule would remain superficial and under threat if the wounds of war were not healed. As in South Africa, the price of state consolidation won by force was entrenched national division within the state. The lack of unity threatened to undermine the fruits of victory and economic growth. The impetus for nation-state building reemerged even more strongly. Central authority and unity had to be backed by popular loyalty, or at least acceptance. The institution of the United States had been reestablished; now the corresponding sentiment would have to be constructed. The state would have to "give us nationality as a people."[26]

To inspire reconciliation where his war machine had reinforced enmity, Lincoln applied his most evocative rhetoric. Having earlier elicited Northern loyalty to the "Union," Lincoln increasingly referred to "the nation," including Northerners and Southerners as victory approached and the need for future reconciliation became apparent. The "United States" became a singular noun in Lincoln's often-repeated, almost religious evocation of unity, just when that unity was submerged in blood. Most notably, the Gettysburg Address was a paean to national resurrection, commemorating that battle, a turning point in the war.[27] Soon thereafter Lincoln established the Thanksgiving holiday as a symbol of shared national heritage. His second inaugural, with victory in sight, disclaimed malice and proclaimed a new goal: "to bind up the nation's wounds."

The issue of race was unavoidably central to the postwar order. The Civil War had been fought to preserve the Union and to end the division over slavery, and in its aftermath resolving how to treat free blacks became all the more pressing with the end of slavery as a distinct category. Abolitionists' pressure for blacks' rights was increased by the war effort of blacks themselves, as it would be in South Africa's Boer War. Lincoln acknowledged that "the North could not have won the war" without 200,000 black troops and 300,000 black "helpers." Du Bois argued that blacks had further contributed to victory by their refusal to work for the South, in what he roughly characterized as the equivalent of a general strike.[28] By war's end, the Republicans had abandoned federal support for recolonization to Africa, reinforcing assumptions of postwar inclusion.[29] Even before the end of the war, Union General William T. Sherman had sought to reward blacks with the provision of "forty acres" in then "liberated" South Carolina. Their efforts on behalf of the North had won for blacks newfound respect, with more radical whites arguing that this contribution to the victory should be rewarded with equal rights. As Justice Harlan would argue in 1896, blacks, having "risked their lives for the preservation of the Union . . . are entitled to participate in the control of the state."[30]

Lincoln had some sympathy for the impetus to grant blacks equal rights after the war. But he well understood that such a policy would directly contradict the pressing need to make peace with the former Confederacy. The South had remained adamant on the need to retain and reinforce racial domination, with abolition having left a sizable black population needed for labor in the region. Freeing the slaves reinforced racism, which Lincoln understood could not simply be crushed. Even in the North, where blacks made up less than 2 percent of the population, early official discrimination and calls for increased white immigration (from Europe and the South) reflected significant social resistance to racial equality.[31] To head off conflict arising from reforms, Lincoln had sought to appease Southerners and welcome them back into the Union. He resisted abolitionists's continued calls for reform, countermanded military orders of abolition that preceded his own Proclamation, and again advocated African recolonization.

Lincoln pragmatically sought to appease the South not only on race, but also with direct efforts of forgiveness, much as the British would seek to appease Afrikaners after the Boer War. The president resisted Congressional pressure to limit the postwar political rights of former Confederates, instead proposing to require of them only that they swear allegiance before resuming citizenship. Death penalties for treason were not imposed. Jefferson Davis himself would be sentenced to only two years in prison.[32] "Lincoln wanted no martyrs . . . he knew, too, that if a vigorous Republican party were to grow in the South it would need the support of many ex-Confederates. That was good politics as well as sweet charity."[33]

Lincoln would not live to see his nation-building project completed. His assassination by an embittered Southerner harshly reaffirmed that the sectional animosity that had spent so much blood would not be easily forgiven or forgotten. Like the Afrikaners later, the South remained proud in defeat and eager to win in peace much of the rights it had lost in battle. Like the British authorities in South Africa, the North won control of the central state and was tempted to use that power to exert revenge. Lincoln's stirring calls for national healing would be drowned out for a decade by the din of the federal machine's postwar retribution and intervention. Given sectional animosity, "the main forces of cohesion in American society, though growing stronger, were still very weak."[34] Such cohesion would be torn further by Reconstruction, picking at the wounds of war, for unlike South Africa there was no external colonial power confidently insisting on appeasement. The Union Lincoln preserved and strengthened would be used as a blunt instrument against the vanquished rather than as a salve for the nation. Ironically, this result was hastened by initial steps in the other direction.

Lincoln's successor ignored the moral imperative of eventually meeting blacks' expectations and instead pursued only the pragmatic need for immediate reconciliation with the South. A Tennessean who had been rewarded for his loyalty to the Union with the vice-presidency, Andrew Johnson used his inheritance of the White House to assist the defeated and economically devastated South.[35] He sought to minimize federal intervention, granting in peacetime states' rights lost in the war. He was also eager to gain support from Southern representatives, who were being readmitted to Congress in the larger numbers implied by allocating House seats by counting still-disenfranchised blacks as full members of the population. Accordingly, besides reversing Sherman's allocation of land, Johnson rejected the extension of Freedmen's Bureau support of blacks and black enfranchisement.[36] Johnson further embraced Southern racism, condemning miscegenation and efforts "to Africanize" the South in violation of "the great difference between the two races."[37] Southern states took up Johnson's concessions, imposing segregationist "black codes" that prefigured post-Reconstruction Jim Crow.

Like Hertzog's premature efforts at Afrikaner–English unity in South Africa, Johnson's efforts at reconciliation were crucially mistimed. His one-sided appeasement of the South provoked an equally one-sided radical response from Congress. If Republicans had been willing grudgingly to follow Lincoln's moderate lead on Reconstruction, they were provoked to greater militancy by Johnson's leniency. The war had not been won in order to lose the peace. The blood of one million casualties and of the Great Emancipator had not been spilt in vain. The South had not been defeated in order to return to the Union more powerful. It was not so much the mistreatment of blacks to which most Northerners objected, given prevalent racism, but rather that such mistreatment flaunted Southern disrespect for the Union's policies and authority. To the Northern eye, "the South had been handed an olive branch and, in the fury of defeat, had shaped it into a whip. . . . [T]he South had failed to appreciate [that] if it did not rein in its excessive intolerance of the freed black man, the North would be forced to do so."[38] Northern sentiment was enraged by Johnson's too quick concessions and the South's seizing the advantage.

The previous century of compromise with the South had been resuscitated, and if civil war was not itself sufficient to kill it, then political action would finish the job – or so the Republicans thought. Like those English in South Africa who would advocate "anglicization" after the Boer War, Congressional Republicans were eager to reject compromise and to impose their will on the defeated. Congress pushed hard for more radical Reconstruction and overturned the black codes with the 1866 Civil Rights Act. The nation-state would be rebuilt on the North's terms. If Johnson had no stomach for it, he was expendable. In 1868 Johnson's obstruction was weakened by his impeachment, though he remained in office.

Congressional Reconstruction was justified by liberal ideology. The North had fought a war ostensibly to replace slaves with free labor and to spread democracy. Constitutional rule had been defended, and under such rule segregation and disenfranchisement seemed to lack legitimacy.[39] The North would be more formally obligated by constitutional amendments to reforms than would be the

English in South Africa, though contradictions remained. Never mind that the North had pioneered its own forms of discrimination. Never mind that recolonization of former slaves back to Africa continued to be discussed and encouraged. Such legacies of racism were purportedly swept aside by the war victory and renewed liberalism. Even the treatment of Native Americans briefly improved under a new Peace Policy during Reconstruction.[40]

A good portion of the motivation for radical Reconstruction was more pragmatic than idealistic. Republicans such as Thaddeus Stevens feared that continued black exclusion would ensure that the South would "send a solid rebel representative delegation to Congress," undermining Republican rule and "the political and economic consolidation that constitutes the fruits of victory."[41] The Republicans thus pursued black enfranchisement for their own advantage, confident that as the party of abolition they would reap black votes. And they needed the black vote to defeat the former Confederates vying for the enlarged number of Southern Congressional seats. The proposed Fourteenth Amendment would ensure black enfranchisement to serve this end, establishing equal rights left vague in the original Constitution. In 1867, those Confederate states readmitted under Johnson were deprived of their status and reduced to military rule from the North within five districts. The return to civil authority was made contingent on granting blacks the vote and ratification of the Fourteenth Amendment. With no formal power within the polity, the former Confederacy had no means of redress short of another secession. The South was forced to concede "the supremacy of the national state and the formal equality under the law of everyone within it. . . ." Citizenship was to be defined nationally, consolidating the United States as a nation-state with the power to impose its will on local authority.[42]

Blacks jumped at the opportunity for inclusion and participation, which they had expected as reward for their war efforts. In the 1867 elections, close to 70 percent of the one million newly eligible blacks registered and black voter turnout was between 70 and 90 percent.[43] The result was far from the "black domination" Southerners feared and decried: only fifteen out of 133 state delegates in North Carolina, for example, were black. But the eventual election of sixteen black U.S. Congressmen and two black senators was indeed dramatic.[44]

Not all the dreams of recently freed blacks were met, but many were. White Southerners awakened to their nightmare. With black enfranchisement consolidating their hold on Congress, the Republicans enacted significant social reform legislation. Only proposals of land redistribution were put aside as inconsistent with basic liberal protection of property.[45] The Freedmen's Bureau provided food rations and established more than forty hospitals and 4,300 schools. Though the Bureau's total expenditure was only $1.25 per capita, at the time it "was the most extraordinary governmental effort at mass upliftment in the nation's history."[46] The results were significant: black literacy rose from 10 to 50 percent between 1865 and 1890, black land ownership rose, and per capita real income of blacks increased 46 percent from 1860 to 1880.[47] And if this intervention to assist blacks were not enough of a shock to Southern whites, a large number of Northern carpetbaggers and Southern scalawags assisted in these efforts or joined the Republican Party. Many Northerners profited from effective colonial rule of the South, leaving Southerners feeling something less than part of a unified nation.

Radical Reconstruction reconfigured political and economic distributions. The reformer Carl Shurz had written in 1865, during the more moderate presidential Reconstruction, that "nothing renders society more restless than a . . . revolution but half accomplished."[48] Radical Reconstruction moved toward completing that social revolution, or as close to one as America had seen. The centrally imposed extension of the franchise and provision of social services to blacks challenged the Southern elite's political monopoly. But such consolidation of reform brought its own restlessness. As Lincoln had understood with his advocacy of balancing reform with reconciliation, to pursue only the former risked reawakening the regional antagonism that had already torn apart the Union. Even Frederick Douglass warned against "special efforts" on behalf of blacks that might "serve to keep up the very prejudices which it is so desirable to banish."[49] Such warnings were ignored, yet proved prescient. "Sowing the wind" of change reawakened the "dragon's teeth" of discord.

With Radical Reconstruction, pivotal American and South African experiences diverged. In both, central state authority was consolidated or formed by military victory. And in both, efforts to appease the vanquished and to unify the nation of whites were initially pursued, by means of backtracking on promised reforms in the treatment of blacks. But there the similarity ends. The South African state generally remained committed to racial exclusion and white unity, pursuing those aims with strong central action impelled by white racism and fear of the black majority. In the United States, the central state did not emerge from the Civil War as strong, but nonetheless was pushed by radicals to impose intervention, in part to win black electoral support. Nothing comparable was attempted in South Africa, where minority white rule would have been threatened by such reforms. As a result, segregation in South Africa was quickly enacted, endured, and was refined; it was not similarly encoded for a generation after the Civil War in the United States. Only after Radical Reconstruction further inflamed regional tensions, thereby undermining the prospect of unified white loyalty to the nation-state, would the salve of racial domination be applied – not by central authority weakened by the failed reform experiment, but by resurgent local authorities. Race making and nation-state consolidation remained linked, but the United States embraced this linkage more fitfully.

Segregation, Party Competition, and Nation-State Consolidation

The United States after the Civil War had not fully embraced the logic of diminishing intrawhite conflict through racial domination, as would be pursued by South Africans after the Boer War. But Reconstruction efforts at reform, and the renewed animosity they provoked, brought even the Republicans around. The nation had to be united, at least for whites, to make a modicum of centralized state rule workable. The South could not be forced to give its loyalty, but would have to be encouraged to do so, if need be by abandoning Reconstruction. But as in South Africa, this arrangement would not immediately erase intrawhite antagonism reflected in the ongoing competition of parties representing divergent interests. And as in South Africa, competing political parties agreed to build or allow further enforcement of racial domination for their electoral advantage. Such competition kept the issues alive, but also contained differences within the preserved polity. Party competition thus emerges again as an intermediate explanation for how nation-state building and racial domination were linked. Such competition reassured divergent groups that the central state remained responsive, at least in allowing for divergent local policies. The result was Jim Crow, with such legal enactments building on past ideology and practice, and with unforeseen consequences.

Central state imposition of Reconstruction backfired in undermining the prospects for nation-state and economic consolidation. What the South most feared were "the nationalizing tendencies in the American government unleashed by the war."[50] Southern whites were aghast when precisely such policies were enacted, condemned by them as "revengeful legislation . . . [that] enfranchised the Negro," seen as "unfit to rule," and "disenfranchised the largest and best portion of the white people."[51] They were further exasperated by their relative economic deprivation and exclusion from "the great barbecue" of postwar federal expenditure.[52] With the perception of "negro domination" causing resentment and reviving regional solidarity and antagonism, Southerners took to the streets. More than forty died in disturbances in New Orleans in 1874.[53] White Southerners also reacted to the threat of rising black rights and competition by taking matters into their own hands and forming the Ku Klux Klan in 1866. With the Union army demobilized, Southern state militias were the strongest military force in the region and appeared ready to resist outgunned federal authorities.[54] Even if there was little prospect of a defeated South returning to formal military conflict, the Civil War had proven that Southern threats of violent resistance could not be taken lightly. By the mid-1870s the air was again thick with such menace, raising the specter of the North's worst nightmare, continued division threatening the Union just recently preserved by force.

If fear of violence was not enough to shake the North's commitment to Radical Reconstruction, economic dislocation further undermined that already wavering commitment. The Panic of 1873 ushered in the greatest depression to date. This economic downturn further exacerbated class tensions in the North, which later exploded with the Great Strike of 1877 and threatened to divide by class a populace united by war.[55] White workers demanded that the social reconstruction extended to blacks "be extended northward" to them.[56] The contagion of a revolution engineered by Congress threatened to expand beyond control, raising fears of a triadic conflict between whites split by region and class, and blacks benefiting from this split. Federal authorities were confronted with the prospect of a two-front conflict, facing both outraged Southerners and Northern workers. And the economic advance that underpinned the growth and consolidation of the recently reunited state was similarly threatened on two fronts. Southern recalcitrance threatened the postwar expansion of cotton production and efforts to build a Southern transcontinental railroad needed for transporting goods were stymied. Strikes and financial panic threatened burgeoning Northern industry. Like any state, the United States needed stability and could not afford to see its economic base again undermined by conflict.

The North faced these challenges with foreboding and weariness. Unionists had expected an easier enjoyment of the fruits of their hard-won war victory. Exaggerating the actual threat, Washington was in no mood to refight the war it had just concluded. Nor were the people. Northern newspapers editorialized that "what this country wants most is a steady period of rest from agitation."[57] Northern business was eager to constrain the "turbulence in the South," which threatened production and investments there.[58] Capital was also eager to diminish Northern workers' expectations raised by Reconstruction social policies. Commitments to black advancement had unsettled both North and South. Even Republicans advocated a reversal of course, back to an emphasis on regional reconciliation and stability. Again Lincoln's more balanced approach was ignored, though now in the opposite extreme. The North's dual aims of racial justice and preservation of a unified and stable Union had come into conflict, forcing a choice.

As national unity and stability had always been the primary goal, the impetus for racial reform would have to be abandoned. Appeasing blacks was not a strong strategic imperative, for they had not proven themselves a major threat to peace. As Justice Harlan argued later, "sixty million whites (are) in no danger from the presence here of 8 million blacks."[59] But this lack of threat, which Harlan hoped would inspire generosity, instead allowed for abandonment. The black minority, historically set-apart and discriminated against, could be deserted with relative impunity. Appeasing the South to reaffirm stability was of greater importance than black rights. The North had tried to achieve both its aims; when it tired of the effort, it turned its attention to more pressing matters than that of the black minority.

Like the British victors in the Boer War two generations later, the North faced the strategic imperative to abandon its commitment to blacks in favor of encouraging white reconciliation and peace. And as in South Africa, pervasive racial prejudice reinforced this impetus.

Even at Gettysburg, Edward Everett had spoken of the need for "reconciliation" among those Northerners and Southerners who share "a substantial community of origin."[60] Blacks were clearly not conceived as part of this ancestral unity, and assisting them had impeded its assertion.

Formal abandonment of Reconstruction was finally forced by political developments. The administration of former Union general Ulysses S. Grant had become mired in corruption fed by the massive increase in federal expenditure. In the South, blacks were blamed for this corruption, which had coincided with the election of black representatives, tarring Reconstruction with the brush of graft. Suffering under the economic depression, Southerners and Northerners looked for an alternative to Republican rule and its Reconstruction. The result was increased electoral support for the Democratic Party, controlled in the South by the former slaveholding planters, aligned with Northern partisans. The Democrats were able to win a Congressional majority in 1874 and to deadlock the presidential election of 1876. The solution to this impasse produced a major turning point in American history.

The stalemated 1876 presidential election exacerbated the already exaggerated but much-feared "menace of war or anarchy" and forced a new settlement.[61] Compromise effectively reaffirmed existing conditions. The North had already lost control of the situation in the South, with little army left mobilized to coerce obedience. The North had also lost interest in exerting such control, for the South provided little economic return and depression made it difficult to pay the costs of federal imposition.[62]

Impasse required a deal. Northern Republicans were willing to concede the restoration of states' rights formally in order to restore stability and preserve Republican control of the White House. In return for the South's acceding to the election of Rutherford B. Hayes, the Republicans agreed to "the appointment of a Southerner to Hayes's cabinet, generous federal aid for internal improvements in the South, federal assistance for completion of the Texas Pacific Railroad, Democratic control of federal patronage in the South, and the withdrawal of the troops in the South."[63] To "promote the pacification of the South," the South would be "redeemed" and the centrally imposed policies of Reconstruction, already in tatters, would be abandoned in favor of restored regional autonomy. Even reformer

Carl Schurz advocated a reassertion of "the rights of local self-government."[64] Southern Democrats and Northern Republicans secretly agreed to the deal, with both hoping to find electoral advantage in such autonomy. Hayes was inaugurated; he committed himself to "reconciliation between North and South," to avoiding further chaos in the South, and to "pacification of the country." He quickly signaled this policy with a dramatic "goodwill tour" of the South.[65] "Effusive Blue and Gray speeches and tearful reunions of old troopers were the order of the day. Hardened South-haters melted . . . the genuineness of the national response to the policy of conciliation and peace was evident."[66] In effect, the old tradition of regional compromise and a constitutional division of power was restored to encourage nation-state consolidation.

The price of this reconciliation was to be paid by African-Americans, much as black South Africans would be sacrificed for white unity. As part of the Compromise of 1877, Southerners had publicly committed themselves to legally required "full and equal protection" of black and white citizens.[67] The emptiness of this rhetoric was quickly revealed by the purposeful disregard of the Fourteenth and Fifteenth Amendments and resurgent efforts to "repatriate" blacks to Africa.[68] Racial inferiority per se was used to justify discrimination and exportation as consistent with adherence to the "democratic creed of the nation" as applied only to whites.[69] The North acceded to this logic. The federal judiciary undermined new constitutional duties to enforce equality and the executive ignored any moral obligation to reward black loyalty in the Civil War. For instance, in 1883 the Civil Rights Act of 1875 was overturned by the Supreme Court.

As the English would find in South Africa, prior commitments to blacks were easily abandoned. To the Southern eye, it seemed that "our Northern fellow citizens begin to feel the race sympathy stilling within their breast."[70] More concerned with restoring stability than with "helping the Negroes," largely "indifferent to the problem" and sharing Southern racial attitudes, the North acceded to the abandonment of Reconstruction efforts. They had become "tired of the worn-out cry of Southern outrages" and the claims of "the everlasting nigger."[71]

The African-American was not just abandoned "as a ward" of the nation "no longer singled out for special guardianship."[72] Following a logic similar to that pursued later in South Africa, blacks were also purposefully discriminated against, with emerging segregationist policies providing a "crucial and final step on the long road to sectional reunion" of former adversaries.[73] According to Du Bois, "all hatred that the whites after the Civil War had for each other gradually concentrated itself on [blacks]. . . . Had there been no Negroes, there would have been no war. Had no Negroes survived the war, the peace would have been difficult because of hatred."[74] Displacing sectional animosity onto blacks helped to pacify the regional antagonism that threatened the Union and its economy. Whites could be and were unified as a race through a return to formal and informal discrimination. Blacks thus served as a scapegoat for white unity, allowing for greater stability and reducing the impediment of regional antagonism standing in the way of further nation-state consolidation. The maintenance of the Union formally won in the war would come to be consolidated with racial domination, which would remain for close to a century. "God wept" as African-Americans returned to a life not so different from slavery, excluded from the polity for which they had fought and from which they had expected more.[75]

Black exclusion was not preordained, but instead emerged from alternatives tried and failed, and from continued intrawhite conflict and competition. Deportation was again considered and abandoned as impractical. Nor can the eventual outcome of official segregation be explained simply as the legacy of earlier racism, for Reconstruction had been attempted. Segregation as it later was codified also cannot be explained as a centrally imposed policy (as in South Africa), for Jim Crow would emerge locally, in fits and starts, not as a result of some grand design. The Compromise of 1877 did not establish the rules of black subordination immediately or finally. But it did signal the trajectory, much as the 1902 peace treaty in South Africa would establish a similar pattern. And as in South Africa, party and class competition led to continued remaking of the "deal" of racial domination to reconcile whites in a unified nation-state.

Party competition played a central role in elaborating racial domination in the post-Reconstruction era. The Republican Party abandoned its earlier attempts to impose racial justice in order to win Southern white support. Hayes committed his administration to ending "the distinction between North and South," overcoming his "anxiety [that] to do something to promote the pacification of the South is perhaps in danger of leading me too far."[76] Republicans remained concerned that appeasing Southern whites ran the risk of losing Civil War gains, were angered by later limits on black suffrage, and even threatened a return to Reconstruction. But partisan efforts to win over enfranchised Southern whites were more pressing than such concerns, not least because many Republicans believed in black inferiority. The gambit failed, with Republican votes in the South falling from 40.34 percent in 1876 to 36.95 percent in 1888. "Republicans actually found their party worse off in the South in 1896 than it had been in 1876, when they sought to redeem it."[77] But even though the Republican Party failed to make inroads in the South, its efforts to do so reinforced its abandonment of black rights.

Southern Democrats successfully contained party challenges by trumping Republican commitments to racial domination, in order to retain their control over the South. The Republican Party in the South was decried as "composed almost exclusively of negroes," backed by the threat of federal force.[78] The greatest threat to the Democratic lock on the South was the Populist movement, which emerged during the depression of the late 1880s and early 1890s, and called for greater federal intervention. Challenging "white solidarity," Populist rhetoric advocated an alliance between small black and white farmers who had been "made to hate each other" for the economic advantage of the "progressive" alliance of planters and capitalists.[79] But the Populists were defeated by fraud and violence and by planters' appeals for regional solidarity of whites against Washington and the Republicans. Racial regulations were gradually reinforced to head off the Populist movement, disenfranchising blacks who had supported this opposition.[80] Racism was a tide against which Populists were not strongly committed and could not swim; instead they eventually joined it.[81]

By the mid-1890s the Populists had been largely eclipsed by Democrats projecting themselves as "the party of the white man." Election to office came to be determined by the Democratic primary, further constraining any opposition. The Democrats enforced party discipline, warning against a triadic conflict of divided whites and blacks, arguing that "if whites split . . . the Negro would hold the balance of power."[82] By 1898, Louisiana Democratic conventioneers were emboldened to proclaim: "What is the state? It is the Democratic Party ... We met here to establish the supremacy of the white race, and the white race constitutes the Democratic Party of this state."[83]

The Democratic Party ensured its lock on the South not only by excluding blacks, but also by selectively disenfranchising those whites who had sided with the Populists. Class and party conflict among whites was eclipsed by the image of consensus enforced by voting limits – the "progressive" era of stable white rule rested upon disenfranchisement. Seen by party leaders as undependable and unworthy or ignorant and brutal, poorer whites had to be eliminated to ensure white Democratic rule, particularly in the Black Belt regions.[84] In a series of state constitutional conventions beginning in the 1890s, poll taxes and property requirements were enacted, excluding many whites.[85] In Alabama, "23.6 percent of the white, male voting-age population was disenfranchised by the poll tax alone."[86] Even the secret ballot ensured that illiterates would get no help in voting. When these legal moves proved insufficient, mob violence and electoral fraud further disenfranchised. Sixty-four percent of adult males voted in the South in the 1880s, but after 1900 participation had fallen to 30 percent.[87] During these decades, the South came to be ruled by whites only, and only by those whites who supported the Democratic Party.

Party rivalry coincided with regional animosity, but actually helped to keep the reunited polity intact. Competing tendencies both saw their interests represented by parties vying for power in a central state not fully captured by either side. And as in South Africa between 1910 and 1948, this dynamic was lubricated by common agreement on racial domination. Superimposed regional and party tensions were contained by white solidarity. Issues other than race might have divided whites and were downplayed.[88]

The major "other issue" contained by racial solidarity was that of divisive intrawhite class antagonism that had emerged after the Civil War. Class conflict had continued to plague development.[89] But the enforcement of racial domination encouraged the unity of whites across class, serving "to transfer class hatred so that it fell upon the black worker."[90] In the South, planters benefited, with Farm Bureau regulations ensuring cheap black labor for cotton and tobacco production when sharecropping diminished.[91] Less developed Southern manufacturers generally went along. Southern white labor's interests were also accommodated. Planters offered personal and economic assistance to reinforce white unity and to deflect worker mobilization or alliances with blacks, as it had earlier.[92] But tensions within and between classes remained just below the surface image of white consensus, and would compel even stronger efforts at unity to preserve the region's political power and stability.[93] As C. Vann Woodward puts it, "Having served as the national scapegoat in the reconciliation and reunion of North and South, the Negro was now pressed into service as a sectional scapegoat in the reconciliation of estranged white classes and the reunion of the Solid South."[94]

The same pattern of using racial domination to diminish intrawhite class conflict also emerged in the North, albeit with important differences. After the Civil War many Northern white workers remained fearful of an influx of black labor from the South. They headed off this threat by imposing their own segregation, reserving for themselves certain jobs and higher wages. As early as 1862, Irish longshoremen in New York called for the dismissal of black competitors. Subsequent waves of European immigrants, themselves discriminated against by nonimmigrants, found employment from which blacks were excluded.[95] Unions affiliated with the American Federation of Labor generally defended their white members against black incursions.[96] Between 1881 and 1900, more than fifty strikes were waged by white immigrants to keep blacks out of their jobs.[97] Resulting segregation helped hold together the diverse parts of the white working class and strengthen it.[98] But for capitalists this was a price worth paying to avoid the even greater threats of sectional conflict and potential unity between white and black workers.

Locally determined segregation policies reflected the distinct regional balance of economic power and demography. In the North, where capital was stronger than labor, employers benefited from paying blacks lower wages than whites.[99] Stricter Jim Crow would have limited the use of such cheaper labor. White workers, including immigrants, were appeased by informal policies of discrimination, in part because blacks were few in number and little threat. Capital did then benefit from a racially segregated labor market enforcing cheaper black wages, but full-scale legal Jim Crow was not imposed upon the relatively small black population. Informal discrimination sufficed, as it would in Brazil. In the post-Reconstruction South, blacks were more numerous. They posed a greater threat to white workers, and their potential alliance with those white workers posed a threat to planter capital. Immediately after abolition, informal discrimination and black codes constrained black opportunities, even in the absence of those more elaborate job and wage color bars of the type later imposed in South Africa. Native white Southerners retained significant bargaining power in shaping Southern segregationist policies as they moved toward greater codification.

The legal expression of racial domination in the South was Jim Crow. The term referred to popular imagery of blacks as "cheerful and merry" in their inferior position, akin to South Africa's tendency to disingenuously label such discrimination as "progressive."[100] Southern elites retained a paternalistic image, with the president of the 1890 Mississippi Constitutional Convention proclaiming that "each race is fond of the other."[101] The reality was vicious segregation, evident earlier but significantly reinforced by legal codes refined through the 1930s.

Most fundamental was the abandonment of the black franchise that had so inflamed, humiliated, and unified Southern whites during Reconstruction. Louisiana state conventioneers were eager "to eliminate from the electorate the mass of corrupt and illiterate voters who have during the last quarter of a century degraded our politics."[102] "Restricted by the Federal Constitution, we have tried to secure more enlightened elective franchise without race discrimination or injustice," the Louisiana conventioneers claimed, though their aim was still "white manhood suffrage."[103] Southern states employed an array of "nonracial subterfuges," including property and literacy requirements, and the poll tax, designed to avoid federal intervention and to deny the vote to blacks.[104] Poorer and less educated whites were also so excluded, as noted, but these measures were most strictly applied to blacks, whose numbers on the voting rolls fell precipitously. For example, black turnout in Tennessee gubernatorial contests fell from 60 percent in 1888 to none in 1890, 1894, and 1898. By 1901 the last black Southern Congressman had lost office.[105] Residential segregation, relatively uncommon before the turn of the century, was enforced and defended by violence.[106] Blacks were also excluded from juries, ensuring that Southern courts would not provide "equal protection."

For all of the subterfuge involved, the race-specific nature of post-Reconstruction social policies was commonly understood. It was perhaps most directly revealed in the application of such policies to mulattoes. Before abolition, a primary social distinction was between slave and nonslave, with freed mulattoes treated as an intermediate category that did not disrupt the basic bifurcation. After Reconstruction, a biracial order was reinforced in order to encourage regional reconciliation, with race replacing bondage as the primary distinction. Segregation, not required to demarcate difference under slavery, was imposed according to race. Mulattoes had to be placed within this new order, to avoid any slippage that might have fed Southern resentment. In 1896, the U.S. Supreme Court declared that even an "octoroon" was subject to segregation within supposedly "separate but equal" facilities.[107] Miscegenation and "mixed marriages" were made illegal.[108] Whites were ever more distinguished from blacks, regardless of mixed ancestry.

Describing the trajectory of post-Reconstruction social policy in this way runs the risk of a false impression. What appears schematically coherent, centrally controlled, and compressed actually developed in a relatively disorganized and protracted process. Reconstruction itself had revealed the limits of the ability of the central government to impose its will on the South. "To enforce [black] rights would have required a concentration of national authority and efficient bureaucratic administration that was beyond the capacity of the American state" at the time, despite state consolidation during the Civil War.[109] The abandonment of Reconstruction signaled the end of attempts at extending such centralized control and interference, and a resurgence of what William Jennings Bryan would describe as states again "sovereign in your local affairs."[110]

Unlike South Africa's centrally imposed policies, segregation would be imposed unevenly and fitfully, resulting in the lag between 1877 and the full elaboration of Jim Crow in the 1890s and thereafter. Even then, Jim Crow was enforced as much by hoodlums as by local authority. Often the two were indistinguishable, as elected judges and other officials turned a blind eye to the mobs who had voted them into office.[111] More than two thousand blacks (and some whites) were lynched during the last two decades of the century, while the federal government declined to intervene.[112]

Lack of a grand design or strong central action did not ameliorate the effect on blacks. As they were largely concentrated in the South, it made little difference in real terms to blacks whether their plight was enforced by Washington, local and state officials, or mobs. With "nothing but freedom," the end of Reconstruction left blacks without the paternalistic security of slavery. To meet the labor needs of planters, they were forced into debt peonage and sharecropping, and in some respects worse off and more subject to racial prejudice.[113] By the 1890s, black codes had been refined, and were applied most strongly in urban areas, where whites and blacks lived more closely.[114] Residential segregation in the North proceeded apace, defended by white mobs and real estate agents.[115] According to a speaker at the Louisiana Constitutional Convention in 1898, "the negro in New York, Boston, Philadelphia, Chicago . . . is no more accepted as an equal than in New Orleans."[116] The term "segregation" came into use by the early twentieth century, and its practice was extended even to the galleries of the U.S. Senate.[117]

The establishment of legal racial domination in the South and continuing discrimination in the North diminished the regional antagonism kept alive by Reconstruction. It also divided the working class along race lines. But these outcomes also produced reverse effects. "The South surrendered claim to substantial economic and political power in the nation in return for social and racial autonomy at home."[118] Such solidified Southern regional autonomy and solidarity also appeased. Confederate spirit was kept alive in subsequent generations by the solid Democratic Party control over the region and continued antagonism against Northern intervention. White working class unity, in both the North and South, was also solidified by white racial solidarity.[119] Such sectionalist party politics and worker mobilization ran counter to the nation-building project of diminishing regional and class antagonism. But these outcomes could not be avoided as consequences of pursuing the larger aim that predominated; allowing such assertions of regional and class interests had the effect of containing more explosive antagonism within overarching white racial solidarity.

Whites were somewhat unified by race, across class. Economic development did bring increased competition, but first among whites and only later with blacks. Intrawhite class conflict grew in both the North and South, together with race conflict.[120] Elites sought to minimize the risk of a triadic conflict, through racial discrimination in its various forms. White workers, including immigrants, were appeased by the exclusion of black competitors and by higher wages. To an extent, capital and workers combined to keep blacks suppressed, forging a kind of class compromise. Business accepted the costs of segregation as a means of allaying white workers' fears of black competition, while occasionally using cheaper black labor to undercut whites and hold down their wages. As Williamson concludes:

> Business exists to make money. Segregated facilities were more expensive than unsegregated facilities so that businesses with unsegregated facilities resisted oncoming segregation. But disorder and violence destroys business altogether. If the violence was to be ended by segregation, business readily adapted and passed the costs along.[121]

Economic development and the tensions it brought did contribute to the reinforcement of racial domination. But white capital and labor had contrary and often internally divided interests. Racial domination cannot then be attributed to narrow or uniform class interests. Instead, class conflict and internal class division help to explain the racial order. Racial domination, helping to unify whites as whites, served to diminish class conflict more than it exclusively served the interests of any one class or fraction thereof. Building on prior ideological and cultural prejudice, both white capital and white workers participated. As Du Bois concluded, "the white workers . . . are just as culpable as the white owners of capital."[122] Particular policies still differed by region, with Washington effectively letting each region go its own way. But in sum, the variegated racial order preserved peace, avoiding the economic dislocation of further regional or class warfare.

Northern Republicans still on occasion pushed for reforms, but their lack of success again demonstrates the impetus to unify whites politically and economically via race. Efforts to repeal the Fifteenth Amendment were resisted and debt peonage was challenged in the early twentieth century, but the amendments and restrictions on "servitude" remained unenforced. The most notable attempt at Northern reforms was the proposed "Force Bill" of the 1890s, which threatened again to send federal officials South to ensure "that every man who is entitled to vote has an opportunity to caste his vote freely." Guaranteeing the franchise was described by the bill's supporters as a national obligation. The bill's leading advocate, Henry Cabot Lodge, argued that blacks deserve "some better reward" for their "loyalty.

... We owe them no more and no less than we owe all American citizens." But even Lodge acknowledged that "the negro question" remained "a matter of party politics, dividing sections and keeping alive sectional animosities and agitation. . . . Each state and each community must work out its own salvation," even as he argued that the franchise "is a different question." The earlier logic of leaving such issues to local authority so as to dampen regional antagonism again won the day. Southern objections against Northern efforts to again "oppress the people" were given greater weight than any moral obligation to blacks.[123] Having passed in the House, the Force Bill was defeated in the Senate, black disenfranchisement proceeded further, and the federal government continued to allow Jim Crow. Enforcing the black franchise continued to be set aside for the larger goal of nation-state consolidation.

By the end of the century, regional animosity had significantly abated, eclipsed by the purposeful allowing of racial domination to encourage regional reconciliation. Symbolizing this victory, President McKinley visited Alabama in 1898, joining a "prolonged celebration of sectional reconciliation . . . singing both Yankee Doodle and Dixie."[124] With the consolidation of Jim Crow in the South, America entered what has been described as "the golden age of racism" in the North as well.[125] The racial order was reaffirmed both domestically and internationally. Immigration was restricted according to race categories, and even Native Americans were subject to renewed repression. Imperialism and the Spanish–American War placed millions of Caribbean and Pacific peoples under American rule, with these subject peoples popularly viewed as "a varied assortment of inferior races."[126]

As the fruits of "the American century" were enjoyed, the scars of the earlier regional conflict began to heal. In 1912 a Southern-born Democrat, Woodrow Wilson, was elected president. Southerners returned to positions of power in Washington, and even black federal civil servants were subjected to segregation.[127] Racial domination, regional reconciliation, national unity and prosperity all grew together. The wisdom of the founding fathers' federalism, balancing central and state powers in order to hold together a diverse nation of whites, was celebrated anew. Reconstruction reforms were retrospectively described as a "blunder," with the "race problem" left to be "worked out in the South."[128] The painful episodes of the Civil War and Reconstruction faded into memory as aberrations.

Centralizing Power and Greater White Unity

With Reconstruction, the United States diverged from the path that South Africa would take. But by the late nineteenth century, the country had reverted to a pattern similar to that in South Africa in encoding or allowing for racial domination to encourage nation-state consolidation among whites. The South was appeased by allowing for Jim Crow. This arrangement had its intended result, gradually diminishing sectional animosity, much as segregation would contain ethnic tension in South Africa. Southerners and Northerners began to converge nationally, economically, and politically. As tensions diminished, central state authority increased and was able to meet economic and geopolitical challenges. Eventually that central authority would return to apply its greater strength to impose an end to Jim Crow, pushed by rising black protest to use its power to "heal the wounds" of race and to contain this new challenge to nation-state unity, as we shall see in Chapter 9. The focus here is on how nation-state consolidation emerged more fully, on the basis of racial domination, and was then turned against it.

Central state authority rapidly expanded to head off the economic dislocation of the Great Depression. The spectacle of widespread "destitution through no fault of their own" encouraged popular support for federal intervention into areas of social policy previously outside of the public realm. Even the South, long committed to states' rights, advocated a stronger central authority to meet pressing needs.[129] President Franklin D. Roosevelt encouraged this view and sought to deliver. His administration expanded the federal machinery, drawing away the autonomy of the states, shifting power toward the center. In the crisis of the moment, federalism was again reconfigured, though the racial order remained largely intact.

The New Deal represented a resurgence of centralized power not seen since Reconstruction. But it also purposefully avoided reawakening the demons of race reform and Southern resistance. While poor blacks suffering disproportionately from the Depression benefited from new forms of assistance and some patronage, they were not targeted by such programs.[130] In fact, they were often implicitly excluded.

Party politics ensured this result. Enjoying dominance in their region, Southern Democrats were often assured reelection, gaining seniority and committee chairmanships in Congress. They used their power to prevent federal economic intervention from threatening racial domination. For instance, agricultural and domestic workers were excluded from Social Security and Old Age Insurance, leaving millions of blacks uncovered. With the federal bureaucracy still underdeveloped, Aid to Dependent Children and other programs were left to states to administer, and Southern states were thereby free to discriminate. Proposed anti-lynching legislation and efforts to extend the franchise to blacks in the South were considered by FDR "too hot to touch."[131] The president feared that addressing such issues would antagonize those Southern legislators on whom he depended to pass the New Deal, which he considered more important than addressing black concerns per se. The South had regained its political foothold in Washington, with Northern Democrats constrained by their alliance with Southern Democrats.

Increased federal power was not applied immediately to race reform, but did create the potential for such reform at a later date.[132] African-Americans embraced this expectation and in gratitude for their limited benefits from the New Deal shifted their support to the Democratic Party, by then the leading advocate of federal intervention. Jim Crow lived on, though the trajectory of growing federal power posed a future threat to local segregation, as it had under Reconstruction. But as long as most blacks remained in the South and disenfranchised, they could not exert the full potential of electoral pressure for reforms, including enfranchisement. This vicious cycle kept race from becoming a more prominent issue at the time.

Economic transition and new migration patterns began to undermine the prior stasis. With dramatic black migration north, particularly after cotton production in the South collapsed, and with decreased white immigration during the First World War, Northern industry was increasingly eager to employ a greater proportion of cheap black labor.[133] And in Northern manufacturing, blacks were used as strikebreakers to diminish working-class bargaining power and to suppress white wages. Capital benefited from such divide-and-rule tactics by deflecting white labor hostility onto blacks and away from employers.[134] This type of resentment exploded in the East St. Louis riots of 1917, when white workers actually attacked blacks. With rising black employment in the North, white unionists began to shift tack, recognizing that their interests would be better served by a cross-race alliance. By 1940, the Congress of Industrial Organizations (CIO) had unionized a half million blacks, insisting on their continued inclusion after merging with the more conservative American Federation of Labor (AF of L).[135] Disagreement over the inclusion of blacks within the union movement remained.

While white workers in the North began to abandon segregation, the centralization of power under the New Deal was further consolidated by the Second World War. The war effort and its aftermath then further undermined the racial order. The war itself brought increased industrial employment for women and blacks replacing white male laborers called into service. Other blacks joined the army, where they "had a chance to compete and showed they could excel."[136] All veterans, including blacks, were rewarded for their efforts with increased educational opportunities provided by the G.I. Bill of Rights. But the impact of the war spread beyond such policies, raising black expectations of reform as a reward for their service and in keeping with the Allies' antiracist rhetoric. The war had broken the isolation of America and of black Americans, with unforeseen consequences.

American embarrassment at the contradiction between the antiracist rhetoric of the war and segregation at home was made all the more acute after the war by the country's emerging international position and concern about its reputation. The war had shaken European colonial control over Africa and Asia, and the United States was eager to win allies among newly independent states that might otherwise be lost to the Soviet Union.[137] The U.S. government was therefore eager to present the best possible image of domestic race relations to the world. President Harry Truman, eager for Northern black votes, appointed a national commission calling for reform and desegregated the army. But after many Southern Democrats bolted the party and refused to support him for election in 1948, Truman was under relatively little pressure on civil rights and largely ignored the issue of race.

When the executive branch faltered, the judiciary took up the lead. From the late 1930s, the U.S. Supreme Court had upheld a number of reforms in education, housing, and electoral design. But the real bombshell came in 1954 with the *Brown* v. *Board of Education* decision, overturning *Plessy* v. *Ferguson* and mandating school desegregation. The Court concluded that "education is the most important function of state and local government" and that discriminatory policies established by such authorities were inconsistent with national norms and requirements for "good citizenship."[138] International reputation, noted for instance in briefs before the Court, certainly had a bearing on this decision; but this was a secondary concern. More to the point, *Brown* was a capstone to the new judicial impetus upholding federal intervention.

A more progressive Court, encouraged by the post–New Deal expansion of central authority, endorsed federal intervention into the last bastion of states' rights. Local authority over race had been granted after Reconstruction. But in the intervening decades, federal power had grown by leaving the divisive issue of race where it lay, and was approaching sufficient strength to address this issue head on. Intentionally or not, the Court acted on this dynamic, helping to set the country on a new trajectory, pushed much further by subsequent black protest demanding inclusion in the nation-state.

Despite national consolidation, sectional animosity remained an impediment, and the promise of federal intervention remained stronger than the reality. The "deliberate speed" of school desegregation did not materialize. But to blacks the Court's decision meant that "for the first time since Reconstruction they felt the federal government was actually on their side."[139] The implication was even broader than school desegregation; *Brown* v. *Board of Education* pronounced segregation per se to be discriminatory and unconstitutional. Blacks henceforth began to engage in direct action.

Even the relatively conservative President Dwight D. Eisenhower could not avoid the shifting terrain of growing central authority and pressure for race reforms signaled by the *Brown* decision and the emergent civil rights movement. Eisenhower himself was reluctant to challenge racial norms, favored gradual change, opposed "social mingling" across race, and was reluctant about federal intervention.[140] But as commander-in-chief he took very seriously any menace of insurrection threatening central state authority. Such a threat was posed by the activities of a resurgent Ku Klux Klan and of White Citizens' Councils, which emerged throughout the South in the wake of *Brown*, and the refusal of Arkansas to implement court-ordered school desegregation in its capital. Eisenhower responded by sending the army to Little Rock, the first such commitment of federal troops since Reconstruction.[141] Southern blacks understood this intervention as a direct challenge to states' rights. Eisenhower subsequently supported the Civil Rights Act of 1957 and created a Commission of Civil Rights, whose representatives were welcomed by Southern blacks as a signal that "the Big Government has really come all the way down here to help us!"[142]

John F. Kennedy shared Eisenhower's political concern that federal intervention on the issue of race would heighten sectional animosity, cost votes, and further divide the nation. Southerners urged Kennedy not to "interfere in the affairs of a sovereign state," and Kennedy himself was concerned about further antagonizing Southern white Dixiecrats. "The Kennedys did not want to rock the boat. They kept their eye on the prize of a solid Democratic Southern vote. They did not want to start another civil war."[143] Kennedy's dilemma was the same faced by FDR, and like Roosevelt he sought to project a progressive image without taking firm action on divisive issues of race. Kennedy had promised an executive order to desegregate federally supported housing with "a stroke of a pen." Blacks sent thousands of pens to the White House, but the order remained unsigned. At the same time, Kennedy continued to use Harris Wofford, his assistant for civil rights, as a buffer to resist pressure for further reforms. The administration later tried to divert such pressure into more manageable activism for voter registration.[144]

Despite his reluctance, Kennedy like Eisenhower was not willing to see central authority defied and was even more ideologically predisposed to consolidating federal intervention in society. Though Kennedy argued that civil rights was "not a sectional issue . . . nor is this a partisan issue,"[145] the history of the United States suggested otherwise. His own liberal rhetoric had raised expectations among blacks that could not then be easily contained despite the political risks. For instance, the day after Kennedy's inauguration, James Meredith became the first black since Reconstruction to register at the University of Mississippi. In the resulting confrontation, Kennedy saw little alternative but to use force to desegregate the university despite resistance from Southern states'-righters of his own party. According to Kennedy, "if the United States government had failed to exert its influence to protect Mr. Meredith . . . that would have been far more expensive [than not acting]. The country cannot survive if the U.S. government and executive branch don't carry out decisions of the court."[146] According to Burke Marshall, "only in the sixties did the Executive Branch see the need to intervene" to exert its authority. Washington's edicts had to be enforced, and administration officials sent South for this purpose had to be protected.[147] Kennedy himself understood his actions in a historical light, describing his efforts to secure black rights as a "Second Reconstruction."[148] He even noted that he had signed the order to enforce desegregation at Ole Miss on General Grant's table. The president urged an aide not to reveal this private aside so as not to "antagonize the South any further with reminders of the Civil War."[149]

Significant black electoral and protest mobilization pushed Kennedy further. His narrow victory in 1960 was attributed to the swing of black votes to the Democrats, indicative of both the continuing party realignment among blacks and the rising proportion of blacks registering to vote as they migrated north. To win these votes, Kennedy had promised to address civil rights more than any previous presidential candidate. Pressure from expectant blacks was reinforced by the concern of the Kennedy administration that discrimination was "making our country look ridiculous before the world."[150] Cold war competition with the Soviet Union heightened this concern. James Forman urged his fellow black activists to play "on the [white] man's politics and the man's fears. . . . [Whites have] to give in to our demands because he's hurting in the cold war."[151]

Kennedy's policies reflected both his slowly fading ambivalence and the growing pressure of black protest. Though he initially resisted fulfilling his campaign promises, in 1961 Kennedy did establish the Committee on Equal Employment Opportunity to enforce desegregation within the government and its contractors. His subcabinet Group on Civil Rights pressed for desegregation of interstate transportation. By 1963, Kennedy had publicly declared that after "one hundred years of delay . . . the time has come for this nation to fulfill its promise."[152] His proposed Civil Rights Act aimed to fulfill that promise.

Kennedy's assassination brought to the presidency a Southerner who emerged as a major advocate of reform, even though cognizant of the political costs. Lyndon B. Johnson recognized that federal intervention that "looks like the Civil War all over again" would force Southerners "right into the arms of extremists."[153] But with massive counterpressure from the civil rights movement he nonetheless persevered, pushed far beyond Kennedy's own ambivalent record to assert central authority. Encouraged by his electoral victory in 1964 against an explicit opponent of civil rights, Johnson embraced the rhetoric of the movement, proclaiming to Congress that "we shall overcome." Later Johnson wrote that "nothing is of greater significance to the welfare and vitality of this nation than the movement to secure equal rights for Negro Americans."[154] The challenge of civil rights had to be met to fulfill "the meaning of our nation" and its promises of rights and citizenship.[155] At the risk of reigniting the sectional divide, Johnson moved to heal the more pressing challenge to nation-state consolidation posed by black protest and violence.

The era of using compromise and delay in order to achieve sectional reconciliation was over. Congress passed the Civil Rights Acts of 1964 and 1966 and the Voting Rights Act of 1965; in 1964 the Twenty-Fourth Amendment ending the poll tax was ratified. Other legislation consolidated civil rights guarantees, with some incorporated into the more general Great Society war on poverty. Reaffirming the historical connection between expanded federal authority and the imposition of civil rights, Johnson's administration represented the high point of both. Federal officials had often cited the strength of "police power and decision making under control of the states" as an impediment to enforcing desegregation from the center.[156] Civil rights activists well understood that reform on "racial issues seems to require a capability for national action," and proceeded to press for precisely such action.[157] According to James Forman, "we saw the powers of the federal government as an instrument to be used over the state governments of the South."[158]

Black protest brought civil rights to the forefront of the national agenda under Johnson, with this issue strongly interconnected with the issue of central state authority. That central authority had expanded from the New Deal until the 1960s, and blacks pressed for its application to their demands. They understood from prior experience that redress rested upon the assertion of federal power, even if that power in part had been centralized precisely by the avoidance of race reform. Blacks pressed for further action, despite continued white resistance. That black demands were gradually met attests not only to the strength of their protest, but also to the strength of central power willing to resist white counterdemands.

Each assertion of such federal authority over the states to force desegregation was resisted by Southern claims to states' rights, and catalyzed their abandonment of the Democratic Party. George Wallace in particular perfected the Southern politician's rhetorical resistance to integration as a violation of the federal balance of powers. "Both themes were popular in Alabama – segregation and against big government," the former governor later recalled.[159] Wallace's appeal, evident in the support for his third-party presidential bids in 1968 and 1972, was "two-pronged – antiblack and anti–federal government," with the two inextricably linked in Southern tradition.[160] Signaling a national shift to come, even some Northerners supported Wallace.

Black rights had been intertwined with federal power since at least the Civil War and Reconstruction. Though Wallace argued that it was "just coincidental . . . that the nation's central power was manifested by matters pertaining to race," it was not.[161] The federal government grew in power and reach, with federal reformist policies and programs of social intervention and regulation over race contributing to this growth. Indeed, the federal budget grew from $92 billion in 1960 to $195 billion ten years later, not so much as a result of the Vietnam War but as a result of the Great Society and civil rights programs.[162] Johnson accepted Southern antagonism as the cost of state consolidation and national incorporation of blacks.

Johnson's legislation signaled a new high-water mark of centralized power, and reinforced concrete changes in the socioeconomic status of black Americans. A disproportionate number of the two million federally funded government jobs created went to blacks, who as early as 1962 had accounted for 13 percent of the federal workforce.[163] Polls showed that blacks saw the government, including the military, as offering prospects for the best jobs.[164] A 1965 executive order requiring nondiscrimination by federal contractors further encouraged black employment.[165] Government policies and hiring, spurred on by general prosperity, dramatically decreased aggregate black poverty levels, which fell to a low point of 30.6 percent below the official nationwide poverty level in 1978.[166]

As in the New Deal, federal economic intervention was profound in its effects, changing the lives of blacks, the federal government itself, and party politics. The advancement of some blacks certainly increased inequality within the black community. Critics pointed out that only a relatively small "black elite" benefited from state-created jobs.[167] Daniel Patrick Moynihan argued that Johnson's policies aimed at serving the poor actually created employment for those working for the programs more than for the target population.[168] Thus, addressing issues of race and poverty served to reinforce central state power via increased government employment. Not surprisingly, federal intervention fed further state consolidation. Meanwhile, the Democratic Party embraced this image as provider of jobs, reaping electoral rewards. Programs of assistance benefited some blacks more than others, but consistently enlarged the federal bureaucracy and power.

Federal intervention for civil rights nurtured the growth of central state authority, but was the direct result of protest and electoral pressure from blacks who had migrated north, urbanized, advanced economically, and registered in increasing numbers. Unlike in South Africa, they could and did vote for reform from within the political system, reinforcing the pressure brought by mobilization and protest. The proportion of U.S. blacks living in the South fell from 89 percent in 1910 to 53 percent in 1970, largely as the result of their own migration and shifting labor demands. The proportion of blacks living in urban areas increased from 27 percent to 81 percent in the same period. Over 64 percent of blacks had registered to vote by 1968, approaching levels not seen since Reconstruction.[169] Later, with the franchise extended to the South, even politicians there were forced to appeal to blacks. Johnson himself urged George Wallace that "like it or not, the niggers are going to vote. You better go home and make some friends."[170] These changing conditions clearly contributed to pressure for reform, most notably by increasing the interest of politicians in winning the black vote. And reforms themselves helped to encourage further migration, urbanization, and voting, reversing the prior vicious cycle of black disenfranchisement and lack of reform. This new cycle of progressive forces added pressure for change upon otherwise reluctant politicians. "Political leaders respond to anxiety," James Farmer observes. "They had to be pressured . . . [since] doing nothing is always safest for politicians."[171]

Black voting reinforced a realignment of political party policies that further undermined the South's ability to resist federal intervention. During the late nineteenth century and thereafter the South had remained solidly Democratic and the North more Republican. This general superimposition of party and regional loyalty had reinforced sectionalism and the South's ability to protect states' rights through Democratic pressure in Washington. Northern Democrats went along. The reformist policies of Democratic presidents such as Roosevelt, Truman, Kennedy, and especially Johnson undermined this arrangement. Democrats began to lose support among white Southerners. Blacks had long seen federal intervention as essential for their advancement, supporting first Republicans and then Democrats who favored such intervention. Recognizing the consequence of his civil rights advocacy, Johnson himself concluded that he had "delivered the South to the Republican Party for a long time to come." The solid South was split: the Democrats lost five Southern states to Goldwater in 1964 and seven Congressional seats in Alabama, Georgia, and Mississippi in 1966.[172] Still, the South was unable to block civil rights and federal intervention, outvoted by the Democratic alliance of liberal whites and blacks.

The end of legal racial domination in the United States was largely the result of these structural changes and protest. But such protest would not have succeeded, perhaps not even emerged as strongly, if a central authority had not grown sufficient to overcome white resistance. Indeed, white racism was somewhat diluted by growing nation-state consolidation and economic change, earlier encouraged by racial domination.

Central government power in the United States had historically been constrained by the individual power of each state, regionally grouped. Growing central authority could only come at the expense of local authority, as it did. The Civil War itself, as well as the two world wars, had reinforced central state capacity to mount a major war effort, each time leaving the central state even stronger after the war. Demobilization never reduced the central state's power to its prewar levels. The crisis of the Great Depression also brought further consolidation of central authority and capacity under the New Deal, establishing the national government's relatively strong intervention in the economy and social policy. The federal machinery – its bureaucracy for social intervention – dramatically expanded. In the half century after 1926, government spending as a proportion of net national product almost tripled.[173] The post–New Deal Supreme Court mostly upheld this increasing federal intervention, and if need be, Washington had the military force necessary to impose its will.

This is not to suggest that assertions of states' rights disappeared, only that they diminished. Efforts to appease the South had largely succeeded, with the South gradually lowering its guard. Southern resentment toward the North and Washington had gradually abated. Common national experiences such as the world wars and New Deal had reinforced national unity further. The South was "Americanized."[174] The growing participation and power of Southerners in Washington, as indicated by FDR's fear of the "Southern veto," further indicates that the South had been incorporated, much as Afrikaners were incorporated in South Africa. And again as in South Africa, representation in party politics, in particular then through the Democratic party, further assured the South that its interests would be defended within the polity.

Appeasement of the South was not only achieved politically, but also through rising prosperity in the region and economic integration of the country as a whole. After abolition, Southern merchants and planters had invested in industry, such as textiles and later iron. Northern industrialists provided some further capital, and federal expenditure for railroads and other services in the region increased, leading to an economic rebirth. The New Deal then forced higher wages and provided assistance, spreading prosperity to Southern workers.[175] In just four years, thanks to war production, Southern manufacturing jobs almost doubled to 2.8 million by 1943.[176] Per capita income in the South exploded after 1940, diminishing the economic disparity between North and South via rising Southern industrialization, urbanization, and cross-regional migration.[177] Much as the Afrikaners reached greater parity with the English in South Africa, the South prospered under Jim Crow.

Ironically, as the South was appeased, developed, and integrated with and increasingly reconciled with the North, it gradually lost the power it had exerted through the continued threat of sectional conflict. Allowing states' rights to be preserved amid party competition preserved the union and quelled resentments, allowing for the gradual diminution of those very states' rights. The nation-state was consolidated among and for whites, as it was in South Africa.

Also as in South Africa, the Union aim of racial justice had been
abandoned in order to secure the primary goal of national unity
through regional appeasement. Southern incorporation suggests that
this strategy had worked, as it had in South Africa. But with the
greater achievement of white unity, blacks increasingly demanded an
end to the racial domination that had helped unify the white nation.
The regional balance of power had had disastrous consequences for
black Americans for as long as central authority remained weak. Federal moves to force the end of Jim Crow in the 1960s were a response
to rising black protest, but also indicated the greater power of the
center made possible by the earlier appeasement.

The South recognized its vulnerability to intervention, foresaw
that accommodation to its racial order was ending and again challenged federal intervention, but it was too late. The indignation of
Presidents Kennedy and Johnson at Southern challenges to national
authority provoked even further imposition of such authority over
local race policies. Racial domination had remained in many ways
the defining component of states' rights, and federal intervention to
meet black demands marked the last step toward consolidation of the
nation-state and of Washington's power. Central authority had
achieved enough strength to finally move forcefully into the last
bastion of states' rights.

By the mid-twentieth century, the central state was strong enough
to consolidate its power more fully, even to impose reforms of the
racial order in the South. Sectionalism was dampened and unity encouraged, allowing for the gradual centralization of political power
sought by the North. Blacks had paid the price of this nation-state
consolidation: their exclusion and domination had appeased the South
and unified whites nationally on racial grounds, thereby diminishing
the sectionalist threat. Later black pressure on the polity was ironically enhanced by the very economic integration, migration, and urbanization made possible by prior racial domination. Such pressure
eventually reinforced a new threat to the nation-state in the form of
black protest, and that could only be defused by ending legal domination. None of this is intended to suggest that Southern regional
loyalty and resistance to the center ever disappeared. To the contrary,
federally imposed reforms rekindled such antagonism. But by then
the South had become much more fully integrated into the nation-

state, could not plausibly threaten to secede, and therefore had little ammunition with which to resist. Racial domination had reinforced the nation-state, which then, under pressure, tried to rid itself of its original sin.

7

"Order and Progress"

INCLUSIVE NATION-STATE
BUILDING IN BRAZIL

In 1822, Pedro I was enthroned as emperor of newly independent
Brazil. The backdrop curtain for the coronation, reproduced in a
print by Regis DeBret, symbolized Brazil's image of itself at this transitional moment. At the center is the Portuguese prince, ruler of the
empire. Grouped around his throne paying homage are representa-
tions of the Brazilian nation, including black and white soldiers, workers, and black slaves. It is an image of state founding remarkable for
its projection of centralized power personified by Pedro, inclusive
unity, and popular loyalty. A comparable image of state founding in
the United States or South Africa would surely have represented the
culmination of conflict, whether the American War of Independence
or Civil War, or South Africa's Boer War. And surely the comparable
American or South African representation would not have included
blacks as symbolic members of the nation represented by that state.
Nor would South African or U.S. imagery have placed at its center a
descendant of the previous colonial power. But Brazil's foundation as
an independent empire had not been the result of conflict, but of a
peaceful transition that retained historical links to the colonial power
of Portugal.

A second image from Brazilian history carries similar symbolism.
In 1889, the son of Pedro I lost his Brazilian throne with the declaration of a republic. Before Pedro II sailed back to his ancestral homeland of Portugal, Brazil threw a party for him on the Ilha das Cobras
in Rio's majestic Guanabara Bay. By all accounts, this was a festive
occasion, including white and some mulatto elites. What is remarkable is that such an inclusive and cordial festivity occurred at all. The
transition from empire to republic, almost simultaneous with aboli-

tion, had been achieved with little rancor. A celebration was in order. It is simply impossible to imagine a comparable party being thrown jointly by Americans and their former colonial rulers to celebrate the forced withdrawal of the British, with Southerners to celebrate the Union's victory and abolition after the Civil War, or by Afrikaners and British to celebrate the founding of South Africa after the Boer War. Brazil was not born of comparably bloody conflict, but rather emerged from a relatively gradual and peaceful transition. Instead of gunpowder smoke and human carnage, Brazil emerged from slavery and empire in a hail of flowers and dancing.

Unity and Discrimination

Brazil's peaceful transitions from colony to empire and then to republic were made possible by, and indicate, the capacity of a state able to finesse change. In part, this relatively unified state was a legacy of the traditions of Portuguese rule. Colonialism had established more centralized rule and greater bureaucratic capability than the decentralized capitalism imported by Britain and Holland to eastern North America and South Africa. The earlier withdrawal of the Dutch and the arrival in Brazil of the Portuguese king fleeing Napoleon had further diminished internal conflict that might have disrupted state coherence. This tradition was then reinforced during the empire. As a result, the Brazilian state remained strong enough to pursue its ideal of "peace and harmony . . . to avoid confrontation." The preservation of authority and relative absence of violent conflict encouraged little mobilization. What regional conflict did emerge consistently ended in compromise.[1]

The Brazilian state's early tendency to conciliate should not be seen as a sign of weakness, but as a signal of a state able and confident enough to bargain away conflict in order to preserve its authority.[2] Patrimonial rule was never seriously challenged, as is reflected in the small number of deaths due to internal conflict. The state and its related elites remained largely hegemonic, even if official authority did not fully penetrate into vast areas of territory.

The state's encouragement of an integrating social order was shaped and reinforced by cultural norms and discourse inherited from Portuguese colonialism. Informed by Catholicism, the Portuguese had constructed an inclusive hierarchy. Unlike in South Africa and the United States, no absolute social or racial dichotomy was enforced. This inclusive hierarchy would be adjusted after abolition, with blacks still at the bottom and mulattoes as intermediaries. By thus maintaining the image of a social and racial continuum, Brazilian culture and policy diminished the prospect of antagonism.[3] This argument was contradicted by discrimination and would be contested among elites and later by Afro-Brazilians (see Chapter 10). But the image of social inclusion remained a strong element of culture, consistent with state policies of incorporation.

The use of compromise to preserve stability guided Brazil in ending slavery, a process so contentious elsewhere. Abolition in Brazil did not disrupt the social hierarchy in which blacks, slave and free, were already incorporated at the bottom. The end of slavery could be achieved gradually, provoking remarkably little of the kind of opposition that elsewhere inflamed racist ideology and practice. Slavery had been a national institution in Brazil, but a regional one in the United States and a more ethnic one among Afrikaners in South Africa. In 1819 "no region had less than 27 percent slave out of its total population. . . . [S]laves continued to be distributed throughout the Empire at a remarkably uniform rate."[4] Similarly, "abolition sentiment and agitation was not limited to any one section of Brazil," with pre-abolition manumission already widespread.[5] When the poorer Northeast eventually did become more committed to abolition and Southerners called for immigration to replace slaves, abolition could be managed by the state with little tension or social disruption, which might otherwise have curtailed emancipation or challenged the state itself. Brazil escaped anything comparable to the American Civil War, and achieved emancipation without civil strife.[6] Indeed, Brazilians were eager to avoid the sort of conflict they had seen erupt in the United States.

Abolition nonetheless did have a significant political impact in Brazil. Former slaveholders angry at the crown for abolition threw their support behind the growing republican movement, already strong among an underpaid and dissatisfied military, advocates of greater religious freedom, and industrialists.[7] Abolition and republic reinforced each other: the military declared the republic a year after abolition. The 1888 prediction that with abolition "your Highness has redeemed a race but lost a crown" proved correct.[8] In some respects, "1889 did not mark a significant break in the Brazilian historical process."[9] The republic was ushered in by the same elites who had prospered under the empire, and with so little violence or rancor as to make possible a pleasant farewell party for the emperor.

Despite the lack of conflict in its founding, republicanism did fundamentally change the form of government. Without the centralizing power and symbolism of the emperor, the republic adopted an American style of federalism, breaking up unitary authority into more autonomous states.[10] Brazil moved in a direction opposite to the greater centralization that characterized the U.S. Reconstruction period and South Africa after the Boer War. In part, the Brazilian ability to shift toward state decentralization demonstrated the greater confidence of Brazilian elites that devolution of power would not bring the sort of conflict already avoided. Despite a major peasant revolt in 1897, decentralization would last until 1930, when the tradition of a more strongly centralized state was reasserted.[11]

Peaceful abolition and republican federalism provided little pressure or capacity for central state intervention to assist freed slaves. Neglect of those slaves earlier manumitted set the pattern. Brazilian abolitionists had rarely raised the issue of how freed blacks would be treated, and once abolition was achieved, most blacks simply continued to work as before, but now for low wages.[12] The long-established social and racial hierarchy remained intact, in contrast to the U.S. South's social order resting on a dichotomy of slave and free shaken by war and abolition. Brazil's "racial order remained almost identical to that which existed under the caste system; and the negro never found in the white man any real support."[13] With no Civil War ushering in abolition, there was also no Reconstruction. Proposed land redistribution was aborted, and in general, the issue of black advancement was eclipsed by the rising tide of republican fever.[14] With no expectation of state intervention to help blacks and little pressure to impose formal segregation already maintained informally, power could be and was diffused for a time. Blacks themselves emerged "from slavery materially and psychologically ravaged," lacking any means to advance themselves or to compete, isolated in rural areas or in the newly emerging urban slums, or favelas.[15]

Not only were blacks abandoned to their fate, but their prospects were diminished by official efforts to further encourage European immigration. The end of slavery and rising industrialization had produced great demand for free labor, which the Brazilian elite preferred to fill with imported whites rather than by training and advancing blacks.[16] Widespread immigration was directly encouraged, with private funds until 1889 and with public funds thereafter used to pay for the passage from Europe.[17] State support for immigration was deemed necessary to overcome reluctance among Europeans to come to Brazil; it was explicitly described as a form of compensation for former slaveholders who had lost their captive labor pool.[18] From 1870 until 1963, over five million immigrants came to Brazil. Eighty percent of the 3.7 million arriving before 1930 settled in the industrial center of the Southeast around São Paulo. By 1920, 50 percent of industrial workers were foreign-born.[19] Those who came brought with them European ideas of white racial superiority, though there is some debate about how influential these immigrants' views were in Brazil.[20] While European immigration was encouraged, resulting advantage was enjoyed without formal, domestic racial domination. And such inequality cannot be explained as being caused by white labor's interests. The preference for importing white labor was established when Brazil still had few white workers, with mulattoes used to fulfill intermediate economic functions elsewhere filled by poorer whites.[21]

Racial prejudice in Brazil was no doubt influenced by European ideas, but it was already well established before the bulk of immigrants arrived. Fears of earlier slave revolts and racially based resistance to dependence on black workers had motivated state support for white immigration as an alternative source of labor. In this sense, Brazil's immigration policies mirrored U.S. policies encouraging black return to Africa. Rather than exporting blacks, Brazil favored importing whites, but the purpose was the same – to dilute the black population. In 1890, Brazil banned the immigration of blacks, a ban again debated and ultimately reinforced in the 1920s and 1930s.[22] As late as 1945, Brazilian legislation stipulated a preference for immigration that would "develop in the ethnic composition of the population the more desirable characteristics of European ancestry."[23] This continued preference for white immigrants was defended, as it had been at the turn of the century, as providing Brazil with a steady "injection of civilization" as a means to "purify the race."[24]

The ban on black and encouragement of European immigration were complementary components of a general policy toward "whitening," shifting the population's color balance toward lighter shades. Encouragement of miscegenation, already pervasive, further reinforced this process. And the image of class mobility for mulattoes encouraged accommodation. Thus, whitening further served to diminish nonwhite solidarity and the prospects for conflict the elites feared. Black solidarity and potential mobilization were diluted; as long as it was possible to become white, there seemed little reason to insist on defining oneself as black, with all of the associated negative stereotypes.

Whitening led to a real increase in the proportion of Brazil's population identifying itself that way. So-called whites rose from 44 percent in 1890 to 62 percent by 1950, with a corresponding fall in the proportion of the population identified as mulatto.[25] Black numbers were relatively diminished by white immigration, intermarriage, low reproduction, and social rewards encouraging people to redefine themselves as lighter.

Whitening as a conscious policy was both explicit and implicit, and a consequence of Brazil's early racial discrimination. The image of Brazilian racial tolerance is directly confronted by the stated post-abolition preference for white immigrants and for a diminution of the Afro-Brazilian presence. Denigration of slaves had clearly shifted post-abolition to a greater explicit focus on racial images, as it had in the United States.[26] At the same time, Brazil's particular history of miscegenation forced a subtle but significant reinterpretation of European eugenics. "They borrowed racist theory from Europe and then discarded two of that theory's principal assumptions – the innateness of racial difference and the degeneracy of mixed bloods."[27] Brazilians embraced their miscegenation, assuming that such mixing would produce ever lighter generations because of the greater strength of white genes.[28] Meanwhile, they encouraged upwardly mobile mulattoes to align themselves and even define themselves with whites, and blacks to define themselves as mulatto.[29] The resulting later increase in mulatto categories, a "browning" more than a whitening of the population, was embraced as consistent with overall lightening.[30] Whitening was thus a reflection of Brazil's racial hegemony, where whites were explicitly preferred, with some flexibility about including mulattoes in that or intermediate categories.[31] Racial prejudice was clearly inscribed into the Brazilian social order and official policies, reflecting white popular ideology and culture.

In light of the U.S. and South African experiences, as well as its own history, Brazil's post-abolition experience of racial prejudice and discrimination is not surprising. What remains remarkable is the constrained and distinct application of these principles. Whitening could be and was achieved without the establishment of biracial categories or official segregation. Indeed, such forced segregation might have discouraged miscegenation, which Brazilians embraced as means to dilute the black presence established by slavery. Instead, integration of a sort was encouraged, not to advance blacks but to absorb and dilute them culturally as a distinct group. White racial domination was still the goal, albeit unstated. But the means of achieving this goal appeared to be the opposite of U.S. and South African policies.

The Persistent Myth of Racial Democracy

Post-abolition Brazil inherited an entrenched social hierarchy and racial prejudice. But instead of enforcing official racial domination, Brazil projected an image of an inclusive nation-state and racial democracy. Compared to South Africa or the United States, Brazil entered the modern age with a more consolidated state apparatus then decentralized in the republic. There had been no major intrawhite conflict that would be resolved through official racism and policies encouraging white unity. Instead of provoking conflict by means of such exclusion, Brazil sought stability and maintenance of its social hierarchy through incorporation of all, consistent with its cultural predilections. Earlier national consolidation required no legal racial crutch for its preservation, but rather was maintained by avoiding policies of segregation, amid debates and challenges.

Post-abolition Brazil's distinctive lack of formal segregation was understood at the time as a significant departure from contemporaneous U.S. official practice. No less a figure than Theodore Roosevelt visited Brazil and in 1914 wrote of Brazil's "tendency to absorb the Negro . . . [and] to draw no line against the Negro." Roosevelt went on to quote approvingly an anonymous Brazilian's comments:

> "You of the United States are keeping blacks as an entirely separate element and you are not treating them in a way that fosters their self respect. They will remain a menacing element in your civilization. . . . [W]e Brazilians have chosen [an alternative that] will in the long run, from the national standpoint, prove less disadvanta-

geous and dangerous than the one you of the United States have chosen."[32]

Roosevelt's quote suggests two elements that help to explain Brazil's alternative racial order. First is the notion of blacks as a potential "menace" to social order. Brazil had directly experienced this threat during its long history of slave revolts, more extensive than those in the United States. With a state and culture fixated on the idea of unity and stability, it is not surprising that they chose to suppress such conflict. They sought to diminish the threat of future unrest by providing a seeming means of inclusion and by avoiding formal segregation, which would likely encourage animosity and protest for redress. By contrast, the post–Civil War United States had experienced a less comparable threat from blacks, a relatively much smaller proportion of the population. U.S. whites were therefore less fearful of the prospect of black revolts and used official segregation to head off any such threat.

Roosevelt's quote from his Brazilian informant also suggests that the American and Brazilian models of race relations were alternatives among which both countries were somehow free to choose. But because in the United States a violent regional conflict was healed, in part, by Northern appeasement of Southern demands for racial domination, the country was not then free to choose the alternative advocated by Theodore Roosevelt. Social order, shaken by war, had to be restored. Abandoning the ideology and practice of racial domination might very well have reopened wounds that had already once torn apart the Union. The imperative for legal racial domination had been so established in America, as it had been in South Africa.

Brazil experienced much less violent regional and no ethnic conflict requiring resolution of the kind elsewhere achieved through the projection of white racial unity. Describing racial domination in the United States and South Africa as the result of such pressure for reconciliation is consistent with Brazil's having less comparable conflict to be reconciled and enacting no official racial domination for this purpose. In Brazil, a consolidated nation-state had long been in place, with civil wars elsewhere in the region reinforcing Brazil's efforts to remain distinguished for its "white," or peaceful, revolutions.[33] This result had significant turning points, and emerged gradually.

Comparison with South Africa and the United States highlights the relatively inclusive nature of Brazil after abolition, and the absence of official racial domination. State-led nationalism was purposefully inclusive. Brazil established no systematic discrimination, and accordingly Jim Crow laws were not enacted.[34] Informal racial discrimination was evident, but official racial domination was not. This was not due to lack of capacity by the Brazilian state, which emerged from a past of centralized power able to manage relatively successfully major transitions with little violence and to support immigration and project nationalist ideology.

Despite republican decentralization, the Brazilian state did act, to some extent by omission, to enforce its particular internal racial order. Racial categories were encoded in the census but not used as the basis of official discrimination. Instead, on occasions when the census was carried out after 1890, it generally encouraged the categorization of as many people as possible in intermediate categories of mixed ancestry, demonstrating that such mixing was leading to increased whitening. Though census categories were official constructs, results were deemed as scientific evidence of Brazil's racial continuum, lightening, and lack of a firm racial divide. Brazilians shared this assumption.[35] State enumeration and popular culture combined to reinforce an image of complexity, countering any sense of biracial distinctions on which segregation might have been constructed.

State actions reinforced a racial order, if not legal domination, but the tensions and conflicts over policy should not be ignored.[36] Black immigrants were banned, though this much-debated official discrimination applied only to outsiders. Official forms of segregation applied to Afro-Brazilians within the country were also debated and then purposefully rejected as heightening the potential for internal conflict.[37] Vagrancy was outlawed and illiterates were not enfranchised, but while these policies adversely affected blacks they were not complemented by racially encoded segregation. Between 1891 and 1907, proposals to establish a formal color bar were debated in the Brazilian parliament, but were not enacted.[38]

The relative preservation of state power coincided with preservation of the social hierarchy, reducing the imperative for legal buttress. Abolition had occurred so gradually that the racial order was not shaken. Blacks were left unable to compete with whites, even in the absence of official racial domination. Slavery had ended with so little disruption that no color line had to be drawn to protect whites.[39]

This left the Brazilian state free to distance itself formally from any official policies of racial domination and instead to claim the higher moral ground by outlawing such practices. The absence of Jim Crow and the existence of laws against such discrimination consistently convinced American visitors, including many prominent blacks, that Brazil was a "racial paradise."[40]

To firmly establish the image of Brazil as such a racial paradise required not only official rejection of present discrimination, but also the purposeful reinterpretation of Brazil's past. For those interested in avoiding racial conflict, it was not enough to establish new laws banning discrimination. The history of discrimination was denied as well, so as to avoid any use of such history to foment antagonism or mobilization. Such prevalent historical reinterpretation is most evident in post-abolition descriptions of slavery, which consistently focused on paternalistic tolerance. There was little intellectual dissent and sufficient earlier rhetoric of historical tolerance to embrace. The actually harsh treatment of the majority of slaves was purposefully brushed under the rug of modern images and "the myth of the benign master."[41] Images of Catholic- or Portuguese-inspired racial tolerance and ease of mixing were celebrated along similar lines, reinforcing cultural assumptions of inclusion.

As further proof of the historical legacy of tolerance, white Brazilians trumpeted the nation's embracing of African culture. African-influenced dance and music, the *candomblé* religion and other cultural forms "sprang back" after 1888, were meshed with European traditions in a variety of synchronism, and then were re-Africanized.[42] But projecting the survival of African culture as a signal of tolerance ignored its roots in the long-maintained slave trade.[43] African culture, together with benign images of slavery and miscegenation, became grist for the mill of revisionism.

The absence of official discrimination and complementary reinterpretations of history emerged as the basic building blocks for a state-supported ideological projection of Brazil as a racial democracy. This term was popularized by Gilberto Freyre, whose interpretations of Brazilian history thus provided the foundation on which other scholars built. According to Carlos Hasenbalg, "Freyre created the most formidable ideological weapon against blacks."[44] He and his followers created an image of history and the present that denied any subordination against which blacks might resist. Inequality remained largely unchallenged by blacks, encouraged to see no barriers to their advancement.

Racial democracy was both a product of and a crucial reinforcement for post-abolition republican nationalism. This was the ideological glue that held together the Brazilian nation. Like the selectively applied liberal creed in the United States, racial democracy was projected as the underpinning for national unity and social peace. These were the paramount concerns of the Brazilian elite who purposefully projected an image of harmony to dampen earlier tensions and to avoid confrontation within a single inclusive culture.[45] Brazilians embraced the view that they had had no problem with race so that there would be no such problem.[46] This ideology of assimilation was embedded in a nationalist celebration of racial tolerance and unity.[47] The Brazilian nation projected itself as analogous to the romanticized image of the big house of the slaveholder, in which everyone had their place in a paternalistic and inclusive hierarchy.

Racial democracy would become a source of Brazilian national pride and criticism of the tolerant image became tantamount to treason.[48] Even numbers that contradicted the image of racial democracy were condemned to oblivion. Freyre himself described "racial statistics as irrelevant."[49] Even before Freyre had refined the official view, racial specifications were simply omitted from the Brazilian census of 1900 and 1920, with no census at all conducted in 1910 and 1930.[50] Later censuses camouflaged the racial divide with categories of mixed "color." Studies of racial discrimination, already hampered by the lack of racially categorized statistics, were later outlawed.[51] Such extreme measures to preserve the image intact suggest that racial democracy resonated with a central core of Brazilian tradition.

The convergence of Brazilian nationalism and the image of racial democracy had the almost magical result of projecting an established social and racial order without conflict. All had their place in a "natural plan," reinforcing social distance.[52] That order clearly reinforced inequalities, but these were generally understood to reflect economic class rather than race, despite the superimposition of black and poor.[53] Undereducated blacks were unable to compete for jobs, and as illiterates were not permitted to vote. But their deprivation and exclusion were not associated with any explicit rules of racial domination.[54] Blacks were formally free to educate themselves, to advance economically, and to become absorbed. They embraced such supposed opportunity, believing in their own mobility despite evidence to the contrary.

Not seeing any official coercion or barriers to their absorption, Afro-Brazilians were encouraged to accept their inferior condition as a "pathology of normality."[55] Racial democracy deprived Afro-Brazilians of any legally explicit cause for their subordination against which they might mobilize. Even contemporary Afro-Brazilian activists have been forced to conclude that purported absorption long worked to discourage blacks from identifying themselves in terms of race, thereby avoiding racial conflict. As we shall see in Chapter 10, until fairly recently Afro-Brazilians did "not even pose a threat to the system."[56] Blacks found themselves in a racial paradise that was indeed heavenly for those elites whose status was seamlessly maintained, but purgatory for the supposed beneficiaries of racial democracy.

Brazil's commitment to an inclusive, nonracial nationalism and to conflict avoidance is underlined by its persistence. Social order was maintained throughout the twentieth century's varied and significant political transitions. The Brazilian polity shifted from republic to dictatorship to democracy to military rule and to more decentralized democracy, but each shift was accomplished relatively peacefully. Official racial domination was consistently avoided, while the effective racial order was left largely unchallenged. The state remained intact, even as it failed to settle firmly on a political expression or form, while the nation itself remained relatively unified. The lack of a founding conflict comparable to the American Civil War or South African Boer War would seem to have allowed a legacy of unity strong enough to withstand institutional rearrangements. And as a central part of that entrenched unity, the image of racial democracy was preserved and continued to deflect potential racial conflict.

As earlier in South Africa and the United States, Brazil embraced state consolidation as a prerequisite for economic development. Decentralized republican rule was abandoned in favor of a resurgent state centralization after the 1930s, a process led by Getúlio Vargas, who served as chief of a provisional government from 1930 to 1934, Congressionally elected president until 1937, dictator until 1945, and again elected president from 1951 to 1954. Faced with minor armed revolts in 1935, Vargas "used the rebellion as a vehicle to enlarge federal power" under a state of siege. He forced the subordination of the states, their governors and militias, and even large landowners weakened by the Depression.[57] Industrialists, the middle class, and the national military generally supported Vargas's centralization, agreeing on the need for state economic intervention and having tired of the costly rivalries that had grown under republican federalism.[58] Appealing to the Brazilian tradition of hierarchy, Vargas convinced many that his efforts to reinforce state and national unity were more important than a divisive "democracy of parties."[59] Support for this position is suggested by the 1937 dictatorship having been established without a shot fired.[60]

Vargas engineered a massive expansion of the centralized state, comparable to that achieved earlier in South Africa and in the United States under the contemporaneous New Deal. The number of public employees rose from 30,000 in 1912 to 65,000 in 1938, and government receipts doubled in the first eight years of Vargas's rule.[61] Various social services were established and by 1951 the state had even moved to take over some industrial activities with the formation of the Petrobrás oil company. Resulting opportunities for massive patronage further reinforced popular support for the regime.[62]

Vargas modernized the Portuguese colonial and Brazilian tradition of a strong state extending its power into society to reinforce the established hierarchy. His *Estado Novo* was the quintessential corporatist regime of state-ordered interest representation.[63] Vargas licensed mandatory trade unions, ensuring their members social benefits such as a minimum wage in return for guarantees against strikes. By 1944, half a million had joined these unions, which continued to operate under the same rules for the next four decades.[64] The FUNRURAL organization established a similar pattern for rural workers.[65] By 1945, Vargas allowed and established political parties, though even these remained influenced by his vision.[66] It is difficult to imagine a more complete convergence of the nation and state, with the state orchestrating popular organization and reinforcing nationalist loyalty through corporatist institutional design.

Brazil under Vargas consolidated the nation-state to an even greater extent than the United States and arguably South Africa without resort to racial exclusion for white unity. Instead, Vargas reached out to Afro-Brazilians and was rewarded with their loyalty. He encouraged the image of racial democracy. And his policies gave credence to the ideology of tolerance. Vargas ended support for white immigrants who competed with blacks. He encouraged expressions of African culture such as samba, *candomblé*, and spiritistic *umbanda*, in which he reportedly participated. In 1934, he supported the first national Afro-Brazilian Congress. He signed the 1951 Arinas anti-discrimination law, and partially opened the civil service.[67] At the same time, Vargas sought state control over black mobilization and religious and cultural practices, consistent with his corporatist philosophy. But "Vargas never spoke [for] racism, allowed *candomblé* . . . created social security . . . so he got black support."[68] This support was only partially diminished when Vargas closed the largest black organization, the Frente Negra, when all such popular organizations were banned in 1937.

Vargas's support for and from blacks and the highpoint of racial democracy rhetoric coincided with a dramatic resurgence of state centralization. The state provided for all, of any color, according to corporatist categories that did not include race.

After a decade of increasingly left-leaning democracy that followed Vargas's death, a 1964 coup brought the military to power for two decades of repressive rule. Adding national security to the traditional emphasis on national unity, the junta crushed divisive popular mobilization and put restraints on what had become an increasingly militant trade union movement.[69] At the same time, the military asserted an economic form of nationalism by breaking with the International Monetary Fund and appropriating foreign investments.[70] State-led investments produced a major economic boom. Phenomenal growth funded a further expansion of the state and a dramatic increase in salary for civil servants and the military.[71] The middle class particularly benefited, but the poor, particularly the black poor, suffered as inequality increased. From 1960 to 1990 the top decile enjoyed an 8.1 percent increase in income, while the bottom half saw their income decrease by 3.2 percent.[72] In short, the military state served the interests of the same elite that had long dominated Brazil. Such rule was maintained with repression but relatively little mass confrontation, consistent with the general pattern of Brazil's historical avoidance of conflict.[73]

Economic growth was built in part on the profits from paying black labor less than whites, as earlier in South Africa and the United States. But because this wage differential was not enforced by law it did not provoke major racial conflict, which might have disrupted growth. Recent analysis reveals pervasive economic inequalities according to race, for instance with black mean income in 1960 less than half of whites, and with mulattoes much closer to the lower black level. In the relatively developed area of Rio de Janeiro, the 1960 average monthly income for blacks was Cr$5,440, for mulattoes Cr$6,492, and almost double that, Cr$11,601, for whites.[74] A leading Afro-Brazilian activist, João Jorge Santos Rodrigues, argues, with some exaggeration, that "Brazil has no black middle class."[75] Such racial inequality was widely attributed to historical legacies and informal discrimination. Inequality purportedly reflected the lower skills of blacks as a class rather than as an officially categorized race.[76] For instance, 53 percent of blacks were illiterate in 1950, compared with 26 percent of whites; educational attainment was correspondingly unequal and occupations were distributed accordingly.[77] The disproportionate number of blacks living in the favela slums, where education and job opportunities have been limited, reinforced this inequality.[78] While dominant white economic interests have been served by depressed black wages, no official racial order was constructed to enforce these interests. Instead, class differences were projected to camouflage racism.

Economic growth under military rule came with increased economic competition and class tensions, and fed growing state centralization, but still without resort to official racial domination. Instead, the ideology of racial democracy was further reinforced as a component of national unity and as a means of avoiding racial conflict.[79] *Candomblé* was sanctioned and even participated in by military officials.[80] But such symbolic gestures were no longer as effective at winning support in light of the declining fortunes of poor blacks. As a result, the junta preserved the image of racial democracy not so much by positive actions but with repression against its critics. In 1969, the National Security Council outlawed studies of racial discrimination as subversive. In 1970 race categories were again omitted from the census. Scholars studying race (including the later president, Fernando Henrique Cardoso) were exiled or at least forced to retire from universities. Even a television debate on race was canceled by the authorities.[81] The very concept of race was effectively banned as an enemy of national security.

The irony of the authoritarian regime using repression to reinforce the image of racial democracy and curtail criticism of it was lost on the generals. But it suggests that the image of racial democracy was more valued for its use in bolstering national unity than as a commitment to real efforts at equal representation and avoiding discrimination. The scholarship and statistical studies squashed by the regime would have demonstrated this contradiction and undermined the projected image. Instead, authoritarianism had the effect of reinforcing white rule under the cover of racial tolerance.

If the persistence of elite power and national unity under military rule is notable, then the same persistence of the social order during the transition toward a federal democracy is even more remarkable.[82] The junta itself began the process of liberalization and by continuing to control this process was able to ensure protection of the military's own interests in the transition. Military representation was secured in the first post-junta cabinet of 1988.[83] The transition process itself was long and cautiously pursued by increments of gradual reform elaborated through "conversations among gentlemen and generals." The result was an elite pact, much as analysts have described the negotiated transition in South Africa after 1990.[84] And also as in South Africa, this negotiated transition was made possible by, and effectively ensured, the maintenance of economic privilege.[85] But unlike South Africa, the Brazilian military was thus able to negotiate a transition with a minimum of violence.[86] Military rule and some central authority were abandoned, but elite power and wealth were preserved. A proliferation of parties further diluted opposition.

This brief description of the Brazilian transition toward democracy in the 1980s runs the risk of understating the extent of popular mobilization and conflict that was evident, albeit contained. Pressure for an end to authoritarian rule emerged via massive strikes in 1978 and 1979. By then numbering more than ten million, these unionized workers were angered by economic decline. Civic organizations, women's groups, churches, and Afro-Brazilian associations further added to this pressure throughout the protracted transition.[87] However, such social mobilization generally followed at least some initial state reforms and remained relatively divided in the face of elite efforts to manage the process from above.[88] More fundamentally, analysts have consistently suggested that civil society mobilization remained isolated and weaker than the Brazilian centralized state.[89] The legacies of "clientalism, co-optation, and corporatism" could not preclude all social mobilization, but the Brazilian state had the strength to contain such protest sufficiently to avoid disruption of an elite-led process of transition.[90]

It is particularly striking that Brazil did not suffer more conflict around issues of race amid growing economic competition and continued inequality. Earlier comparisons with South Africa and the United States suggested that Brazil's relatively slow growth and the persistence of a precapitalist social hierarchy constrained potential black–white competition that otherwise might have provoked more explicit racial domination and conflict.[91] But Brazil did not remain the economic laggard implied by such analysis.[92] Even in the Southeast, where industrialization and immigration produced high levels of competition by the 1930s, legal discrimination was not used, though "social practices were clearly discriminatory."[93] More recently, the proportion of the population engaged in manufacturing has doubled, rising from 12.9 percent in 1960 to 24.4 percent in 1980. At the same time, GDP per capita increased by 60 percent, while income inequality and competition grew markedly.[94] Still, expectations that economic development would replace the old hierarchy with competition-inspired formal racial segregation and conflict have not proven correct. "During the twentieth century Brazil has moved from its old paternalistic type of race relations toward the competitive model,"[95] yet Brazil has not imposed official racial domination. Even if a Jim Crow equivalent would have been difficult to impose in the 1930s or during later growth, some movement in this direction would have been possible. But the post-abolition legacy of tolerance was maintained. White capital and white labor advanced without formal segregation or major racial conflict. As a result, social hierarchy and order were preserved.

Economic (and social) discrimination is pervasive in Brazil, but without formal racial domination. The absence of legal segregation was connected to the absence of any major early intrawhite conflict that might have required rapprochement via white unity. The Brazilian state was less challenged by regional or ethnic conflict than South Africa and the United States. Even Brazilian trade union activism was long contained by corporatism.[96] Indeed, the relative lack of regional and ethnic conflict, which elsewhere was superimposed with class, reduced overall antagonism. And racial democracy, like corporatism more generally, conveyed an image of everyone's interests being served. Employers faced no formal color bar that might impede their flexible use of the cheapest available labor. White workers benefited from relatively higher wages. Black workers who saw no official racial impediment could believe that they might advance, even though they generally did not. A flexible and inclusive racial order purportedly served the interests of all and therefore encouraged unity. Until recently, all Brazilian sectors have avoided the issue of race. Racial democracy thus helped unite the nation, forging a class compromise as in South Africa and the United States, but a compromise that did not take the form of racial domination, which elsewhere provoked conflict.

What emerges most starkly from this historical overview is a picture of the resilient Brazilian state containing and avoiding conflict. This state has consistently been able to maintain national unity of a sort and to protect the interests of a well-established elite and hierarchy. The forms of rule have varied significantly, from colony, empire, republic, and military dictatorship to more federal democracy. But these transitions, all managed from above, produced remarkably little change in the fundamental social order. The "Order and Progress" inscribed on the Brazilian flag have been maintained. Social movements and conflicts have emerged, but have been largely tamed by absorption into the social and institutional framework dominated by the state and elites. The state remained the expression of a remarkably unified nation, using its power to shape national loyalty and obedience. Brazil emerges as a quintessential example of hierarchical rule and state-led nationalism.

As a significant portion of the population, Afro-Brazilians were inescapably absorbed into the impressive project of Brazilian nation building orchestrated by the state. After abolition, the Brazilian elite was concerned about the prospect of racial conflict, which might have disrupted national unity and state building. To avoid such conflict, the elite consciously avoided imposing antagonistic racial exclusion. It instead gradually refined an image of racial democracy as a fundamental component of Brazilian nationalism, consistent with cultural assumptions of inclusion. Blacks were embraced, at least rhetorically, to avoid division. African culture was celebrated, though more substantive political and economic rights did not follow. Laws were enacted penalizing color discrimination in public places, not as an acknowledgment that there was such discrimination but ostensibly to prevent it.[97] Constitutional assurances that "racism constitutes a crime" were later enacted, though no enabling laws were passed and few prosecutions of such a crime were pursued.[98] The state proclaimed itself the representative of all Brazilians, though few blacks were employed as civil servants.[99] Many blacks were long deprived of the franchise, but on the basis of illiteracy, and not race per se. The murder of street children and police brutality suggests significant violence against blacks continuing with impunity, but not as official policy.

In official terms, the rule was racial democracy. In practice, the state was often far from democratic in general terms. Laws were selectively enforced. Policies toward blacks were more notable for the lack of legal discrimination than for any positive assertions of black political, economic, or social rights.

The two themes of nation-state unity and racial democracy are interconnected. National unity was proclaimed by the Brazilian elite to contain and avoid disruption to its continued privilege and its efforts at state building. Racial democracy was projected as a central component of that national unity, in order to avoid the sort of race conflict Brazilians had experienced with the slave revolts and watched in dismay unfold in the United States. Having accomplished abolition without a conflict comparable to the Civil War, the elite was eager to maintain the benefits of unity by projecting an image of inclusiveness. And as no regional or ethnic conflict comparable to that in the United States or South Africa had impelled the need to unify whites through racial exclusion, this strategy was consciously rejected. This relative absence of violent intrawhite struggle and the persistence of a unified nation-state made it possible for the upper classes to rule without legally racializing their hegemony. Instead, the image of unity and inclusiveness preserved and protected the social order, more than it was an outcome of that order. Afro-Brazilians did not benefit from this ideological project. As we shall see, they were largely deflected from protest against social discrimination. The lack of any official rules for such discrimination deprived them of a target for mobilization that might have forced redress of inequality. The elite did benefit; it preserved its place at the top of the hierarchy.

Racial democracy was an ingenious form of social engineering, largely through omission rather than commission. The Brazilian state ruled without official racial domination. White interests were protected. To reinforce the social order, racially distinct legal treatments were not encoded and racial conflict was largely avoided. The Brazilian nation-state emerged relatively unscathed from a century in which racial conflict tore at the fabric of the United States and South Africa.

Comparative Racial Domination
AN OVERVIEW

European descendants in South Africa, the United States, and Brazil established early legacies of racial discrimination against African descendants, despite dramatic differences in population mix and mixing. Slavery in all three countries reinforced pervasive images of inequality. By the time slavery ended, such discrimination was often buttressed by pseudo-science and encoded in varying forms of legislation, evident even in Brazil, where later interpretations of Portuguese rule, Catholicism, slavery, and miscegenation were purposefully shaped to deny this inheritance and to project an image of racial tolerance. But Brazil's self-image as an exception to the discourse, culture, and practice of racial discrimination was more creative than historical.

Historical legacies of discrimination were not automatically or thoughtlessly brought forward into the modern era. All three countries came to junctures at which the preexisting social order and relations between blacks and whites had to be consciously reconfigured. Of course, the resolution of race relations would not be fully decided at any single moment, and was instead elaborated over decades of conflict, political and economic competition, and varying policies. But the establishment of the post-abolition, formally unified nation-state in all three countries did crystallize the issue of race relations, forcing decisions that set the course of those relations for generations.

In South Africa and the United States, the conflict-ridden process of nation-state consolidation set the terms of official racial domination. Ethnic conflict between Afrikaners and English-speakers in what became South Africa, and regional conflict between South and North in the United States, came to a head in the dramatic violence of the Boer and Civil wars. In both, the relatively liberal industrializing power won, only to face the challenge of how to reconcile with its former adversaries, incorporating them as productive citizens rather than allowing their separate and destabilizing self-determination. Further conflict had to be contained to avoid instability undermining the primary fruit of victory, which was control over the newly unified or reunified state as an organ of economic development. In South Africa, the British concluded that abandoning commitments to enfranchising and advancing blacks was the surest way to appease the Afrikaners and to consolidate union – deletion of a commitment to the native franchise in the 1902 peace treaty symbolized this deal. Continued Afrikaner nationalism reinforced English efforts at appeasement, leading finally to Afrikaner rule and apartheid. In the United States, the North was gradually forced to a similar conclusion about how to appease its former adversary. The North's efforts to impose reforms under Reconstruction brought sufficient Southern antagonism to persuade the North to abandon the effort. Sectional tensions were then diminished by allowing the South to impose Jim Crow, with blacks again paying the price of white reconciliation.

For all their dramatic differences, these patterns linking nation-state consolidation and formal racial domination were similar in the United States and South Africa. In both, the nation-state was divided and policies of racial domination were designed to diminish such division. Earlier racial discrimination and the racist ideology developed to defend it were encoded or allowed by state action to reinforce institutional power and white loyalty to it. Legal exclusion of blacks helped to gradually unify the core constituency of whites.

Brazil was "exceptional," not in its lack of racial discrimination, but in failing to establish official racial domination. Brazil suffered nothing comparable to the Boer or Civil War, and was not as riven by overarching antagonisms. Its colonial legacy of a strong state and established hierarchy produced less pressure for regional and none for ethnic reconciliation encouraged elsewhere by white racist ideology and black exclusion. With less pressure for intrawhite reconciliation, no racial domination was constructed. Instead, the Brazilian elite feared regional division and conflict with blacks, present in large numbers and previously prone to revolt. To head off this threat, the elite purposefully projected a form of nationalism that included blacks under an official racial democracy, despite ongoing discrimination. The established hierarchy remained in place.

This schematic description of the different challenges to nation-state consolidation and the resulting official racial domination or racial democracy is artificially neat. Such analysis projects fixed subjects – Afrikaners, British, North and South – whose conscious unity was not simply given or ascribed. Each was divided internally by political and economic differences. But the violent process of nation-state building in South Africa and the United States solidified antagonistic ethnic and regional identities. And as these conflicting identities were reinforced, their competing interests repeatedly had to be reconciled to maintain the stability needed for further nation-state building. Continued tension exacerbated antagonism, solidifying the units to be reconciled in repeated iterations and official responses to the social conflicts in which states were embedded. It was precisely because the nation-states were not united that policies to encourage such consolidation were enacted and refined. Specific policies varied according to the individual characteristics of this messy, ongoing dynamic. National unity in Brazil was also achieved in an ongoing process, but was not riven by comparable levels of violent conflict. The predominant solidarity was a unified nation, with conflicts over the form of rule but with each regime encouraging dependence on the state.

It must be acknowledged that identifying the historical process of identity constructions and efforts at reconciliation does not do justice to the complexity of the comparative experience. For instance, the post–Boer War South African state imposed segregation and exclusion relatively quickly and centrally, while such policies in the post–Civil War United States were imposed after a lag, locally and unevenly. In large part, this difference was due to varying state structures, the form and level of central state power, and types of challenges to it.

South Africa quickly became a strong state, backed by the British Empire and by agreement among English-speakers and Afrikaners regarding the benefits of centralized power. These ethnic groups, solidified within themselves by their prior conflict, continued to compete for control of the state. But they did not dispute the power of or the need for the central prize over which they wrestled. Nor did they disagree over the need to maintain and reinforce centrally imposed racial domination. The perceived threat from the African majority impelled such a consensus, as compared with the lesser threat posed by the African-American minority.

The contrasts with the United States are marked. The Civil War did not produce a consensus for centralized power, but instead reinforced the dispute with advocates of states' rights. The balance of federal power had been and remained the central issue of political competition. After the North's imposition of Reconstruction intensified continuing sectional animosity, racial domination was imposed locally. The weaker central authority in the United States gradually and grudgingly ceded the issue of black rights to the states, restoring the balance of federal authority and states' rights as a compromise necessary for national unity. The weakness of central power forced its own solution of federal withdrawal. While the North, like Brazil, discriminated informally rather than imposing legal Jim Crow, it was a party to and allowed for Jim Crow in the South.

Brazil again differs, with central state authority preserved until the republic, and a balance of central and regional power established thereafter. Political competition remained largely under the control of an elite, vying over whether the state should be democratic or dictatorial. The power of that state was not as disputed as in the United States and the lack of official racial domination was countrywide.

In all three cases, race making was tied to the imperative of nation-state building and challenges to it. Elites sought consolidation of state institutions and popular loyalty to them to ensure stability and development, using race selectively as a means to that end. Having fought in part – or so they alleged – for blacks' rights and won, both the Northerners and the South African English abandoned this commitment in order to pursue in peace the more pressing goal of intra-white reconciliation. Blacks were expendable, useful as scapegoats for core white unity, a choice that crucially coincided with existing prejudice and racist ideology. The Brazilian state and social hierarchy faced no challenges comparable to those posed by the Afrikaners or South, and so nation-state consolidation could proceed without racial domination but with informal discrimination.

The role of war in nation-state building was also shaped by and in turn shaped racial dynamics. Earlier in Europe, state consolidation had been achieved through warfare. And as formative states had united and called upon the populace to fight, they had extended citizenship rights accordingly. In the United States, South Africa, and Brazil, war making again led to extensions of the franchise, albeit to whites only, though blacks had expected that their participation in the military would also be rewarded by better treatment and inclusion. But after helping the victorious British in the Boer War, the North in the Civil War, and Brazil against the Dutch in 1630–54, blacks in each case subsequently returned to subordination. By contrast, in later external wars, blacks fighting for Brazil against Paraguay in the 1860s did help bring abolition, and blacks fighting for the United States in the Second World War helped inspire some reforms of segregation. Thus, while external war generally reinforces national loyalty and encourages inclusion, internal war more often exacerbates subnational loyalties that may be healed through specific exclusion.

Democracy itself played a role in these processes, though this form of rule did not produce the same policies in different contexts. Selective inclusion in democracy continued to reinforce and reflect racial orders. Racially specified democracy in South Africa and the United States enabled white voters to ensure their dominance over outvoted or nonvoting blacks. Party competition in South Africa from 1910 to 1948 preserved the polity while leading to further black disenfranchisement and segregation to bolster white unity. Post-Reconstruction party competition in the United States had similar results. In the South, even some whites were disenfranchised to preserve state and local Democratic Party power and the image of white unity. Democrats and Republicans then vied for national power, again preserving the polity amid deepening racial domination. Limited democracy in republican Brazil and from 1945 to 1964 did not produce the same outcomes: blacks were disenfranchised by subterfuge and no official racial domination was enacted. Thus, democracy served as a kind of transmission belt for reinforcing the distinct directions of racial policy.

And what was the role of economic forces in shaping divergent legal racial orders? Earlier comparative studies argued that in the United States and South Africa, industrial expansion brought competition for jobs between blacks and whites, with whites then acting to protect themselves with legal color bars.[1] By contrast, goes this explanation, Brazil's relatively slower economic development brought little competition between blacks and whites, even amid European immigration, so that whites perceived less need to impose a harsh racial order to protect themselves. Paternalistic race relations were preserved.

There are numerous problems with such an economistic account. Racial domination was evident before industrialization and heightened black–white competition. And the legacy of slavery and past discrimination itself contained the threat whites felt from black advancement. Though competition was often stronger between whites, particularly with rising immigration, blacks became the primary target of discrimination.[2] Regional and demographic differences also intruded. Both the more industrial regions of the U.S. North and Brazilian Southeast had fewer blacks than the less developed regions in which blacks were more concentrated, the U.S. South and Brazilian Northeast. But amid informal discrimination, rising industrial development and competition did not produce fully fledged Jim Crow or apartheid anywhere in Brazil or in the U.S. North, even when blacks later migrated there. In the U.S. South, as late as 1930 more than 40 percent of black males were employed in agriculture.[3] Yet it was in the less industrialized South that Jim Crow came of age, with the acquiescence of the North. And Jim Crow was most strictly enforced in the deep South, as in Mississippi, where industrial competition was at its lowest. If industrial competition causes segregation, then Jim Crow should have been born a Yankee in the early twentieth century, not a rural Southerner in the late nineteenth.

Racial domination was perhaps then impelled by capital's efforts to maintain a split labor market, reducing the cost of labor. Dominant economic interests benefited from rules ensuring a lower wage scale for blacks and from the racial division of workers, who then found it more difficult to unify in demanding higher wages. According to this argument, business reinforced racial antagonism, pressed for more rigid forms of racial domination, and reaped the fruits of official segregation.[4] Florestan Fernandes and others in the São Paulo School in Brazil similarly argued that capital there discriminated against blacks to reduce wages, but without official edict.[5]

Explaining racial domination as a tool of capitalist exploitation over labor recognizes the central role of intrawhite class competition, but such analysis falsely assumes that capital alone determines state policy. Not only were capital's demands often rebuffed, but capital itself was often divided by sector. For instance in South Africa, agrarian capital consistently resented the efforts of mining interests to pull labor off the farms and into the pool of cheap, forced migrant labor.[6] And English manufacturers' calls for reform of the color bar as an impediment to economic growth were resisted by Afrikaner employers. While Marxists pointed to the mining sector and Afrikaner capital to blame business for apartheid and liberals hailed manufacturers' calls for reform, neither argument about the role of capital could be generalized, for capital remained divided.[7] In the United States, business was uncertain of its interests and also divided, often according to region. Businessmen in the North advocated concessions to the South to avoid the instability of Civil War but then later attacked President Andrew Johnson's accommodationist policies.[8] Northern capital was wary of the instability provoked by Congressional Reconstruction, but these concerns were diluted by expectations of profit from military rule of the South, and were subordinated to ideology and party political imperatives for reform until Reconstruction was abandoned to restore stability. Primary and agricultural producers did benefit from cheap black labor. But capital's interests were not consistently served, for the exclusion of blacks was often and in many ways costly, particularly for manufacturers. Fractions of capital were forced to "adjust to the requirements of a racially stratified labor force" ensuring higher wages for whites.[9]

A related argument suggests that white labor enforced segregation to ensure its advantage over black labor. Certainly in South Africa, and arguably in the United States, white workers used their popular strength and votes (more numerous than white business) to deny blacks equal justice. They forged a racially bounded working class and supported parties that were committed to preserving whites' economic position above their black competitors.[10] As C. Vann Woodward concluded, Jim Crow was enforced by the Democratic Party "to please the crackers,"[11] much as South African segregation can be described as having enforced by the National Party to serve poor Afrikaners.

Reducing racial domination to specific white working-class interests overstates the power of such pressure. White workers rarely determined state policy on their own; nor were their demands always consistent, for as more sophisticated Marxists acknowledge, working-class solidarity cannot be assumed as given.[12] For instance, U.S. white labor was divided over Jim Crow by region. And even within each region, labor's interests and advocacy varied. Many Southern white workers supported populism, while others supported segregation. Even Northern unions shifted in their policies toward blacks. White labor also suffered under Jim Crow, with segregation dividing the working class as a whole, making it possible for capital to pay lower wages and to use racially divided workers against each other. White workers were often willing to pay the price of racial domination by accepting division by race and a lower rate of economic growth.[13] The fact that there were costs to such policies suggests that narrow working-class interests did not consistently produce racial policies.

Official racial orders were shaped by, but cannot then be reduced to, specific class interests. Capital and white labor were often in conflict, for instance in South Africa's 1922 Rand revolt. Indeed, had racial domination been determined by one class's interests, then class conflict and related party competition would have disrupted the racial order. No interests were sufficiently dominant or uniform to produce the persistent outcome of racial domination. And classes were often internally divided into ethnic, regional, or sectoral factions with distinct interests and predilections and party representatives, undermining a strict class dichotomy. That whites were united neither within nor between classes argues against any effort to reduce racial domination to such a narrow interpretation.

Comparative analysis then suggests some refinement of the conclusion that "racial domination . . . is essentially a class phenomenon."[14] Class interests were significant, but this alone does not tell us very much. The interrelation between racial order and class interests is more complex than can be described by reducing the former to the latter. Instead, racial domination has been constructed with or without serving distinct economic interests, and not because of them. And racial orders varied over time, mixing informal economic discrimination, political exclusion, and legal segregation.

Specific class interests were not determinant, but economic interests were relevant to the construction of racial domination. What was determinant was an overriding white interest in peace and stability as essential for economic development. Growth could proceed only if competition did not provoke open conflict, thereby threatening the market. Karl Polanyi has argued that this overriding economic interest in avoiding conflict accounts for "the long peace" engineered by the great powers during the nineteenth-century economic and trade expansion.[15] A similar process took place within countries, where growth depended on avoiding domestic unrest as well. Much as the balance of power provided for peace among the major European powers, consolidation of the nation-state within countries was impelled by the necessity of avoiding internal conflict that otherwise would have disrupted the economy, if not destroyed it. In South Africa and the United States, racial domination was formally constructed and reinforced to avoid such further disruptive conflict between regions, ethnic groups, or classes. Such policies did constrain economic development, but less than open violent conflict would have. In Brazil, racial democracy served not so much to heal previous conflict as to avoid its further emergence. The imperative of stability as a precondition for growth provided an overarching economic incentive for conflict control or avoidance through either racial domination or racial democracy.

Specific racial orders were constructed and refined by a process of class compromise rather than the serving of one class. As described by political scientist Adam Przeworski, for such a compromise to become hegemonic in establishing an explicit social order, a minimum of objective conditions of development must have been reached.[16] With such development, the pressure to satisfy and coordinate competing interests grows, for instance with capital demanding a minimum of profits.[17] The way in which such compromise is achieved is uncertain and variable, rather than implying a static solution, much as racial orders have been reinforced and reformed. The specific terms of compromise vary according to shifting pressures. According to Gramsci, such compromise repeatedly emerges

> as a continuous process of formation and superseding of unstable equilibria (on the juridical plane) between the interests of the fundamental group and those of subordinate groups – equilibria in which the interests of the dominant group prevail, but only up to a certain point, i.e. stopping short of narrowly corporate economic interests.[18]

The pressure for continual compromise remains, particularly where the alternative is open conflict. "The decision to compromise depends, in the end, on a comparison of the best compromise that can be obtained with the consequence of no compromise."[19] In South Africa and the United States, racial domination emerged out of such a class compromise to avoid further conflict. The Rand revolt was not repeated and U.S. Southern populism was contained.

This argument helps to combine political and economic analyses of racial domination. Racial orderings are constructed to diminish conflict *and* to allow for economic growth, in a mutually reinforcing way. Racial domination and its refinement diminished overlapping and ongoing intrawhite regional or ethnic and class conflict dividing the nation and threatening growth. Indeed, race was a long-standing "central ideological underpinning" of each of the developing nation-states discussed here, though subsequent social orders differed.[20] Each such construct was shaped by economic interests, for ideology or state action and policy do not emerge in a vacuum. And such particular interests and their impact on policy vary. But the overriding interest served by racial orders was not class-specific, but more general: to preserve the overall state and its economy, in which industrialization and related social changes could and did proceed.

This argument fits with a more general analysis of the role of the state in constructing class compromise. Development heightens class conflict at the same time that it provides resources to build state capacity. For such conflict to be diminished, for the polity to be preserved and consolidated, the state must act.[21] The policies of the state then make explicit the terms of the class compromise it engineered, in historically specific forms.[22] The varying institutions of segregation in South Africa and the United States and the ideology of racial democracy in Brazil were constructed in a political process. Conflict remained, forcing variations in such outcomes and underlining the difficulties of achieving stability. Economic interests and related demands had to be tamed and met. When this was not sufficient, state force was used, in wars or to put down revolts or strikes.[23]

The state was the instrument for conflict management, using racial order as a tool. Economic development exacerbated the potential for conflict among whites, which the state then had to manage to ensure revenues. And with such stability, growth provided the state with resources to so manage society. Capital, white labor, and fractions thereof all lent

> legitimacy to the racial order and race domination. Each calls on the state to take control of the subordinate worker, to draw racial lines. . . . The well developed racial state, very much the product of

capitalist development and the period of intensification, does not wither away with its feckless business, farm and perhaps trade-union supporters.[24]

In other words, state-imposed racial domination helped to prevent class warfare, meeting a general interest in preserving a functioning economy.[25] A class reductionist argument, for instance in assuming the policy determination of capitalists, ignores both that states do make policy and that such policy often contradicts dominant class interests.[26] The actual process of state action again differed according to state structures.

The state's own interest was not autonomous but shaped by varying popular interests that had to be satisfied enough to preserve peace and maintain growth. States themselves were not unitary. Rather than being insulated from class and related interests, "the state itself was penetrated and structured by the very interests whose conflicts it seeks to stabilize and control."[27] In South Africa, capital and white workers were served by racial domination, which helped to contain intra- and interwhite class and ethnic conflict. With a more porous state in the United States, capital and white workers were similarly served by segregation, taking different forms in North and South. In Brazil, racial democracy and corporatism more generally long contained significant class conflict, not as aggravated by regional or any ethnic tensions. Solutions to conflict via differing racial orders were thus determined by overlapping political and economic challenges needing to be addressed. That the state could provide such solutions served as well to reinforce its own power. But such outcomes that appeared functional were refined in response to varying pressures. Particularly where tensions between ethnic groups or regions reinforced class divisions, conflicts were fitfully addressed by purposeful and varying state action and policies of racial domination aimed at preserving the nation-state and its economy. Despite economic costs of segregation, growth could and did proceed, bringing structural changes that would contribute to further refinements of the racial order.

Ongoing party and economic tensions thus kept alive and reengaged the same dynamic that determined racial order, providing an intervening explanation for refinements of that order. Under political and economic pressures, state elites continually remade racial domination or racial democracy. In South Africa and the United States, state action convinced whites in different parties, classes and class factions that their interests were being met. In Brazil, some blacks even believed they were being included. In all three cases, the nation-state and its economy were thus preserved by purposeful state action and responses to social pressures.

This analysis suggests not only the process that led to the elaboration of racial domination or racial democracy, but also part of the complex process by which apartheid or Jim Crow later came to be abandoned. In South Africa, Afrikaner Nationalists came to power first under Hertzog and again after 1948 under the National Party. They used their control of the strong state to bolster Afrikaner cultural, social, and economic standing until greater parity with the English was achieved. With ethnic and class antagonism diminished, the strategic imperative for racial domination to encourage white unity faded. Nation-state consolidation, at least for whites, had been largely accomplished. Similarly in the United States, localized racial domination via Jim Crow appeased the South, which over the course of a century was reincorporated into the nation-state and its economy. With diminished sectional and class antagonism, white unity no longer needed to be reinforced by racial domination. In this sense, in both countries racial domination served the strategic purpose for which I argue it had been enacted.

Institutionalized racial domination did not end simply because it was no longer needed; practices were not so functionally enforced or abandoned. As institutionalized reflections of racist ideology, apartheid and Jim Crow had a life of their own, beyond their strategic purpose to encourage white unity. As I will discuss in Part Three, such racial domination also had the unintended consequence of provoking greater mobilization, agency, and protest by subordinated blacks, bringing a new and increasing threat to the nation-state that could only be defused by ending official racial domination. The nation-state in both South Africa and the United States had been strongly enough consolidated to abandon its racial crutch. A more muted form of black protest emerged in Brazil, where there was no official racial domination to challenge or demolish.

Racial orders as class compromise also provided the conditions for nation-state preservation and for growth to proceed. But unforeseen consequences would gradually undermine racial orders and impel new forms of class and political compromise. Growth brought significant changes in systems of production and society, with industrialization requiring more skilled and urbanized labor, and consumption by blacks. Migration expanded to areas of opportunity. These changes were made possible by racial orders, though the costs of segregation also grew. Economic development also consolidated and empowered blacks, setting the conditions for blacks to challenge established patterns of racial domination.

The significant implication of this analysis is its emphasis on the political determinance of racial domination. Earlier historical legacies, discourse, and culture were important, but their later influence was not direct but rather depended upon subsequent interpretations. Demographic factors were also important, but again how such physical differences were interpreted in varying forms over time was shaped by political processes. The imperative for nation-state consolidation produced explicit and varying forms of official domination where ethnic or regional and class combatants sought resolution of their conflict by projecting white unity and black exclusion. Where nation-state consolidation faced fewer such obstacles of regional or ethnic conflict, Brazilian ruling classes did not encode racial domination to unify whites. They instead projected racial democracy to unify an increasingly mixed populace, heading off internal conflict. Racial domination was constructed and imposed (or not) according to these contexts, framed by the goal of nation-state consolidation, until black demands and contestation grew to challenge this consolidation.

PART THREE

Race Making from Below

ANALYSIS OF RACE MAKING must address both racial ordering from above and opposition from below. Neither alone can be understood without the other, for the two emerge in an ongoing dialogue. Racial domination is shaped by its subject population, and that population's beliefs and actions are shaped by rules impinging upon it. Out of such continual contestation, identities, discourse, and practice are reinterpreted and reconfigured. But acknowledging this dynamic does not in itself tell us very much about why and how race making proceeds. I here turn to specifying this process from below, having outlined the process from above. The order of this analysis is not meant to suggest that the racial identity, ideology, and mobilization of blacks can be reduced to a mere response to racial ordering from above. Such identity and action is self-determined, evident before racial domination is fully established, and continuing after such rules are abandoned. For the purposes of this book, this placement of analysis allows an assessment of the relationship between the two sides of race making with the framework of officially imposed racial ordering clearly established.

Racial identity among blacks has deep historical and cultural roots. Much as white prejudice existed before modern political and racial orders were constructed, and helped shape them, so a degree of black solidarity and mobilization predates the modern era. Early black identity and activism informed later processes, though it was not itself fully determinant of varying outcomes. For instance, before abolition Brazilian slaves identified themselves as such and acted accordingly, though these protests declined during the heyday of racial democracy.

Still, race making from below in Brazil, as in South Africa and the United States, built upon past foundations.

Where it was enacted by state policy, racial domination further solidified black racial identity and provoked and influenced mobilization. Enforced boundaries and formal exclusion from the nation-state reinforced black solidarity in opposition to adversity, informed by cultural resources and social practices. Analysts of social movements have often ignored this crucial issue of identity formation, which I argue is prior to and determines the effects of resource allocation and political opportunities, more often the focus of study. And once identity is more consolidated, the strategy, tactics, and goals of black protest – my shorthand for opposition to racial domination that often included white allies – were themselves in part shaped by imposition from above, in an ongoing dynamic. As racial orders were refined in response to party politics and economic conflict among whites, blacks also refined their solidarity as the basis for action. Not coincidentally, when racial domination was consolidated, black solidarity and protest also reached their high points, though divisions remained. In contrast, the absence of official rules of racial domination in Brazil may have muted racial identity and thereby constrained mobilization. But even there, opportunities for protest were both created and exploited by blacks, building on traditions and institutions.

Analysis of race making must also include an assessment of the "endgame" and its aftermath. Black protest and white vulnerability to such protest were heightened by industrialization, migration, and urbanization, which concentrated blacks and increased their leverage against the racial orders under which such structural changes had occurred. Rising black protest in South Africa and the United States then succeeded in forcing an end to apartheid and Jim Crow respectively, albeit in a protracted and uneven process. And just as white racism and discrimination remain, so do black racial identity and protest. In the absence of official rules of racial domination against which blacks united and acted, many African-Americans in particular have tended to assume their own solidarity as natural, much as whites had done earlier. Such efforts to essentialize race can only be understood in the context of ongoing structure and political contestation. And what about Brazil? Racial identity and protest appear to be on the rise there, albeit still at lower levels than during the South African anti-apartheid and U.S. civil rights movements. Race making in its various forms continues; identity formation is never complete.

8

"We Are a Rock"

BLACK RACIAL IDENTITY, MOBILIZATION, AND THE NEW SOUTH AFRICA

Early protest by black South Africans was both strengthened and weakened by its indigenous nature. Ties to the land and existent social structures provided the basis for early identity and organization, but these were largely divided by persistent language, regional, and ethnic distinctions, and as elsewhere even more broken up by dispersion. Only as white rule and a unified state were consolidated fully did black South Africans find commonality in their experiences. Cross-language, cross-ethnic, and cross-class identity emerged, as did more united mobilization. Contacts with African-American activists and growing industrialization and urbanization continually reinforced black South Africans' efforts. Divisions remained, but were gradually eclipsed by racial identity and action in opposition to white rule, to which state authorities were forced to respond.

Consolidation of Racial Identity and Protest

Indigenous resistance to white domination predates the formal establishment of a unified South African state. Africans often either fought or sought to escape from the imposition of white rule and exploitation after the arrival of the Dutch and later the British. Africans north of the Kei River waged war against the British during the nineteenth century, a conflict resulting in considerable bloodshed. Most notably, in 1879 an entire British regiment was defeated by the Zulus.[1] In that same year, the "semi-political" Native Education Association was founded, with one of its early presidents also serving as editor of the *Isigidimi Sama Xhosa* newspaper. Later John Tengo Jabavu used his editorship of *Isigidimi*, and then of his own paper, *Imvo Zabantsundu*

(Native Opinion), to coordinate African political activity.[2] By the 1880s, a separatist religious movement of Ethiopianism had emerged, encouraged by earlier-established U.S. black churches and an 1898 visit to South Africa by Bishop Henry Turner.[3] Such mobilization was described in 1905 as evidence of "an aggressive spirit" with which white South African officials had little sympathy.[4]

Such early resistance was generally neither described nor understood by participants as being based on racial identity. It in no sense diminishes the significance of such resistance to note that it remained scattered throughout what was to become South Africa and was understood by blacks and whites as various expressions of disparate ethnic assertiveness. As colonial policies played "tribal" rulers and factions off against each other, they reinforced such groupings and provoked divided responses.[5] With no central state authority yet imposing pervasive racial domination per se, little unifying cross-ethnic racial identity or mobilization emerged. Nevertheless, practical barriers to representation and unequal treatment "aroused African self-consciousness through protest."[6] For instance, 1882 saw the founding of Imbumba Yama Nyana, an explicitly political African organization.[7] But despite such efforts, self-consciousness and protest still remained largely localized and ethnically distinct in form, amid pervasive deprivation, oppression, and early discrimination. With potential black resistance so divided, the expansion of white rule proceeded.

The end of the Boer War proved a turning point in establishing pervasive official racial domination to reconcile Afrikaners and English within a unified white racial identity and nation. A unified and strong state acted to refine the racial order, assuming that long-divided blacks could be suppressed. Belittling the viable threat from blacks and acting accordingly, the state enacted policies that gradually consolidated the racial identity of its own adversary. Official policy reinforced the nationwide category of racially defined natives, gradually unifying and provoking further mobilization among Africans. Racial domination constructed the category of a subordinated race as such, in effect forcing previously disparate groups into a common identification. In accordance with the Treaty of Vereeniging and British efforts to unify the white races, the South Africa Act effectively excluded "natives" from the franchise, though Cape coloureds retained the vote. The rude shock of entrenched exclusion and white racist unity further propelled unified African responses and protest. Noting the oppression of blacks in America, South African blacks described themselves as being Jim Crowed.[8]

In the aftermath of the founding of a consolidated state, an opposition based on race emerged more strongly. Blacks well understood that the union of 1910 united only the whites.[9] In anticipation, what was to become the African National Congress (ANC) was formed in 1909. According to the ANC's founding president at its first meeting, the Congress was

> for the purpose of creating national unity and defending our rights and privileges as subordinated Africans rather than as distinct tribes. ... The white people of this country have formed what is known as the Union of South Africa – a union in which we have no voice ... We have called you therefore to this Conference ... for the purpose of creating national unity and defending our rights and privileges.[10]

ANC President Pixley Seme further called for "all the dark races ... to come together," overcoming interethnic "divisions ... [and] jealousies."[11]

A consolidated state reinforcing racial domination not only brought together Africans across ethnicity, but also gradually united Africans and coloureds sharing common grievances. ANC membership was open only to Africans, but discrimination also imposed on coloureds, albeit in different forms, encouraged cooperation between the ANC and the predominantly coloured African Political Organization.[12] The common destiny of those suffering from some form of political exclusion and segregation was portrayed as the basis for united action in response.[13] The urban mixing of Africans from different ethnic groups and provinces, along with coloureds, further encouraged a sense of solidarity undermining the divide-and-rule tactics of the state.[14] The solidifying of racial domination had begun to foster a common racial identity and protest among those dominated, buttressed by earlier organization. Race was imposed and then embraced as a basis of resistance.

In its early years, the ANC remained hopeful that earlier British commitments to reform would be honored. The result was a relatively constrained form of protest. Dominated by lawyers, other mission-educated professionals, and chiefs, the ANC petitioned the British crown as "loyal and humble subjects."[15] Only the most polite references were made to Africans' services for the British in the First World War and to the expectation that these services would be rewarded.[16] As it had after the Boer War, such mild petitioning fell on deaf ears. Still, the ANC remained in loyal opposition, later calling for "the ultimate creation of a South African nation . . . [and] the extension of the rights of citizenship to all groups."[17] The ANC recognized that "the colour bar struck the death-knell of Native confidence in what used to be called British fair play. That cow of Great Britain has gone dry."[18] But still influenced by earlier British promises, they remained expectant and did not quickly or easily abandon their polite efforts. Popular support for the Congress remained low, with expectations of reform from above mollifying the populace and restraining mass protest demanding such reform.

Consistent with earlier divisions and its call for inclusion in a polity implicitly recognized as legitimate, the ANC kept its distance from non-Africans and more radical groups. Most notable among these was Clement Kadalie's Industrial and Commercial Workers' Union (ICU), a militant union that sought to unify coloured and African workers brought into the workforce by increased demands for labor during and after the First World War.[19] Kadalie proclaimed that "we natives . . . are dealing with rascals – the Europeans are rascals," and criticized the "good boys" of the ANC for remaining respectful of the British.[20] Prime Minister Hertzog later sought to co-opt the ICU and its coloured constituency by advocating further preferences for coloureds aimed at dividing the potential unity of nonwhites. Meanwhile, Indians organized separately, following Gandhi's early efforts at mobilization in South Africa.[21]

Somewhat mollified by the growth of a small black middle class amid emerging industrialization, the best the ANC could muster was to call again for common citizenship.[22] But with white party competition bringing further reinforcements of segregation and exclusion, even this modest effort failed, bringing the ANC to the nadir of its influence.[23] Mobilization remained muted under elite African leadership more interested in reconciliation with whites than in challenging consolidated white rule.

As in the United States, the Second World War further raised expectations for reform among black South Africans, who became increasingly vocal in their demands. Hertzog lost power to Smuts, who brought South Africa into the war against Nazism, aligning it, among other things, with the Atlantic Charter reaffirming the Allies' antiracism. As Smuts pulled back from reforms after 1943, a new generation of ANC leaders sought to increase the pressure with a shift from polite petitioning to mass mobilization. The ANC Youth League, formed in 1944, advocated "Africanism" and "national consciousness and unity," revitalizing the ANC.[24] The Youth League pushed for further unification of subordinated Africans and encouraged greater mass participation by an increasingly urbanized population, expecting that the greater reliance on black labor would provide leverage with the state.

The ANC's long-standing patience in requesting reforms was most dramatically abandoned after the 1948 election of the National Party and its imposition of apartheid. White nation-state building and racial domination reached a high point. Segregation was reinforced, systematized, and extended. Prior petitioners were convinced that they had been protesting too feebly, reinforcing the Youth League's argument for a more assertive strategy of opposition.[25] Led by the Youth League, this more militant stance was advocated and implemented. In 1949, the Youth League's Programme of Action, calling for massive protests and nonviolent disobedience, was approved. This eventually led to the Defiance Campaign of protests in 1952, which boosted ANC membership above 100,000.[26] By then the Youth League officials had taken control of the ANC as a whole.

The more apartheid was entrenched, the more the opposition coalesced. Race was fast becoming the sine qua non of South African society.[27] The reinforced racial order further fostered a common identity among its victims and a more formal coalition of its opponents. As segregation applied in varying forms also to coloureds and Asians, representatives of these groups moved increasingly toward an opposition alliance with the ANC.[28] The banned Communist Party joined this alliance, assuming that racial domination would have to be ended before class exploitation could be challenged, an objective not necessarily shared by all within the alliance. That such varying goals were incorporated within "the great tent" of what became the Congress Alliance suggests that many shared Mandela's view: "I was far more certain in those days of what I was against than what I was for."[29] In 1955, the Alliance adopted the Freedom Charter, calling clearly for nonracial democracy, but somewhat vague on the potentially divisive issues of tactics and economic redistribution. Opposition in itself provided a firm foundation for unity, feared by state officials who were increasingly concerned that Africans were becoming more and more politically conscious.[30] When such unity found expression in a further explosion of protest after the Sharpeville massacre of peaceful pass law protestors in 1960, the state banned the major opposition groups. The ANC then established itself in exile as a nascent guerrilla movement.

Despite more militant tactics, the ANC and its allies still remained relatively modest in their goals. On economics, the Freedom Charter called for nationalization of the mines, but not for a more general challenge to basic property relations. The Communist Party advocated a national democratic revolution as a precondition for a more fundamental economic transformation. The ANC embraced the former without committing itself to the latter.[31] The pragmatic logic of this position was that redistribution could only be planned and carried out after the poor majority had been included in the polity, and that only limited change could be achieved at once.[32] Critics suggested that the omission of economic redistribution from immediate ANC goals instead suggested a continued appeasement of the white establishment, but the ANC argued that its demand for political inclusion was by itself a radical challenge to the racially ordered state and white privilege.

The ANC did not simply call for inclusion of those racial categories excluded by apartheid, but also advocated that all such categories be abandoned in a nonracial state. This idealistic stance did not preclude the ANC from recognizing racial categories as they had been imposed. Racially defined, distinct groups were incorporated into the ANC alliance. But the goal of nonracialism did imply that such distinctions would be abandoned after inclusive national democracy had been achieved. And Marxists assumed that class then would become the more pressing identity and issue, forcing economic transformation. A more radical ideological challenge to racial domination is difficult to imagine, but nonracialism can also be seen as a response to state policies. The ANC remained committed to the principle of nonracialism, confident that with a black majority the extension of democracy in itself would ensure redress.

Even within the opposition, not all agreed with the ANC's ideology and strategy. More militant African nationalists within the Youth

League were dismayed by the ANC's alliance with non-Africans. In 1959, this group broke away from the ANC to form the Pan Africanist Congress (PAC), open only to those giving "primary loyalty" to Africa and thereby effectively excluding coloureds, Asians, and whites. The PAC attacked the ANC's lack of commitment to economic change, but also dismissed Communism as a white ideology inconsistent with African traditions of communalism and sharing. They also disparaged nonracialism for its abandonment of African nationalism, which the PAC embraced as a powerfully assertive mobilizing ideology. The Africanists assumed that their rhetoric would inspire mass insurrection, which later the PAC's small guerrilla activities were intended to spark. The ANC also used violence, concluding that a minority regime held in power by force would not succumb to previously attempted Gandhian tactics. In later years, the ANC maintained civil disobedience while it pursued an organized guerrilla campaign, targeting state installations not so much to foment insurrection as to unsettle the white regime.

Ideological and strategic disagreements and basic organizational competition produced considerable ill will between previous allies divided in the ANC and PAC.[33] In part, this tension reflected the defensiveness of those within the ANC who earlier had been or remained sympathetic to African nationalism. They well understood the emotional drawing power of Africans acting alone as a response to heightened repression. And in its early years, the PAC did give the ANC much to worry about, growing quickly in size. But during the decades of exile that followed its banning with the ANC in 1960, the PAC was torn by leadership disputes, corruption, and lack of funding, leaving it weakened by the time it was again legalized in 1990. By contrast, the ANC remained well funded and organized, its popularity bolstered by more effective guerrilla activities and by the carefully nourished image of Nelson Mandela in prison. The ANC would emerge from banning and exile with much greater strength and popularity.

The 1960s were the high point of the apartheid state. Opposition had been largely crushed and Verwoerd's systematic design of racial domination was put into place with the construction of separate homelands for excluded Africans. Asians and coloureds found themselves increasingly subject to apartheid regulations that treated them more as subordinates than intermediaries. Demands for skilled industrial labor fed the growth of urban areas, schools, and universities, all officially separated by racial groups. For instance, the number of Africans enrolled in separate residential universities rose from 619 in 1959 to 2,604 in 1971 and to 12,204 by 1982, with the number of such institutions growing from one in 1959 to five by 1982. The number of Africans employed in manufacturing grew from 308,332 in 1960 to 780,914 by 1980.[34] Such development and dependence on black labor were seen by the state as consistent with, or at least containable within, apartheid.

Unintentionally, however, apartheid and economic growth served to concentrate blacks, exacerbating long-standing white fears of the black majority. Concentration in urban areas made organization more feasible; in segregated townships, factories, and educational institutions, blacks met across ethnic lines, providing a locus and unifying target for seeing in each other a common identity. Speaking on behalf of a new generation of blacks coming of age under apartheid, Steve Biko argued that

> every . . . facet of my life [has] been carved and shaped within the context of separate development. . . . What blacks are doing is merely to respond to a situation in which they find themselves the objects of white racism. We are in the position in which we are because of the color of our skin. We are collectively segregated against – what can be more logical than for us to respond as a group?[35]

The Black Consciousness movement founded by Biko in 1969 embraced imposed racial identity as a basis for resistance, defining and including as "black" all those subject to apartheid. Thus, state consolidation of racial domination also consolidated opposing racial identity cutting across cultural differences and the official categories of African, coloured, and Asian. Self-deluding official views and biased survey findings that most coloureds did not favor an alliance with blacks missed the powerful emergence of just such an alliance.[36] The high-water mark of racial domination produced a correspondingly high point of unified racial identity, thereby inspiring mobilization.

The Black Consciousness (BC) movement had organizational components, but was most prominently an ideological expression of racial unity and opposition. BC employed the state's own rhetoric to reinforce popular consciousness of racial domination and the separation of black and white. Official projections of inferiority were reversed by positive expressions of black unity. The movement spread the message that being black didn't mean being inferior. BC asserted racial identity as a basis for mobilization, using the experience of imposed domination as its defining and unifying force rather than defining race with a vision of biological or cultural coherence. Black Consciousness was intended "to cope with colour oppression located in power. We are a group of the oppressed," as Bishop Mames Buthelezi later said.[37] Fearing a more direct mass confrontation with the repressive state, the BC movement focused on spreading racial identity defined by and opposed to domination.

At first the authorities saw BC's exclusion of whites as an acceptance of the racial distinction imposed by apartheid, as compared with the ANC's advocacy of nonracialism. "The government hailed the formation of [BC] as consistent with separate development."[38] But as the true meaning of Black Consciousness became clearer, the state moved to crush this positive assertion of racial opposition and to denigrate it as an ideological import inspired by the Black Power movement in the United States. The idea of BC was not as easily crushed as its organizational expressions, for the state's own ideology and repressive policies reaffirmed racial unity. By 1976, BC rhetoric converged with student opposition to the state's imposition of Afrikaans school instruction for blacks, leading to the widespread Soweto uprising.

The state violently repressed the Soweto uprising and later banned the BC movement, forcing a reevaluation within the opposition. The very fact of the uprising suggested that the goal of inspiring greater assertiveness and unity had largely been achieved. But its supression also demonstrated that such assertiveness provided little cover once bullets started flying. Many BC activists, influenced by growing links with the ANC, concluded that a less ideological and more mass-based, locally organized resistance was now necessary. The state unintentionally encouraged this new strategy when in 1979, seeking to appease its opponents, it instituted reforms that provided breathing space for greater mass organization. Ironically, the emerging mass organizations benefited from reforms while publicly rejecting them to further bolster their popular appeal. For example, when P.W. Botha later proposed a new tricameral parliament intended to attract back the loyalty of coloureds and Asians by giving them limited representation, activists used the proposal as the impetus for a national unification of localized resistance under the United Democratic Front (UDF), founded in 1983. The state's gambit to win over coloureds and Asians subsequently failed, with a majority of those constituents refusing to vote for the new parliament, thereby reaffirming the unity forged under BC and in the process channeling it into a highly organized national movement.

The UDF was distinguished from BC not only by its greater focus on mass organization over ideology, but also by its conscious return to the tradition of nonracialism. UDF affiliates included African, coloured, Asian, *and* white groups. In part, this return to nonracialism was pragmatic: by including whites, the UDF could attract financial support needed for its mass organization and publicity. It also demonstrated a return to prominence of ANC loyalists, though "the UDF was afraid to openly claim ties to the ANC," which was still banned.[39] And nonracialism reflected the Marxist leanings of the many within the UDF, the ANC, and the unions who saw any retained focus on race as an impediment to class consciousness and mobilization.

Resurgent nonracialism was also influenced by a shift in state policy. Reforms of petty apartheid and the inclusion of nonwhites in the new parliament signaled a loosening of racial domination and an effort by the state to reach out for new allies across the color line. The UDF responded by denigrating these reforms but also offered a countereffort at inclusion, inviting whites instead to join in the opposition to apartheid. At the same time, the UDF was careful not to distance itself too much from the mobilizing potential of racial assertiveness. The resulting ideological vagueness allowed the UDF to incorporate diverse interests and motivations, much as the ANC had benefited from a vague inclusiveness to attract a wide alliance.

Mass mobilization exploded throughout the 1980s, including rent and consumer boycotts, worker stayaways, protest meetings, and marches. Ensuing destabilization caused more than $69 million in damage by 1986 alone, and left more than a thousand dead each year from 1985 through 1989.[40] But the more the state attacked UDF activists, even violently, the more it created sympathy and gave credibility to the opposition, feeding further mobilization. And when state of emergency regulations and bannings reduced UDF activity, legalized trade unions representing more than two million workers took the lead in maintaining popular pressure through massive stayaways that disrupted the economy. White labor in the mines and elsewhere had been replaced steadily by cheaper blacks, and so had lost some of its previous leverage. Where before a white labor force had posed a threat, now a black one did.[41]

Rising black solidarity and protest, itself shaped by the prior nation-state configuration, now challenged the white nation-state. Africans were increasingly unified by the racial terms of their domination, with coloureds and Asians joining in black identity as segregation and apartheid were applied to them. The more the state sought to unify whites by harsher exclusion of blacks, the more it forced blacks to identify themselves as such. Mobilization building on this black identity also responded to the patterns of domination. When the racial order remained relatively fluid, protest remained polite and elitist, but when the state responded to party competition by reinforcing the racial order to unify whites further or to encourage Afrikaner nationalism, black protest became more widespread and assertive. Reforms of apartheid encouraged the inclusion of whites in the opposition, though the continued exclusion of blacks from full citizenship maintained racial solidarity and mass mobilization. Finally, the rock of solid black protest threatened the very state stability that had been built on racial domination.

Black Protest Forces Inclusive Nation-State Building

By the late 1980s, the confrontation between white racial unity and domination on one side and rising black unity and resistance on the other had produced a crisis. Black popular and labor mobilization had reached unprecedented levels, challenging the legitimacy and control of the nation-state and undermining an economy ever more dependent on blacks, mirroring the instability earlier intrawhite conflict had brought. To head off this rising challenge, ruling elites would abandon apartheid while hoping to preserve the polity, restore growth, and thereby retain long-entrenched white advantage. Other pressures and events were important, such as the end of the cold war, new leadership, and international sanctions. But geopolitical changes would have been less meaningful in South Africa without already rising black opposition within the country. Protest shook the economy, scared domestic and foreign capital, inspired the international pressure, and brought new leaders to the state. Disagreement over reform did not disappear, but protest forced fundamental change. The result was what the state's mainstream opponents sought, though the end of apartheid then brought new challenges to nation-state building.

The South African state was unable to contain the protests its own policies had provoked, as it wavered between reforms and repression.[42] Former parliamentarian Helen Suzman describes the reaction: "Further escalation of black resistance would have meant continuous repression. [The National Party] took the necessary steps to contain the rebellion. Some said we cannot keep doing this."[43] The state's military and repressive apparatus had remained strong, reinforced by ethnic loyalty among the army's officers, 85 percent Afrikaners.[44] But this loyal force was unable to halt popular unrest, and the greater use of force only threatened further economic dislocation. Broederbond Chairman P. J. de Lange concedes that "the unrest was important" in forcing a reconsideration of the viability of continued minority rule. And Beyers Naude adds that "the 1980s couldn't have been avoided" and were needed for state "leaders to be confronted by the reality of the depth of black feelings."[45] Certainly the level of mass protest engendered by state repression shook the commitment to minority rule among many whites.

The central thrust of the UDF and related mobilization was a demand for inclusion in South African citizenship, unifying the opposition despite other disagreements. The state had set the agenda in excluding blacks from the new constitution and formal citizenship. Opposition movements rejected the creation of separate homelands, as they had rejected the tricameral constitution. Even within the homelands themselves, the artificial construct of non-South African citizenship was challenged. Most notably, the Inkatha movement in Kwazulu under Chief Buthelezi rejected formal independence, even as it distinguished itself from national black unity and movements.

Despite Buthelezi's rejection of independence, Inkatha distanced itself from mainstream opposition. Buthelezi himself had earlier been sympathetic to both BC and the ANC. But in accepting the government post of homeland leader he had shifted to a more ambivalent position toward the state, blurring the distinction between homeland semi-autonomy and formal independence. He now used patronage, and later coercion, to bolster his support, primarily among Zulus, with the state providing the resources.[46] The National Party increasingly viewed Buthelezi as an anti-ANC ally. "We are natural allies," said Nationalist Gerrit Viljoen. Inkatha "has emphasized the free market, was against violence, and opposed foreign sanctions."[47] In response, the ANC's Oliver Tambo denigrated Buthelezi for "defending the system. . . . [H]e embraces tribalism, plays into the hands of the enemy."[48]

Buthelezi's Inkatha encouraged loyalty with images of ethnic Zulu nationalism, differentiating it from the black unity projected by BC and the national anti-apartheid, nonracialism of the UDF and ANC. This difference exacerbated basic political competition. Conflict emerged between Inkatha and the UDF and ANC, exploding into massive violence in Natal by the mid-1980s and in the Transvaal thereafter. Such internecine fighting served the interests of the state, in keeping with the old tradition of divide and rule, though the conflict in Natal pitted Zulu against Zulu. The state and media described the violence as "black on black," hiding or ignoring the state's role in fanning divisions and the greater emergence of unified opposition to apartheid. By thus projecting blacks as prone to violence and unprepared for democracy, the state hoped to diminish support for reform.

The other major counterpressure against inclusive citizenship came from the white, largely Afrikaner, right wing. Representing up to one-third of the white electorate, the right wing claimed that "apartheid was another word for self-determination."[49] According to Afrikaner stalwart Jaap Marais, since "every nation on this earth should have its own ground," Afrikaners deserved to rule South Africa.[50] The right wing therefore continued to advocate the Afrikaner ethnic separatism of Hertzog and the early National Party. They resented the reformist impulses of British manufacturers and *verlighte*, or reformist, Afrikaners. The right wing sought to represent the interests of poorer Afrikaners, grudgingly incorporating sympathetic English who shared "a common cultural heritage" not shared by blacks.[51] In their view, apartheid had successfully produced a great industrial revolution; its continuation was necessary because "Africans cannot run their own country."[52] While disingenuously denying that South Africa was suffering any great disorder, the right wing did acknowledge that black militancy might prevent them from holding all of South Africa. They retreated to advocating a separate white homeland, or *volkstadt*. Right-wingers like Pieter Mulder who participated in the inclusive 1994 elections did so on the understanding that they would gain such "self-determination" if they garnered "sufficient support."[53]

With rising black protest matched by repression and some division among both blacks and whites, how then can we account for the dramatic shift of state policy toward negotiation? In part, the answer lies with events external to South Africa. Decolonization in Africa, and particularly the liberation of neighboring Mozambique and Angola in 1975, added to the perceived threat to the regime. It also gave confidence to black South Africans that the tide was turning their way.[54] According to then-Minister Gerrit Viljoen, the results of the negotiated independence of Namibia in 1988 were "influential." Pretoria officials were encouraged by their "positive experience" of former adversaries who "got along well with each other" and successfully managed a transition.[55] More generally, "the end of Communism in 1989 was the ultimate key," according to Viljoen.[56] The collapse of the Communist bloc deflated white fears that majority rule would bring Soviet domination, and further undermined Western support for Pretoria as an anti-Communist bulwark. And with the end of Western cold war strategic interest in South Africa, Pretoria feared a heightening of international sanctions and condemnation. Whereas state officials had earlier argued that international pressure would "have the effect of strengthening [white] determination to retain their right of self-preservation,"[57] in an age of international economic integration this bluster became hollow.

These practical and psychological pressures from outside were shaped by and combined with internal pressures. Most notably, protest and disorder had brought capital flight and added to pressure on foreign lenders and governments to impose significant informal and state sanctions. In particular, images reminiscent of its own civil rights movement inspired U.S. domestic protestors to demand punitive actions against South Africa. Economic disruption threatened the white privilege apartheid had served, as real GDP growth, for example, fell from 3.7 percent to 2.1 percent just from 1988 to 1989.[58] Unemployment rose to dramatic levels, further threatening general prosperity and unrest. Because whites had become increasingly dependent on black labor and markets with rising industrialization, black strikes and boycotts hit home. Finally, the costs of enforcing apartheid had risen to unbearable levels as the black population had grown in both size and willingness to challenge the state.

Despite rising domestic mobilization and international and economic pressures, Pretoria still retained the military resources to resist change. But the state was under extreme pressure, and many within the National Party concluded that the challenge would be better addressed from a position of relative strength, for instance while the police force retained its ability to "combat violence."[59] According to Nelson Mandela, State President F. W. de Klerk pragmatically bowed to the pressure for reform not "with the intention of putting himself out of power ... [but] to ensure power for the Afrikaner in a new dispensation."[60] De Klerk acted before he fully lost control of the situation. Economic and international pressure had forced many whites to conclude that the status quo could not be maintained and that the time was ripe to get the best deal possible. Many Afrikaners in particular, conscious of being a minority, supported de Klerk's reform efforts. A compromise was needed to ensure survival and the preservation of social and economic gains made by Afrikaners since 1948.

That many Afrikaners were rethinking their commitment to apartheid does not mean that all shared such reforming impulses. The simultaneous rise of the right wing and *verlighte* reformers suggests a significant split within the Afrikaner population, which in itself further weakened its domination. According to Allan Boesak, protest aimed at "making black townships ungovernable" had also "made white South Africa ungovernable. . . . [We] achieved a division of white politics."[61] By 1986, 35 percent of Afrikaners polled described current reforms as proceeding "too fast," 40 percent supported reforms, and 15 percent described reforms as going "too slow."[62]

Division among Afrikaners was not new, for there had been a long debate about whether to unify with the English or to assert a separatist Afrikaner nationalism. What was new was that the focus of the debate had shifted to the pressing question of whether or how to incorporate blacks, an issue raised forcibly by black protest. This shift indicates that many Afrikaners had concluded that English domination was no longer their greatest problem. They were now primarily concerned about the threat posed by blacks themselves. Even the white right wing advocated a separate *volkstadt* to protect themselves not primarily from the English, but from the black majority. The central issue of white politics, and the most pressing challenge to the nation-state, had shifted from Afrikaner–English conflict to the rising white–black conflict, reflecting greater white unity.

Black South African racial identity and mobilization had been provoked by the imposition and elaboration of racial domination designed to unify whites. Racial domination used as a means to unify whites had also reinforced black identity, unity, and mobilization, largely cutting across ethnic distinctions. The price of Afrikaner–English reconciliation was rising black protest. The state's shift to negotiations was in large part a response to this rising threat. According to the ANC's Walter Sisulu, as a result of the pervasive experience of apartheid "people are very much politicized in this country. . . . They will challenge anybody."[63] In addition, many black South Africans were unified and inspired by their support for Nelson Mandela, whose "charisma and [living] martyrdom" led many to proclaim "he is our God."[64] Mass mobilization generally rested on such popular imagery and direct experience more than on ideological points over which diverse opposition groups differed; "Masses don't see the ideological differences," remarked Natal professor Fatima Meer. "For the common man, all opposition groups are 'out there' and supportable for opposing the state."[65] Though ideological divisions remained, fueled by leadership competition, the varying opposition tendencies all pressed together. With the ANC acknowledging that a military victory was out of reach, popular protest was seen as a way to destabilize the regime.[66]

Rising popular protest was used by mainstream opposition leaders to project a threat against the state sufficiently strong to force negotiations. But they were also eager to contain that threat in order to avoid scaring whites into a defensive retreat, into circling the wagons in a *laager*, or into greater use of force. The state's shift toward negotiations was therefore encouraged by opposition pragmatism, itself informed by the prospect of negotiations. In effect, the regime's primary opponents offered to collude in reconfiguring the nation-state, avoiding a full-scale civil war that would destroy both the state and its economy. Most prominently, the ANC took pains to reassure whites that democratic inclusion would not jeopardize existing property rights and economic privilege entrenched under apartheid. In meetings with businessmen, the ANC distanced itself from nationalization and socialism.[67] Such reassurances were consistent with the ANC's long-standing advocacy of national democracy and its avoidance of demands for radical economic redistribution. For such practical reasons, ANC-aligned unionist Cyril Ramaphosa concluded that the struggle would "have to be in two stages," using the language of the Communist Party.[68] Such pragmatism also reflected the interests of the growing black middle class, well represented among the ANC leadership. The very existence of such an African bourgeoisie sharing an interest in economic stability and growth itself reassured whites.

Opposition efforts to reassure whites would continue even after formal negotiations began. The ANC formally abandoned the armed struggle, if not mass protest. Afrikaners in particular were mollified by the prospect of continued civil service postings, guaranteed both in the negotiations and by necessity. According to former National Party Minister Gerrit Viljoen, "blacks will come to power but will need Afrikaners [to run the state], just as the British were essential to the Afrikaners. Afrikaners cannot now be marginalized."[69] Surveys reaffirmed that most blacks had relatively moderate expectations about economic change.[70]

Symbolism was also reassuring. Mandela himself was only the most visible figure advocating forgiveness and reconciliation. "After 1990, there was a sudden appearance on television of blacks," P. J. de Lange recalled in 1994. "They were sophisticated and articulate. The seclusion of white and black under apartheid was breached. [We] saw people on both sides as rational and capable," and thus less threatening.[71] Whites took solace in such moderation.

South African politics converged on the center, propelled by the threat of further instability, protest, and dislocation, which the mainstream opposition promised to contain. The National Party leadership concluded that continuing apartheid was impossible, and eagerly looked for a compromise deal despite right-wing condemnations. The Nats were particularly eager to strike a deal with Nelson Mandela, whose secret meetings with government in the late 1980s assured state ministers that he was a moderate prepared to compromise.[72] These officials pressed for negotiations before Mandela was replaced by the next generation of ANC leadership, which they saw as likely to claim his legacy for more militant aims. "If Mandela died he would be a permanent martyr. Everyone would claim him and he wouldn't be able to say no," argued Gerrit Vilgoen. "[Our] greatest fear was the high expectations of the youth. . . . We need Mandela for quite some time."[73] The ANC itself was also eager for a deal, tired of its years of exile, fearful of losing popular support if it failed to deliver. If negotiations faltered, the ANC might have been swept aside by popular anger, so it was eager to take up the state's invitation to join talks. A corresponding convergence developed on the military front: "the South African Defense Force knows the ANC can cause mayhem and the ANC knows the right can cause mayhem. That balance of power is a basis for national unity."[74] The army certainly retained the ability to repress, but at a high cost to both the opposition and themselves. Blacks and whites both had an interest in preserving the state and its economy. The result among whites was, in Viljoen's words, "a shift from confrontation to negotiations, with a realization that neither can we win, nor can the ANC win."[75]

Stalemate and convergence on the center pushed both state and opposition elites to negotiate; they lacked any viable alternative. De Klerk and Nelson Mandela seized this opportunity, forging a tenuous and often tense partnership testing their diplomatic skills. The result was an extended period of negotiations from 1990 until 1994. But South Africa's transition was not controlled from above, as a comparison with Brazil's transition from dictatorship suggests.[76] Negotiations proceeded amid the din of continued mass mobilization and pressure, which increased as talks proceeded. Whenever negotiations faltered, resurgent mass protest forced a return to the table. Violence was not eliminated; instead, its occasional outbreak pressed the negotiators forward. Between 1990 and 1993, more than 9,000 people died in conflict between the ANC and Inkatha, with the latter bolstered by secret state support and seen by the ANC as an opponent of change to be headed off in negotiations, if not by force. In 1992, the bloody Boipotang massacre of peaceful marchers and rising protests thereafter brought the ANC back to the table with greater strength.[77] In short, the continuation of negotiations was driven by mass mobilization and violence, much as their start was. A consensus on the need to contain instability and to preserve the nation-state and its economy provided the essential common ground, much as it had fitfully brought together Afrikaners and English earlier in the century.

The results of negotiations and even the following elections were carefully balanced to reduce tensions. The Nats and ANC finally agreed upon a five-year interim Government of National Unity, with representation of all parties that reached a minimal threshold of popular support in the April 1994 election.[78] Both sides sought to deal with images of tribalism, most notably that of Inkatha: the Nats until 1992 hoped to forge an alliance with Inkatha, and the ANC sought to diminish the division of the African electorate.[79] At the last minute, Inkatha agreed to participate in elections, with the Zulu king enticed to support this participation by a controversial grant of land.[80] Amid some claims of fraud, Inkatha was rewarded with an equally controversial electoral victory in Natal. The National Party was able to win a majority in the Western Cape. The other provinces were won by the ANC, falling just below the overall two-thirds majority needed for absolute control over the subsequent process of constitution writing. Even ANC supporters confessed, though, that it was not in the interests of any party to gain absolute control; a government of national unity was essential.[81] In May 1994, South Africans celebrated the inauguration of Mandela as president. Thereafter the potentially more militant UDF was disbanded, union demands and more militant parties were largely pushed aside, and the official Reconstruction and Development Program avoided pitting redistribution against growth.[82]

Efforts to encourage newly inclusive national unity prevailed. The suspiciously neat election results, appeasing the National Party and Inkatha and giving the ANC a majority short of two-thirds, raised liberals' accusations of deception and election tampering.[83] But the result was just the sort of balance the elites had hoped for, providing an incentive for all major parties to remain within the newly inclusive government. These parties recognized that the negotiation and election results would reaffirm the image of the state as autonomous, with varied representation in government ensuring popular loyalty. Much as intrawhite party competition had earlier helped to preserve the polity amid deepening racial domination, inclusion of an array of parties within the new government helped to preserve the polity and unify the newly inclusive nation-state.

The transition process and form of the interim government reflected the pressing need to encourage national unity. Given the history of ethnic and racial antagonism, National Party and ANC elites were eager to ensure that their efforts contributed to a healing of prior conflicts. The imperative for nation-state consolidation to avoid disruptive conflict, earlier applied exclusively among whites, now applied across the racial divide. The historically inclusive election of April 1994 was anticipated and did serve as a nation-building experience. Until 1996, the resulting Government of National Unity was purposefully inclusive, at the price of precluding any parliamentary opposition, generally an ingredient of democracy.[84] The framers of the interim constitution did not believe that South Africa could contain a system of partisanship likely to exacerbate conflict. Instead, they forced all major parties together into the governing cabinet to encourage cross-ethnic and cross-racial compromises and alliances. Debate was shifted to within parties and the government, whose structures contained conflict.

Even with institutional incentives for unity, the legacy of past divisions would not be easily or quickly overcome. F. W. de Klerk sought to finesse the issue rhetorically, arguing, in Viljoen's words, for "nation-building . . . without denying the existence of [separate] nations in the cultural sense, just like Hertzog saw two streams without denying togetherness."[85] Certainly the end of formal racial domination opened the possibility of inclusive nationalism cognizant of cultural diversity. But no institutional arrangement could magically produce this result, for antagonisms had been long entrenched by prior institutional rule.[86] According to activist Neville Alexander, "in South Africa, building a nation has to be a conscious process; it won't just happen. . . . Previously no government tried. To the contrary, they divided. . . . Blacks identified themselves more as African, denied South African nationality. . . . Now people are proud of being South African."[87] Many hoped that unity would be reinforced by common interest in economic growth, which would require stability within a newly consolidated nation-state. "The glue is the comfortable living of whites and the hopes of comfortable living of blacks," according to Helen Suzman,[88] though for most blacks such hopes remained unfulfilled, even as a few were greatly enriched by corporate concessions. Despite the slow pace of reforms, education was also generally seen as an essential tool for encouraging such national unity, together with meeting some minimal expectations of concrete change in the living conditions of the majority. But no one was sanguine about the prospect of quick redress, easy unity, and reconciliation. As described by anti-apartheid stalwart Beyers Naude:

A nation in a full sense is not possible without conflicts and disagreement. A nation is a product of cultural conflicts that have been
resolved. In South Africa, we are all talking about a South African
nation. We don't yet have a South African nation, but we are mov-
ing in that direction. We must be careful not to talk too glibly
about a South African nation. It is a process, sometimes very ago-
nizing. . . . [E]thnic groups each want to establish their own language and culture. Certain groups are more privileged. [Nation
building] will require a conscious education of our peoples, but it
can be done. I fear we won't understand the significance of the
process and will allow old forces of distrust to prevail.[89]

Ethnic, class, and racial tensions, building on historical legacies,
remained just under the surface of the newly democratized South
Africa. "Latent ethnic conflict is always there, as in any multicultural
and linguistic society"; for instance, the rising use of English as the
common language generated some resentment among Afrikaners.[90]
Spokesmen for the increasingly marginalized white right wing continued to maintain that "there is no [common] South African language" (Pieter Mulder) and to proclaim that "we want a Boer
republic. Sooner or later, we will fight" (Fred Rundle).[91] Fear remained that Afrikaners, Zulus, and others might further embrace such
separatism.[92] Middle-class fears that reforms would bring a further
influx of the unemployed into urban areas raised the possibility that
inclusive nation building would be swamped by a class antagonism.
And among "marginalized" people, resentment over the lack of jobs
and services and over the perks enjoyed by new government officials
was evident after the 1994 election.[93] Such resentment did not coa-
lesce into a strong, organized opposition to the ANC, but it raised
the future possibility of a class or ideological division within the ANC
ranks.

Neither could long-entrenched racial animosity easily be defused
by democratic inclusion and nonracialism. According to one activist,
"it is difficult for people to overcome distrust of whites. . . . A lot of
hatred between black and white has been created and will remain after
liberation."[94] Such tension could be manipulated among whites or
blacks. For instance, the majority of coloureds in the Western Cape
voted for the National Party in 1994, induced by Nationalist elec-
tioneering to fear that an ANC victory would undermine coloureds'
relative privilege.[95] Zulu supporters of Inkatha similarly feared a loss

of autonomy and distanced themselves from others. As in the past, issues of race and ethnicity were enmeshed with the definition and encouragement of national unity. Democracy in itself could give voice to such potential divisions, without neccessarily or quickly leading to redress or uniform loyalty. Divergent groups fearing the interference of the ANC-controlled central state called for greater local authority.

Prior nationalism had been constructed and reinforced through antagonism; it was defined by who was excluded, and following an ethnic rather than a civic logic. Afrikaner nationalism had emerged in response to British domination, and had vied with white South African national unity for the first half of the twentieth century. To the extent that English and Afrikaners had unified, they had done so by agreeing to exclude the black majority. Such domination had further enforced and then been challenged by black identity and provoked protest, adopting its own form of exclusivity in the case of African nationalism, or incorporating all supporters of nonracialism as advocated by the ANC. But even the ANC defined and projected its nationalism in opposition to supporters of apartheid; the ANC was "based on uniting those 'against,' without examining what they are 'for.' "[96] With the loss of a unifying target of opposition, many felt the loss of identity more than they immediately adopted an inclusive nationalism. "The people are shattered into a thousand pieces. Everyone is just running with his own little piece of hatred."[97]

Given the history of Afrikaner, white, African, and anti-apartheid nationalism, the transition to an inclusive form of nationalism remained uncertain. The onus for this transition fell on the new government and its president, Nelson Mandela, who faced the challenge of redirecting past forms of exclusive nationalism. According to Broederbond chairman P. J. de Lange:

> We need to forge mutual respect for various cultures. . . . We have to eat a few bags of salt. . . . The experience of struggle has created a certain mind-set. We have to get beyond that. While chasing the bus, people could shout. Once you catch the bus, you have to drive it and prevent it from going over the cliff. A major shift in attitude is needed, an acceptance of responsibility.[98]

This challenge of forging national unity not only had to overcome the particular pattern of South African antagonisms, but also the more general tendency to define and construct a nation in opposition to some "other." Nationalisms had long been expressed in antagonistic terms. A newly inclusive South African nation was envisioned and could only be constructed without vindictiveness or the crutch of exclusion used so pervasively for nation building. National unity required grappling with the past, led by the Truth and Reconciliation Commission. Beyond that, "we need the state to give incentives to allow for unification, for a national consciousness," says Neville Alexander. "Not 'nationalist,' as usually against something. National is for something. Statesmen must ensure 'national' doesn't become 'nationalist.' "[99] How to define and encourage such national unity without revenge or reference to some ethnic, racial, or class exclusion remained the fundamental challenge of the new South Africa.

Negotiated transition to a nonracial democracy in 1994 brought to the fore challenges remaining from past antagonism. Ethnic and racial policies of divide and rule had coalesced with assertions of tradition and culture. Elites then sought to define and reinforce an inclusive nationalism, to heal divisive legacies that continued to impede such nation-state consolidation. As the South African nation-state had been built on the basis of racial exclusion, ending such exclusion required a fundamental change in the form and constitution of the state. But institutional change ending formal racial domination did not immediately end entrenched inequality or bring a change in popular loyalties. The nation's wounds remained open amid continued violence, notably in Kwazulu. Encouraged by their democratic inclusion, the majority of black South Africans would continue to look for further substantive changes in their lives. The potential threat remained that they might return to protest for such change, or fissure into ethnic, class, or regional blocks. Arguably this threat would continue to offer leaders pragmatic incentive for further redress and nation-state consolidation in its new, inclusive form.

9

Burying Jim Crow

BLACK RACIAL IDENTITY, MOBILIZATION, AND REFORM IN THE UNITED STATES

As in South Africa, black identity and protest against racial domination in the United States built upon earlier solidarity, culture, and shared experience. African-Americans were long constrained by repression and regional division, if not the ethnic divisions evident in South Africa. Over the long run, however, central state abandonment of Reconstruction, which allowed for heightened racial domination imposed locally, also provoked greater efforts at forging black unity as the basis for protest. Economic changes made possible by stability then further reinforced African-American solidarity and potential power. Black identity was affirmed, not received, in a contested process. Such identity consolidation had to and did precede actions by such a self-conscious group in response to resources and opportunities, the more conventional focus of study. And opportunities for mobilization were both taken and made, forcing responses from white authorities. Even before black protest reached its high point with the civil rights movement, the dynamic between state policy and black activism was evident.

Toward Racial Solidarity

Well before Jim Crow, blacks were conscious of their common distinctive experience and culture. They had earlier formed separate Methodist churches. But before abolition, the prominent identity among African-Americans was as slaves, and the pressing issue was freedom. Bondsmen engaged in various forms of resistance, and on occasion revolted. Most slaves or freedmen saw no option for or attraction to inclusion in American society. Emergent racial identity was evident in such acts as Denmark Vesey's leadership of an 1822 slave revolt (although he himself was a free man) and the attack of Nat Turner's rebels against every white person they encountered.[1] By the 1830s a small number of early black nationalists had emerged, advocating a separate territory, self-determination, or return to Africa. In 1835 and 1847, national black conventions were held, and after 1850 Northern blacks were impelled to protest the Fugitive Slave Law, which threatened their protection from reenslavement.[2] Informed by such efforts, "Afro-Americans invented themselves, not as a race, but as a nation," describing themselves as a "poor nation of colour."[3] But distinctions among blacks by color, place of origin, or culture remained. Many then linked themselves with the United States, even going so far as to fight for the Union in the Civil War.

During Reconstruction, free African-Americans did engage in an inclusive American polity for which they had fought, and they later resisted the foreclosure of such participation. Having gained the franchise in the South, they voted and gained office. When Reconstruction was abandoned, blacks joined with whites in the populist movement. And when the Democratic Party began to undermine populism through disenfranchisement, blacks protested their loss of rights.[4] But as a minority subject to pervasive discrimination, they were unable to block party political moves to unify the white South. Subjected to poll taxes, property requirements for voting, and violence, black voting declined precipitously in the late nineteenth and early twentieth century, falling for instance in Georgia presidential elections from 55 percent in 1876 to 5 percent in 1904.[5] The nation-state and "solid South" were consolidated by allowing or enforcing Jim Crow; blacks were excluded.

The enforcement and then abandonment of black rights directly affected black views. During the Civil War and Reconstruction, with expectations of reform at their peak, separatist black nationalism was abandoned in favor of supporting the Union. But the end of Reconstruction showed America to be unwilling to continue enforcing the inclusion of blacks and many blacks responded in kind, advocating a return to Africa or living separately. For instance, leading black nationalist Martin Delany advocated migration to Africa until the Civil War, joined the Union army in the hope of winning civil rights, and then again advocated migration in response to the disappointing end of Reconstruction.[6] African churches, established in large numbers after Reconstruction, supported both a return to Africa and self-isolation in the United States. Such separatism, writes William Julius Wilson, "represented a retreat from, rather than an attack against the social order."[7] With racial discrimination so pervasive, blacks saw little chance of incorporation, retreating to enforced disillusionment.

Even as radical and significant a figure as Frederick Douglass appears in retrospect to have been somewhat uncertain of how to identify and mobilize blacks after abolition. Douglass advocated "assimilation through self-assertion," and condemned the hypocrisy of America's celebrations of freedom amid continued black disenfranchisement.[8] But Douglass also rejected the notion of racial pride, separatist nationalism, and calls for a return to Africa, advocating instead self-reliance and extension of the franchise.[9] He wanted blacks to seek inclusion, though he knew that such demands were unlikely to be met. Having acknowledged the unifying effect of slavery,[10] Douglass seemed less certain of what held blacks together after abolition, and the best means to seek redress for their new grievances. Unsure of the basis for continued mobilization, Douglass saw his power dwindle after Reconstruction, though he lived until 1895.[11] In his wake, the next generation of black national leaders would continue to wrestle with how to consolidate black identity, mobilization, and advancement.

The leadership mantle was taken up by Booker T. Washington, who stressed the assimilationist aspect of Douglass's message rather than any popular assertion of black identity. Washington pursued a dual agenda of local black self-reliance in the South while garnering federal patronage and white financial support from Northern liberals still eager to help. To the extent his strategy was consistent with racial separatism, Washington's Africanism remained covert and conservative, at least by most measures.[12] Seeing no opportunity for their political inclusion in the South where most blacks remained, Washington focused on separate economic advancement as a practical necessity, largely ignoring the link between such advancement and political rights.[13] While Washington may have provided an example for racial pride, he did nothing to channel that pride into mass mobilization. Commentators and later activists would rebuke him – perhaps unfairly – for capitulation to racial domination.[14]

Committed to building his own institutional base at the Tuskeegee Institute for black education, Washington abandoned political assertiveness and demands for equal citizenship. He accepted segregation and remained silent on the 1890 Force Bill, which, had it passed, would have required black enfranchisement.[15] In return, he expected continued financial support, black economic advance, and reduced repression.

Washington's near-contemporary and eventual successor on the national stage, W. E. B. Du Bois, argued that whites had failed to fulfill their part of Booker T. Washington's bargain. Rather than allowing blacks to advance on their own, Jim Crow segregation and disenfranchisement had caused further black impoverishment.[16] Du Bois concluded that blacks would have to agitate for the preservation and expansion of their rights and for integration, rather than accept isolation. He assumed that "the talented tenth" of a Northern-concentrated black elite he represented would lead this effort, expecting they would forgo the temptations of accommodation. Yet even Du Bois would compromise at times, for instance in accepting separate training for black officers in the First World War as preferable to no training at all. When his own support of Woodrow Wilson and black participation in the war effort were left unrewarded, Du Bois began to rethink his position.[17]

Du Bois had long been conflicted over the "double self" he described as dividing the loyalties of blacks between America and their race.[18] Concluding that America had abandoned blacks, Du Bois shifted to a greater emphasis on race pride, self-segregation, and avoidance of self-denigrating protest.[19] In this sense, his radicalism echoed Washington's conservatism. But in the Northern tradition, he also became a staunch advocate of black nationalism, using the terms race and nation interchangeably as identities based on common blood and shared experience.[20] Du Bois condemned any mixing of blood that would dilute the black race and create division. He feared that fellow mulattoes would see themselves as intermediaries or even white, rather than join the black cause. Racial identity had not yet consolidated to the point where such concerns over absorption would diminish.[21] Blacks remained trapped in the "double self" of a distinct minority within, yet spurned by white America.

The National Association for the Advancement of Colored People (NAACP), which Du Bois helped to found, reflected his elitism. The organization evolved from Du Bois's Niagara movement, which never had more than four hundred members, and remained relatively focused on the small black middle class, though the association's newspaper did achieve a circulation of 100,000.[22] Du Bois initially supported the interracial nature of Niagara and the NAACP board, both of which enjoyed considerable white financial support. But he would later resign from the NAACP, criticizing it for a lack of commitment to Pan Africanism; in 1944 he rejoined. Having joined the Communist Party, he had become increasingly disillusioned with the NAACP's continued and largely unsuccessful efforts to encourage integration with white America, though he later saw no viable alternative to the association.[23]

The NAACP itself had no ambivalence about its aims, consistently focusing on appeals to whites and to the federal authorities for decency and redress. According to one longtime official, "the government was always the key. . . . The NAACP program is to obtain all rights to which we are entitled . . . [pushing for] changes in the courts without protests."[24] The association remained focused on blacks' gaining rights as Americans rather than asserting racial identity or engaging in protest. It pressed for the end of debt peonage and against repeal of the Fifteenth Amendment. Though the organization would later claim credit for the 1960s civil rights mobilization in the South, where the NAACP did have major branches, it long remained stodgily distant from such mass protests.[25] The NAACP gradually declined in influence until its use of the courts began to bear fruit in the 1950s.[26] A similar fate would befall the Urban League, focused not on court battles or on mass protest, but on easing the transition and encouraging the economic advance of blacks migrating North. As mass protest later emerged, those organizations not involved in such protest were eclipsed.

White America simply did not respond to black appeals for redress, which would have disrupted white unity encouraged by racial domination. Jim Crow expanded in the South, provoking many blacks to migrate North in search of opportunity, a process later crucial in undermining racial domination. While Northern blacks were not isolated in separate townships, as in South Africa, they were increasingly segregated in poor urban ghettoes.

With the NAACP remaining relatively elitist and focused on judicial redress, the major mass movement among blacks before the middle of the twentieth century was that led by Marcus Garvey. Advocating racial purity and nationalism, Garvey combined an urban and less accommodationist version of Booker T. Washington's focus on economic advance with the inspirational message of a return to Africa. Among the new potential mass constituency of urban poor blacks migrating North, he found a receptive audience increasingly convinced that whites were not open to persuasion for redress, leaving blacks to fend for themselves. As Garvey concluded, "upon ourselves depends our own destiny."[27] This view was reinforced by America's spurning of black veterans after the First World War and by a series of riots in 1917–19, in which white workers objected to the rising use of black labor. These experiences and trends converged to boost the following of Garvey's Universal Negro Improvement Association, which by 1923 had close to a million members. Meanwhile, an increasing sense of black self-empowerment also emerged out of the Harlem Renaissance and later the unionization of black Pullman railroad porters.

Though Garvey was imprisoned for tax violations and his movement collapsed, its legacy was to demonstrate that blacks could be mobilized on a mass level. By 1941, railroad porter unionist A. Philip Randolph would call for a blacks-only march on Washington, the mere threat of which was sufficient to force President Roosevelt to create the Committee on Fair Employment Practices, aimed at ending job discrimination in war industries. Blacks were still often excluded from social programs throughout the New Deal and endured continued disenfranchisement.

The sixty or more years after Reconstruction marked a period of early black attempts at ideological refinement and mobilization, but did not produce long standing mass protest for inclusion. According to Du Bois, the majority of blacks still in the South remained mired in hypocritical compromise.[28] With segregation entrenched, impoverished Southern blacks also were intimidated by mob violence. Northern blacks did engage in small-scale riots and even in the Garveyite mass movement. But Garveyite abandonment of an American-based identity remained largely a form of escape rather than a direct challenge. Blacks were spurned by white America, but still did not collectively assert themselves as a race demanding inclusion in the American nation.

The continued distinction between regional trends in itself demonstrates a lack of consolidated nationwide racial identity despite the efforts of leading intellectuals. The North–South divide, which had ripped apart the nation, had also divided blacks, whose experiences varied according to region. That division reflected the post-Reconstruction reassertion of states' rights, with localized race policies providing no nationally unifying target for protest. No nationwide race policy was imposed, and little nation-wide racial identity or protest emerged. Federal toleration of local policies did not have the unifying effect of the South African central state's acts of commission. As a result, for all the intellectual activity of the black elite, Garvey, the black porters' union, and the threatened 1941 march, the period from 1877 to 1955 remained one of relative quiescence and division among black masses. Even mobilization during the 1920s was Northern and focused on separatism and a return to Africa, rather than inclusion and redress, and the planned 1941 march was abandoned through compromise. Meanwhile, the racial order was further consolidated in response to party pressure.

That this period did not produce nationwide mass mobilization for inclusion is not to suggest that nothing of significance occurred. For all of their disagreements, the efforts of Douglass, Washington, Du Bois, Garvey, and others provided a rich legacy of ideological identity formation. This legacy gradually helped to inspire further nationwide racial consciousness, as did rising industrialization, migration to the North, and urbanization. But structural conditions still did not provide the opportunity for the ideological spark to light the tinder of mass mobilization.

Throughout this period regional reconciliation and nation-state consolidation among whites proceeded. The tension between North and South abated, the economy grew, and centralized authority could be and was expanded as the disruption posed by regional conflict faded. By mid-twentieth century the central state had solidified sufficiently to have won two world wars and sustained the interventions of the New Deal. By the 1950s, the federal government had accumulated enough power to intervene again, this time in the defining bastion of regional autonomy, race relations. And African-Americans, conscious of this development, would press for just such an intervention. With the consolidation of a centralized instrument of social intervention, demands would rise for the use of this instrument to fulfill the aspirations of the previous generations.

Rising Black Protest Forces State Reforms

By mid-century, African-Americans were becoming more united, particularly in the South, where blacks were further solidified by long-entrenched social, religious, and economic ties, and by the inspiring efforts of leadership. Black density had fed white fears of political and economic competition, headed off by Democratic Party and local authority efforts at disenfranchisement and legal segregation, which in turn created further racial unity. As whites were unified in the "solid South" by racial domination, blacks increasingly consolidated as a self-conscious group ready to act for themselves. Black communities pressured local authorities, while national organizations pressed for intervention by federal authority consolidated in the New Deal and world wars. This combined pressure would force federal action against Jim Crow, first through the judiciary and then the executive branch. Such intervention capped the trend of growing central power over state and local government, but it was the growing protest that forced central power to bear. Consolidation of power and pressure for the application of that power converged, in an ongoing dynamic.

Racial domination diminished regional intrawhite conflict and bolstered nation-state consolidation, which in turn provided the necessary conditions for tremendous economic growth. Not only did such growth increase the power of the state, but it also enlarged the urbanized and educated black middle class, a trend later encouraged by state policies. Black family income was 41.1 percent of whites' in 1940, but 61.2 percent by 1970. The number of blacks with white-collar jobs grew with the explosion of government employment and support services.[29] It is not surprising that such economic advance should have fed rising expectations, but it is also conceivable that rising class distinctions within the black community could have divided more than unified, as it had in the past.[30] Distinctions by class and color remained salient. But the emerging black middle class gradually took a leading role in asserting unified racial identity, with greater militancy evident at higher levels of job status and education.[31]

Du Bois's expectations for activist leadership from the talented tenth proved prescient, though such engagement emerged only once the black elite actually grew closer to that proportion. When the civil rights movement developed in the 1950s and 1960s, it was led primarily by the black middle class, much as earlier attempts at mobilization had been led by an elite.[32] Relative economic security and growing size provided the emergent class with the confidence and resources to pursue such political mobilization, but it does not explain why the class did so.

Racial domination and discrimination forced the black middle class to identify itself racially across class, and to see its fate tied to that larger identity. As Congressman Charles Rangel of New York puts it, "segregation and racism caused the black middle class to stay with blacks," and quantitative studies confirm that blacks remained uniquely isolated together, regardless of income.[33] Prominent legal segregation in the South and discrimination in the North defined all blacks and forced them together, forging collective identity in the most practical manner. "As long as segregation was the law, it didn't make any difference if you had gone to Harvard Law. . . . No matter how rich you were, you had to live in a certain section."[34] Whereas whites were divided socially and politically by class and ethnicity, blacks had no alternative but to increasingly focus on race, the official category that bound them together and down. Middle-class blacks were acutely aware that their opportunities were limited by their race, making them all the more conscious of their collective responsibility and peer pressure. Even better-off blacks could not escape the logic that "black people have not suffered as individuals but as members of a group; therefore, their liberation lies in group action."[35] The resources gained from economic advance would be applied to collective action.

Enforced racial domination inescapably imposed race as the over-riding category of identity and mobilization for blacks, while segregation itself helped to create a black middle class whose businesses benefited from a captive black market.[36] Middle-class blacks then began to focus their concern and action on the continued constraints of racial domination from which their money provided little escape.[37] This was particularly true for small black business people, preachers, and undertakers, for whom segregation had provided some protection from white sanctions. These entrepreneurs and professionals serving blacks were more interested in avoiding group ostracism they might face if they ignored their fellows than they feared whites who already segregated them. By comparison, teachers and others employed by public authorities remained susceptible to economic pressures from whites, and tended to avoid confrontation.[38]

Given imposed racial unity, the rise of the black middle class reinforced the indigenous black organizations that would provide the foundation for protests, initially in the South. Economic advance brought together larger numbers of relatively well-off blacks within churches, universities, and local NAACP branches, which would become the locus and initiators of mobilization. Churches in particular would shift from conservative bulwarks of the status quo to sites of movement organization.[39] This shift not only reflected greater economic security, but the greater autonomy enjoyed by the black middle class and their organizations. According to Andrew Young, "with the second or third generation out of poverty, they were secure enough [to provide] leadership . . . independent of the white power structure."[40]

That the emergence of mass mobilization would occur first in the South is not surprising. That region was where black social networks were entrenched and where formal segregation provided for autonomous organizational centers, unified blacks most strongly, and offered a clear target for protest. The South was "where blacks were, Jim Crow country, the heart of the enemy," recalls George Houser. "There were plenty of issues in the North, but the thing that attracted most attention was the petty apartheid in the South."[41] Thus, while the absence of nationwide Jim Crow still impeded nationwide racial unity and protest, its regional imposition would reinforce unity and protest in the South, developed through social networks and cultural ties. Localized state policy provoked initially localized response.

If Jim Crow reinforced the potential for Southern mobilization, the image of a more liberal North and the increased central authority in Washington provided another crucial ingredient for the protests to come. Southern black protest would not only be the result of the push of unifying local oppression and black solidarity, but the pull of protection and vindication that might be called upon from the North. Southern blacks recalled that the North, at least for a time, had imposed abolition and Reconstruction on the South. Indeed, the New Deal signaled that the federal government and the Democratic Party in particular favored social intervention that might yet be directed toward blacks.[42]

The Allies' antiracist rhetoric in the Second World War further encouraged blacks, as it had in South Africa. African-Americans were inspired to a greater hopefulness and national loyalty that largely eclipsed the separatist nationalism that had emerged during the decades of post-Reconstruction abandonment. Veterans in particular returned from war expecting their national service and loyalty to be rewarded. "Black men had been in the . . . fight against Hitler's racial theories," says James Farmer. "Fighting against racism over yonder [made them] more sensitized about racism at home. They observed racism here as quite alive and it hit them harder than ever before because they knew their buddies had died."[43] It was not uncommon for black veterans to encounter segregation upon their return home with a new sense of shock. Percy Sutton recalls, "I was thrown off a train in my captain's uniform. It was a castration I remembered for a long time. I fought a war to stop that."[44] Black veterans responded with occasional small protests.[45]

Rising expectations of change helped to move Du Bois's dilemma of the double self to greater resolution. Blacks recognized their racial distinction – even the middle class could not escape. But they had also served their country. If America would reward such service and fulfill its promise of equal rights, then blacks could be loyal both to race and country. The trick was to force such fulfillment, and only the North was likely to help, if not out of generosity toward blacks then to resolve the North's own ambivalence between allowing for regional autonomy and encouraging national consolidation. Many blacks assumed that if only the North were forcibly reminded of the conditions in the South, they would move to correct it, for the South was part of the same country.[46] Blacks expected the circle to turn. If the South had forced the North to withdraw and allow for Jim Crow, the North might now be ready to revisit the issue and fulfill its earlier promise.

In 1954, Washington sent the clearest signal since Reconstruction that it was again ready to impose reforms on the South. Where party politicians had prevaricated, nine white justices of the U.S. Supreme Court spoke as one, finding in *Brown* v. *Board of Education* for the plaintiff that the Constitution demanded the end of segregation in the crucial area of public education. Constitutional vagueness was replaced by constitutional imperative, in effect nullifying the deal of 1877. Federal authority would no longer fully appease the South in allowing for Jim Crow.

Brown v. *Board of Education* did not mark the first time the Court had moved against segregation, but it was the strongest such decision to date. Nor was the *Brown* order for school desegregation quickly or uniformly implemented. Indeed, the decision provoked considerable moves and countermoves, including the formation of the first local anti-integration White Citizens' Council two weeks later, the segregationist Congressional Southern Manifesto the next year, and local black efforts to force implementation.[47] But such contestation only reaffirmed that the battle had been joined. Washington had effectively promised a second Reconstruction, again provoking Southern white resistance that had defeated the first attempt a century earlier. But *Brown* would help spark a movement that this time would counter white Southern resistance to reform and reconfigure America's racial order, thereby reordering American politics as well.

The *Brown* decision signaled federal receptivity to extending civil rights, inviting mobilization. In 1955, blacks in Montgomery, Alabama, were well prepared to take up the invitation, for local authorities had already proved somewhat open to reform, and the local bus company was vulnerable to the economic pressure of a boycott by its urban black constituency.[48] A strong base of church organizations proved crucial in uniting black elites, not bus riders themselves, to support poorer members of their congregations, particularly a cohort of courageous women who were.[49] Indeed, the Church was crucial as then the only institution "we controlled."[50] It also provided legitimacy during the McCarthy era, for it was difficult to accuse the Church of Communism.[51] Further cover was provided by the *Brown* decision itself, as suggested by the more modest demands and result of a 1953 bus boycott in Baton Rouge before that decision. In his first boycott speech in Montgomery, the Rev. Dr. Martin Luther King, Jr., made explicit reference to this effect of the *Brown* decision: "if we are wrong, the Supreme Court of this nation is wrong."[52]

The Montgomery bus boycott was not the spontaneous event of later myth. Nor was it, as Andrew Young argues, "the bus driver [who] started the movement," for segregated seating had been long practiced.[53] When Rosa Parks decided not to give up her seat for a white, she knew what she was doing, having been trained in civil disobedience at the Highlander School and having long served as an NAACP official.[54] Still, the boycott began with modest aims. "At the outset, it was just for more equal treatment," James Farmer says. "They demanded more courteous treatment, hiring more black drivers, seating by first come first served, but not for desegregation."[55]

The widespread observance of the boycott encouraged its participants to push their leaders to demand more, and after more than a year the buses were desegregated. Popular protest against daily indignity, encouraged by *Brown*, had advanced the impetus for integration beyond courts and classrooms.

Montgomery provided not only a signal victory, but also a new leader. At the first boycott meeting, as James Farmer remembers it, local civic leader E. D. Nixon charged, "you preachers are all cowards." Martin Luther King replied, "Nobody calls me a coward," to which Nixon responded, "I nominate Dr. King as president."[56] King was perfect for the role. Scion of a leading family, he had recently arrived at the pulpit, independent of both white patronage and prior intrablack competition. His Gandhi-inspired faith in nonviolence resonated:

> His was a heady gospel. Though you hit us, we will love you and we will wear you down with our capacity to suffer. These were beautifully crazy words that moved them, especially whites. He was plucking the tenets of faith in which we all believe – the Judeo-Christian and American faith.[57]

King was a true believer in the promise of the religiously inspired American dream, who eloquently could and did demand that it be fulfilled for blacks with full citizenship. He used the promise of federal intervention to demand not that the social order be overthrown but that it live up to its ideals of incorporation.[58] He understood the federal dynamic and played on it, inviting local Southern repression that would provoke federal action and Northern white liberal support.[59] King remained convinced that gaining concessions from the federal government was possible and essential for the movement's success in overcoming Southern black fear. When this dynamic required him to engage in sit-ins or other forms of direct action himself, he often did so reluctantly. He encouraged black protest and demanded action from a receptive federal government that, by acting, could thereby avoid an explosion.

King and his movement sought to speak to all of America, and the mass media now made this possible. As one activist noted later, the civil rights movement was "the first social movement on television. . . . After a while we saw how to use TV [so that] people saw the reality."[60] Former Assistant Attorney General Burke Marshall attests to the impact of the media: "Television and communications technology educated the rest of the country to what was an intolerable situation. This is an important part of what makes the political system run."[61] As an early example, the 1955 lynching of young Emmett Till was unlike any previous lynching in the national publicity it received. According to activist Bob Mants in Alabama's Lowndes County, "I remember seeing the pictures of [Till's] battered body. . . . [It] put spark to the fire."[62] The media thus further consolidated black unity and national attention, while simultaneously inspiring white liberal support and encouraging federal intervention.

In a nation more self-consciously unified by the media, America's "can do" sensibility informed a popular response that such injustice had to be and could be redressed anywhere. "When fire hoses were brought down to a church, that was put on TV. Middle-class whites were incensed – they can't do that in a church."[63] But this tactic also brought its own problem of escalation, or "what to do for an encore," as James Farmer explains. "The second protest always had to exceed the first to get more attention, otherwise the press will yawn and if so, the nation yawns."[64]

In the aftermath of Montgomery, the Southern Christian Leadership Conference (SCLC), founded in 1957 as a church-based coalition, struggled to find an encore to the bus boycott, amid ongoing local efforts. Black college students then took the initiative through the use of peaceful sit-ins, beginning in Greensboro in 1960.[65] Later that year, they formed the Student Non-violent Coordinating Committee (SNCC), with SCLC support and the prominent advice of activist Ella Baker. Women remained an important movement constituency.

Though most of the students were close to middle-class status, they identified themselves racially (as would those in South Africa's Black Consciousness movement), because of the direct experience of legal segregation. Indeed, these students sought to distance themselves from middle-class concerns, postponing their own studies, receiving little funding or reimbursement, by which they feared they would be corrupted, and purposefully adopting an anti-organization and nonhierarchical structure.[66] To further identify themselves with the general black public they later moved the SNCC national office to Mississippi, and began to focus on rural community organizing, spreading the doctrine of black solidarity and protest.[67] According to activist Bob Mants:

> By 1964–65, we left the urban centers and had gone to the field where racism was more overt. Lots of idealism was left at the lunch counters. In the bayou and the Black Belt, it was a different ball game – hardball. Where there was more violence, there was more movement. Violence organized people, gave people more solidarity. It became a tidal wave.[68]

Even in such relatively low-profile local activities, SNCC still followed King's basic strategy of provoking federal intervention against localized repression.[69] Reflecting in 1966 on the early 1960s, SNCC activists acknowledged that "it was assumed that if the country was informed, there would follow certain reforms," reflecting an ongoing "confidence in the government."[70]

Inspired by the students, SCLC returned to direct action, repeatedly seeking to provoke local repression, invoke federal intervention, and negotiate redress. When officials in Albany, Georgia, failed to respond to protests with repression, publicity wavered and the federal government failed to intervene. The lesson learned was to pick a protest cite where the authorities would respond violently, preferably in front of cameras. Birmingham, Alabama, with its vociferously segregationist and states'-rights Sheriff Bull Connor, was perfect for furnishing an opportunity for the movement to dramatize itself before the national media.[71] Connor responded with dogs and hoses, provoking national dismay and federal intervention. Where Albany had been a failure, Birmingham was "the pinnacle," says James Farmer. "If the object was to change the mind of a nation and a president, then it was a great success. The public came to our side."[72]

Of course, the dynamics of mobilization success were not always so straightforward. Segregationists also learned the lesson of Birmingham. King himself acknowledged that after that episode there would be "fewer overt acts to aid us; naive targets . . . will be harder to find."[73] Some potential targets were also purposefully avoided; for instance, "the black power structure" of Atlanta, "closely aligned with whites and not wanting a confrontation," was able to "call the leadership together to get King not to mess with Atlanta."[74] According to activist Hosea Williams, "if there was a town King wanted to start a movement in, it was Atlanta, but every time he started to, the white folks would get Daddy King and the folks Martin respected to stop him."[75] SCLC's link to the black middle class thus served as a brake as well as a resource.

The other main organization of the movement was the Congress of Racial Equality (CORE), founded in 1942 under white leadership and later led by James Farmer. Early CORE protests failed to take off, for "there was nothing to back us up." But after 1960, CORE also learned to target its actions to provoke federal intervention.[76] In addition to sit-ins and marches, CORE engineered the Freedom Rides, which used integrated buses to provoke unrest throughout the South. In one instance, mobs beating Freedom Riders were watched with approval by the Alabama attorney general, provoking the federal attorney general, Robert Kennedy, to intervene, a dramatic example of the dynamic of states'-rights repression prompting federal intervention.[77] Wary of the explosive nature of this dynamic, federal authorities sought to divert CORE and the other leading organizations from protest into more manageable voter education and registration drives, but the protests continued alongside the voting projects.[78]

By 1963, civil rights protests had emerged as the most pressing issue on the political agenda, with protests challenging white national unity and provoking an official response. On 11 June 1963, despite Southern resistance, President Kennedy abandoned his earlier reluctance to embrace the issue, arguing in a nationally broadcast speech that "one hundred years of delay have passed since President Lincoln freed the slaves, yet their heirs, their grandsons, are not fully free. ... Now the time has come for this nation to fulfill its promise."[79] As if in rebuke to such imposition from Washington, that same night the NAACP's Medgar Evers was killed in Mississippi.

Two months after Kennedy's June speech, the large-scale March on Washington culminating at the Lincoln Memorial riveted the nation. Martin Luther King's soaring "I have a dream" speech pressed for the dismantling of Jim Crow. But the march also signaled a rise in black expectations. SNCC's John Lewis used the occasion to goad Kennedy by asking "which side is the federal government on?" – explicitly invoking the issue of the division of power in which race had long been enmeshed.[80] Lewis was pressured against being even more confrontational in a last-minute meeting held in the Lincoln Memorial itself. The statue of the Great Emancipator silently watched over this debate and the ensuing speeches in a moment filled with historical poignancy. This transitional moment was further symbolized by the death of W. E. B. Du Bois, news of which came the very morning of the march. The architect of a civil rights movement that only emerged at the end of his lifetime passed on just as the movement came to fruition.

Under continued pressure, President Lyndon Johnson advocated further reforms, including the landmark 1964 Civil Rights Act. In 1965 he declared that "nothing is of greater significance to the welfare and vitality of this nation than the movement to secure equal rights for Negro Americans."[81] The architect of the Great Society understood that federal authority had to be exerted over the defining issue embedded in states' rights, that of race, if the nation-state and his centralized social policy were to be consolidated and further disruption avoided. When a controversial march in Selma, Alabama, was attacked by local police, Congress was provoked to pass the 1965 Voting Rights Act, which led to massive black voter registration.[82] Not coincidentally then, the high-water mark of centralized state authority and power came together with the peak of protest demanding federal civil rights intervention in 1964 and 1965. Jim Crow was finally legally dead.

A century after the Civil War, the issues that had torn apart the Union finally seemed to be reaching a resolution. The South still resisted federal imposition of civil rights – for instance with a resurgence of the Ku Klux Klan – but such sectionalism and mob action no longer threatened to destroy the Union. The South had been appeased with Jim Crow and increasingly reintegrated into the nation-state. Racial domination had served the purpose of regional reconciliation. By the mid-twentieth century, that central authority was strong enough to turn its power back to race relations, the issue on which its very growth had been forged by earlier avoidance of intervention. Racial domination had allowed Washington to gain enough power to challenge that very racial order and thereby finally consolidate central control.

Of course, describing federally enforced reforms of Jim Crow as simply the culmination of a dynamic between states and the center ignores the popular pressures that catalyzed this outcome. Politicians had long been accustomed to appeasing sectional animosity by allowing for Jim Crow. While this policy allowed for the gradual incorporation of the South, it also had gradually further solidified prior racial identity and new forms of opposition, at least in the South where Jim Crow was strongest. Politicians' frame of reference was shaken by popular pressure posing a new threat to stability, if not to the state's coercive power. According to longtime activist Willie Ricks, speaking with some exaggeration, "institutions opened up and passed rules of fairness [only] when [the movement] became a physical threat to the United States government."[83] Even as sympathetic a president as Lyndon Johnson had to be pressed to use federal power to fulfill the promise of reform. According to Andrew Young, "LBJ told us he could not give us voting rights in 1964, so we created a crisis."[84] That crisis of mass mobilization forced Johnson to give what he had thought he could not. Southern resistance was overcome; racial domination unifying whites had been met with rising black protest, forcing the end of legal Jim Crow. The circle closed.

National Black Protest and White Backlash

The demise of Jim Crow did not end inequality nor foreclose black protest, which then shifted North, where blacks inspired by the traditions of Du Bois and Garvey had been increasing their numbers as they migrated from the South. Pervasive discrimination and urban segregation concentrated and united blacks, whose cross-class mobilization was further inspired by Southern activism. As the central state consolidated its authority and the national media spread images of discrimination, nationwide black identity and protest emerged more forcefully. Protest in the North now exploded, taking a different form than in the South, reflecting continued regional differences of experience, institutions, and culture. Northern blacks also lived in a society in which race was entrenched, and in a state where racial domination had been regionally enforced, but without legal Jim Crow comparable to the South. Northern blacks had no official racial order enforcing their unity. In a sense, they found themselves in a situation similar to Afro-Brazilians, in an official racial democracy of strong, informal discrimination. As a result, Northern black activism tended to focus on separatist identity building to challenge liberal images of inclusion. In a vicious cycle, riots then discouraged white support for reform, provoking greater black militance. Whereas the federal government had earlier acted against the violence of Southern segregationists, it now shifted to act against black violence.

The federal embrace of civil rights had the unintended effect of reinforcing an emerging spread of the movement to the North. When President Johnson declared to Congress in 1965 that there was "no Negro problem . . . only an American problem," he implicitly nationalized the movement.[85] Activists had already begun to shift their focus accordingly, for once "segregation had fallen, now you see the system as not just about Southern segregation, but also more national."[86] Indeed, democratic inclusion with the end of Jim Crow did not bring an end to discrimination and black economic deprivation nationally. This further convinced many that racism was a national attitude reflected also in Northern black urban poverty, which the civil rights movement had not yet begun to address.[87]

That race was an issue outside of the South was not news to Northern blacks. But the explosion of the civil rights movement in the South both raised expectations of change in the North and inspired Northern black mobilization. In the words of activists: "People in the North saw us being beaten up,"[88] and as "heroic activity was seen on TV [involving] people who look like them being brutalized, . . . in the North they also wanted to struggle."[89]

Between 1940 and 1970, five million blacks had migrated North in search of opportunities, a prominent example of black agency predating mass protest.[90] This migration, made possible by the preservation of a united polity allowing for racial domination, also diminished the sectional focus of race issues, creating a more nationwide racial identity. Northern blacks retained links with their Southern roots, which added to the diffusion: "We went South every summer. We felt connected. . . . People were coming up from the South and telling stories. . . . [Those] Southern experiences enraged us" (Barbara Omalade).[91] Northern blacks responded by saying "let's check out this civil rights stuff and began attending CORE and SNCC meetings and listening" (James Farmer).[92]

The then-established civil rights organizations were primed to take up the challenge in the North. SNCC's 1964 Freedom Summer project had brought South a thousand volunteers, who returned North with a newly radicalized vision reinforced by the murder of three volunteers, two whites and a black. That radicalization was reinforced by the experience of the activists' Mississippi Freedom Democratic Party's (MFDP) failed attempt to be recognized at the Democratic Party convention of 1964. "Disappointed and betrayed" by their abandonment by Johnson and the Democratic Party, SNCC concluded that their previous success at gaining federal support had been "played out."[93] Rising Southern Congressional resistance to civil rights reaffirmed this conclusion.[94] Activists still hoped that protests in the North would force federal support as they had in the South, but they understood, in Marvin Rich's words, that "the struggle in the North would be more complex. The cities were too big for community organizing."[95] The hypocrisy of Northern liberalism – the absence of legal Jim Crow amid pervasive informal discrimination – also made it "difficult to unite the forces and consolidate the attack upon so elusive a target. . . . [We were] unable to zero in on a clearly defined enemy. . . . In the North, the enemy was diffuse, scattered, and often concealed" (James Farmer).[96]

Martin Luther King's 1966 Chicago campaign was the most notable attempt by the Southern-based civil rights organizations to shift their operations North. In the absence of explicit formal segregation as a target of mobilization, King focused on economic opportunity.[97] The difference of concerns from the South was marked. As one Northern activist, Livingston Wingate, noted, "the black cat in [the North] wasn't worried about no damn bus – he'd been riding the bus for fifty years. What he didn't have was the fare."[98] But poverty and exploitation had no single cause that could be easily dramatized in a way comparable to the legal inequities of Jim Crow. Informal residential segregation in Chicago limited blacks, but was not legally codified.[99] And local authorities under Mayor Richard J. Daley were then unlikely to be provoked into serving as advertisements for mobilization comparable to Bull Connor.[100] Veteran activists warned King not to try a Chicago campaign, and when that campaign faltered for lack of a clear focus or victory, King's allies advised, "For God's sake, Martin, this is getting you nowhere! Settle for something" (Willie Ricks).[101] But there was no one thing to settle for, and no external intervention forthcoming.

In the absence of Jim Crow or illegal activity by local officials, the federal government initially saw little or no role in Northern race issues. Disputes over class and poverty were not embedded in the balance of federal power as was the South's official racial segregation.

Activists complained that federal officials told them that the government was very limited in what it could do.[102] The Supreme Court had mandated an end to legal segregation, which the executive could enforce. But there was no comparable mandate for equal economic outcomes, both more difficult to ensure and inconsistent with liberal images of meritocracy. This difference left the movement unable to engage the same dynamic of federal intervention upon which its Southern success had depended.

By 1965, Johnson had apparently concluded that the movement had achieved its aims. Further pressure seemed to Johnson ungrateful and likely to feed a countershift among whites to the right.[103] Even within the movement itself, A. Philip Randolph concluded that "the civil rights revolution has been caught up in a crisis of victory," and activist James Bevel even declared that "there is no more civil rights movement. President Johnson signed it out of existence when he signed the voting-rights bill."[104] Other activists did not see it that way and still held expectations of greater victories, amid declining white and federal support that might have provided such victories.[105]

Having declared victory over Jim Crow and consolidated its power, the federal government lost interest in civil rights. The Democratic Party, having already lost Southern white support, saw no advantage in now antagonizing Northern whites. Instead, Johnson shifted his focus from civil rights to the Great Society, which many whites opposed as a veiled attempt to further help blacks. Later Johnson even lost interest in his poverty programs, shifting his focus to the Vietnam War. Covert surveillance by the FBI – long noted for its opposition to the civil rights movement – fed Johnson's growing resentment and distrust of the movement.[106]

Stokely Carmichael, among others, argued that the increasing fervor of the movement was unfairly blamed for the backlash of federal withdrawal, but it did contribute.[107] The movement's disillusionment and pique exacerbated Washington's withdrawal. Activists spurned Johnson's 1965 conference on civil rights, criticized his appointment of Thurgood Marshall to the Supreme Court, and even launched personal attacks on the wedding of the president's daughter.[108] By 1966, many in the movement had lost all hope of federal support, concluding with SNCC staff conferees that whereas "we asked the federal government to hand us solutions . . . [now] we see the government willing to perpetuate white supremacy."[109] Jim Crow was dead, but racism and socioeconomic discrimination beneficial to whites remained significantly unchanged by public intervention.

Much as the first Reconstruction had been reversed by Redemption, the second Reconstruction led to a second Redemption amid demands for an end to civil rights reforms. By 1964, Republican presidential candidate Barry Goldwater was attacking federal intervention and civil rights to boost his campaign. In the South, George Wallace and other white politicians sought to benefit from white resentment at federal intervention, using attacks on Washington and on black protest, despite the rise in black voting.[110] Northerners joined Southerners in this backlash, in part reflecting dismay over the movement's unwillingness to accept victory and its incursions into the North, where most whites believed there was no problem. According to Percy Sutton, "we began to step on the toes of some of our friends who had been with us. It was frightening to whites when we began challenging where we lived" in the North.[111] Or as Hosea Williams explains in retrospect, "most of our support had come from the North. If we went there, I knew they would defect."[112]

White backlash, the federal government's inability or unwillingness to redress Northern discrimination, and rising black Northern mobilization all contributed to a volatile mix. Riots exploded in New York in 1964, eighteen days after Johnson signed the Civil Rights Act, as if to signal that such legislative redress was insufficient to meet Northern expectations and needs. Shortly after the Selma march in 1965, the Watts area of Los Angeles rioted, leaving thirty-six dead. In 1967, Newark, Detroit, and thirty-eight other cities erupted in violent riots, leaving eighty-four dead. Within three days of King's assassination in 1968, 125 cities and towns burned.[113] Between 1964 and 1969 there were more than four hundred "disorders"; the contagion spread from larger cities to smaller and diminished only after potential centers of unrest had already burned and police had increased patrols and curfews.[114]

The direct causes of the riots are difficult to specify. Certainly, experiences of discrimination, police brutality, unemployment, inadequate housing, and the like contributed to their potential. But such conditions were all too common in Northern ghettoes, and the actual participants in riots were generally not the most economically underprivileged members of the community.[115]

The context of the civil rights movement may have been more

directly relevant. Roger Wilkins argues that "the riots emerged out of seeing [what was happening in] the South. Spirits were stirred, [while] nothing was happening with them" in the North.[116] Northern blacks "saw changes in the South, they saw the president signing the Civil Rights Act with all the Negro leaders in attendance, but they saw no changes in their own lives."[117] Such disillusion reflected both federal inaction in the North and a rising nationalization of black identity and aspirations following migration north and spreading images of activism. These circumstances did not provoke riots in the South, where the recent end of Jim Crow was widely celebrated by blacks. And in the North, recent migrants seeing greater opportunity than in the South were themselves less prone to riot. But more established Northern blacks were angered by the lack of opportunity compared to whites and retained ties to the South that may have inspired a desire to somehow associate themselves with the mobilization in the South.[118] Bob Mants argues that there was a direct relationship: "Every time there was a major demonstration in the South, there was a sporadic reaction in the North. In the North, they saw their kinfolk in the South getting beaten. There were Southern roots to the urban riots. It was the violence in the marches they saw that united people in a common belief."[119] Given the time lag between Southern marches and most Northern riots, such a direct causation seems overdrawn, but the riots did reflect national developments as much as local conditions. Southern protest had inspired Northern activism, which ultimately expressed itself in riots.

Though blacks in the North were less subject to Jim Crow, they had clearly come to identify themselves racially, across regions, with the civil rights movement. They lacked an organized movement themselves, in the absence of an explicit legal target and federal response which had strengthened organizations in the South.[120] The absence of direct federal intervention in the North against a diffuse target of poverty raised resentment among a black populace that now expected such intervention and did not appreciate its limits. According to Martin Luther King, "our summers of riots have been caused by our winters of delay."[121] But what King hopefully saw as delay reflected what others saw as a more fundamental unwillingness and inability to intervene. And in the absence of such intervention, riots were an assertion of black identity and anger, with surveys suggesting that the majority of Northern blacks felt greater racial pride as a consequence of the riots[122] The riots indicated and reinforced that racial identity and mobilization had become national in scope.

In their own way, the riots were akin to the Southern movement as an appeal for federal intervention, though they elicited a different response. Washington had intervened against the violence inflicted by Southern Jim Crow officials, in keeping with the fundamental imperative to restore peace. But mass violence in the North provoked intervention against blacks there and their challenge to social peace. Furthermore, the riots undermined the majority's perception of the movement's legitimacy. Whereas most blacks viewed the riots as spontaneous protests against real grievances, most whites viewed them as conspiratorial or criminal acts.[123] And federal officials now expressed concern that earlier reforms and social programs had raised unreasonable expectations. They were eager not to appear to reward the rioters with further such programs, though some increased social spending from Washington was targeted at optimistically designated "model cities."[124] But by then the Great Society, which had raised expectations of change, was already losing funds to the Vietnam War effort.

The most direct outcome of white backlash against rising black militancy was to help elect a Republican president. With white resentment strong, Richard Nixon's "Southern strategy" of appeasement and a commitment to restore "law and order" helped him to capture the White House in 1968. Voted in by Southern whites abandoning the Democrats and by Northern conservatives, Nixon did not owe anything to the black community.[125] His later cuts in civil rights implementation programs, including his own "Philadelphia Plan," underlined this lack of electoral debt.[126] Expenditures were shifted from social programs to law enforcement.[127] Furthermore, Nixon's policy of "benign neglect" toward blacks and his encouragement of black capitalism as an alternative to protest encouraged a newly resurgent black nationalism.[128] Having previously appealed to America, they now questioned America. By the mid- to late 1960s, many activists had concluded that white America was again more concerned with domestic peace than racial justice. They saw what was described as a backlash as actually representing a racist status quo. Frustrated by the federal government's reluctance to interfere in the North, they increasingly blamed "the system" for continued inequality and injustice, concluding that "the federal government ain't nothing but a white man.''[129] And so they turned to the tradition of separatism, using their exit from the mainstream as a shock tactic designed to gain attention and to force further redress from a system that had spurned them.[130]

The rise of black nationalism not only reflected a shift of the dynamic between the movement and federal government, but also a regional realignment within the movement itself. Northern blacks had become further engaged in the movement and had outpaced the South in protests by the latter half of the 1960s.[131] They were less concerned with ending formal segregation than with achieving greater economic opportunity, which was being blocked by informal discrimination. Federal legislation had made little impact on their lives. Localized boycotts and sit-ins were unlikely to result in major structural change. And so Northern blacks instead turned from King's approach to assertions of separatism to gain political and economic power. Such Black Power had its roots in Southern experiences. According to Bob Mants, Lowndes County, Alabama, "taught us Black Power," for it was there that SNCC activists listened to rural blacks' suspicions of whites and launched the Black Panther Party. In Mississippi the Black Power slogan was first used on a march in 1966, but it soon came to be seen as a Northern development, signaling both some regional convergence and the rise of Northern activism.[132]

Class realignment coincided with regional shift. The Southern civil rights movement had fundamentally involved the black middle class and had benefited them most directly, for instance with the provision of government jobs. But this relatively better-off group in the North was pushed to reaffirm its solidarity with the larger group of black poor who had not so benefited.[133] Activists described Black Power as "a call to the black middle class to come home . . . so that all blacks, haves and have nots, can have more."[134] Black Power was both ennobling and empowering in providing a link to the black middle class, unifying Northern blacks on the basis of racial identity and their common experience of discrimination.

The focus on encouraging racial identity was at the core of the Black Power movement. The most notable symbolic move was the expression of positive racial identity, which did not require white support. Seeking a form of less tangible but real psychological power, the Black Power movement focused on black self-identification.[135] In part, this assertion of identity was cultural, for instance in the wearing of dashikis and Afro hairstyles. Black nationalists claimed a tie to Africa, then itself proclaiming independence.[136] Beyond cultural separatism, some advocates of Black Power stressed the need for self-determination, or for separate black capitalism, ironically in the tradition of Booker T. Washington.[137] Alternatively, Black Power was described as consistent with American pluralism, following the logic that "before a group can enter the open society, it must first close ranks. . . . What we have needed most has been the opportunity for the whole group."[138]

Though Black Power remained vaguely defined, focusing on varying mixes of culture, politics, and economics, it was unified by a focus on asserting a positive racial identity, with strategy adjusted accordingly. Symbolizing this focus was the replacement of the old term "Negro" with "black," embracing unity based on physical traits and shared experience. Integration as a demand or tactic was rejected as a middle-class preoccupation unlikely to meet the needs of the majority of blacks and destructive of black pride and independence.[139] Consistent with this reasoning, and similar to South Africa's Black Consciousness movement, whites were increasingly excluded from the movement, in part to "convey the revolutionary idea . . . that black people are able to do things themselves."[140] As the movement shifted from demands of concrete redress through appeals to allies to a focus on black identity, whites were no longer needed or wanted. And the shift away from integration was consistent with a diminished strategic commitment to nonviolence, which had so appealed to whites. Many blacks had become frustrated at seeing peaceful protests violently repressed, and had become more willing to countenance or use counterviolence.[141] And as the Black Power movement was eager to embrace the urban riots as expressions of racial identity, for some "Black Power became the cry for burning down the cities."[142] In the tradition of Algerian revolutionary writer Franz Fanon, violence was seen as a positive expression of identity.

For all of its ideological and strategic distinctiveness, there remains some dispute as to how widespread or significant the Black Power movement was. According to Daniel Patrick Moynihan, "there was no transition to Black Power, other than among a few elites and in the media."[143] Kwame Ture (aka Stokely Carmichael) counters that whites "always pretend that the nationalist tendency doesn't exist," and former activist Marvin Rich warns against "denigrating Black

Power [proponents] for being few."[144] Polls suggest that in 1966 black nationalist leaders such as Carmichael enjoyed a 19 percent popularity rating among blacks. In 1970, 42.2 percent of blacks viewed Black Power favorably, compared to only 10.7 percent of whites.[145] Before his death, King himself acknowledged the need to increase racial pride and acknowledged the rising influence of Black Power while at the same time criticizing it.[146]

Perhaps the best indicator of the significance of Black Power was its rising influence within existing movement organizations, and the rise of new leaders and groups associated with its ideology. As early as 1965, SNCC's John Lewis argued for a black-controlled movement.[147] The next year, Stokely Carmichael became chair of SNCC, arguing for a shift from nonviolent fieldwork to more assertive black identity as a means to positive racial identification. Carmichael sought to awaken "the black community to an awareness of blackness, that is black consciousness," and to unify the black bourgeoisie and youth.[148] White participants were seen as an impediment to this assertion of black identity, and so their SNCC membership was first limited in 1964, and then prohibited in 1967.[149] A similar development occurred within CORE, which by 1964 had begun to focus more on ideology than a concrete program, and insisted on having a black chair. Eventually CORE adopted enough Black Power rhetoric to lead most whites to drift away without being formally expelled.[150]

The shift to Black Power was also demonstrated by the emergence of new organizations, most notably the Black Panthers.[151] Founded in 1966 in the 85 percent black Lowndes County, Alabama, and then spreading to the north and California, the Panthers rejected "the degrading begging which has gone hand in hand with the civil rights movement when it has been subordinated to white liberalism."[152] At the same time it effectively discouraged white membership, while still receiving liberal white donations. And while Panthers dismissed nonviolence, even openly carrying guns, this show of force was more psychological assertion and media attention grabber than a viable option of armed resistance.[153] Even their organized provision of community service was designed primarily as a propaganda tool to win trust and prove their competency, again similar to the Black Consciousness movement in South Africa.[154] In 1968, the Panthers had 5,000 members, but by the following year it was largely in disarray,

the result of internal divisions, ideological disputes and power struggles encouraged by law enforcement officials' surreptitious efforts to
sow discord and direct police assaults.[155]

The Panthers, like many other black nationalists, were inspired by
the words and life of Malcolm X, whose original base was the rising
Nation of Islam separatist religious movement.[156] Informed by the
Black Muslim ideology, Malcolm was an early proponent of ending
black self-hate through a positive assertion of an inclusive black racial
identity and self-determination. His and the Nation of Islam's stance
was an American version of Fanon and a precursor of South Africa's
Black Consciousness movement. This philosophy offered a prototype
of Black Power, advocating a return to Africa more as a philosophical
assertion than as a practical proposal. And Malcolm purposefully used
separatist militancy to attract media attention to spread his message.[157] Spreading that message of identity was his aim, not the immediate results pursued by the civil rights leadership. Still, Malcolm's
militancy may have strengthened the bargaining position of more
moderate leaders in a radical flanking effect.[158] But whereas King had
appealed to and believed in the American dream, Malcolm saw America as a nightmare from which he sought to awaken both blacks and
whites.[159] Though this basic difference remained, by the end of his
life Malcolm began to shift toward a more programmatic focus and
an alliance with King and civil rights organizations such as SNCC,
after being expelled by the Nation of Islam for violating orders.[160]
But the prospect for convergence was lost with the assassinations that
followed. Malcolm was killed by Black Muslims in 1965, before the
white backlash and the height of the movement that evoked his memory.

Though the movements symbolized by King and Malcolm X remained distinct, together they demonstrated the emergence of nationwide black unity and protest. The Southern-based civil rights
movement succeeded at pressing for federal intervention and for the
end of Jim Crow. Bolstered by migration, the more Northern-based
Black Power movement focused on consolidating black identity and
gaining socioeconomic redress. As the nation-state had been consolidated, so had black identity and protest. Regional distinctions remained, but a two-front movement applied strong pressure on the
federal government to overturn racial domination and then to encourage greater economic equality.

The Movement Fractures

Even in the wake of historic success, black unity and protest eventually faltered. The target of legal Jim Crow had fallen and federal intervention for ending poverty had peaked, then begun to diminish. But Washington's efforts to meet black demands and to contain their challenges to nation-state stability had profound if unforeseen consequences. Though discrimination and segregation continued, anti-poverty and related programs further advanced the black middle class, exacerbating the class rift among blacks. Growing electoral participation incorporated black voters, but also diluted their impact within the larger electorate. More militant blacks sought to reinforce black unity with calls for separatism and claims of cultural distinction, which moderates belittled as counterproductive for integration. Issues of race continued to tear at the national fabric, but with less ideological coherence or organizational force. The nation-state had become more inclusive, at least officially, dissipating and co-opting black protest.

To the extent that the civil rights movement and Black Power were intended to identify and unify blacks across class lines, government policy responses worked against such unity. Increased social services and education, affirmative action, minority contracting, and government employment all tended to bolster and benefit the black middle class than the poor, with the former doubling in proportion during the 1960s alone.[161] During the 1970s and 1980s, income differences among blacks grew considerably, with the rising black middle class eager to retain their jobs and income, particularly as they had not accumulated a cushion of assets.[162] While such co-optation may not have been purposefully intended by government planners, mobility for some, gained by unified protest, cut against racial solidarity. As the better off "moved up and out, they accommodated themselves," encouraging many whites to believe that discrimination no longer existed.[163] But remaining inequality and black poverty, no longer legally encoded, was then blamed by many whites on black inferiority, tarring the black middle class as well. Thus, the end of legal segregation and rise of the black middle class somewhat diminished racial unity, but the reality and perception of a linked fate did not disappear.[164]

Meanwhile, the black urban poor remained poor and isolated, subject to discrimination and alienated from the mainstream. Close to a third of blacks remained stuck below the poverty line throughout the 1970s and 1980s, suffering from a decline in industrial jobs and rising crime. Black male workers' average earnings in proportion to whites, which had risen from the 1940s to 1970s, stagnated after 1973.[165] Even in Alabama's rural Lowndes County, where the Black Panthers originated, most blacks remained in abject poverty.[166] Blacks remained consistently more likely to be unemployed, more likely to fall below official poverty lines, unable to get home mortgages, and stuck in poor neighborhoods.[167] This continued poverty also led some young ghetto residents to condemn more moderate and well-off blacks for having abandoned the less well-off, exacerbating the class division.

Particularly during the 1970s and 1980s, participation in electoral politics was seen by many as the way to avoid a class rift within the black community and to advance that community as a whole. Enfranchised in the South by the 1965 Voting Rights Act and in the North via migration, more than 50 percent of African-Americans voted during the early 1970s. The number of black elected officials rose to more than three thousand in the same period.[168] Ironically, informal segregation encouraged such participation by effectively creating racial voting blocks able to elect their own representatives.[169] Civil rights activists saw such participation as a logical outcome of their demands for the franchise, and even Black Power advocates embraced the prospect of greater representation as a form of self-determination.[170] Such participation indicated a continued belief in integration, with those blacks feeling more integrated in American society also more likely to vote. In Malcolm's words, they preferred the "ballot to the bullet."[171] Most black votes continued to flow toward the Democrats, following the New Deal transition of that party to the leading adherent of federal social intervention from which blacks hoped to and did benefit.[172]

Over time, many blacks became disillusioned with electoral participation. Much as legislative reform had led to disenchantment for lack of concrete change, many later concluded, in activist Hosea Williams's words, that "all these black politicians haven't meant a damn thing."[173] As a minority, blacks could not outvote whites, who were increasingly voting for conservative Dixiecrats and Republicans. The exception remained those black-majority urban districts where political power was consolidated, but such victories still did not translate into improved living conditions.[174] Resulting black voter apathy was overcome temporarily by the enthusiasm for Jesse Jackson's 1984 and 1988 presidential races, but disillusionment quickly returned thereafter, and black voter participation fell precipitously.[175]

Rising black disillusionment with electoral politics was reinforced during the 1980s and thereafter by the continued backlash of white sentiment and government policy. The limited impact of earlier reforms reinforced white racists' arguments about the futility of official redress, ignoring the impact of past and ongoing discrimination. During the Reagan and Bush administrations, black federal employment and budgets for civil rights implementation were reduced while the black poor lost further ground.[176] This trajectory ultimately led to a shift back to further states' rights after the 1994 Republican Congressional victory. As the federal balance of power was again reconfigured toward less central power, blacks suffered under a second Redemption. Much as they had after the first Reconstruction, many blacks felt abandoned by Washington. Past reforms were rescinded amid the end of progress, with earlier commitments to change ignored and expectations dashed.[177]

Backpedaling of policy, omission of further gains, and discrimination provoked a black separatist response similar to that of the late 1960s, but with less coherence. Some blacks expressed their disillusionment with the prospect for a better life in the North by returning to the South. Others rioted, most notably in 1992 in Los Angeles, where black anger over rising poverty and crime was turned against Asians and Latinos. Urban youth joined a resurgence of interest in the thought and imagery of Malcolm X, thereby hoping to reassert black identity, purity, unity, and conviction. This shift was denigrated by more established blacks as "a feel good thing . . . of barking at the moon" (Charles Rangel).[178] But militant rhetoric appealed nonetheless, evident in a popular surge of interest in and assertions of multicultural distinctiveness tied to race. This interest was perhaps most evident in the rising popularity of the Nation of Islam leader Louis Farrakhan, in the lyrics of Rap music, and in popular theories about antiblack conspiracies that embraced "victimology."[179] Some blacks even advocated the return of a "one drop of blood rule" to distinguish and unify all blacks, thereby effectively seeking to replace Jim Crow's unifying definition with a self-imposed equivalent. Former civil rights activists were led to wonder, "Why do they want segregation back?"[180] To preserve group solidarity and some minority power, many blacks reverted to assertions of essentialist difference.

The recent rise of separatist black identity reflects not only black disillusionment with white America, but also a collective black interest in defining and asserting a category no longer imposed by the state. If previously the state had done the work of reinforcing identity via imposed racial domination, such formal rules had now ended. Racial identity had been refined by Jim Crow and related policies; that target was now lost. At the same time, many African-Americans concluded that "anti-discrimination law . . . has largely succeeded in eliminating symbolic manifestations of racial oppression, but has allowed the perpetuation of material subordination of Blacks," despite class differences.[181] Blacks remained linked by informal discrimination and indeed, the black middle class's greater contact with whites led them to experience this discrimination most directly, producing widespread disillusionment.[182] To challenge continued subordination, "the most valuable political asset of the Black community has been its ability to assert a collective identity."[183] Physical distinctions of race that had earlier been categorized to enforce racial domination were now embraced as a basis for black unity and power. But in the absence of "clear simple issues [and] . . . a visible enemy which stirs the emotions and stiffens resistance" (Joseph Lowery), assertions of identity become more difficult.[184] With the implementation of such reforms, not only did many whites conclude that there was nothing else the law could do, but a defining target of black identity formation was lost.[185]

Official racial domination's imposed racial categories had created shared experiences according to which blacks defined themselves, building on prior cultural and social ties. Many of the early intellectual efforts of the black elite during the twentieth century had been aimed at turning the category of racial domination into a basis for a more positive assertion of identity, efforts that were hindered by continued regional or related distinctions and Southern repression.

Only when federal authority was pressed to impose nationwide reforms of the racial order was corresponding national racial identity finally consolidated. The possibility of such reforms also provided the opportunity for further mobilization around racial identity, giving rise to the civil rights movement, creating still further opportunities. Again regional distinctions remained. Washington had allowed the

South to impose Jim Crow until the mid-1950s before, pressed by protest, it imposed reforms. As a result, Southern blacks remained optimistic, inspiring a moderate form of mobilization for integration. No such dynamic applied to the North, where there was less formal Jim Crow and less legal and historical basis for federal intervention. Northern blacks received no encouragement regarding intervention, and so turned away from white allies toward more separatist and cultural movements.

As the racial order was officially dismantled, the target of identity formation and mobilization faded. The recent result has been a crisis of uncertainty and some fracturing of racial identity, though efforts at retained solidarity have continued, informed by continued discrimination. White racism and black racial solidarity persisted, in an ongoing dynamic. Black solidarity remains evident in both electoral politics and cultural assertions, but divisions have grown and mass collective protest has diminished.

10

Breaching Brazil's Pact of Silence

Race making from above and below also has been an interactive process in Brazil. If legal racial domination elsewhere reinforced racial identity and provoked protest among blacks, then did the relative absence of such official domination in Brazil reduce the salience of racial identification and restrain mobilization there? Certainly a minimum of identity formation is an essential basis for mobilization, prior to the influence of resources or opportunities. Without consolidation of an identity, mobilization is less likely. Indeed, Brazil's racial order has not been challenged by assertions of black solidarity and protest comparable to the anti-apartheid or civil rights movements. Despite significant discrimination, racial democracy has engendered more muted protest, suggesting that state actions are more consequential for race relations than informal social practices. This general argument can be assessed against Brazilian experience, as a negative test of the patterns found in South Africa and the United States.

That there has been rising black protest in modern Brazil demonstrates that racial identity and mobilization are not simply reactions to state policy. Instead, Afro-Brazilian solidarity has built upon particularly strong cultural and religious traditions and been reinforced by evident discrimination and inequality. Identity has been asserted and protests pressing the state to act have been made. But as elsewhere, state policy has often shaped particular outcomes. For instance, state receptivity has provoked more moderate forms of mobilization, and greater repression and hardening of state policies have produced greater militancy. Brazil thus also gives us a positive way of testing the patterns suggested in the other two cases.

Constrained Afro-Brazilian Solidarity under Racial Democracy

Brazilian experience both before and shortly after abolition demonstrates a tradition of black protest as well as some constraints. Slaves continually imported in large numbers retained social and cultural ties augmenting a vibrant tradition of revolts and *quilombos*. To contain such unrest, nineteenth-century Brazilian authorities encouraged large-scale manumission, creating an intermediate category of freed slaves, often mulatto. More preferential treatment for these intermediaries discouraged nonwhite solidarity, with some freed slaves even resisting the end of the slave trade out of fear that decreased supply would lead to their own reenslavement. By the 1870s, some freedmen supported slavery in general as a way to ensure their greater privilege.[1] In response to earlier protests, the authorities had learned to dampen the potential for further mobilization through differential treatment, co-optation, and the projection of prospects for mobility.

Brazil's post-abolition racial order did not impose official racial domination. Brazilians instead claimed to live in essentially peaceful relations, for instance avoiding the lynchings and race riots seen elsewhere.[2] A more critical view, that of Anani Dzidzienyo, suggests that "the official Brazilian ideology of non-discrimination, by not reflecting reality and indeed by camouflaging it, achieves without tension the same results as do overtly racist societies."[3] The relevant point is that the ideology of racial democracy and absence of official Jim Crow or apartheid had the effect on Afro-Brazilians of "numbing them from the inside . . . barring almost definitively any possibility of their self-affirmation, integrity or identity" (Abdias do Nascimento).[4] Informal discrimination did not consolidate identity and protest comparably to what official exclusion provoked elsewhere.

Comparison with official segregation in South Africa and the United States clarifies the argument. In the absence of legal racism, informal discrimination via customs and consensus is less defining, less explicit in its origin, and more difficult to challenge.[5] With no defining or unifying legal racial order, Afro-Brazilians were "compelled to face prejudice in a state of great psychological confusion and without the means to group themselves into integrated racial minorities."[6] As described by Afro-Brazilian historian Clóvis Moura, "our biggest, fundamental problem is a lack of united identity. . . . [A]ll is fragmented here."[7]

State policies encouraged such fragmentation by constructing diverse categories and using them in a manner that discouraged racial solidarity. Since 1890 the official census has categorized Brazilians as black, white, and at least two intermediate groups, with the latter growing proportionately and thereby "scientifically" validating whitening.[8] No strict biracial boundaries were enforced, and racial categories were not used as the basis for segregation or other forms of racial domination that would have contradicted the image of fluidity. Instead, the state embraced a cultural focus on "color" more than "race," thereby reinforcing the salience of a wide array of physical differences rather than potentially antagonistic larger groupings. Surveys consistently found multiple self-identifications reflecting the physical variations produced by generations of miscegenation.[9] But while such a physical continuum has been forced into dichotomous categories by state policies and practices elsewhere, this has not occurred in Brazil. Multiple identities have been allowed and encouraged, avoiding polarized conflict inconsistent with the prevalent ideology of tolerance.

Brazil's racial democracy encouraged submissiveness to a social order in which there is no legal racial domination against which identity formation and mobilization can be targeted. Brazil's inclusive yet rigid social hierarchy was preserved amid party rivalries, transitions between democracy and authoritarianism, and growing class competition. As a result, many Afro-Brazilians long accepted notions of their own inferiority reflected in the established white value-based hierarchy, seeking incorporation and advancement within that hierarchical order more than they challenged it.[10] To advance in that hierarchy, "lots of blacks don't want to be black," and "every black wants to be white."[11] Racial identity was rejected as an impediment to purportedly open mobility, rather than embraced as a basis for challenging blocked mobility. Jobs are still advertised with a preference for "a good appearance," which means white, encouraging blacks to hope for economic advance through passing and a denial of racial distinction.[12]

Rather than seeking to advance collectively, Afro-Brazilians tended to seek incorporation as individuals and to avoid any racial identification that would constrain them. Black hopes for advancement through denial of race effectively incorporated Afro-Brazilians in a pact of silence that long preserved the informal racial order.

The relative lack of consolidated racial identity and its debilitating effect on collective action are indicated by the divisions the social order encouraged among Afro-Brazilians. As long as most blacks believed in racial democracy and in the possibility of individual advancement, they tended to see other blacks as potential competitors more than fellow victims of discrimination. Class divisions and alienation thus curtailed the prospect of racial unity, for instance with the rare successful black often disclaiming any racial association, identity, or protest.[13] Such class division tended to reinforce and be reinforced by overlapping physical distinctions. Lighter-colored peoples, marginally more likely to rise to the middle class than darker, sought to distance themselves from blacks and even themselves mistreated blacks.[14] In the absence of enforced segregation, racial unity across class was elusive. Most Afro-Brazilians long saw their deprivation as a reflection of class status rather than race. They sought redress within the union movement and from the corporatist state, rather than through protest.

The relative absence of unified racial identity among Afro-Brazilians has been remarkable, given the commonality of Afro-Brazilian experience. General inequality in Brazil has long remained among the most marked in the world. And though studies of racial distinctions were long suppressed, recent analysis demonstrates that such general inequality has consistently followed race lines of informal segregation and discrimination. For instance, the average income for whites in 1976 was double that of nonwhites, a greater differential of income by race than in the United States.[15] Afro-Brazilians are still disproportionately unemployed or employed in lower-skilled and lower-paying job categories, and generally receive lower wages than whites.[16] Whites are eight times as likely to be employers than are blacks, and one-third as likely to be manual laborers.[17] Such differences between nonwhites and whites are vastly greater than any differences between mulattoes and blacks.[18] Accordingly, Afro-Brazilians tend to have a shorter life expectancy, and are more likely to live in distinct neighborhoods reinforcing lower-class status.[19]

Socioeconomic inequalities in Brazil have not been the result of official racial segregation, but reflect long-standing informal discrimination. State policies did exacerbate inequality, for instance with the earlier selective encouragement of white immigration displacing black labor, but such official discrimination was not applied domestically. Income differentials in part reflected lower levels of literacy and education among Afro-Brazilians. Among Afro-Brazilians, the proportion who can read is roughly half that of whites, and the porportion who complete nine years of school is less than one-third that of whites. The result is higher black unemployment or lower-paying jobs and residence in poorer neighborhoods.[20] But statistical studies have demonstrated that up to half of the lower economic status of Afro-Brazilians cannot be accounted for by education or jobs held, and can be attributed to racial discrimination.[21] Thus, while the adage that "money whitens" may be true, it is largely irrelevant, as few Afro-Brazilians have gained the resources to enjoy such fluidity.[22]

The persistence of inequality was not by itself sufficient to provoke a high degree of racial identity and mobilization. The lack of legal racial domination was highly consequential. Though black fates are linked, they were not generally so perceived. Deprivation according to race did not engender corresponding levels of solidarity or protest comparable to that in South Africa or the United States. Certainly inequality and experiences of informal discrimination were and are widely recognized among Afro-Brazilians, but in the absence of formal rules enforcing such inequality, many long believed that their own lack of advancement was due to other causes, such as lack of education or their own failings.[23] Racism was rarely blamed, though such an explanation of poverty would be less self-damaging and is commonplace in the United States and South Africa.

The myth of racial democracy was the major impediment to black identity formation and mobilization.[24] Even for blacks, the psychological investment in this myth has been profound: "when you are black and poor, you think your problems are due to being poor. That is more comfortable, since I can be not poor, say if I win the lottery, but there is no escape from being black" (activist-official Carlos Alberto Medeiros).[25] To retain hope, racism was underemphasized, even by its victims. As a result, few blacks saw any need for racial separatism or activism that might reinforce a distinct identity.[26] And as "whites say there is no racism, they give no support to black movements."[27] Not surprisingly then, efforts at racial mobilization were stunted, small in number, and deprived of white allies.[28] Race long did not provide an identity, issue, or basis for mass action.

Afro-Brazilian Activism Emerges

Despite the constraints of racial democracy and purported mobility, black Brazilian identity has been asserted and mobilized, particularly during transitions in state rule. With the consolidation of corporatism, such activism sought promised inclusion. Gradually, as discrimination and limits on advancement remained, activists turned to more aggressive assertions of racial identity and grievances. By the late 1980s, amid democratization and industrialization, the image of racial democracy was ever more contested. Still, the lack of official racial domination reinforcing racial identity left the Afro-Brazilian movement to form such an identity more fully for itself. Cultural and essentialist distinctions were asserted, gradually forcing the Brazilian ruling elite to reconsider the implications of national inclusion.

Those Afro-Brazilian movements that have emerged have been constrained by both economic factors and political context. As was initially true in the United States and South Africa, Brazilian racial movements have begun with the black, urban, emergent middle class.[29] Not only do wealthier blacks have access to education, international influences, and the resources with which to begin such mobilization, but they are less likely to attribute lack of mobility to being poor. "When you are not poor and still facing problems, then (racial) consciousness is unavoidable" (Carlos Alberto Medeiros).[30] As a higher proportion of the black middle class lived in the more developed Southeast, much black mobilization has been centered there, though the overall proportion of blacks is higher in the poorer Northeast.[31] And reflecting this small elite base, much black protest long remained a "revolution within the order," relatively respectful of the well-entrenched social hierarchy in which blacks hoped to advance.[32]

The first major post-abolition black movement in Brazil was the Frente Negra Brasileira, founded in 1931 during the height of state efforts to construct an image of racial democracy. Inspired by discussions in the newspaper *Clarim da Alvorada*, the Frente established its own newspaper in 1933, *A Voz da Raça*. It advocated equal rights through assimilation, at least among the literate black elite suffering from rising deprivation during the Depression.[33] This elite focus limited the Frente to a relatively small constituency – those who could read the newspapers and expected greater advancement; there were fewer than six thousand members in its largest chapter in São Paulo. And the moderate tone of the Frente reflected the interests of a black elite more eager to become part of the social order than to challenge it.[34]

The Frente remained highly patriotic, claiming allegiance to "God, country, race and family," in that order, and disclaiming any form of separatism.[35] Though divided, it remained largely loyal to the regime of Getúlio Vargas (provisional president, 1930–4; constitutionally elected president, 1934–7 and 1951–4; dictator, 1937–45), who had provided the "climate of a general opening" in which the Frente had grown.[36] And consistent with its patriotism and support for Vargas, the Frente embraced racial democracy, calling for its more complete elaboration.[37] Rather than challenge the racial order, the Frente reaffirmed it.

By 1936 the Frente was sufficiently confident of being accepted into the Brazilian mainstream to transform itself into a political party. The following year, Vargas seized dictatorial power and banned all parties. Just short of the fiftieth anniversary of peaceful abolition, organized Afro-Brazilians had affirmed their loyalty to the state. Official edict then subordinated the most prominent black association to the emerging corporatist order, in which race was not a category of representation. According to the state, black needs would be met together with the needs of all Brazilians, and would not require any separate mobilization or efforts.

During the restored democracy of 1945 to 1964, others took up where the dismembered Frente had left off. Learning from the banning of 1937 to avoid party politics, Abdias do Nascimento and his followers instead focused on an assertion of black culture. Most notably, his Teatro Experimental do Negro used drama to "redeem black African values," as a sort of informally political "group therapy."[38] According to do Nascimento, the purpose was "to assert African heritage. . . . People didn't have an identity. . . . First we must say 'I am black,' and increase visibility, to facilitate mobilization."[39] But again, do Nascimento's efforts remained relatively elitist in encouraging "negritude" among the small black middle class of Rio de Janeiro. He purposefully avoided any class rhetoric that might have attracted a wider following but would have diminished the focus on race and culture.[40]

Do Nascimento's focus on African culture was part of a more general trend felt among all Afro-Brazilians, who had retained ties to African culture from slavery. But such a focus remained double-edged in its assertion of a distinct black culture and in its demands for the incorporation of such distinctiveness within a heterodox Brazilian national culture. Samba, macumba, *umbanda*, and *candomblé* had all retained and reinforced aspects of African culture. But these practices had also gained white followings and emerged as symbols of national unity encouraged by Vargas and his successors.[41] By the 1940s, the Brazilian state had sought to control these cultural expressions, for instance by subsidizing *carnaval* (the Brazilian Mardi Gras), already generally inclusive and hierarchical, and mandating "pro-Brazilian" themes in the *carnaval* competitions.[42] Such penetration worked the other way as well, with *umbanda* groups and leaders serving as patrons able to negotiate for state services, thus reinforcing the social hierarchy at least as much as they challenged it culturally.[43] Even the African religious aspects of *umbanda* were merged with Catholic symbolism in a process of synchronism, and generally avoided party politics. Separate black associations within the Catholic Church, aimed at helping to stem falling church popularity, were similarly incorporating. And by the 1970s, the Black Soul movement, which tried to provide for a separate cultural expression, was also controlled and highly commercialized.[44] Afro-Brazilian culture was continually folded into a Brazilian culture celebrating tolerance consistent with the ideology of racial democracy.

If purely cultural expressions remained somewhat ambivalent between asserting racial distinctiveness and incorporating with the overall population, the Movimento Negro Unificado (MNU) finally broke through to somewhat greater militancy and a national following in the 1970s. The MNU was based on local *centros de luta* coordinated by a national executive and annual congresses; though informed by events in the United States, it remained a response to local conditions of continued repression and inequality that had finally raised skepticism about the validity of racial democracy.[45] With the reforms and initial mobilization for democracy of the late 1970s, in which the MNU played a role, gradual opening allowed for criticism of racial democracy to be expressed more openly than previously. But continued repression forced the MNU to retain a focus on culture while at the same time "legitimating the struggle against racism."[46]

The major thrust of the MNU was to work for black self-esteem and to establish that racial discrimination and "marginalization" was a fact of life that had to be challenged. Though often combined with Marxist analysis, race remained the central issue of the movement. And just proclaiming race a national question was a radical stance in Brazil.[47] Still, the focus on asserting black solidarity attests to a recognition that such racial identity remained unsolidified. The "individual solution" of integration and advancement advocated earlier by the Frente was rejected in favor of a more conflictual approach, focused on ideology rather than mass mobilization.[48] The state had left the terrain of identity formation to activists, but also thereby restrained mass mobilization.

The strengths of the MNU also suggest its limits. The movement was and has remained relatively intellectual, elitist, and middle-class, with fewer than two thousand active members.[49] At its height in 1982, none of the MNU's candidates for public office was elected, suggesting a general view that it was too elistist and "too advanced" to gain broad popularity.[50] Its ideological concern appealed to elites but not others, particularly after the economic decline of the 1980s raised more concrete concerns than those it addressed. Given its intellectual and cultural focus, the MNU did not mobilize and has failed to gain popularity in the favela slums and among the large population of illiterates.[51]

With the return to democracy in the mid-1980s, mobilization around race could potentially be directed into electoral politics. The constituency of such electoral efforts was expanded by the 1985 abandonment of a literacy requirement for voting.[52] For instance, 31.9 percent of the 1988 candidates for Salvador's municipal offices were Afro-Brazilian. Out of thirty-five positions, five blacks were elected, though most of them generally denied the existence of racial discrimination and sought support among both blacks and whites by avoiding any explicit racial identification.[53] Such denial was particularly evident in Bahia, where Afro-Brazilians remained reluctant to identify themselves and their interests in racial terms even when they were in the majority.[54] According to do Nascimento, "all the [black] politicians are afraid to use race. The ones who use this speech are the target of repressive forces . . . [and] the great part of blacks don't want racial discourse. The number of conscious people is very small."[55]

An exception to this avoidance of race issues was offered by Rio de Janeiro's Benedita da Silva, elected to the National Congress as its first black woman in 1986 and later elected to the Senate. Her explicit denunciations of racism have directly challenged the image of racial democracy. But as a politician she remained concerned about explicitly addressing racial issues, recognizing that the myth of inclusion was still widely believed by her own constituency. Da Silva acknowledges that racial identification can be more of an electoral impediment than a useful base of support:

> When we use race, we have more difficulties. . . . In Brazil, it doesn't help to use race; the identity is not strong. . . . Even blacks say we have no racism. . . . [They say] we are poor, not because we are black. . . . In my campaign it was the intellectuals who raised the question of race.[56]

Certainly, the general lack of any explicit use of racial politics to win votes in a setting of tremendous inequality remains striking.

The avoidance of race by most candidates for elected office was consistent with the platforms of most left-leaning parties and organizations. While the Workers' Party (PT) has put forward prominent blacks for election, including Benedita da Silva, the party itself has avoided any strong commitments on race, seen as divisive and a deflection from the primary focus on class. The PT's leader, Luiz Incío "Lula" da Silva, has been criticized by black activists like Luis Alberto for "having a consciousness of class and not a consciousness of race."[57] This bias follows that of the increasingly powerful unions out of which the PT emerged. The major union federation, Central Única dos Trabalhadores (CUT), officially supported the black movement, while at the same time retaining a focus on class. Only in the 1990s did CUT explicitly condemn racial discrimination.

There have been some party organizations willing to engage the subject of race. The Partido Democrático Trabalhista (PDT), influenced by prominent black members such as do Nascimento and Joel Rufino dos Santos, has been eager to appeal to the strong black popular culture movement in Rio and elsewhere. The PDT has "recognized the race issue as central," included a condemnation of racism as one of the key planks of its platform, and advocated *socialismo moreno* (brown socialism), mixing race and class rhetoric.[58] But other leftists have argued against the idea of *socialismo moreno*. According to Benedita da Silva of the Workers' Party, her party advocates "just socialism. There is no color to socialism."[59]

In general, the Brazilian left has remained primarily focused on class issues or gender, seen as a more likely basis for mobilization than race. Popular ambivalence about racial identity and the resulting unlikelihood of winning votes with such an appeal justifies fears among leftists that race would divide classes.[60] Afro-Brazilian activists complain that the left "sees us as paranoid, fighting an enemy that doesn't exist."[61] By contrast, issues of gender have been more readily adopted by the left.[62]

Despite these fundamental constraints, assertions of Afro-Brazilian identity and protest have been on the rise, significantly contesting the dominant racial discourse. Activists have challenged the assumption that the state is an inappropriate site to voice racial demands, countering official views of the state's tolerance with the argument that the apparatus of government has been deeply involved in the maintenance of racial distinctions.[63]

To apply pressure on the state, activists have had to confront the impediments of lingering legacies of racial democracy. Most notably, in 1991 a campaign was launched by a coalition of black activists to encourage Afro-Brazilians to identify themselves as black on the upcoming census, in an effort to consolidate a racially defined pressure group. The long tradition of "whitening," inclusion, and social disincentives to black self-identification was challenged. This effort became a "battle over where the boundaries of national identity end and where those of distinct racial identities begin."[64] Whereas the South African and U.S. government had reinforced such boundaries, in Brazil activists faced an uphill struggle to consolidate racial self-identification on which further mobilization could build. To meet this challenge, activists turned to essentialist claims of African origins,[65] trying to counter long-entrenched images of a physical continuum diluting racial identity.

A focus on African roots among black activists again built upon interpretations of cultural activity as an assertion of racial consciousness.[66] But culture can be used to reinforce both domination and resistance. Afro-Brazilian activists have tended to assume that assertions of African culture are a central component of resistance and identity formation. For instance, they have highlighted the history of the *quilombos* as evidence of such African resistance. But the state has consistently sought to absorb such cultural assertions. The result has been that expressions of African culture have given many activists the sense that they are mobilizing, without posing a real challenge to the state or informal racial order. For instance, the leader of the largest African cultural group in Salvador, Bahia, OLODUM, embraces the use of culture as "an indirect route" to political activity and assertion.[67] Yet there remains little evidence that such cultural activity has produced greater political assertiveness or power, even in Bahia where blacks are the majority; it may instead serve to reinforce the official Brazilian image of inclusiveness.

For all of this ambivalence and ideological constraint, the rising discourse about race has been acknowledged by the state. Officials have moved to incorporate any proto-movement among Afro-Brazilians. For instance, the centenary of abolition was widely celebrated in 1988. President Sarney used the opportunity to embrace the African component of Brazilian culture. The general tone of the celebration remained self-congratulatory about Brazil's racial democracy, despite the efforts of activists to use the occasion to highlight continued discrimination and inequality.[68] As an example of more substantive reform, state and provincial offices established to represent Afro-Brazilians have both acknowledged a racial distinction and promoted incorporation. For instance, in the state of Rio de Janeiro, the PDT established a Secretariat for the Promotion and Defense of Afro-Brazilians headed by do Nascimento. The Secretariat supported plaintiffs in cases of racial discrimination. Critics have suggested that this agency was largely ineffectual and was actually intended to co-opt activists within state functions.[69] And constitutional guarantees of equality and policies of affirmative action have since been hotly debated, with President Cardoso in 1996 acknowledging the need to explore such policies without committing to implementation.[70]

What is striking about recent efforts to address Afro-Brazilian concerns within the reestablished Brazilian democracy is the extent to which this incorporation has followed traditional patterns. Brazil has long remained a hierarchical society of cordial clientalist relations, in which everyone is expected to know his or her place.[71] All are at least theoretically included in the social order, and encouraged to participate, particularly as individuals, not as more potentially disruptive groups.[72] The tradition of pluralist democratic practices was not strong in a rigid form of *democradura*.[73] Thus, as Afro-Brazilians have increasingly asserted their identity as a group and raised demands for participation and redress, the political system has moved to incorporate them, if only to avoid any disruption to the most highly prized traditions of national unity and social peace.[74] Such compromise has been primarily aimed at containing potential disruption, rather than inviting more fundamental change. That the social order is maintained amid considerable levels of violence, including the murder of black street children and police brutality, somehow does not diminish the belief in a working order.[75]

Given the large population of Afro-Brazilians, their inclusion is essential for more general democracy. But this requirement was long met by maintaining the myth of racial democracy rather than by making it a reality. By avoiding explicit rules of segregation and categories of exclusion, Brazil maintained the myth, constraining racial identity formation and potential conflict. Even activists ironically concede that "the only thing Brazil got right was race" (Januário Garcia).[76] For instance, given the lack of formal segregation, "it is hard to go to the favelas and talk about racism, since blacks and whites live there together."[77] Without a more fully consolidated, widespread, and assertive racial identity, continued informal discrimination and inequality remain relatively unchallenged and without redress. In this sense, racial democracy has worked; the myth has been lived.

This context has presented a major challenge to those activists who seek to mobilize Afro-Brazilians. With no formal rules of racial domination, Brazil's social order has been maintained without presenting an explicit target for identity formation that might otherwise have provided an external basis for mobilization and redress. This has presented activists with the difficult task of seeking to consolidate such an identity unilaterally, which in the United States and South Africa had been enforced by state policy and could be exploited by popular leaders. Thus, the greatest task and achievement of the Movimento Negro has been to establish the fact of racism.[78] Consumed by this task, the movement has been largely unable to move beyond it to actually organizing much in the way of mass action. As a high-ranking black police official, Jorge da Silva, notes, "there has never been a riot here," or for that matter any other form of major collective action focused on race per se.[79] Class mobilization has long been more prominent.

Afro-Brazilian mobilization has occurred, but on a small scale and primarily focused on ideology and identity consolidation. When the state was receptive to such efforts, black activists remained relatively moderate in tone, seeking fulfillment of the promise of racial democracy, as with the Frente or more recent electoral politics. When the state was more repressive, activists became more militant, as with the MNU at the end of the dictatorship in the late 1970s. And under democracy, Afro-Brazilians have pressed for redress. But even these variations occurred within the overriding context of constraint. Only during political crises or transitions did these black movements emerge, for instance at the start of the Vargas regime, during the *abertura* (democratic opening), and with the shift toward democracy in the late 1970s and thereafter. During most of the past century, the social order has not been so open, state rule has been more firm, and little black mobilization has emerged to puncture the image of national unity.

Comparative Overview

Black protest relates to nation-state consolidation built through racial domination; the state-led process of race making proves to be double-edged. Official policies of exclusion according to race have drawn boundaries solidifying subordinated racial identity, which then forms a basis for collective action in response to shifting state policies. Such identity formation is prior to and necessary for the logic of resource allocation and political opportunities to produce social movements. Formal exclusion so defines and unifies who is subordinated, building on past solidarity and inviting pressure for inclusion. Racial domination thus punished its victims, but also reinforced and legitimized racial identity and protest, by which subordination could be and has been challenged to gain the expected rewards of formal inclusion. The relative lack of such legal racial domination, as in Brazil, appears less hurtful in a direct sense, but also constrains the prospect for racial identity, mobilization, and redress even when cultural and informal discrimination still provide some basis for racial identity and protest.

This general argument is affirmed by the linkage between levels of racial domination and of identity consolidation and protest responses. The South African state, founded after the Boer War and strengthened by British support, inflicted early, pervasive, and nationwide segregation. Opposing racial identities and efforts at protest emerged quickly, gaining strength over time. In the United States Jim Crow was established locally while the central authority remained weak and withdrew. Under such circumstances, racial identity and protest emerged more gradually and long remained regionally divided. In Brazil, with no legal segregation, racial identity and protest long remained muted despite persistent inequality. Yet, in all three cases, activists reinforced racial identity as a basis for potential mobilization, evoking images of past solidarity and building on existing networks to overcome divisions.

Given relative identity formation, the timing and tactics of black mobilization were also tied to shifts in state policies, in turn reflecting varying efforts to encourage white unity through racial domination. When states reinforced such domination, blacks saw no hope of redress or escape from repression, and mobilization was limited. When white unity had been consolidated, reforms by the state tended to invite more moderate black activism, often aimed at integration. Reversal or failure of reforms provoked more militant responses, often aimed at separatism. Both reform and repression were turned into opportunities for mobilization, taking different but related forms. This is not to suggest that state policy in itself was fully determinant of opposition responses. For instance, black identity and protest predated official racial domination. Demography was also relevant to outcomes. South Africa's black majority gave the ANC confidence that inclusive democracy in itself would bring substantive redress, without requiring continued racial distinctions. As a result, the ANC long has been committed to nonracialism. At the same time, the use of force by the minority regime to hold onto power diminished commitments to Gandhian nonviolence. In the United States, the African-American minority was less confident that democratic inclusion in itself would bring redress, and nonracialism was not widely adopted. Violence was used at times, but often seen as illegitimate in the context of possible democratic change. And in South Africa, the United States, and Brazil, rising industrialization and migration also shaped black protest, though arguably such development rested upon the preservation of a polity and stability in which growth and migration were possible.

Protests eventually forced those legal changes at which they had aimed. Apartheid and Jim Crow were abandoned, not by revolution but by protest that raised the specter of instability and thereby forced reconfiguration of the nation-state into more inclusive official forms, though discrimination remained. Elites saw the most pressing challenge to stability shift from intrawhite conflict to black protest against racial domination. In South Africa, the end of apartheid came only with massive popular protest, forcing a fundamental change and the creation of a new political form. In the United States, blacks remained a minority, regionally divided, and yet often more confident than South Africans that rhetorical guarantees of equality would eventually be enforced within the existing polity. Their powerful protest was sufficiently destabilizing to force federal authorities to intervene against Jim Crow. A new political order was not necessary or enacted; instead, blacks were at least officially admitted into the existing order. And in Brazil, more limited black protest has brought somewhat greater incorporation long promised by the state.

This overview provides a corrective or refinement of earlier theories of social movements applied to race. Most notably, racial identity must be consolidated before this identity can be turned to action. And in this process, state policies have notably enforced lines of race on which identity has been built. Deprivation, resources, or opportunities in themselves do not establish such an identity and basis for protest and may be present without provoking protest. In the absence of state-imposed segregation, such identity and mobilization may be weaker. Only when identity is consolidated does the logic of response to structural conditions apply. Deprivation or absence or reversal of reforms angers. Economic advance, reforms, and resources mollify, provoking more moderate protest. But again the state plays a major role in these processes, heightening or alleviating deprivation, diminishing or providing resources, and creating opportunities by race-specific policies. Not surprisingly then, black protest generally emerges during periods of transition in state rule and race policies, when there are perceived openings or fluidity. But its emergence and strength depend upon the consolidation of identity and solidarity of a group then able to act for itself.

11

Conclusion

State actions were highly consequential in shaping the template of modern race relations. Where and when states enacted formal rules of domination according to racial distinctions, racism was reinforced, whites were unified as whites, challenges from those subordinated eventually emerged, and major racial conflict ensued. Where racial domination was not encoded by the state, issues and conflicts over race were diluted. These dynamics were central to the very different experiences of South Africa, the United States, and Brazil during this century.

Elites encoded racial domination in pursuit of nation-state building, selectively reinforcing earlier prejudice. In South Africa and the United States, blacks were sold out to encourage white unity and nationalist loyalty to the state, precisely because such loyalty was divided. Major intrawhite conflict impelled strong policies to build a coalition, restoring stability and thereby allowing for preservation of the polity and economic growth. Ongoing party and economic conflict brought refinement of ideology and policies toward this end, not in a functionalist manner but as a result of such conflict. Divided white identities were eroded by unifying whites racially as a nation, with elites using the instrument of the state to encourage such unity, and thereby to reinforce the power of the state itself. In contrast, Brazil's early legacy of relatively little intrawhite conflict produced neither an ideology of racism to unify whites nor policies of racial domination to encourage such unity. An assimilationist Brazilian nation was unified inclusively, despite marked discrimination, inequality, and later class tensions.

For all the similarity in the strategic use of racial domination in

South Africa and the United States, actual policy outcomes diverged according to differences in state structure and demography. Describing state action requires disaggregating the form of the state and pressures upon it. In South Africa, a strong centralized state was formed to protect whites from the indigenous black majority. Ongoing political and economic competition among whites reinforced racial domination and the power of the state, which ethnic and class factions sought to control. The central state in the United States was weaker, countered by local authorities in a structure designed to contain conflict, a structure that failed notably with the Civil War. Ongoing regional, party, and class competition after Reconstruction then recalibrated the federal balance of power. The polity was preserved after Reconstruction by central authority allowing for locally imposed Jim Crow. Washington acted by withdrawal. In both South Africa and the United States, the state served its own ends by preserving itself while meeting competing and varying pressures to appease and unify. Selective democracy reinforced these outcomes.

Not only did states reinforce race to unify the nation, but race also made nation-states. The political production of race and of particular forms of nation-state were linked processes. In South Africa, fears of the black majority informed efforts to build a strong central state and to unify whites as whites. In the United States, a decentralized and weaker central state preserved the polity by allowing for differences among whites. White unity was encouraged and built more fitfully. Brazilian elites, earlier more fearful of black revolts and less of intrawhite conflict, projected images of racial democracy in order to create the appearance of a more inclusive nation-state not of whites alone but of all Brazilians. In all three countries, political structures, solidarities, and racial constructions were continually contested.

These different constructions made preservation of the state and economic development possible in each of the three countries. Conflicts between and within capital and labor were contained by racial exclusion or inclusion, unifying white South Africans and Americans by race and all Brazilians as Brazilians. There were costs to these efforts, particularly from segregation, but less than the higher cost of conflict. With continued refinements of the racial order, growth and industrialization proceeded, a process that itself changed the situation in which costs and benefits were assessed.

Unmaking Legal Racial Domination
and the Continuing Legacies of Discrimination

Just as the construction of racial orders emerged from a dynamic of nation building from above and real or potential challenges from below, changes in those racial orders emerged from the same general dynamic. It was black protest that forced the end of apartheid and Jim Crow, with international pressures and macroeconomic changes also playing an important role. However, in both cases reform would have been stymied had militarily strong, central state authority retained an ideological and strategic commitment to enforcing or allowing racial domination. The end of legal subordination thus came only after the impetus for race making had been reversed by further developments.

The gradual decline of intrawhite conflict did not by itself bring an end to apartheid and Jim Crow. Effectively reducing one conflict had served to exacerbate another. As the intrawhite conflict had diminished, reconciliation through racial domination provoked rising black assertions of solidarity and protest, which built upon sociocultural ties and shared experience. The strategic impetus of nation-state consolidation then shifted from resolving intrawhite conflict to resolving the increasingly pressing black–white conflict provoked by racial domination. In both South Africa and the United States, racial domination brought greater white unity, and then provoked black unity and protest that achieved legal inclusion in reconfigured nation-states. The dynamics of race making from above and from below come together to explain the end of official racial domination.

This argument can be presented in schematic form. The thesis of institutionalized racial domination provoked its antithesis of consolidated black identity and rising protest. These conflicting forces eventually produced a new synthesis of legal racial inclusion. Institutional exclusion had shaped and provoked assertions of identity and rights, which then forced a reconfiguration of those same institutions. But this schema must be clarified and refined according to particular histories. Change was driven by emerging pressures and agency, not by some abstract Hegelian determinacy. What appears in a schema as neat was far from it.

In South Africa, the cost of white unity was rising black protest. Conflict between Afrikaners and English remained but gradually diminished as a central political concern. Racial domination had worked to diminish intrawhite conflict by bolstering the privilege and status even of poorer Afrikaners. But the costs of segregation had risen with major black protest, elite division, industrialization, sanctions, and lost opportunities for market growth. With economic development increasingly dependent on blacks, these costs became unbearable. And black protest had by then replaced the English–Afrikaner conflict as the dominant threat to the state. Official racial domination had worked and then backfired, and was finally abandoned, despite white right-wing resistance. And as the South African state had been explicitly designed on the basis of racial domination, this transition required a new constitution, something not required in the United States.

In the United States, the South had been appeased after Reconstruction by allowing formal, localized, racial domination. A greater degree of state consolidation and white national unity was then largely achieved. By the mid-twentieth century, industrialization and prosperity had begun to spread to the South; increased black protest encouraged by and pushing for further reforms impelled central intervention in localized racial policies despite Southern resistance. Black protest did not threaten to destroy the polity but did threaten stability and growth. The central state had gained capacity by earlier appeasing the South, and then under pressure turned its new strength against that region's racial order to enforce greater uniformity. Formal inclusion fulfilled the promise of the existing political form. The Union victory in the Civil War was finally consolidated a century later with a second Reconstruction, in which the racial order was remolded. Regional tensions that had encouraged a white coalition of supremacy persisted, but this intrawhite conflict was gradually replaced as the most pressing threat to national unity and stability by the black–white conflict it had engendered. To curtail the rising disruption of black protest, legal racial domination was ended by strong action from the center, though inequality remained.

The same process of ending legal racial domination is not applicable to Brazil. No comparable legal racial domination had been constructed to be reformed. This does not mean that social discrimination or economic inequality were less evident in Brazil. Instead, the lack of an official racial order that might have provoked stronger protest has left such discrimination largely unchanged.

Summarizing the argument in this way specifies the ongoing processes of race making as a consistent explanation of both legal racial domination and its end. Segregation was encoded to diminish threats to the nation-state posed by intrawhite conflict. By so diminishing ethnic or regional and class conflict, it allowed for core nation-state consolidation, reinforcing central authority. As long as such intrawhite conflict remained prominent, emerging black protest did not result in reform but instead provoked a hardening of domination. Apartheid or Jim Crow could be ended only once those intrawhite threats to the united polity diminished and central authority had gained the capacity to force reforms. With white nation-state consolidation and reconciliation largely achieved, the imperative for racial domination faded. But racial domination nonetheless remained in place until black protest eclipsed intrawhite conflict. Again, the need for stability asserted itself, but this time it forced greater official inclusion. State power consolidated through racial domination was then turned on its head to dismantle that same domination.

The end of formal Jim Crow and apartheid does not mean that race has disappeared or will easily disappear as a salient issue in the United States or even South Africa. Official racial domination ran its course, but that is not the end of the processes it reinforced. Whites defined themselves as whites and reinforced racism in varying forms of post-abolition segregation for their own strategic purposes and benefit. Once race has been so constructed, whites cannot easily dismantle this awful creation. As Joseph Schumpeter observed, "Social structures, types and attitudes are coins that do not readily melt. Once they are formed they persist."[1]

Unmaking racial domination does not unmake the prejudice upon which domination was built and then reinforced, nor dissolve a now-consolidated racial identity. The scars of race remain deeply embedded. Legal apartheid or Jim Crow have ended, but the historical foundation and entrenched legacies of discrimination and inequality persist. Racial identities, ingrained through painful experience and embedded in everyday life, do not quickly fade even if the institutions that reinforced them change. In the United States, racial identities remain salient, not least because the African-American minority views its solidarity as a vital resource for protecting its interests and for combating discrimination or countering threats to race-specified reforms. In post-apartheid South Africa, blacks are more confident that as the majority their interests will be served under democracy. Still, the previous ideological project of interpreting culture, ancestry, and economic interests according to race has left a deep scar. Even in Brazil, nascent racial identity and conflict encouraged by information about the former two cases is evident, with Afro-Brazilians pressing for further political and economic incorporation. In all three cases, democracy did not and has not brought equality, though it does allow for expressions of racial discontent accordingly.

The end or absence of official racial domination does not end racial identity or mobilization, but it may militate against them. Without apartheid, South Africans may increasingly focus on class or ethnic grievances and protest, with militant black nationalism largely eclipsed thus far by democratic inclusion of the majority. Race politics may diminish in salience, amid economic advance for some blacks and a resurgence of ethnic politics. But nonracial democracy did not immediately bring fundamental change in the lives of most South Africans. White privilege remains, effectively having been guaranteed in order to encourage the end of apartheid. Populist leaders have sought to retain a focus on race, combined with class or ethnicity, to challenge the new order or to assure their standing. Continued black deprivation may swing more people to support such efforts, building on remaining resentment over racism.

In the United States, race was long entrenched in issues of federalism, constructed in large part to contain divisions over slavery and recalibrated to contain divisions over the treatment of freed blacks. The interrelated issues of racial justice and states' rights have remained unresolved despite the end of Jim Crow. Federal intervention for racial justice has provoked white resistance, as it had in the past, feeding a continued process. Indeed, a resurgence of states' rights during the 1980s and especially after 1994 has threatened previous reforms. African-Americans may no longer be united by opposition to Jim Crow, but their fate remains linked by discrimination and threats to policies of redress. Indeed, white racism has in some ways been reinforced by the end of Jim Crow: continued deprivation of blacks has been attributed to innate inferiority rather than to discrimination, now falsely assumed by many whites to have ended. To resist this trend, African-Americans have sought to contain class or related divisions and to retain their solidarity and electoral blocs. Racial politics remains salient, though less organized as such than during the fight against Jim Crow and its aftermath.

The end of apartheid and Jim Crow has left South Africa and the United States in a situation in some ways similar to that of Brazil. In the absence of formal categories used for legal segregation, racial identity is somewhat diluted, but it endures. Discrimination evident before the institutionalization of racial domination continues after its end, reinforcing racial identity. But such identity is no longer defined and reinforced in opposition to official rules. Where no longer used as an explicit tool of domination and resistance to such domination, race may be transformed into an expression of cultural distinction. Blacks may then themselves project their distinctiveness as primordial, with assertions of their own difference replacing prior state enforcements of such difference. African nationalists and populists in South Africa make such cultural appeals. In the United States, activists have increasingly turned to cultural messages and claims of essentialism as a means of retaining black solidarity in the face of continued discrimination. The more long-standing focus on cultural assertiveness among Afro-Brazilians suggests the salience of this approach. But Brazil also suggests that such culturalism does not necessarily pose a fundamental challenge to polities committed to absorption of difference. Multiculturalism seen by activists as a challenge to national unity may instead be turned by others into a signal of national incorporation.

Racial solidarity in South Africa and the United States, long entrenched by now-abandoned official policy, retains a stronger trajectory than in Brazil. But if prior intrawhite conflict in South Africa and the United States had made the Brazilian option of racial democracy long inapplicable, the healing of those conflicts and the end of legal racial domination have now "Brazilianized" South Africa and the United States. The U.S. result has arguably been some decline in the significance of race, or at least less black unity and mass protest. Given continued and relatively unchallenged racial discrimination and inequality in Brazil, a comparable situation in South Africa and the United States is not cause for unrestrained celebration. "Colorblindness" in Brazil has been devastating for Afro-Brazilians; recent calls for such color-blindness in the United States, for instance by the Supreme Court, may also prove devastating to efforts at redress by African-Americans. What appears liberal is not. Meanwhile, Brazil seems to be headed in the opposite direction, with racial salience rising to challenge the image of liberalism and entrenched discrimination.

Racial identity is not primordial, but a remnant of past institutional arrangements and ongoing informal social practice shaping and shaped by those institutions. What appeared as cultural determinants of emergent racial orders were reinforced by institutional rules. Similarly, what remains now as cultural identity also is tied to structure. Until long-entrenched social discrimination ceases, race will remain as a historical legacy. Institutions must reinforce racial justice or race conflict will continue to shake the constructions of social order built on and still tied to foundations of racial discrimination.

General Implications

What emerges is a consistent pattern of efforts at institutionalized coalition building as a central component of racial dynamics. The evolution of Du Bois's "problem of the color line" during the twentieth century was inextricably connected to the political dynamics of conflict resolution and avoidance. Alliances were forged, framed by the ideal of the nation-state. The institutions of the polity were applied to reinforce a nationalist identity and loyalty. Brazil did so directly and inclusively. South Africa and the United States could not. Entrenched internal conflict led to reinforcing nationalism by means of a racial identity employed to encourage white unity. Rules excluding blacks emerged to unify whites as dominant. And in the process black racial identity was also further consolidated, then acted upon, requiring a reconfiguration of national identity as more inclusive. The strategic calculations differed, either impelling racial domination and conflict or not, but the imperative of nation-state consolidation was evident in each situation. And throughout, South Africa, the United States, and Brazil suffered from the burdens of real or potential internal conflict.

That race making and nation-state building were so connected is not surprising, for these two processes were among the dominant social processes of the twentieth century. Nor is it surprising that these processes were contentious, since both race making and nation state building emerged as means to contend with internal conflict.

The more contentious the internal conflict, the harder the state had to work for resolution through heightened racial domination. In Brazil, the state did not use the same techniques, but still had to contain conflict. In more general terms, states inheriting major internal conflict often fall back on constructing racial or ethnic justifications for loyalty. Without such contested loyalty, states can afford to be more "civic," or at least to project themselves as such in official policy.

From the nineteenth through the twentieth century, elites and much of the populace have generally shared one political assumption: nation-state building was the overriding imperative for achieving internal stability, growth, and geopolitical standing. Disputes over polity boundaries emerged, but in any polity development required domestic peace. Internal conflicts had to be diminished or avoided and unified loyalty to the nation built where it was not inherited. Such solidarity would allow the state to rule, playing its essential role in further containing conflict, providing protection, and managing growth. This goal was imported from Europe to other countries where states had been earlier constructed by colonialism, and also was reinforced domestically by reminders of the cost of ongoing internal conflict.

Official and informal imaginings of a unified nation often have rested upon vicious demarcations that solidified those included by distinguishing those excluded. Shared allegiances were forged on the basis of common and enforced enmity. The advantages of unifying via internal exclusion were evident – selectively building on inherited prejudices reinforced unity among those sharing a particular prejudice – though at the cost of also reinforcing social cleavages, inequality, potential mobilization, and conflict. Countering prejudice to build a truly inclusive or "civic" nation was more difficult. When internal conflict emerged and reemerged, the crutch of exclusion was too handy to ignore. The nation-states of South Africa and the United States were built upon this logic. Brazil instead allowed formal inclusion, while retaining significant informal discrimination.

This argument is more broadly applicable. The image of the nation-state implies a convergence of the polity and of unified and inclusive loyalty to it, thereby supposedly overwhelming or healing subnational social cleavages. But nations have all too often been built through purposeful racial, ethnic, religious, class, or other internal exclusions. Official allocations and boundaries of citizenship rights have demarcated who is part of the nation and encouraged the loyalty of a core constituency, shaping and provoking later conflict. Such exclusion of specified others has been central to nation-state building, rather than tangential. What particular form of institutional exclusion was used depended upon historical prejudice and embedded conflictual issues informing elites about which encoded identity would unify core allegiance. Much as regional or ethnic conflict was diminished by racial exclusion and unity, ethnic conflict was contained by class exclusion and unity, and class conflict was contained by ethnic exclusion and unity. State structures and ideologies were similarly configured according to imperatives for selective nation-state building. An overview of other cases can here suggest such broader application of this argument.

Perhaps the most obvious extension of my argument about race is to the issue of ethnicity more generally. Spain had been unified with exclusion of its Jews. Much later many African states built upon colonial policies of ethnic exclusion to consolidate their independent rule, reforming such exclusion only after states were consolidated. But arguably the most notable instance of such a use of ethnic exclusion during this century was the anti-Semitism of Nazi Germany. The interwar period in Germany had brought significant and highly stratified internal class and related conflict, threatening to tear apart the nation-state. As my study of race suggests, did the Nazis then gain popularity by using anti-Semitism as a way to unite Germans against a common enemy? This would help to explain why Jews were so singled out and why anti-Semitism elsewhere, in the absence of equally threatening internal divisions, did not lead to comparable legal enactments, even if it does not explain the later genocide.

Expanding further, has legal exclusion by class been used for selectively reinforcing unity? The most prominent instance of the use of class exclusion for purposes of building a united polity is that of the Soviet Union, a case which potentially expands my framework beyond nation-states to a multinational state. Again, Russia before 1917 was torn by multifaceted, major internal conflict. Did the Bolsheviks use Communist ideology to gain unified support, and then once in power use vilification of the aristocratic upper class and exclusion of capitalists to consolidate pervasive loyalty? This argument takes seriously the class-based ideology of the Communist Party as a tool for building an expansive polity. Russia being a less developed industrial power, capitalists could more readily be excluded there than in Germany, though with later costs and ultimate failure. But is the case of the Soviet Union, in which national/ethnic distinctions were partially legitimated, comparable to nation-states?

Of course, class and related conflict did not always produce legal ethnic exclusions to heal such internal rifts. For instance, Mexico around 1910 experienced a violent internal revolution. But post-Revolution reconciliation was not based upon any official exclusions of "others." In a sense, Mexico's inclusionary corporatism is similar to that of Brazil, but unlike Brazil was founded amid bloody conflict that elsewhere produced more exclusion. After the 1920s, Mexico's ruling party did not represent only the peasants of landed elite, but instead sought compromise, combining limited land reforms with capitalism. Does Mexico then demonstrate that legal exclusion was not preordained by internal conflict, suggesting some Latin American exceptionalism, or is there something different about how class conflict has been contained?

Class is different from race or ethnicity. Contrary to traditional class analysis, economic cleavages in themselves have rarely led to major conflict. Such conflict in this century has more often emerged where and when a class divide has coincided with and been aggravated by ethnic, race, religious, or other cleavages. Does the potentially fungible nature of economic disparity, allowing for compromise, leave class less salient than cleavages that are projected as more primordial, fixed or zero-sum? Certainly belief in potential class mobility, co-optation of working class leadership, ambivalence of middle classes, and the "extralegal processes" of class differentiation may diminish class antagonism per se.[2] Does this account for how nation-states with major economic disparity but less ethnic or related conflict have remained intact?

And what does this tell us about democracy, which was long seen as either inapplicable to instances of great poverty, or likely to reduce such poverty, and yet has been maintained (more or less) amid extreme inequality? Certainly the cases explored in this book demonstrate that democracy neither is necessarily inclusive nor ensures that the interests of all will be met. Who is included in the nation and able to effectively use democratic citizenship largely determines substantive outcomes.[3] This issue is now particularly pressing in the newly democratic South Africa, confronted by the challenges of inequality and potential class conflict.

My argument is suggestive in regard to these cases and issues, raising fruitful further questions. Exploring such extensions of my thesis beyond race demonstrates that various selective legal exclusions have often been used to reinforce nation-state unity.

Successful examples of constant civic inclusiveness are much more rare. Rather than benign inclusive nationalism, specified exclusion was the predominant logic of nation-state building in a century obsessed with stability and growth. The result has been institutional reinforcement of racial, ethnic, and other distinctions of identity, which people embrace as primordial, retain, and act upon even after institutional boundaries have been reformed. The full costs of such dynamics, in the form of resurgent conflict and hatred, are still being paid.

Notes

Chapter 1. Introduction

1. W. E. B. Du Bois, *The Souls of Black Folks* (New York: McClurg, 1903), p. 1.
2. See Rogers M. Smith, "Beyond Tocqueville, Myrdal and Hartz: The Multiple Traditions in America," *American Political Science Review* 87.3 (September 1993), pp. 550–6.
3. Edward Said, *Orientalism* (New York: Random House, 1978); Frantz Fanon, *Black Skin, White Masks* (New York: Grove Press, 1967), p. 17; Reginald Horsman, *Race and Manifest Destiny* (Cambridge, Mass.: Harvard University Press, 1981), p. 62; Leon Poliakov, *The Aryan Myth: A History of Racist and Nationalist Ideas in Europe* (New York: Basic Books, 1971); Walker Connor, *Ethnonationalism* (Princeton: Princeton University Press, 1994), p. 94; Robert Miles, *Racism* (London: Routledge, 1989), pp. 31, 113.
4. Jacques Barzun, *Race: A Study in Superstition* (New York: Harper, 1937), p. 6.
5. Charles Darwin, *The Descent of Man* (London: J. Murray, 1871); Nancy Stepan, *The Idea of Race in Science: Great Britain 1800–1960* (London: Macmillan, 1992); Michael D. Biddiss, ed., *Gobineau: Selected Political Writings* (New York: Harper and Row, 1970); Michael D. Biddiss, *The Father of Racist Ideology* (New York: Weybright and Talley, 1970).
6. UNESCO, *Statements on Race and Race Prejudice* (Paris: UNESCO, 1950, 1951, 1964, 1967); Ashley Montagu, *Man's Most Dangerous Myth: The Fallacy of Race* (New York: Oxford University Press, 1974), p. 125.
7. Karl Marx and Friedrich Engels, "The Communist Manifesto," in David McLellan, ed., *Karl Marx: Selected Writings* (Oxford: Oxford University Press, 1977), p. 224.
8. See David E. Apter, *The Politics of Modernization* (Chicago: University of Chicago Press, 1967); Clifford Geertz, "The Integrative Revolution," in *Old Societies and New States* (New York: Free Press, 1963); Crawford

Young, *The Politics of Cultural Pluralism* (Madison: University of Wisconsin Press, 1976), pp. 11–22; George M. Fredrickson, *The Arrogance of Race* (Middletown, Conn.: Wesleyan University Press, 1988), p. 5. The assimilation argument applied to race was advanced by the Chicago School, led by Robert Park.

9. Ira Katznelson, *Liberalism's Crooked Circle* (Princeton: Princeton University Press, 1996), p. 105.

10. See Manning Marable, *Black American Politics* (London: Verso, 1985), p. 2; Katherine O'Sullivan See and William Julius Wilson, "Race and Ethnicity," in Neil J. Smelser, ed., *The Handbook of Sociology* (Newbury Park, Calif.: Sage, 1988), p. 227.

11. Max Weber, "Class, Status, Power," in H. H. Gerth and C. Wright Mills, eds., *From Max Weber* (New York: Oxford University Press, 1946), p. 184.

12. See Peter Evans, *Embedded Autonomy* (Princeton: Princeton University Press, 1995), p. 19.

13. See Theda Skocpol, "Bringing the State Back In," in Peter Evans, Dietrich Rueschemeyer, and Theda Skocpol, eds., *Bringing the State Back In* (Cambridge: Cambridge University Press, 1985), pp. 7, 14; Katznelson, *Liberalism's Crooked Circle*, pp. 125, 178.

14. See Charles Tilly, "Reflections on the History of European Statemaking," in Charles Tilly, ed., *The Formation of National States in Western Europe* (Princeton: Princeton University Press, 1975), pp. 1–83. Tilly notes that such nationalism was encouraged with selection of personnel, control of groups, education, and other policies.

15. Bertrand Badie and Pierre Birnbaum, *The Sociology of the State* (Chicago: University of Chicago Press, 1983), p. 37.

16. Quoted in Katznelson, *Liberalism's Crooked Circle*, p. 119.

17. Benedict Anderson, *Imagined Communities* (London: Verso, 1983).

18. Anderson himself revised his earlier work to make a similar argument about the purposeful actions of states, underemphasized in his first edition. See Anderson, *Imagined Communities* (1989 ed.), p. 163. For a more state-centered analysis of nationalism, see Ernest Gellner, *Nations and Nationalism* (Ithaca, N.Y.: Cornell University Press, 1983); John Breuilly, *Nationalism and the State* (Chicago: University of Chicago Press, 1982).

19. Connor, *Ethnonationalism*, p. 48.

20. Paul Starr, "Social Categories and Claims in the Liberal State," in Mary Douglas and David Hull, eds., *How Classification Works* (Edinburgh: Edinburgh University Press, 1992), p. 169. This argument follows Tocqueville, as discussed in Skocpol, "Bringing the State," p. 21.

21. Eric Hobsbawm, "Some Reflections on 'The Break-up of Britain,' " *New Left Review* 105 (1977), p. 5; Gellner, *Nations and Nationalism*, p. 63.

22. Frank Parkin, *Max Weber* (London: Travistock, 1982), p. 100; Frank Parkin, *Marxism and Class Theory: A Bourgeois Critique* (New York: Columbia University Press, 1979), p. 95.

23. T. H. Marshall, *Citizenship and Social Class* (London: Pluto, 1992); and as quoted in Katznelson, *Liberalism's Crooked Circle*, p. 119.

24. Judith N. Shklar, *American Citizenship: The Quest for Inclusion* (Cambridge, Mass.: Harvard University Press, 1991), p. 3; Sidney Tarrow, *Power in Movement* (Cambridge: Cambridge University Press, 1994), p. 62.

25. Tarrow, *Power in Movement*, p. 76; Shklar, *American Citizenship*, p. 28; Charles Tilly, *Popular Contention in Great Britain, 1758–1834* (Cambridge, Mass.: Harvard University Press, 1995); Michael Lipsky, "Protest as a Political Resource," *American Political Science Review* 62 (1968), pp. 1144–58; Craig Calhoun, *Social Theory and the Politics of Identity* (Cambridge: Blackwell, 1994), p. 25; Margaret R. Somers, "Citizenship and the Place of the Public Sphere," *American Sociological Review* 58.5 (October 1993), p. 589.

26. Aldon Morris and Carol McLurg Mueller, eds., *Frontiers in Social Movement Theory* (New Haven: Yale University Press, 1992), p. 189.

27. Albert O. Hirschman, *Exit, Voice and Loyalty* (Cambridge, Mass.: Harvard University Press, 1970).

28. Barbara Fields, "Slavery, Race and Ideology in the United States of America," *New Left Review* 181 (1990), p.101. For a related discussion of racism as a "pitfall of nationalism," see Frantz Fanon, *The Wretched of the Earth* (New York: Grove, 1968), pp. 125–31.

29. Herbert S. Klein, *African Slavery in Latin America and the Caribbean* (New York: Oxford University Press, 1986), p. 10. Europe, with its absence of major domestic slaveholding, and history of ethnic exclusion, is not included in this comparative study.

30. See, for example, Pierre Van den Berghe, *Race and Racism* (New York: Wiley, 1967); Stanley B. Greenberg, *Race and State in Capitalist Development* (New Haven: Yale University Press, 1980); George M. Fredrickson, *White Supremacy* (Oxford: Oxford University Press, 1981); John W. Cell, *The Highest Stage of White Supremacy* (Cambridge: Cambridge University Press, 1982); Carl N. Degler, *Neither Black nor White* (Madison: University of Wisconsin Press, 1971).

31. C. Vann Woodward, *The Strange Career of Jim Crow* (New York: Oxford University Press, 1957), p. 97; George Reid Andrews, "Comparing the Comparers: White Supremacy in the United States and South Africa," *Journal of Social History* 20 (1987) p. 588; George M. Fredrickson, "Black–White Relations Since Emancipation: The Search for a Comparative Perspective," in Kees Gispen, ed., *What Made the South Different?* (Jackson: University Press of Mississippi, 1990), p. 141.

32. George M. Fredrickson, *Black Liberation: A Comparative History of Black Ideologies in the United States and South Africa* (New York: Oxford University Press, 1995).

33. See Gilberto Freyre, *The Masters and the Slaves* (Berkeley: University of California Press, 1986); Gilberto Freyre, *The Mansions and the Shanties* (Berkeley: University of California Press, 1986).

34. Nina Rodrigues, *Os Africanos no Brasil* (São Paulo: Cia Ed. Nacional, 1977), pp. 29–30.

35. For discussion, see the Commission for the Socio-Economic Development of the Bantu Areas within the Union of South Africa (Tomlinson Commission), *Summary of the Report* (Pretoria: Government Printer, 1955), p. 9; Marvin Harris, *Patterns of Race in the Americas* (Westport, Conn.: Greenwood, 1964), p. 84. The United Nations has estimated that up to 80% of the Brazilian population have some African ancestry, as reported in I. K. Sundiata, "Late Twentieth Century Patterns of Race Relations in Brazil and the United States," *Phylon* 48.1 (1987), p. 69.

36. Degler, *Neither Black nor White*, p. 3; E. Bradford Burns, *A History of Brazil* (New York: Columbia University Press, 1970), p. 50.

37. Frank Tannenbaum, *Slave and Citizen* (New York: Knopf, 1946).

38. Eugene D. Genovese, *Roll, Jordan, Roll* (New York: Random House, 1972), p. 177; Winthrop D. Jordan, *White Over Black* (New York: Norton, 1968), p. 206.

39. C. R. Boxer, *Four Centuries of Portuguese Expansion, 1415–1825* (Berkeley: University of California Press, 1969), p. 42; Perry Anderson, "Portugal and the End of Ultra-Colonialism 2," *New Left Review* 16 (July–August 1962); Gerald J. Bender, *Angola Under the Portuguese* (Berkeley: University of California Press, 1978).

40. Degler, *Neither Black nor White*.

41. Nelson do Valle Silva, "Updating the Cost of Not Being White in Brazil," in Pierre-Michel Fontaine, ed., *Race, Class and Power in Brazil* (Los Angeles: Center for Afro-American Studies, University of California, 1985), pp. 42–55.

42. Elie Kedourie, *Nationalism* (Oxford: Blackwell, 1960), p. 70. For a more general discussion, see Ian Lustick, "History, Historiography, and Political Science," *American Political Science Review* 90.3 (September 1996), pp. 605–18.

43. Greenberg, *Race and State*, p. 24; Joel Williamson, *The Crucible of Race* (New York: Oxford University Press, 1984), p. 495; Rebecca J. Scott, "Defining the Boundaries of Freedom in the World of Cane," *American Historical Review* (February 1994), p. 70.

44. See Charles Tilly, "To Explain Historical Processes," Center for Studies of Social Change, New School for Social Research, New York, Working Paper no. 168 (July 1993); Gary King, Robert O. Keohane, and Sidney Verba, *Designing Social Inquiry* (Princeton: Princeton University Press, 1994), p. 226.

45. See Etienne Balibar and Immanuel Wallerstein, *Race, Nation, Class: Ambiguous Identities* (London: Verso, 1991), p. 81.

46. Ira Katznelson, "The State to the Rescue?" *Social Research* 59.4 (Winter 1992), p. 732.

47. Donald Pierson, *Negroes in Brazil* (Chicago: University of Chicago Press, 1942), p. 335.

48. See Andrews, "Comparing the Comparers," p. 589; A. Leon Higgin-botham, Jr., "Racism in American and South African Courts: Similarities and Differences," *New York University Law Review* 65.3 (June 1990), p. 491; Richard M. Valelly, "Party, Coercion, and Inclusion: The Two Re-constructions of the South's Electoral Politics," *Politics and Society* 21.1 (March 1993), pp. 37–67.
49. Aristide Zolberg, "Moments of Madness," *Politics and Society* 2 (1978).
50. See V. O. Key, Jr., *Southern Politics in State and Nation* (New York: Knopf, 1949), p. 15.
51. See Michel Foucault, *Power/Knowledge* ed. Colin Gordon (New York: Pantheon, 1980), p. 90.
52. Arthur Stinchcombe, "Social Structure and Politics," in Nelson W. Polsby and Fred Greenstein, eds., *Handbook of Political Science* (Reading: Addison-Wesley, 1975), vol. 3.
53. Kimberlie Crenshaw, "Race, Reform and Retrenchment," *Harvard Law Review* 101.7 (May 1988), p. 1360; William Julius Wilson, *Power, Racism and Privilege* (New York: Free Press, 1973), p. 35; George M. Fredrick-son, *The Black Image in the White Mind* (Middletown, Conn.: Wesleyan University Press), p. 151; Connor, *Ethnonationalism*, p. 94.
54. Donald Denoon, *A Grand Illusion* (London: Longman, 1973), p. 158.
55. Cell, *Highest Stage*, p. 248.
56. For a general discussion, see Jon Elster, *Nuts and Bolts for the Social Sciences* (Cambridge: Cambridge University Press, 1989), pp. 99–100, 123.
57. See van den Berghe, *Race and Racism*, pp. 27–30; Cell, *Highest Stage*, p. 104; Susan Olzak, *The Dynamics of Ethnic Competition and Conflict* (Stanford: Stanford University Press, 1992).
58. Edna Bonacich, "A Theory of Ethnic Antagonism: The Split Labor Mar-ket," *American Sociological Review* 37 (October 1972), pp. 547–59.
59. Michael Burawoy, "The Capitalist State in South Africa," in Maurice Zeitlin, ed., *Political Power and Social Theory* (Greenwich: JAI Press, 1981), vol. 2, p. 282.
60. See Donald L. Horowitz, *Ethnic Groups in Conflict* (Berkeley: University of California Press, 1985); Ralf Dahrendorf, *Class and Class Conflict in Industrial Society* (Stanford: Stanford University Press, 1959), p. 314.
61. See Balibar and Wallerstein, *Race, Nation, Class*, p. 33.
62. See Louis Hartz, *The Founding of New Societies* (San Diego: Harcourt Brace Jovanovich, 1964).
63. Fredrickson, *Black Liberation*, pp. 5, 8.
64. See Carlos Hasenbalg, "Race Relations in Post-Abolition Brazil," Ph.D. dissertation, University of California at Berkeley, 1978, p. 258; Carlos Hasenbalg, "Desigualdades Raciais no Brasil," *Dados* 14 (1977), p. 7; Roberto Da Matta, *Carnivals, Rogues and Heroes* (Notre Dame, Ind.: Uni-versity of Notre Dame Press, 1991), pp. 139–40; Florestan Fernandes, *The Negro in Brazilian Society* (New York: Columbia University Press, 1969), pp. 180–1.
65. Scott, "Defining the Boundaries of Freedom," p. 96; Gilberto Freyre,

Brazil: An Interpretation (New York: Knopf, 1945), pp. 120–1. See also Hartz, *Founding of New Societies*, pp. 78, 124.

66. Célia Marinho de Azevedo, *Onda Negra, Medo Branco* (Rio de Janeiro: Paz e Terra, 1987).

67. Hasenbalg, "Race Relations in Post-Abolition Brazil," p. 260.

68. Brazil's informal racial order is an example of what Foucault describes as the "effects of power which don't pass directly via the state apparatus yet often sustain the state more effectively than its own institutions, enlarging and maximizing its effectiveness." See Foucault, *Power/Knowledge*, p. 73.

69. See Rogers Brubaker, *Citizenship and Nationhood in France and Germany* (Cambridge, Mass.: Harvard University Press, 1992).

70. Ibid., p. 21.

71. Gunnar Myrdal, *An American Dilemma* (New York: Harper and Row, 1944), p. 466.

72. See Michael Dawson, *Behind the Mule* (Princeton: Princeton University Press, 1994).

73. Kedourie, *Nationalism*, p. 134.

74. Perry Anderson, *Lineages of the Absolutist State* (London: Verso, 1974), p. 11.

75. See Skocpol, "Bringing the State," p. 21.

76. See Anthony W. Marx, *Lessons of Struggle: South African Internal Opposition, 1960–1990* (New York: Oxford University Press, 1992).

77. John and Jean Comaroff, *Ethnography and the Historical Imagination* (Boulder: Westview, 1992), p. 50.

78. See Ted Robert Gurr, *Why Men Rebel* (Princeton: Princeton University Press, 1970); Bob Blauner, *Black Lives, White Lives* (Berkeley: University of California Press, 1989), p. 17; Tarrow, *Power in Movement*, p. 81.

79. John D. McCarthy and Mayer N. Zald, "Resource Mobilization and Social Movements," *American Journal of Sociology* 82.6 (May 1977); Aldon Morris, *The Origins of the Civil Rights Movement* (New York: Free Press, 1984). See also Pamela Oliver et al., "A Theory of Critical Mass," *American Journal of Sociology* 91.3 (November 1985), pp. 522–86.

80. Doug McAdam, John D. McCarthy, and Mayer N. Zald, "Social Movements," in Neil J. Smelser, ed., *The Handbook of Sociology* (Newbury Park, Calif.: Sage Press, 1988), p. 702; Doug McAdam, *Political Process and the Development of Black Insurgency, 1930–1970* (Chicago: University of Chicago Press, 1982), ch. 2.

81. McAdam, *Political Process*; Tarrow, *Power in Movement*, pp. 31, 61–2. See also Pierre Birnbaum, *States and Collective Action* (Cambridge: Cambridge University Press, 1988); Charles Tilly, "How to Detect, Describe and Explain Repertoires of Contention," Center for the Study of Social Change, New School, New York, manuscript (October 1992); Dennis Chong, *Collective Action and the Civil Rights Movement* (Chicago: University of Chicago Press, 1991); Sidney Tarrow, "Struggling to Reform," Western Societies Program Working Paper no. 15 (1983), Cornell Uni-

versity; Doug McAdam, "Tactical Innovation and the Pace of Insurgency," *American Sociological Review* 48 (December 1983), pp. 735–54.

82. Wilson, *Power Racism and Privilege*, p. 47.

83. Rupert Taylor, "Racial Terminology and the Question of Race in South Africa," manuscript (1994).

84. See Jean Cohen, "Strategy or Identity," *Social Research* 52.4 (Winter 1985); Calhoun, *Social Theory and the Politics of Identity*; Charles Tilly, "Models and Realities of Popular Collective Action," *Social Research* 52.4 (Winter 1985), pp. 717–48; Morris and Mueller, *Frontiers*, p. 308.

85. See Russell J. Dalton and Manfred Kuechler, *Challenging the Political Order* (New York: Oxford University Press, 1990).

86. Karl Marx, "The Poverty of Philosophy," in David McLellan, ed., *Karl Marx: Selected Writings* (Oxford: Oxford University Press, 1977), p. 214.

87. See Michael Mann, "The Autonomous Power of the State," *Archives Europeennes de Sociologie* 25 (1984), p. 189; Skocpol, "Bringing the State," pp. 21–8.

88. See Ernesto Laclau and Chantal Mouffe, *Hegemony and Socialist Strategy* (London: Verso, 1985), pp. 93, 67.

89. Hasenbalg, "Race Relations in Post-Abolition Brazil," p. 210; Degler, *Neither Black nor White*, p. 275.

90. Williamson, *Crucible of Race*, p. 505.

91. Blauner, *Black Lives*, p. 11; Elijah Anderson, *Streetwise: Race, Class and Change in an Urban Community* (Chicago: University of Chicago Press, 1990), p. 40. For case studies of such strategic interaction and learning, see Herbert H. Haines, *Black Radicals and the Civil Rights Mainstream, 1954–1970* (Knoxville: University of Tennessee Press, 1988); James A. Cone, *Martin and Malcolm and America* (Maryknoll, N.Y.: Orbis, 1991); Marx, *Lessons of Struggle*.

92. Interview with Kwame Ture (aka Stokely Carmichael), New York, 19 March 1993.

93. Tarrow, *Power in Movement*, p. 62; Birnbaum, *States and Collective Action*, p. 73.

94. Nelson Mandela, *Long Walk to Freedom* (Boston: Little, Brown, 1994), pp. 144, 468.

95. Leonard A. Cole, *Blacks in Power* (Princeton: Princeton University Press, 1976), p. 18; See and Wilson, "Race and Ethnicity," p. 227; Chong, *Collective Action*, pp. 11, 173.

96. Tarrow, *Power in Movement*, p. 172.

97. See Manning Marable, *Race, Reform, and Rebellion* (Jackson: University Press of Mississippi, 1991), p. 4; William Brink and Louis Harris, *Black and White* (New York: Simon and Schuster, 1966), p. 242.

98. David Laitin, "Hegemony and Religious Conflict," in Peter B. Evans, Dietrich Rueschemeyer, and Theda Skocpol, eds., *Bringing the State Back In* (Cambridge: Cambridge University Press, 1985), pp. 287, 308.

99. Fredrickson, *Black Image*, p. 135. See Fields, "Slavery, Race and Ideology"; Hartz, *Founding of New Societies*, p. 53.

100. Laitin, "Hegemony and Religious Conflict," p. 311.
101. Evans, *Embedded Autonomy*, p. 18.
102. Ibid., p. 18.

Part One. Historical and Cultural Legacies

1. Louis Hartz, *The Founding of New Societies* (San Diego: Harcourt Brace and World, 1964).

Chapter 2. Trajectories from Colonialism

1. Gerald J. Bender, *Angola Under the Portuguese: The Myth and the Reality* (Berkeley: University of California Press, 1978), pp. xxi, xix.
2. Ibid., p. xxii.
3. Gilberto Freyre, *The Masters and the Slaves* (Berkeley: University of California Press, 1986), pp. xii, 199.
4. Ibid., pp. xiii, 208. See also Gilberto Freyre, *Brazil: An Interpretation* (New York: Knopf, 1945), pp. 4, 20; Donald Pierson, *Negroes in Brazil* (Chicago: University of Chicago Press, 1942), pp. 326–7.
5. Louis Hartz, *The Founding of New Societies* (San Diego: Harcourt Brace and World, 1964), p. 52.
6. C. R. Boxer, *Four Centuries of Portuguese Expansion, 1415–1825* (Berkeley: University of California Press, 1969), p. 4. See also George M. Fredrickson, *The Black Image in the White Mind* (Middletown, Conn.: Wesleyan University Press, 1971), p. 131, n. 1.
7. Freyre, *Masters and Slaves*, p. 189.
8. Vianna Moog, *Bandeirantes and Pioneers* (New York: George Braziller, 1964), p. 67; David Brion Davis, *The Problem of Slavery in Western Culture* (New York: Oxford University Press, 1966), p. 274.
9. H. Hoetink, *The Two Variants in Caribbean Race Relations* (London: Oxford University Press, 1967), p. 14–5. For contrary views, see Michael Mitchell, "Racial Consciousness and the Political Attitudes and Behavior of Blacks in São Paulo, Brazil," Ph.D. dissertation, Indiana University, Bloomington, July 1977, p. 13; Leslie B. Rout, Jr., "The African in Colonial Brazil," in Martin L. Kilson and Robert I. Rotberg, eds., *The African Diaspora* (Cambridge, Mass.: Harvard University Press, 1976), p. 132.
10. Perry Anderson, "Portugal and the End of Ultra-Colonialism 2," *New Left Review* (16, July–August 1962), pp. 93, 110.
11. Boxer, *Four Centuries*, pp. 6–13, 72; Moog, *Bandeirantes*, pp. 17, 92; James Lang, *Portuguese Brazil: The King's Plantation* (New York: Academic Press, 1979), pp. 12–28, 37, 57, 71.
12. Boxer, *Four Centuries*, p. 51; Lang, *Portuguese Brazil*, p. 31; Helio Jaguaribe, *Economic and Political Development* (Cambridge, Mass.: Harvard University Press, 1968), p. 102.

13. E. Bradford Burns, *Nationalism in Brazil* (New York: Praeger, 1968), p. 15. See also Clóvis Moura, *História do Negro Brasileiro* (São Paulo: Atica, 1989), p. 57; Leslie Rout, "The African in Colonial Brazil," p. 168; A. J. R. Russell-Wood, *The Black Man in Slavery and Freedom in Colonial Brazil* (London: Macmillan, 1982), p. 74; Nicholas Canny and Anthony Pagden, *Colonial Identity in the Atlantic World, 1500–1800* (Princeton: Princeton University Press, 1987), p. 16.

14. Leslie Bethell, "The Independence of Brazil," in Leslie Bethel, ed., *Brazil: Empire and Republic, 1822–1930* (Cambridge: Cambridge University Press, 1989), p. 41.

15. Boxer, *Four Centuries*, p. 75; Bethel, "Independence," p. 3; Herbert S. Klein, *African Slavery in Latin America and the Caribbean* (New York: Oxford University Press, 1986), p. 68; Lang, *Portuguese Brazil*, pp. 121, 153.

16. Rout, "The African in Colonial Brazil," p. 151; E. Franklin Frazier, "Some Aspects of Race Relations in Brazil," *Phylon* 3.3 (1942), p. 289; Kenneth R. Maxwell, *Conflicts and Conspiracies: Brazil and Portugal, 1750–1808* (Cambridge: Cambridge University Press, 1973), p. 87.

17. Bethell, "Independence," pp. 6, 86; Klein, *African Slavery*, pp. 90, 119; Richard Graham, "1850–1870," in Leslie Bethel, ed., *Brazil: Empire and Republic, 1822–1930* (Cambridge: Cambridge University Press, 1989), pp. 84, 116; Burns, *Nationalism in Brazil*, p. 72.

18. Lang, *Portuguese Brazil*. p. 108.

19. Boxer, *Four Centuries*, p. 76.

20. Maxwell, *Conflicts and Conspiracies*, pp. 83, 116, 134, 199, 210.

21. Ibid., pp. 61, 177.

22. Lang, *Portuguese Brazil*, p. 195; Bethell, "Independence," pp. 15–16; Maxwell, *Conflicts and Conspiracies*, p. 239.

23. Jaguaribe, *Economic and Political Development*, pp. 114, 121; Emilio Viotti da Costa, *The Brazilian Empire* (Chicago: University of Chicago Press, 1985), pp. xviii, 69; Bethell, "Independence," pp. 18, 22, 81; E. Bradford Burns, *A History of Brazil* (New York: Columbia University Press, 1970), p. 215.

24. Doris Sommer, *Foundational Fictions* (Berkeley: University of California Press, 1991), p. 146.

25. Costa, *Brazilian Empire*, pp. 47, 68; Maxwell, *Conflicts and Conspiracies*, p. 134; Leslie Bethell and José Murilo de Carvalho, "1822–1850," in Leslie Bethel, ed., *Brazil: Empire and Republic, 1822–1830* (Cambridge: Cambridge University Press, 1989); Luiz Felipe de Alencastro, "Proletários e Escravos," *CEBRAP–Novos Estudos* (21 July 1988), p. 34.

26. Burns, *History of Brazil*, pp. 172–6.

27. Lang, *Portuguese Brazil*, p. 231.

28. Costa, *Brazilian Empire*, pp. 59, 181; Freyre, *Master and Slaves*, p. xi; Freyre, *Brazil*, pp. 37, 79; Moog, *Bandeirantes*, p. 83; Hartz, *Founding of New Societies*, p. 27.

29. Boxer, *Four Centuries*, p. 81.

30. Stein Rokkan, "Dimensions of State Formation and Nation-Building," in Charles Tilly, ed., *The Formation of National States in Western Europe* (Princeton: Princeton University Press, 1975), p. 581. See also Hartz, *Founding of New Societies*, pp. 126, 152; Riordan Roett, *Brazil: Politics in a Patrimonial Society* (New York: Praeger, 1984).

31. Donald Pierson, *Negroes in Brazil*, p. 170; Burns, *History of Brazil*, pp. 258–9; Clóvis Moura, *História*, p. 57.

32. Freyre, *Master and Slaves*, p. 185.

33. George Reid Andrews, "Race and the State in Colonial Brazil," *Latin American Research Review* 19.3 (1984).

34. Costa, *Brazilian Empire*, p. 53; Maxwell, *Conflicts and Conspiracies*, p. 95; Canny and Pagden, *Colonial Identity*, p. 34.

35. Rout, "The African in Colonial Brazil," p. 166; Boxer, *Four Centuries*, pp. 42–4; Burns, *History of Brazil*, p. 149.

36. Boxer, *Four Centuries*, p. 42.

37. Bender, *Angola*, p. 3.

38. Perry Anderson, "Portugal," pp. 110, 115, 113.

39. Bender, *Angola*, p. 5. See also Peter Fry, *Para Inglês Ver* (Rio de Janeiro: Zahar Editores, 1982).

40. Boxer, *Four Centuries*, p. 13; W. A. de Klerk, *The Puritans in Africa: A History of Afrikanerdom* (Harmondsworth: Penguin, 1975), p. 4; C. W. De Kiewiet, *A History of South Africa* (London: Oxford University Press, 1941), p. 3.

41. Leonard Thompson, *A History of South Africa* (New Haven: Yale University Press, 1990), p. 33; de Klerk, *Puritans*, p. 8; George M. Fredrickson, *White Supremacy* (New York: Oxford University Press, 1981), pp. 17–18, 66.

42. Commission for the Socio-Economic Development of the Bantu Areas within South Africa (Tomlinson Commission), *Summary of the Report* (Pretoria: Government Printer, 1955), p. 18; I. D. MacCrone, *Race Attitudes in South Africa* (Johannesburg: University of the Witwatersrand Press, 1937), pp. 41, 73.

43. Jonathan Neil Gerstner, *The Thousand Generation Covenant* (Leiden: E. J. Brill, 1991), pp. 246–50; Heribert Adam and Hermann Giliomee, *Ethnic Power Mobilized: Can South Africa Survive?* (New Haven: Yale University Press, 1979), p. 86; de Klerk, *Puritans*, p. 12; Donald Harmon Akenson, *God's People* (Montreal: McGill and Queens University Press, 1991), p. 14.

    For an argument that the idea of Afrikaners as "chosen people" only developed later, see Andre du Toit, "No Chosen People: The Myth of Calvinist Origins of Afrikaner Nationalism and Racial Ideology," *American Historical Review* 88.4 (October 1993), pp. 920–52.

44. De Kiewiet, *History of South Africa*, p. 24; Howard Lamar and Leonard Thompson, *The Frontier in History* (New Haven: Yale University Press, 1981), p. 309; Thompson, *History of South Africa*, p. 38; South African

Native Affairs Commission, *Report of the Commission* (Cape Town: Government Printer, 1905), p. 3.
45. Thompson, *History of South Africa*, p. 52; Leonard Thompson, "The South African Dilemma," in Louis Hartz, ed., *The Founding of New Societies* (New York: Harcourt, 1964), p. 191; De Kiewiet, *History of South Africa*, p. 29; Donald Denoon, *Settler Capitalism* (Oxford: Clarendon Press, 1983), p. 43; Monica Wilson, "Cooperation and Conflict," in Monica Wilson and Leonard Thompson, eds., *The Oxford History of South Africa* (New York: Oxford University Press, 1969, volume 1), p. 369.
46. De Kiewiet, *History of South Africa* p. 46; Marianne Cornevin, *Apartheid: Power and Historical Falsification* (Paris: UNESCO, 1980), p. 59.
47. T. Dunbar Moodie, *The Rise of Afrikanerdom* (Berkeley: University of California Press, 1975), pp. 3–6; Peter Walshe, *The Rise of African Nationalism in South Africa* (Berkeley: University of California Press, 1971), p. 3; Andre Odendaal, *Vukani Bantu!* (Cape Town: David Philip, 1984), p. 5; George M. Fredrickson, *Black Liberation* (New York: Oxford University Press, 1995), pp. 15–20.
48. Jeff Guy, *The Destruction of the Zulu Kingdom* (London: Longmans, 1979); James O. Gump, *The Dust Rose Like Smoke* (Lincoln: University of Nebraska Press, 1994), p. 126.
49. Thompson, *History of South Africa*, p. 66; Akenson, *God's People*, pp. 62, 299.
50. Hermann Giliomee and Lawrence Schlemmer, *From Apartheid to Nation-Building* (Cape Town: Oxford University Press, 1989), p. 6; De Kiewiet, *History of South Africa*, p. 142; Saul Dubow, *Racial Segregation and the Origins of Apartheid in South Africa, 1919–1936* (Hampshire: Macmillan, 1989), p. 21; John W. Cell, *The Highest Stage of White Supremacy* (Cambridge: Cambridge University Press, 1982), p. 53; Thompson, *History of South Africa*, p. 97.
51. Moodie, *Afrikanerdom*, pp. 3–6; de Klerk, *Puritans*, p. 31; Hermann Giliomee, "The Beginnings of Afrikaner Ethnic Consciousness, 1850–1915," in Leroy Vail, ed., *The Creation of Tribalism in Southern Africa* (Berkeley: University of California Press, 1989), p. 27.
52. Quoted by de Klerk, *Puritans*, p. 33.
53. Donald Denoon, *A Grand Illusion* (London: Longman, 1973), p. 3.
54. De Klerk, *Puritans*, p. 23. See also Thompson, *History of South Africa*, pp. 67, 87; Leonard Thompson, "Cooperation and Conflict," in Monica Wilson and Leonard Thompson, eds., *The Oxford History of South Africa* (New York: Oxford University Press, 1969), vol. 1, p. 409; C. W. De Kiewiet, *The Imperial Factor in South Africa* (Cambridge: Cambridge University Press, 1937), p. 3.
55. South African Native Affairs Commission, *Report*, pp. 5–6.
56. Moodie, *Afrikanerdom*, p. 31; De Kiewiet, *History of South Africa*, p. 132.
57. Julius Lewin, *The Struggle for Racial Equality* (London: Longman, 1967), p. 5.

58. Fredrickson, *White Supremacy*, pp. 219, 228–9.
59. South African Native Affairs Commission, *Report*, pp. 5–6; Leonard Thompson, *The Unification of South Africa* (London: Oxford University Press, 1960), p. 3; Leonard Thompson, "Great Britain and the Afrikaner Republics," in Wilson and Thompson, eds., *Oxford History of South Africa* vol. 2, pp. 289–300.
60. De Kiewiet, *History of South Africa*, p. 114.
61. J. D. Kestell and D. E. van Velden, *The Peace Negotiations* (London: Richard Clay, 1912), p. 74. Afrikaner concern about the moral threat of wealth is consistent with the Dutch tradition of such concerns, as discussed in Simon Schama, *The Embarrassment of Riches* (Berkeley: University of California Press, 1988).
62. Shula Marks and Stanley Trapido, "Lord Milner and the South African State," *History Workshop* 8 (Autumn 1979), p. 60.
63. Thompson, *History of South Africa*, p. 138; De Kiewiet, *Imperial Factor in South Africa*, p. 10; Iain R. Smith, *The Origins of the South African War, 1899–1902* (London: Longman, 1996), p. 44.
64. De Kiewiet, *History of South Africa*, p. 89.
65. South African Native Affairs Commission, *Report*, p. 10.
66. James Lang, *Conquest and Commerce: Spain and England in the Americas* (New York: Academic Press, 1975).
67. Edmund S. Morgan, *American Slavery / American Freedom* (New York: Norton, 1975), pp. 269, 344.
68. Quoted in Fredrickson, *Black Image*, p. 1.
69. Joel Williamson, *The Crucible of Race* (New York: Oxford University Press, 1984), p. 16; Alexander Saxton, *The Rise and Fall of the White Republic* (London: Verso, 1990), p. 136.
70. Winthrop D. Jordan, *White Over Black* (New York: Norton, 1968), p. 332.
71. Eugene D. Genovese, *Roll, Jordan, Roll* (New York: Vintage Books, 1972), p. 92; Saxton, *White Republic*, pp. 385–8; Williamson, *Crucible of Race*, p. 81.
72. Quoting Frederick Douglass, in Genovese, *Roll, Jordan, Roll*, p. 64. See also J. William Harris, *Plain Folk and Gentry in a Slave Society* (Middletown, Conn.: Wesleyan University Press, 1985), p. 95.
73. Ulrick Bonnell Phillips, *The Course of the South to Secession* (New York: Hill and Wang, 1939), p. 165.
74. V. O. Key, Jr., *Southern Politics in State and Nation* (New York: Knopf, 1949), p. 315. See also Du Bois, *Black Reconstruction*, p. 39; Saxton, *White Republic*, p. 1; Michael Banton, *Race Relations* (London: Tavistock, 1967), p. 120.
75. Seymour Drescher, "Brazilian Abolition in Comparative Perspective," *Hispanic American Historical Review* 68.3 (1988), p. 438.
76. Fredrickson, *Black Image*, p. 5; Eric Foner, *Free Soil, Free Labor, Free Men* (London: Oxford University Press, 1970), p. 261; James M. McPherson,

The Struggle for Equality (Princeton: Princeton University Press, 1964), pp. 25, 333.

77. Alexis Tocqueville, *Democracy in America* (Garden City, N.Y.: Anchor/ Doubleday, 1969), p. 343.

78. Reginald Horsman, *Race and Manifest Destiny* (Cambridge, Mass.: Harvard University Press, 1981); Alexis Tocqueville, *Democracy in America*, p. 318; Saxton, *White Republic*, pp. 11, 54; McPherson, *Battle Cry*, p. 46; Lamar and Thompson, *Frontier in History*, p. 47.

79. Du Bois, *Black Reconstruction*, p. 47; Carl N. Degler, *The Other South* (New York: Harper and Row, 1974), p. 99.

80. Charles Tilly, *Coercion, Capital and European States, AD 990–1992* (Cambridge, Mass: Blackwell, 1990), p. 92.

81. Immanuel Wallerstein, *The Modern World-System II* (New York: Academic Press, 1980), pp. 39, 118, 184; Julia Adams, "Trading States, Trading Places," *Comparative Studies in Society and History* 36.2 (April 1994).

82. Tilly, *Coercion, Capital*, p. 93.

83. Wallerstein, *Modern World-System*, pp. 166, 192.

84. Freyre, *Masters and Slaves*, p. 81.

85. Mauricio Solaun and Sidney Kronus, *Discrimination with Violence* (New York: Wiley, 1973), p.1.

Chapter 3. Lessons from Slavery

1. David Brion Davis, *The Problem of Slavery in Western Culture* (New York: Oxford University Press, 1966), pp. 31, 66, 73.

2. Robert Shell, *Children of Bondage* (Hanover, N.H.: University Press of New England, 1994), p. 404; George M. Fredrickson, *White Supremacy* (New York: Oxford University Press, 1981), p. 74; Donald Denoon, *Settler Capitalism* (Oxford: Clarendon Press, 1983), p. 28.

3. Stanley B. Greenberg, *Race and State in Capitalist Development* (New Haven: Yale University Press, 1980), p. 36.

4. Shell, *Children of Bondage*, p. 143.

5. Ibid., p. 413; Leonard Thompson, *A History of South Africa* (New Haven: Yale University Press, 1990), p. 42.

6. Thompson, *History of South Africa*, pp. 57–8; Franklin W. Knight, *The African Dimension in Latin American Societies* (New York: Macmillan, 1974), p. 58.

7. Herbert S. Klein, *African Slavery in Latin America and the Caribbean* (New York: Oxford University Press, 1986), pp. 140–2; Herbert S. Klein, *The Middle Passage* (Princeton: Princeton University Press, 1978), pp. 37, 67–8, 85.

8. Davis, *Problem of Slavery*, p. 9.

9. Carl Degler, *Neither Black nor White* (Madison: University of Wisconsin Press, 1971), p. 3.

10. Frank Tannenbaum, *Slave and Citizen* (New York: Knopf, 1946), pp. xvi–xvii.

11. E. Bradford Burns, *A History of Brazil* (New York: Columbia University Press, 1970), p. 41. See also Roger Bastide, *The African Religions of Brazil* (Baltimore: Johns Hopkins University Press, 1978), p. 32; C. R. Boxer, *Four Centuries of Portuguese Expansion, 1415–1825* (Berkeley: University of California Press, 1969), p. 71; Gilberto Freyre, *The Masters and the Slaves* (Berkeley: University of California Press, 1986), p. 250.

12. Freyre, *Masters and Slaves*, p. 179.

13. Richard M. Morse, "The Heritage of Latin America," in Louis Hartz, ed., *The Founding of New Societies* (New York: Harcourt Brace and World, 1964), p. 138. See also Caio Prado, Jr., *The Colonial Background of Modern Brazil* (Berkeley: University of California Press, 1969), p. 115; Klein, *African Slavery*, pp. 22–3, 26, 41.

14. Burns, *History of Brazil*, p. 50; Robert Conrad, *The Destruction of Brazilian Slavery* (Berkeley: University of California Press, 1972), p. 26; Klein, *African Slavery*, p. 38.

15. Clóvis Moura, *História do Negro Brasileiro* (São Paulo: Atica, 1989), pp. 7–12. See also Robert Brent Toplin, *The Abolition of Slavery in Brazil* (New York: Atheneum, 1972), p. 119; Thomas E. Skidmore, *Black into White* (New York: Oxford University Press, 1974), p. 43. Klein notes that by 1850 and thereafter, slaves were increasingly concentrated in Rio de Janeiro, Minas, and São Paulo, but such concentration occurred only in the last decades of slavery. See Klein, *African Slavery*, p. 130; Klein, *Middle Passage*, pp. 95–111.

16. Robert Fogel and Stanley L. Engerman, *Time on the Cross* (Boston: Little, Brown, 1974), pp. 17–20.

17. Tannenbaum, *Slave and Citizen*, p. 39. See also Prado, *Colonial Background*, p. 406.

18. Davis, *Problem of Slavery*, p. 46.

19. Leslie B. Rout, Jr., "The African in Colonial Brazil," in Martin L. Kilson and Robert I. Rotberg, eds., *The African Diaspora* (Cambridge, Mass.: Harvard University Press, 1976), pp. 136–43; Tannenbaum, *Slave and Citizen*, p. 28.

20. Tannenbaum, *Slave and Citizen*, pp. 46, 89.

21. Alma Guillermoprieto, *Samba* (New York: Vintage, 1990), p. 51; Rout, "The African," p. 148.

22. Roberto da Matta, *Relativizando* (Petrópolis: Vozes, 1984), p. 75.

23. Tannenbaum, *Slave and Citizen*, p. 53. See also Klein, *African Slavery*, p. 191.

24. Tannenbaum, *Slave and Citizen*, p. 62; Pierre L. Van den Berghe, *Race and Racism* (New York: Wiley, 1967), p. 67; Donald Pierson, *Negroes in Brazil* (Chicago: University of Chicago, 1942), p. 92; Perry Anderson, "Portugal and the End of Ultra-Colonialism 2," *New Left Review* 16, (July/August 1962), p. 114; Winthrop D. Jordan, *White Over Black* (New York: Norton, 1968), p. 198.

25. Bastide, *African Religions of Brazil*, p. 52; Burns, *History of Brazil*, p. 53; Rout, "The African," pp. 134, 144; Abdias do Nascimento, *Brazil: Mixture or Massacre?* (Dover: Majority Press, 1979), p. 69. See also Stuart B. Schwartz, *Slaves, Peasants and Rebels* (Urbana: University of Illinois Press, 1992).

26. H. Hoetink, *The Two Variants in Caribbean Race Relations* (London: Oxford University Press, 1967), pp. 5, 21; Freyre, *Master and Slaves*, p. 193; Boxer, *Four Centuries*, p. 43; da Matta, *Relativizando*, p. 64.

27. Prado, *Colonial Background*, p. 327; Michael Mitchell, "Racial Consciousness and the Political Attitudes and Behavior of Blacks in São Paulo, Brazil," Ph.D. dissertation, Indiana University, Bloomington (1977), pp. 87, 98.

28. Tannenbaum, *Slave and Citizen*, p. 62; Emilia Viotti da Costa, *The Brazilian Empire* (Chicago: University of Chicago Press, 1985), p. xix; Diana DeG. Brown and Mario Bick, "Religion, Class and Context: Continuities and Discontinuities in Brazilian *Umbanda*," *American Ethnologist* 14.1 (February 1987), p. 75; Toplin, *Abolition of Slavery*, p. 119; Eugene D. Genovese, *Roll, Jordan, Roll* (New York: Random House, 1972), p. 177.

29. Tannenbaum, *Slave and Citizen*, p. 49; Stanley Elkins, *Slavery* (Chicago: University of Chicago Press, 1959), p. 73; Robert Conrad, *Children of God's Fire* (Princeton: Princeton University Press, 1983), p. 101; Robert Conrad, "Nineteenth Century Brazilian Slavery," in Robert Brent Toplin, ed., *Slavery and Race Relations in Latin America* (Westport, Conn.: Greenwood, 1974), p. 162.

30. Conrad, "Nineteenth Century Slavery," p. 165; Robert Brent Toplin, *The Abolition of Slavery in Brazil* (New York: Atheneum, 1972), p. 48.

31. Klein, *African Slavery*, pp. 128. 194.

32. Tannenbaum, *Slave and Citizen*, p. 49; Toplin, *Abolition of Slavery*, p. 199; Conrad, *Destruction*, p. 237; Guillermoprieto, *Samba*, p. 185.

33. Freyre, *Master and Slaves*, p. 378; Laura Foner and Eugene Genovese, eds., *Slavery in the New World* (Englewood Cliffs, N.J.: Prentice Hall, 1969), p. 199.

34. Tannenbaum, *Slave and Citizen*, pp. 54, 69.

35. Rout, "The African," p. 162.

36. Toplin, *Abolition of Slavery*, p. 24; Tannenbaum, *Slave and Citizen*, p. 100; Richard Graham, "1850–1870," in Leslie Bethell, ed., *Brazil: Empire and Republic, 1822–1930* (Cambridge: Cambridge University Press, 1989), p. 124; Conrad, "Nineteenth Century," p. 152; Charles Wagley, *Race and Class in Rural Brazil* (Paris: UNESCO, 1952), p. 143; Thomas E. Skidmore, "Toward a Comparative Analysis of Race Relations . . . ," *Latin American Studies* 4.1 (1972); Carlos Hasenbalg, "Race Relations in Post-Abolition Brazil: The Smooth Preservation of Racial Inequalities," Ph.D. dissertation, University of California, Berkeley (1978), p. 125; Carlos Hasenbalg, "Desigualdades Raciais no Brasil," *Dados* 14, (1977), p. 12.

37. Tannenbaum, *Slave and Citizen*, p. 55.

38. Degler, *Neither Black nor White*, p. 84; Jocélio Teles dos Santos, "Ex-Escrava Proprietária de Escrava," Programa de Estudo do Negro na Bahia (Salvador: Federal University of Bahia, 1991); Stuart B. Schwartz, "Patterns of Slaveholding in the Americas," *American Historical Review* 87.1 (February 1982), p. 79. Freed blacks in the United States also on occasion owned their own slaves.

39. Conrad, "Nineteenth Century," pp. 154–5; Robert Conrad, "Neither Slave nor Free: The Emancipados of Brazil, 1818–1868," *Hispanic American Historical Review* 53.1 (February 1973), pp. 50–3.

40. A. J. R. Russell-Wood, "Colonial Brazil," in David W. Cohen and Jack P. Greene, eds., *Neither Slave Nor Free* (Baltimore: Johns Hopkins University Press, 1972), pp. 90–2.

41. Degler, *Neither Black nor White*, p. 71; Richard Graham, "Economics or Culture," in Kees Gispen, ed., *What Made the South Different?* (Jackson: University Press of Mississippi, 1990), p. 120; do Nascimento, *Brazil*, p. 43; Clóvis Moura, "Organizações Negras," in Paul Singer and V. Caldeira Brant, eds., *São Paulo: O Povo em Movimento* (Petrópolis: Ed. Vozes, 1980), p. 143; Clóvis Moura, *Brasil: Raízes do Protesto Negro* (São Paulo: Global, 1983), p. 47; Conrad, "Neither Slave nor Free," p. 60; George Reid Andrews, "Race and the State in Colonial Brazil," *Latin American Research Review* 19.3 (1984), pp. 208–9.

42. Pierson, *Negroes*, p. 73; Van den Berghe, *Race and Racism*, p. 61. See also Elkins, *Slavery*, pp. 102–3.

43. Do Nascimento, *Brazil*, p. 3. See also Davis, *Problem of Slavery*, p. 243, n. 26; A. J. R. Russell-Wood, *The Black Man in Slavery and Freedom in Colonial Brazil* (London: Macmillan, 1982), pp. 95–6.

44. Charles H. Wood and Jose Alberto Magno de Carvalho, *The Demography of Inequality in Brazil* (Cambridge: Cambridge University Press, 1988), p. 140.

45. Degler, *Neither Black nor White*, pp. 65, 74; Luiz Felipe de Alencastro, "Qui parle de démocratie raciale?," *Brésil* 44 (November 1982), pp. 102–5.

46. Charles Boxer, *The Golden Age of Brazil, 1695–1750* (Berkeley: University of California Press, 1962), p. 174; Moura, *História do Negro Brasileiro*, p. 14.

47. Conrad, *Destruction*, p. 150. See also Conrad, *Children of God's Fire*, p. 100; Costa, *Brazilian Empire*, p. 134.

48. Costa, *Brazilian Empire*, p. 144; Hasenbalg, "Race Relations in Post-Abolition Brazil," pp. 135–52.

49. Degler, *Neither Black nor White*, pp. 52–7; Klein, *African Slavery*, p. 168; Clóvis Moura, *Rebeliões da Senzala* (São Paulo: Livraria Editora Ciências Humanas, 1981); Eugene D. Genovese, *From Rebellion to Revolution: Afro-American Slave Revolts in the Making of the Modern World* (Baton Rouge: Louisiana State University Press, 1979), pp. 11–12.

50. Burns, *History of Brazil*, p. 54; Freyre, *Masters and Slaves*, p. 69.

51. C. L. R. James, *The Black Jacobins* (New York: Random House, 1963);

Célia Maria Marinho de Azevedo, *Onda Negra, Medo Branco* (Rio de Janeiro: Paz e Terra, 1987), p. 35.

52. Russell-Wood, *Black Man*, p. 81; Moura, *História*, p. 43; do Nascimento, *Brazil*, p. 32; Pierson, *Negroes*, p. 7; Genovese, *From Rebellion to Revolution*, p. 32; Robert M. Levine, "Turning on the Lights," *Latin American Research Review* 24.2 (1989), p. 207; Conrad, *Children*, p. 406–11; Klein, *African Slavery*, p. 212.

53. Thomas Flory, "Race and Social Control in Independent Brazil," *Journal of Latin American Studies* 9.2, p. 216. See also Célia Maria Marinho de Azevedo, "Sinal Fechado para os Negros na Rua Liberdade," *Humanidades* 5.17 (1988), p. 10; Azevedo, *Onda Negra*, pp. 35, 120, 180; Burns, *History of Brazil*, p. 271.

54. Azevedo, *Onda Negra*, pp. 43–5.

55. Roger Bastide, "The Development of Race Relations in Brazil," in Guy Hunter, ed., *Industrialization and Race Relations* (London: Oxford University Press, 1965), p. 9; Conrad, *Destruction*, p. 35; Skidmore, *Black into White*, p. 19.

56. Azevedo, *Onda Negra*, p. 60; Seymour Drescher, "Brazilian Abolition in Comparative Perspective," *Hispanic American Historical Review* 68.3 (1988), pp. 433–8; Carlos Hasenbalg and Suellen Huntington, "Brazilian Racial Democracy: Reality or Myth?" *Humboldt Journal of Social Relations* 10.1 (Fall/Winter 1982–3), p. 130; Emilia Viotti da Costa, "1870–1889," in Leslie Bethell, ed., *Brazil: Empire and Republic, 1822–1930* (Cambridge: Cambridge University Press, 1989), p. 199.

57. Toplin, *Abolition of Slavery*, p. xi. See also Azevedo, *Onda Negra*, pp. 52, 215–22; da Matta, *Relativizando*, p. 68; Azevedo, "Sinal Fechado," p. 9.

58. Toplin, *Abolition of Slavery*, p. 39; Leslie Bethell, "Independence," in Leslie Bethell, ed., *Brazil: Empire and Republic, 1822–1930* (Cambridge: Cambridge University Press, 1989), pp. 20–39; Burns, *History of Brazil*, p. 182; Conrad, *Destruction*, pp. 21–3.

59. Drescher, "Abolition," p. 445; Costa, *Brazilian Empire*, p. 144; Conrad, *Destruction*, pp. 31, 49.

60. Toplin, *Abolition of Slavery*, p. 216; Eugene D. Genovese, *The World the Slaveholders Made* (New York: Pantheon, 1969), p. 94; George M. Fredrickson, "Reflections on the Comparative History and Sociology of Racism," manuscript (1994), pp. 9–10; Degler, *Neither Black nor White*, p. 77; Skidmore, *Black into White*, p. 8.

61. Azevedo, "Sinal Fechado," pp. 10–11; Célia Maria Marinho de Azevedo, "Batismo da Liberdade," *História: Questões e Debates* 9.16 (January 1988), pp. 38–44; Azevedo, *Onda Negra*, p. 257; Hasenbalg, "Race Relations in Post-Abolition Brazil," p. 154; Thomas E. Skidmore, "Racial Ideas and Social Policy in Brazil, 1870–1940," in Richard Graham, ed., *Brazil: Empire and Republic, 1822–1930* (Austin: University of Texas Press, 1990), p. 9; Toplin, *Abolition of Slavery*, p. 74; Knight, *The African Dimension*, p. 88.

62. Skidmore, *Black into White*, p. 20; Harris, *Patterns of Race*, p. 93.

63. Conrad, *Destruction*, p. 211; Klein, *African Slavery*, p. 256.
64. Thomas E. Skidmore, "Brazilian Intellectuals and the Problem of Race, 1870–1930," Vanderbilt University, Nashville, Occasional Papers Series no. 6 (1969).
65. Skidmore, *Black into White*, p. 16; Conrad, *Destruction*, p. 91; Graham, "1850–1870," p. 158; Burns, *History of Brazil*, p. 268; Azevedo, "Batismo," p. 47; Jan Fiola, "Race Relations in Brazil," Program in Latin American Studies, University of Massachusetts at Amherst, Occasional Paper Series no. 24 (1990), p. 2.
66. Florestan Fernandes, "Luta de Raças e de Classes," *Teoria e Debate* 2 (March 1988), p. 7; Burns, *History of Brazil*, p. 278.
67. Drescher, "Abolition," p. 459.
68. Prado, *Colonial Background*, p. 1, n. 1. See also Costa, "1880–1889," p. 202; Costa, *Brazilian Empire*, p. 169.
69. Joaquim Nabuco, *O Abolicionismo* (São Paulo, 1938), p. 130.
70. Vincent Harding, *There Is a River* (New York: Harcourt Brace Jovanovich, 1981), p. 7.
71. Fogel and Engerman, *Time on the Cross*, p. 248.
72. W. E. B. Du Bois, *Black Reconstruction in America* (New York: Atheneum, 1992), p. 12. See also J. William Harris, *Plain Folk and Gentry in a Slave Society* (Middletown, Conn.: Wesleyan University Press, 1985), p. 38; Edmund S. Morgan, *American Slavery / American Freedom* (New York: Norton, 1975), p. 369.
73. Davis, *Problem of Slavery*, p. 154.
74. Fogel and Engerman, *Time on the Cross*, p. 154; Genovese, *Roll Jordan, Roll*, p. 57. In Virginia, earlier mortality for whites and blacks had been higher, as discussed in Morgan, *American Slavery*, p. 297.
75. Ulrich Bonnell Phillips, *Life and Labor in the Old South* (Boston: Little, Brown, 1951), pp. 194, 200.
76. Fogel and Engerman, *Time on the Cross*, pp. 40, 57, 149; Claudia Dale Goldin, *Urban Slavery in the American South, 1820–1860* (Chicago: University of Chicago Press, 1976), pp. 1, 40, 65, 123.
77. Du Bois, *Black Reconstruction*, p. 10. See also Elkins, *Slavery*, p. 59.
78. Phillips, *Life and Labor*, p. 162; Joel Williamson, *A Rage for Order* (New York: Oxford University Press, 1986), p. 9; Genovese, *Roll, Jordan, Roll*, pp. 41, 561; Alexis Tocqueville, *Democracy in America* (Garden City: Anchor/Doubleday, 1969), p. 317; Van den Berghe, *Race and Racism*, p. 83
79. Davis, *Problem of Slavery*, p. 57.
80. Degler, *Neither Black nor White*, p. 83; Tannenbaum, *Slave and Citizen*, pp. 65, 69, 95; Williamson, *Rage for Order*, p. 25; Fogel and Engerman, *Time on the Cross*, pp. 37, 150.
81. Genovese, *Roll, Jordan, Roll*, p. 51.
82. Du Bois, *Black Reconstruction*, p. 40; William Julius Wilson, *The Declining Significance of Race* (Chicago: University of Chicago Press, 1978), p. 33; James C. Scott, *Weapons of the Weak* (New Haven: Yale University Press, 1985); Harding, *There Is a River*, pp. 49, 162.

83. Genovese, *Roll, Jordan, Roll*, Book 4; Degler, *Neither Black nor White*, p. 47; Genovese, *From Rebellion to Revolution*, pp. 4, 42–6; Harding, *There Is a River*, p. 58.
84. Fogel and Engerman, *Time on the Cross*, p. 230; Phillips, *Life and Labor*, pp. 160, 195.
85. Goldin, *Urban Slavery*, pp. xi, 49.
86. Richard Kluger, *Simple Justice* (New York: Random House, 1976), pp. 36–7.
87. James M. McPherson, *The Struggle for Equality* (Princeton: Princeton University Press, 1964), pp. 222–4.
88. George M. Fredrickson, *The Black Image in the White Mind* (Middletown, Conn.: Wesleyan University Press, 1971), p. 27.
89. Du Bois, *Black Reconstruction*, p. 147; Edwin S. Redkey, *Black Exodus* (New Haven: Yale University Press, 1969), p. 18.
90. Harold Holzer, ed., *The Lincoln–Douglas Debates* (New York: Harper Collins, 1993), p. 189; Fredrickson, *Black Image*, pp. 150, 166; Fredrickson, *White Supremacy*, p. 158.
91. Holzer, *Lincoln–Douglas Debates*, p. 42; Genovese, *Roll, Jordan, Roll*, p. 437.
92. Fredrickson, *Black Image*, pp. 321, 43. See also Du Bois, *Black Reconstruction*, p. 39; Fredrickson, *Black Image*, p. 321.
93. Fredrickson, *Black Image*, pp. 69, 255. See also Nancy Stepan, *The Idea of Race in Science* (Hamden: Archon, 1982), p. 47.
94. Jordan, *White over Black*, p. 131.
95. Eric Foner, *Free Soil, Free Labor, Free Men* (London: Oxford University Press, 1970), p. 224.
96. Alexander Saxton, *The Rise and Fall of the White Republic* (London: Verso, 1990), p. 247.
97. Holzer, *Lincoln–Douglas Debates*, p. 49.
98. Foner, *Free Soil*, pp. 219, 224–5; Holzer, *Lincoln–Douglas Debates*, p. 94.
99. Foner, *Free Soil*, pp. 310–11; James M. McPherson, *Battle Cry of Freedom* (New York: Oxford University Press, 1988), p. 223.
100. Genovese, *The World the Slaveholders Made* (New York: Pantheon, 1969), p. 99.
101. Skidmore, *Black into White*, p. 44.
102. Louis Hartz, *The Founding of New Societies* (San Diego: Harcourt Brace Jovanovich, 1964), p. 56.

Chapter 4. The Uncertain Legacy of Miscegenation

1. Marvin Harris, *Patterns of Race Relations in the Americas* (Westport, Conn.: Greenwood, 1964), p. 68.
2. E. Bradford Burns, *A History of Brazil* (New York: Columbia University Press, 1970), p. 37; Caio Prado, Jr., *The Colonial Background of Modern Brazil* (Berkeley: University of California Press, 1969), p. 119.

3. A. J. R. Russell-Wood, *The Black Man in Slavery and Freedom in Colonial Brazil* (London: Macmillan, 1982), p. 30.
4. David T. Haberly, *Three Sad Races: Racial Identity and National Consciousness in Brazilian Literature* (Cambridge: Cambridge University Press, 1983), p. 168; Roberto da Matta, *Relativizando* (Petrópolis: Vozes, 1984), pp. 72–3.
5. Thomas E. Skidmore, "Bi-racial U.S. versus Multi-Racial Brazil: Is the Contrast still Valid?" Conference on Racism and Race Relations in the Countries of the African Diaspora, Rio de Janeiro (June 1992), manuscript, p. 4; Frank Tannenbaum, *Slave and Citizen* (New York: Knopf, 1946), p. 35; Herbert S. Klein, *African Slavery in Latin America and the Caribbean* (New York: Oxford University Press, 1986), p. 147.
   For a general discussion, see Ann L. Stoller, "Making Empire Respectable," *American Ethnologist* 16.4 (November 1989); Frantz Fanon, *Black Skin, White Masks* (New York: Grove Press, 1967), ch. 6.
6. Burns, *History of Brazil*, p. 55; Carlos Hasenbalg, "Desigualdades Raciais no Brasil," *Dados* 19.7 (1983), p. 14; Nelson do Valle Silva and Carlos Hasenbalg, *Relações Raciais no Brasil Contemporâneo* (Rio de Janeiro: Rio Funda, 1992), p. 26.
7. H. Hoetink, *The Two Variants in Caribbean Race Relations* (London: Oxford University Press, 1967).
8. Pierre L. Van den Berghe, *Race and Racism* (New York: Wiley, 1967), p. 71.
9. Ben Zimmerman, "Race Relations," in Charles Wagley, ed., *Race and Class in Rural Brazil* (Paris: UNESCO, 1952), p. 95.
10. Karl Friedrich Philipp Von Martius, "Como se Deve Escrever a História do Brasil," *Revista do Instituto Histórico e Geográfico Brasileiro* 6 (1844), pp. 381–403 (reprinted in translation in E. Bradford Burns, *Perspectives on Brazilian History* [New York: Columbia University, 1967], pp. 21–41). See also Thomas E. Skidmore, *Black into White* (New York: Oxford University Press, 1974); Winthrop R. Wright, *Cafe con Leche* (Austin: University of Texas Press, 1990); Peter Wade, *Blackness and Race Mixing* (Baltimore: Johns Hopkins University Press, 1993).
11. Harris, *Patterns of Race*, pp. 86–9; H. Hoetink, *Slavery and Race Relations in the Americas* (New York: Harper and Row, 1973), p. 21; Célia Maria Marinho de Azevedo, *Onda Negra, Medo Branco* (Rio de Janeiro: Paz e Terra, 1987), p. 80; Katia de Quierós Mattoso, "Slave, Free and Freed Family Structures in Nineteenth Century Salvador, Bahia," *Luso-Brazilian Review* 25.1 (1988); Russell-Wood, *Black Man*, p. 63; Carl N. Degler, *Neither Black nor White* (Madison: University of Wisconsin Press, 1971), p. 84.
12. Degler, *Neither Black nor White*, pp. 195, 225.
13. Harris, *Patterns of Race*, p. 54.
14. Van den Berghe, *Race and Racism*, p. 71.
15. Florestan Fernandes, "Negro and Mulatto in Brazil," in *Slavery and Race Relations in Latin America* (Westport, Conn.: Greenwood, 1974), p. 293.

16. Thomas E. Skidmore, "Race and Class in Brazil: Historical Perspectives," in Pierre-Michel Fontaine, ed., *Race, Class and Power in Brazil* (Los Angeles: Center for Afro-American Studies, University of California, 1985), p. 19.

17. Abdias do Nascimento, *Brazil: Mixture or Massacre?* (Dover: Majority, 1979), p. ix; Degler, *Neither Black nor White*, p. 192.

18. George Reid Andrews, *Blacks and Whites in São Paulo, Brazil, 1888–1988* (Madison: University of Wisconsin Press, 1991), p. 253.

19. Tannenbaum, *Slave and Citizen*, p. 4.

20. Da Matta, *Relativizando*, p. 84. See also Sérgio Buarque de Holanda, *Raízes do Brasil* (Rio de Janeiro: José Olympio, 1983).

21. Degler, *Neither Black nor White*, pp. 102–3.

22. Nelson do Valle Silva, "Updating the Cost of Not Being White in Brazil," in Pierre-Michel Fontaine, ed., *Race, Class, and Power in Brazil* (Los Angeles: Center for Afro-American Studies, University of California, 1985), p. 54. See also Silva and Hasenbalg, *Relações Raciais no Brasil*; Charles H. Wood and Jose Magno de Carvalho, *The Demography of Inequality in Brazil* (Cambridge: Cambridge University Press, 1988); Andrews, *Blacks and Whites*, pp. 250–3.

23. Degler, *Neither Black nor White*, p. 235.

24. George M. Fredrickson, *White Supremacy* (New York: Oxford University Press, 1981), pp. 101–4; F. James Davis, *Who is Black?: One Nation's Definition* (University Park: Pennsylvania State University Press, 1991), pp. 33–6.
    Miscegenation was already condemned in Virginia in the late 1600s, as discussed in Edmund S. Morgan, *American Slavery/American Freedom* (New York: Norton, 1975), p. 335. Louisiana outlawed miscegenation only in 1908.

25. Davis, *Who is Black?*, p. 36; Virginia R. Dominguez, *White by Definition* (New Brunswick, N.J.: Rutgers University Press, 1986); W. E. B. Du Bois, *Black Reconstruction in America* (New York: Atheneum, 1992), p. 12.

26. Robert William Fogel and Stanley L. Engerman, *Time on the Cross* (Boston: Little, Brown, 1974), p. 132.

27. Davis, *Who is Black?*, pp. 25, 40; E. Franklin Frazier, *Black Bourgeoisie* (New York: Collier Macmillan, 1957), p. 116; Genovese, *Roll, Jordan, Roll*, p. 414; Du Bois, *Black Reconstruction*, p. 3; Elizabeth Mullins and Paul Sites, "The Origins of Contemporary Eminent Black Americans," *American Sociological Review* 49 (October 1984), p. 673.

28. Joel Williamson, *A Rage for Order* (New York: Oxford University Press, 1986), p. 25.

29. Joel Williamson, *New People* (New York: New York University Press, 1984), p. 3; Skidmore, "Bi-racial U.S. versus Multi-Racial Brazil," p. 12; Mullins and Sites, "Origins," p. 672.

30. Do Nascimento, *Brazil*, p. 65.

31. Davis, *Who is Black?*, p. 21; Frazier, *Black Bourgeoisie*, p. 116; Verna M. Keith and Cedric Herring, "Skin Tone and Stratification in the Black

Community," *American Journal of Sociology* 97.3 (November 1991), pp. 760–78; Michael Hughes and Bradley R. Hertel, "The Significance of Color Remains," *Social Forces* 69.1 (1990).

32. Commission for the Socio-Economic Development of the Bantu Areas within the Union of South Africa (Tomlinson Commission), *Summary of the Report* (Pretoria: Government Printer, 1955), p. 18.

33. Fredrickson, *White Supremacy*, pp. 112–15.

34. George M. Fredrickson, *The Arrogance of Race* (Middletown, Conn.: Wesleyan University Press, 1988), p. 242.

35. Leonard Thompson, *A History of South Africa* (New Haven: Yale University Press, 1990), p. 66.

36. Commission of Inquiry into Matters Relating to the Coloured Population Group (Theron Commission), *Report* (Pretoria: Government Printer, 1976), p. 343. See also Sheila Patterson, *Colour and Culture in South Africa* (London: Routledge and Kegan Paul, 1953), p. 40.

37. Ian Goldin, *Making Race* (Cape Town: Maskew Miller Longman, 1987), p. 32; Shula Marks and Stanley Trapido, eds., *The Politics of Race, Class, and Nationalism in Twentieth Century South Africa* (London: Longman, 1987), pp. 158, 162.

38. Leonard Thompson, "The Compromise of Union," in Monica Wilson and Leonard Thompson, eds., *Oxford History of South Africa* (Oxford: Clarendon, 1971) vol. 2, p. 356; Leonard Thompson, *Unification of South Africa* (Oxford: Clarendon, 1960), p. 110; Patterson, *Colour and Culture*, p. 32.

39. Thomas Karis and Gwendolen M. Carter, eds., *From Protest to Challenge* (Stanford: Hoover Institution Press, 1973), vol. 2, p. 91.

40. Gavin Lewis, *Between the Wire and the Wall* (Cape Town: David Philip, 1987), p. 207; Marks and Trapido, eds., *Politics of Race, Class, and Nationalism*, pp. 29, 163, 165–6.

41. Theron Commission, *Report*, pp. 344, 439; Goldin, *Making Race*, pp. 87, 97; Lewis, *Between the Wire and the Wall*, p. 147.

42. Theron Commission, *Report*, pp. 489, 503, 519.

43. Ibid., p. 38.

44. Ibid., pp. 449–50; Lewis, *Between the Wire and the Wall*, p. 249.

45. Central Statistical Service, *South African Statistics* (Pretoria: Government Printer, 1988), Tables 1.7, 7.7.

46. Degler, *Neither Black nor White*; Harris, *Patterns of Race*, p. 54.

47. Lewis, *Between the Wire and the Wall*, p. 3.

48. Theron Commission, *Report*, p. 23.

49. Alexis Tocqueville, *Democracy in America* (Garden City: Anchor/Doubleday, 1969), p. 356.

50. Fredrickson, *White Supremacy*, p. 134.

51. Ibid., p. 86.

52. Harris, *Patterns of Race*, p. 56.

53. Hoetink, *Slavery*, p. 27.

Part Two. Racial Domination and the Nation-State

Chapter 5. "We for Thee, South Africa"

1. W. A. de Klerk, *The Puritans in Africa* (Harmondsworth: Penguin, 1975), p. 67.
2. Shula Marks and Stanley Trapido, "Lord Milner and the South African State," *History Workshop* 8 (Autumn 1979), pp. 60–3; C. W. De Kiewiet, *A History of South Africa* (London: Oxford University Press, 1941), pp. 100, 141.
3. J. A. Hobson, *The War in South Africa* (New York: Howard Fertig, 1969), pp. 47–9. See also Iain R. Smith, *The Origins of the South African War, 1899–1902* (London: Longman, 1996).
4. Quoted in G. H .L. LeMay, *British Supremacy in South Africa, 1899–1907* (Oxford: Clarendon Press, 1965), p. 27.
5. Ibid., p. 3.
6. Ivor Wilkins and Hans Strydom, *The Super Afrikaners* (Johannesburg: J. Ball, 1978), p. 38.
7. Thomas Packenham, *The Boer War* (New York: Random House, 1979), p. 607; Leonard Thompson, *The Unification of South Africa* (Oxford: Clarendon Press, 1960), p. 12; Wilkins and Strydom, *Super Afrikaners*, p. 38.
8. Pakenham, *Boer War*, p. xix.
9. J. D. Kestell and D. E. van Velden, *The Peace Negotiations* (London: Richard Clay, 1912), pp. 22, 30, 68.
10. Ibid., pp. 73–4, 89.
11. LeMay, *British Supremacy*, p. 21.
12. Kestell and van Velden, *Peace Negotiations*, p. 189.
13. Ibid., p. 144; LeMay, *British Supremacy*, pp. 77, 82, 139.
14. LeMay, *British Supremacy*, pp. 154, 111.
15. Ibid., p. 112.
16. Kestell and van Velden, *Peace Negotiations*, pp. 116–18.
17. Ibid., p. 208. See also LeMay, *British Supremacy*, p. 42.
18. Leonard Thompson, "The Compromise of Union," in Monica Wilson and Leonard Thompson, eds., *The Oxford History of South Africa* (Oxford: Clarendon Press, 1971), vol. 2, p. 326; LeMay, *British Supremacy*, p. 101; Pakenham, *Boer War*, pp. 424, 608.
19. Ian Goldin, *Making Race* (Cape Town: Maskew Miller Longman, 1987), pp. 19–20. See also Gavin Lewis, *Between the Wire and the Wall* (Cape Town: David Philip, 1987), p. 15; Donald Denoon, *A Grand Illusion* (London: Longman, 1973), p. 111.
20. Denoon, *Grand Illusion*, p. 4.
21. Kestell and van Velden, *Peace Negotiations*, pp. 54–6, 195. See also LeMay, *British Supremacy*, p. 55.
22. Kestell and van Velden, *Peace Negotiations*, p. 112 (a facsimile of the

original text, with handwritten edits, is presented facing this page). See also Denoon, *Grand Illusion*, p. 25.

23. Shula Marks, "Review Article: Scrambling for South Africa," *Journal of African History* 23 (1982), pp. 97–113.
24. Thompson, "Compromise of Union," p. 331; Denoon, *Grand Illusion*, p. 97.
25. Ralph Horowitz, *The Political Economy of South Africa* (New York: Praeger, 1967), p. 58, quoting A. J. P. Taylor.
26. Leonard Thompson, *A History of South Africa* (New Haven: Yale University Press, 1990), p. 146. See also John W. Cell, *The Highest Stage of White Supremacy* (Cambridge: Cambridge University Press, 1982), p. 266.
27. Peter Walshe, *The Rise of African Nationalism in South Africa* (Berkeley: University of California Press, 1971), p. 23.
28. Kestell and van Velden, *Peace Negotiations*, pp. 91, 176.
29. LeMay, *British Supremacy*, pp. 174, 213. See also Shula Marks and Stanley Trapido, eds., *The Politics of Race, Class and Nationalism in Twentieth Century South Africa* (London: Longman, 1987), p. 1; Rene de Villiers, "Afrikaner Nationalism," in Monica Wilson and Leonard Thompson, eds., *The Oxford History of South Africa* (Oxford: Clarendon Press, 1971), vol. 2, p. 367.
30. Thompson, "Compromise of Union," p. 341.
31. Thompson, *Unification*, pp. 30–2.
32. Denoon, *Grand Illusion*, pp. 14, 242.
33. Thompson, *History of South Africa*, p. 71.
34. Lewis, *Between the Wire and the Wall*, p. 13; Thompson, "Compromise of Union," p. 345.
35. South African Native Affairs Commission, *Report of the Commission* (Cape Town: Government Printers, 1905), vol. 1, p. 35. See also Adam Ashforth, *The Politics of Official Discourse in Twentieth Century South Africa* (Oxford: Clarendon Press, 1990), p. 28.
36. Thompson, "Compromise of Union," p. 364.
37. Pakenham, *Boer War*, p. 612.
38. Lewis, *Between the Wire and the Wall*, p. 37.
39. Nelson Mandela, *Long Walk to Freedom* (Boston: Little, Brown, 1994), p. 541.
40. As quoted in LeMay, *British Supremacy*, pp. 11–12.
41. Hobson, *War in South Africa*, pp. 281, 246.
42. Commission for the Socio-Economic Development of the Bantu Areas within the Union of South Africa (Tomlinson Commission), *Summary of the Report* (Pretoria: Government Printer, 1955), p. 8; Ashforth, *Politics of Official Discourse*, p. 23.
43. Hermann Giliomee and Lawrence Schlemmer, *From Apartheid to Nation-Building* (Cape Town: Oxford University Press, 1989), p. 11.
44. Dan O'Meara, *Volkskapitalisme* (Johannesburg: Ravan, 1983), p. 25.
45. South African Native Affairs Commission, *Report*, vol. 1, pp. 35, 96, 10.

46. Basil Williams, ed., *The Shelborne Memorandum* (London: Oxford University Press, 1925), pp. 27, 109–10, 170–4.
47. Donald Denoon, *Settler Capitalism* (Oxford: Clarendon Press, 1983), p. 200.
48. Thompson, *Unification*, p. 402.; Julius Lewin, *The Struggle for Racial Equality* (London: Longmans, 1967), pp. 32–7.
49. Thompson, *Unification*, p. 187.
50. George M. Fredrickson, *The Arrogance of Race* (Middletown, Conn.: Wesleyan University Press, 1988), p. 264. Though I disagree with Fredrickson's argument that South Africa had no conflict comparable to the U.S. Civil War, I agree that even if one sees the Boer War as comparable, the overall experiences of the two countries cannot be "lumped" together.
51. Thompson, *History of South Africa*, p. 150. See also Horowitz, *Political Economy*, p. 74; Thompson, "Compromise of Union," p. 351.
52. South African Native Affairs Commission, *Report*, p. 35; Ashforth, *Politics of Official Discourse*, p. 28.
53. See Walshe, *African Nationalism*, p. 44.
54. Thomas Karis, "South Africa," in Gwendolen Carter, ed., *Five African States* (Ithaca, N.Y.: Cornell University Press, 1963), p. 481.
55. South African Native Affairs Commission, *Report*, p. 95. See also Horowitz, *Political Economy*, p. 78; Martin Legassick, "The Frontier Tradition in South African Historiography," in Shula Marks and Anthony Atmore, eds., *Economy and Society in Pre-Industrial South Africa* (London: Longmans, 1980), p. 259.
56. Thompson, "Compromise of Union," pp. 338, 356.
57. Cell, *Highest Stage*, p. 62; De Kiewiet, *History of South Africa*, p. 146.
58. Tomlinson Commission, *Summary of the Report* p. 9; Cell, *Highest Stage*, pp. 62–7; Francis Wilson, *Labour in the South African Gold Mines, 1911–1969* (Cambridge: Cambridge University Press, 1972), p. 15.
59. South African Native Affairs Commission, *Report*, vol. 1, p. 80.
60. Hobson, *War in South Africa*, p. 240. See also Le May, *British Supremacy*, p. 30.
61. South African Native Affairs Commission, *Report*, vol. 1, pp. 35, 80–1, 87. See also Martin Legassick, "South Africa: Forced Labor, Industrialization, and Racial Differentiation," in Richard Harris, ed., *The Political Economy of Africa* (New York: Wiley, 1975), pp. 242–6; Colin Bundy, *The Rise and Fall of the South African Peasantry* (Berkeley: University of California Press, 1979), p. 213; David Yudelman, *The Emergence of Modern South Africa* (Westport, Conn.: Greenwood Press, 1983), pp. 33, 55; John Rex, "The Plural Society: The South African Case," *Race* 12.4 (1971), p. 406; Deborah Posel, "Rethinking the Race–Class Debate in South African Historiography," *Social Dynamics* 9.1 (1983), p. 60.
62. Yudelman, *Emergence*, p. 5.
63. Quoting Milner in LeMay, *British Supremacy*, p. 8.
64. C. M. van den Heever, *General J. B. M. Hertzog* (Johannesburg: APB

Bookstore, 1946), p. 121; T. Dunbar Moodie, *The Rise of Afrikanerdom* (Berkeley: University of California Press, 1975), p. 10.

65. Thompson, *Unification*, p. 16.
66. Jan Smuts, "The White Man's Task," (1917), in *Greater South Africa* (Johannesburg: Truth Legion, 1940), p. 14.
67. Moodie, *Rise of Afrikanerdom*, p. 10. See also de Klerk, *Puritans*, p. 85; van den Heever, *Hertzog*, p. 200.
68. De Klerk, *Puritans*, p. 102; Moodie, *Rise of Afrikanerdom*, p. 16.
69. Smuts, "White Man's Task," p. 18; Walshe, *African Nationalism*, p. 53.
70. Giliomee and Schlemmer, *Apartheid to Nation-Building*, p. 53.
71. Fredrick A. Johnstone, *Class, Race and Gold* (London: Routledge, 1976), pp. 105, 93; David Yudelman, "Industrialization, Race Relations and Change in South Africa," *African Affairs* 74.294 (January 1975), p. 87; F. Wilson, *Labour*, p. 10; Yudelman, *Emergence*, pp. 21, 134.
72. George M. Fredrickson, *White Supremacy* (Oxford: Oxford University Press, 1981), p. 232.
73. Yudelman, *Emergence*, p. 217; Fredrickson, *White Supremacy*, pp. 232-3.
74. Moodie, *Rise of Afrikanerdom*, pp. 73-4; Wilkins and Strydom, *Super Afrikaners*, p. 55.
75. Van den Heever, *Hertzog*, pp. 147-8; Heribert Adam and Hermann Giliomee, *Ethnic Power Mobilized* (New Haven: Yale University Press, 1979), p. 106; Moodie, *Rise of Afrikanerdom*, p. 76.
76. Interview with Breyten Breytenbach, Johannesburg, 28 April 1994; Henry Kenney, *Architect of Apartheid: H. F. Verwoerd* (Johannesburg, Jonathan Ball, 1980), p. 39.
77. O'Meara, *Volkskapitalisme*, pp. 36-7.
78. Adam and Giliomee, *Ethnic Power*, pp. 149, 151; Kenney, *Architect*, p. 40; Thompson, *History of South Africa*, p. 166.
79. Interview with P. J. de Lange, Johannesburg, 2 May 1994.
80. Horowitz, *Political Economy*, p. 145; Ashforth, *Politics of Official Discourse*, p. 69; Saul Dubow, *Racial Segregation and the Origins of Apartheid in South Africa, 1919-1936* (London: Macmillan, 1989), p. 142.
81. Johnstone, *Class, Race and Gold*, p. 93; Ashforth, *Politics of Official Discourse*, p. 198. After 1937, the Chamber of Mines granted to white miners a "closed shop" arrangement. See Stanley Greenberg, *Race and State in Capitalist Development* (New Haven: Yale University Press, 1980), p. 169.
82. Robert Davies et al., "Class Struggle and the Periodization of the State in South Africa," *Review of African Political Economy* 7 (September-December 1976), p. 19; Walshe, *African Nationalism*, p. 111; Giliomee and Schlemmer, *Apartheid to Nation-Building*, pp. 15-16; Dubow, *Racial Segregation*, p. 114.
83. van den Heever, *Hertzog*, p. 224; Kenney, *Architect*, p. 40. Hertzog's shift was consistent with his original formulation of the "two streams" coming "together in the distant future," as quoted in van den Heever, *Hertzog*, p. 148.
84. Dubow, *Racial Segregation*, pp. 133, 15.

85. Walshe, *African Nationalism*, pp. 262, 269; de Klerk, *Puritans*, p. 195; Leo Kuper, "African Nationalism in South Africa," in Monica Wilson and Leonard Thompson, eds., *The Oxford History of South Africa* (Oxford: Clarendon Press, 1971), vol. 2, p. 454.

86. Davies et al., "Class Struggle," p. 23; Giliomee and Schlemmer, *Apartheid to Nation-Building*, p. 21; Kenney, *Architect*, p. 69.

87. Interview with P. J. de Lange, Johannesburg, 2 May 1994.

88. Interview with Gerrit Viljoen, Pretoria, 28 April 1994; Thompson, *History of South Africa*, p. 181.

89. Kenney, *Architect*, p. 70; Ashforth, *Politics of Official Discourse*, p. 118.

90. Moodie, *Rise of Afrikanerdom*, p. 102; O'Meara, *Volkskapitalisme*, p. 60.

91. Wilkins and Strydom, *Super Afrikaners*, pp. 140–4; Moodie, *Rise of Afrikanerdom*, p. 189; Interview with P. J. de Lange, Johannesburg, 2 May 1994.

92. De Klerk, *Puritans*, p. 115; Interview with Helen Suzman, Johannesburg, 11 May 1994.

93. Kenney, *Architect*, p. 73.

94. Dubow, *Racial Segregation*, p. 22; Deborah Posel, *The Making of Apartheid, 1948–1961* (Oxford: Clarendon Press, 1991), p. 50.

95. Interview with Walter Sisulu, Johannesburg, 2 May 1994.

96. Interview with Carel Boshoff, Jr., Pretoria, 4 May 1994; de Villiers, "Afrikaner Nationalism," p. 374.

97. De Klerk, *Puritans*, p. 218.

98. Marianne Cornevin, *Apartheid: Power and Historical Falsification* (Paris: UNESCO, 1980), p. 61.

99. De Villiers, "Afrikaner Nationalism," p. 393.

100. Tomlinson Commission, *Report*, p. 34; Thompson, *History of South Africa*, p. 154.

101. Lewin, *Struggle for Racial Equality*, p. 74, quoting Malan in 1954; Posel, *Making Apartheid*, p. 62.

102. Tomlinson Commission, *Report*, pp. 105–8; Ashforth, *Politics of Official Discourse*, p. 178.

103. For official discussions of the difficulty in refining racial categories, see the South African Native Affairs Commission, *Report*, pp. 11–13; Commission of Inquiry into Matters Relating to the Coloured Population Group (Theron Commission), *Report* (Pretoria: Government Printer, 1976), p. 23.

104. De Villiers, "Afrikaner Nationalism," pp. 370, 394.

105. Interview with Jaap Marais, Pretoria, 3 May 1994. See also Harold Wolpe, "Capitalism and Cheap Labor Power in South Africa," *Economy and Society* 1.4 (November 1972), p. 426.

106. See Tomlinson Commission, *Report*, pp. 179, 192; Posel, *Making Apartheid*, p. 231; Martin Legassick and Harold Wolpe, "The Bantustans and Capital Accumulation in South Africa," *Review of African Political Economy* 7 (September–December 1976), pp. 87–107.

107. Kenney, *Architect*, pp. 238–9. See also Greenberg, *Race and State*, p. 173.
108. Goldin, *Making Race*, p. 123.
109. Lewin, *Struggle for Racial Equality*, pp. 124–8; Kenney, *Architect*, pp. 177–9.
110. Tomlinson Commission, *Report*, p. 10; Interview with P. J. de Lange, Johannesburg, 2 May 1994; Kenney, *Architect*, pp. 202, 209.
111. Moodie, *Rise of Afrikanerdom*, pp. 277–8, 284. See also Ernesto Laclau, *New Reflections on the Revolution of our Time* (London: Verso, 1990), pp. 139–40.
112. Tomlinson Commission, *Report*, p. 17.
113. F. Wilson, *Labour*, p. 46; Central Statistical Services, *South African Statistics, 1986* (Pretoria: Government Printer, 1986), Table 7.6.
114. Posel, *Making Apartheid*, pp. 12–14, 19; Kenney, *Architect*, p. 140; Dubow, *Racial Segregation*, p. 66.
115. Stephen Lewis, *The Economics of Apartheid* (New York: Council on Foreign Relations, 1990), p. 41.
116. Bonacich, "Capitalism and Race Relations in South Africa," p. 258. See also Kenney, *Architect*, p. 31; Donald Harman Akenson, *God's People* (Montreal: McGill and Queen's University Press, 1991), p. 225; Yudelman, *Emergence*, p. 281; Adam and Giliomee, *Ethnic Power*, p. 165.
117. Interview with P. J. de Lange, Johannesburg, 2 May 1994.
118. O'Meara, *Volkskapitalisme*, p. 250–1.
119. As quoted in Cornevin, *Apartheid Power*, p. 74. See also Moodie, *Rise of Afrikanerdom*, p. 292.
120. Interview with Gerrit Viljoen, Pretoria, 28 April 1994; Commission of Inquiry into Matters Relating to the Coloured Population Group, *Report*, p. 519.
121. Heribert Adam and Kogila Moodley, *The Opening of the Apartheid Mind* (Berkeley: University of California Press, 1993), p. 40; Robert Schrire, *Adapt or Die* (New York: Ford Foundation, 1991), p. 66. See Robert M. Price, *The Apartheid State in Crisis* (New York: Oxford University Press, 1991).
122. Ashforth, *Politics of Official Discourse*, p. 202.
123. Adam and Moodley, *Opening*, p. 41; Interview with Carel Boshoff, Jr., Pretoria, 3 May 1994.
124. N. E. Wiehahn, *The Complete Wiehahn Report* (Johannesburg: Lex Patria, 1982), p. 28. See also Alan Brooks and Jeremy Brickhill, *Whirlwind Before the Storm* (London: International Defense and Aid Fund for Southern Africa, 1980), p. 113; Thompson, *History of South Africa*, p. 224; Steven Friedman, *Building Tomorrow Today: African Workers in Trade Unions, 1970–1984* (Johannesburg: Ravan, 1987), pp. 154–69; Ashforth, *Politics of Official Discourse*, pp. 198–232; Price, *Apartheid State in Crisis*, pp. 101–51; Donald L. Horowitz, *A Democratic South Africa?* (Berkeley: University of California Press, 1991), p. 18.
125. Interview with Gerrit Viljoen, Pretoria, 28 April 1994. See also Com-

mission of Inquiry into Legislation Affecting the Utilization of Manpower (Riekert Commission), *Report* (Pretoria: Government Printer, 1979); Ashforth, *Politics of Official Discourse*, pp. 203–32.

126. Schrire, *Adapt or Die*, pp. 147–55.

127. Interview with Carel Boshoff, Jr., Pretoria, 3 May 1994.

128. Schrire, *Adapt or Die*, pp. 62, 82; Goldin, *Making Race*, p. 182; Timothy Sisk, *Democratization in South Africa* (Princeton: Princeton University Press, 1995), p. 68.

129. "North Coast UDF Meeting," Verulan Civic Hall, (18 July 1984, police transcript), p. 2.

130. Neville Alexander, *Sow the Wind* (Braamfontein: Skotaville, 1985), p. 171.

131. Letter from Bishop Desmond Tutu to P. W. Botha, 1 May 1988, reprinted in the program of the *Emergency Convocation of Churches in South Africa*.

132. Schrire, *Adapt or Die*, p. 155.

133. "Tasks of the Democratic Movement in the State of Emergency," *Isizwe* 1.1 (November 1985), p. 8.

134. Oliver Tambo, *Address to the Nation* 22 July 1985, leaflet.

135. Letter from P. W. Botha to Frank Chikane, 24 March 1988, in *Emergency Convocation of Churches*.

136. Akenson, *God's People*, p. 299.

137. Interview with P. J. de Lange, Johannesburg, 2 May 1994.

138. Adam and Moodley, *Opening*, p. 149.

139. Interview with P. J. de Lange, Johannesburg, 2 May 1994; Wilkins and Strydom, *Super Afrikaners*, pp. 143–4.

140. Interview with Pieter Mulder, Pretoria, 3 May 1994.

141. Sisk, *Democratization in South Africa*, p. 60.

142. Allan Boesak, *Black and Reformed* (Braamfontein: Skotaville, 1984), p. 128.

143. Sisk, *Democratization in South Africa*, p. 137.

144. Interview with Alec Erwin, Johannesburg, March 1988.

145. Schrire, *Adapt or Die*, p. 25; Interview with P.J.de Lange, Johannesburg, 2 May 1994. See also Akenson, *God's People*, p. 301; Horowitz, *A Democratic South Africa?* p. 81.

146. Adam and Moodley, *Opening*, p. 2.

147. Wiehahn, *Weihahn Report*, pp. 11, 31–3; Merle Lipton, *Capitalism and Apartheid* (London: Wildwood, 1985); Posel, *Making of Apartheid*, p. 101; Greenberg, *Race and State*, pp. 177, 184; Price, *Apartheid State in Crisis*, pp. 88–90; Horowitz, *A Democratic South Africa?* p. 12.

148. Tomlinson Commission, *Report*, p. 27.

149. Commission of Inquiry into Legislation, *Report*, pp. 133, 159.

150. Price, *Apartheid State in Crisis*.

151. Yudelman, *Emergence*, p. 281.

152. Adam and Giliomee, *Ethnic Power*, pp. 165–80; Edna Bonacich, "Capitalism and Race Relations in South Africa," in Maurice Zeitlin, ed.,

Political Power and Social Theory (Greenwich, Conn.: JAI Press, 1981), vol. 2, p. 256; Giliomee and Schlemmer, *Apartheid to Nation-Building*, p. 120; Sisk, *Democratization in South Africa*, p. 137.

153. Interview with Gerrit Viljoen, Pretoria, 28 April 1994.
154. Willem de Klerk, *The Second (R)evolution* (Johannesburg: Jonathan Ball, 1984), p. 21; Interview with P. J. de Lange, Johannesburg, 2 May 1994.
155. O'Meara, *Volkskapitalisme*, p. 241.
156. F. Wilson, *Labour*, p. 11.
157. Cell, *Highest Stage*, p. 234. See also Michael Banton, *Race Relations* (London: Tavistock, 1967), p. 174.
158. Greenberg, *Race and State*, p. 129; Rex, "Plural Society," p. 404.
159. Michael Savage, "Costs of Enforcing Apartheid and Problems of Change," *African Affairs* (1977).
160. Steve Biko, *I Write What I Like*, ed. Aelerd Stubbs (San Francisco: Harper and Row, 1986), p. 91.

Chapter 6. *"To Bind Up the Nation's Wounds"*

1. George M. Fredrickson, *The Black Image in the White Mind* (Middletown, Conn.: Wesleyan University Press, 1971), p. 22, n. 45.
2. Robert William Fogel and Stanley L. Engerman, *Time on the Cross* (Boston: Little, Brown, 1974), p. 3.
3. See W. E. B. Du Bois, *Black Reconstruction in America* (New York: Atheneum, 1992), p. 39; Barrington Moore, Jr., *Social Origins of Dictatorship and Democracy* (Boston: Beacon, 1966), p. 118; Eric Foner, *Free Soil, Free Labor, Free Men* (London: Oxford University Press, 1970), p. 263.
4. 60 *U.S. Supreme Court* (1857), p. 407.
5. Harold Holzer, ed., *The Lincoln–Douglas Debates* (New York: HarperCollins, 1993), pp. 54, 189, 254; Du Bois, *Black Reconstruction*, p. 147. Abolitionists objected to recolonizing blacks back to Africa as a "proslavery plot" to get rid of free blacks and thereby reinforce slavery for those who remained. See Fredrickson, *Black Image*, p. 27.
6. James McPherson, *The Struggle for Equality* (Princeton: Princeton University Press, 1964), p. 135.
7. Du Bois, *Black Reconstruction*, p. 49; Holzer, *Lincoln–Douglas Debates*, p. 65; Foner, *Free Soil*, p. 311.
8. Eric Foner, *Reconstruction* (New York: Harper and Row, 1988), p.1; Du Bois, *Black Reconstruction*, p. 84; Garry Wills, *Lincoln at Gettysburg* (New York: Simon and Schuster, 1992), p. 142; Kenneth M. Stampp, *The Era of Reconstruction* (New York: Random House, 1965), p. 44; McPherson, *Struggle for Equality*, pp. 62–3, 118.
9. Alexis Tocqueville, *Democracy in America* (Garden City, N.Y.: Anchor/Doubleday, 1969), p. 344.
10. Moore, *Social Origins*, pp. 125–6. See also James M. McPherson, *Battle Cry of Freedom* (New York: Oxford University Press 1988), p. 12; Du Bois, *Black Reconstruction*, p. 581; John Hope Franklin, *Reconstruction*

After the Civil War (Chicago: University of Chicago Press, 1961), p. 177; Stephen Skowronek, *Building a New American State* (Cambridge: Cambridge University Press, 1982), p. 124; C. Vann Woodward, *Reunion and Reaction* (Boston: Little, Brown, 1951). The economic causes of the Civil War are discussed in Charles A. and Mary Beard, *The Rise of American Civilization* (New York: Macmillan, 1927), pp. 3–54; Foner, *Free Soil*, p. 2; Kenneth Stampp, *The Causes of the Civil War* (New York: Simon and Schuster, 1959), pp. 85–106.

11. Stampp, *Causes*, pp. 88, 95; Woodward, *Reunion and Reaction*, p. 59.
12. Moore, *Social Origins*, p. 136.
13. Holzer, *Lincoln–Douglas Debates*, pp. 53, 84.
14. Lincoln to Horace Greeley, 22 August 1862, published in the *New York Tribune* 25 August 1862. See also Du Bois, *Black Reconstruction*, p. 85.
15. Stampp, *Causes*, p. 48.
16. For a discussion of the institutional dynamics leading to the Civil War, see Barry R. Weingast, "Institutions and Political Commitment: A New Political Economy of the American Civil War," manuscript (November 1994).
17. Stampp, *Causes*, p. 59.
18. Gunnar Myrdal, "An American Dilemma," *Race* 4.1 (November 1962), p. 4; C. Vann Woodward, "Editor's Introduction," in McPherson, *Battle Cry*, p. xix; Shelby Foote, *The Civil War: A Narrative* (New York: Vintage Books, 1986), vol. 3, p. 1040.
19. Skowronek, *Building a New American State*, p. 86; Foner, *Reconstruction*, p. 23.
20. Richard F. Bensel, *Yankee Leviathan: The Origins of Central State Authority in America, 1859–1877* (Cambridge: Cambridge University Press, 1990), pp. 96, 124, 268; Foner, *Reconstruction*, pp. 21, 469; David Montgomery, *Beyond Equality* (New York: Knopf, 1967), p. 345.
21. Foner, *Reconstruction*, pp. 21–3; Skowronek, *Building a New American State*, p. 49; Bensel, *Yankee Leviathan*, p. 165; Theda Skocpol, *Protecting Soldiers and Mothers* (Cambridge, Mass.: Harvard University Press, 1993).
22. Stampp, *Causes*, p. 222.
23. Quoted in John Hope Franklin, *Reconstruction*, p. 4.
24. Woodward, *Reunion and Reaction*, p. 237.
25. George M. Fredrickson, *The Inner Civil War* (Urbana: University of Illinois Press, 1965), p. 65; Foner, *Free Soil*, p. 310. See also McPherson, *Struggle for Equality*, p. 46.
26. *New York Courier and Enquirer* 1 December 1860, quoted in Stampp, *Causes*, p. 75.
27. Wills, *Lincoln at Gettysburg*.
28. Du Bois, *Reconstruction*, pp. 55, 80; Montgomery, *Beyond Equality*, p. 95; McPherson, *Struggle for Equality* ch. 9.
29. Alexander Saxton, *The Rise and Fall of the White Republic* (London: Verso, 1990), p. 261; Du Bois, *Black Reconstruction*, p. 149; McPherson, *Struggle for Equality*, p. 156.

30. *Plessy* v. *Ferguson*, 163 *U.S. Supreme Court* (1896), p. 537.

31. Foner, *Reconstruction*, pp. 25–6; Manning Marable, *Race, Reform and Rebellion* (Jackson: University Press of Mississippi, 1991), p. 8; Foner, *Nothing but Freedom* (Baton Rouge: Louisiana State University Press, 1983), p. 47.

32. Stampp, *Era of Reconstruction*, pp. 10, 43; Franklin, *Reconstruction*, pp. 17–20.

33. Stampp, *Era of Reconstruction*, p. 43.

34. Moore, *Social Origins*, p. 141.

35. Woodward, *Reunion and Reaction*, p. 52.

36. Franklin, *Reconstruction*, p. 27; Foner, *Reconstruction*, pp. 190, 199, 215, 247, 252; Stampp, *Era of Reconstruction*, pp. 80, 125; Foner, *Nothing But Freedom*, p. 49. The South's Congressional representation was increased after the Civil War by counting each black no longer as three-fifths of a person but instead as a full unit.

37. Foner, *Reconstruction*, p. 179; Fredrickson, *Black Image*, p. 190. Johnson had never been an advocate of blacks' rights, and was concerned that enfranchising blacks would actually empower the Southern planters to whom he had long been opposed. See McPherson, *Struggle for Equality*, pp. 317, 346.

38. Richard Kluger, *Simple Justice* (New York: Knopf, 1976), p. 46. See also McPherson, *Struggle for Equality*, p. 335; James C. Cobb, *The Most Southern Place on Earth* (New York: Oxford University Press, 1992), p. 57.

39. George M. Fredrickson, *White Supremacy* (Oxford: Oxford University Press, 1981), p. 250.

40. Francis Paul Prucha, *The Great Father* (Lincoln: University of Nebraska Press, 1984), Part 5.

41. Stampp, *Era of Reconstruction*, p. 93; Fredrickson, *White Supremacy*, p. 183. See also Lerone Bennett, Jr., *Black Power USA* (Chicago: Johnson, 1967), pp. 42–3.

42. Barbara J. Fields, "Ideology and Race in American History," in J. Morgan Kousser and James M. McPherson, eds., *Region, Race and Reconstruction* (New York: Oxford University Press, 1982), p. 163.

43. Woodward, *Reunion and Reaction*, p. 15; A. Leon Higginbotham, Jr., "Racism in American and South African Courts," *New York University Law Review* 65.3 (June 1990), p. 496; Franklin, *Reconstruction*, p. 80; Foner, *Reconstruction*, p. 314.

44. Franklin, *Reconstruction*, p. 105; George M. Fredrickson, *Black Liberation* (New York: Oxford University Press, 1995), p. 28.

45. Marable, *Race, Reform*, p. 6; Stampp, *Era of Reconstruction*, p. 127; McPherson, *Struggle for Equality*, p. 407.

46. Franklin, *Reconstruction*, pp. 37–8; Kluger, *Simple Justice*, p. 51.

47. Fredrickson, *Black Liberation*, p. 99; James M. McPherson, "Comparing the Two Reconstructions," *Princeton Alumni Weekly* 79 (26 February 1979), p. 18.

48. Foner, *Reconstruction*, p. 411.

49. Ibid., p. 68.
50. Montgomery, *Beyond Equality*, p. 58.
51. Constitutional Convention of the State of Louisiana, *Official Journal of the Proceedings* (New Orleans: H. J. Hearsey, 1898), p. 31; Constitutional Convention of the State of Mississippi, *Journal of the Proceedings* (Jackson: E. L. Martin, 1890), p. 702.
52. C. Vann Woodward, *Origins of the New South, 1877–1913* (Baton Rouge: Louisiana State University Press, 1951), p. 111; Woodward, *Reunion and Reaction*, pp. 59–60.
53. Paul Lewinson, *Race, Class and Party* (New York: Grosset and Dunlap, 1932), pp. 46, 56.
54. Saxton, *White Republic*, p. 258.
55. Foner, *Reconstruction*, p. 585; Montgomery, *Beyond Equality*, pp. 335–6. For a discussion of how the Civil War unified cross-class national loyalty prior to Reconstruction, see Martin Shefter, "Trade Unions and Political Machines," in Ira Katznelson and Aristide Zolberg, eds., *Working Class Formation* (Princeton: Princeton University Press, 1986), p. 247.
56. Montgomery, *Beyond Equality*, p. ix.
57. Ibid., p. 338.
58. Stampp, *Era of Reconstruction*, pp. 206–7. See also Vincent P. DeSantis, *Republicans Face the Southern Question* (New York: Greenwood, 1959), p. 47.
59. *Plessy v. Ferguson*, U.S. Supreme Court, 163 (1896), p. 560.
60. Wills, *Lincoln at Gettysburg*, p. 245.
61. Woodward, *Reunion and Reaction*, pp. 4, 10.
62. Vincent P. DeSantis, "Rutherford B. Hayes and the Removal of the Troops," in J. Morgan Kousser and James M. McPherson, eds., *Region, Race and Reconstruction* (New York: Oxford University Press, 1982), p. 432; Richard M. Vallely, "Party, Coercion and Inclusion," *Politics and Society* 21.1 (March 1993), p. 47; Bensel, *Yankee Leviathan*, p. 403; Gunnar Myrdal, *An American Dilemma* (New York: Harper and Row, 1944), p. 226.
63. DeSantis, "Rutherford B. Hayes," p. 421. See also Woodward, *Reunion and Reaction*, pp. 91, 104, 208, 225; DeSantis, *Republicans*, pp. 75–7.
64. Woodward, *Reunion and Reaction*, p. 168; Stokely Carmichael and Charles V. Hamilton, *Black Power* (New York: Vintage, 1967), p. 36; Joel Williamson, *The Crucible of Race* (New York: Oxford University Press, 1984), p. 507; DeSantis, *Republicans*, p. 54.
65. DeSantis, "Rutherford B. Hayes," pp. 437, 445; DeSantis, *Republicans*, p. 34; Stampp, *Era of Reconstruction*, p. 210.
66. Woodward, *Reunion and Reaction*, p. 228.
67. DeSantis, "Rutherford B. Hayes," p. 436.
68. Edwin S. Redky, *Black Exodus* (New Haven: Yale University Press, 1969), pp. 18, 21, 59, 74; Edward G. Carmines and James A. Stimson, *Issue Evolution: Race and the Transformation of American Politics* (Princeton: Princeton University Press, 1989), pp. 30–1.

69. Myrdal, *American Dilemma*, pp. 87, 97. See also E. Franklin Frazier, *On Race Relations* (Chicago: University of Chicago Press, 1968), p. 89.
70. Constitutional Convention of Louisiana, *Proceedings*, p. 9.
71. Myrdal, *American Dilemma*, p. 226; Stampp, *Era of Reconstruction*, p. 15.
72. DeSantis, *Republicans*, p. 128.
73. C. Vann Woodward, *The Strange Career of Jim Crow* (New York: Oxford University Press, 1957), p. 6; Fredrickson, *White Supremacy*, p. 191.
74. Du Bois, *Black Reconstruction*, pp. 125, 238. For a similar remark by Frederick Douglass, see McPherson, *Struggle for Equality*, p. 431.
75. Du Bois, *Black Reconstruction*, p. 634.
76. DeSantis, *Republicans*, pp. 70–1.
77. Ibid., pp. 191, 261.
78. Constitutional Convention of Louisiana, *Proceedings*, p. 375. See also V. O. Key, Jr., *Southern Politics in State and Nation* (New York: Knopf, 1949), pp. 8, 286; Bensel, *Yankee Leviathan*, p. 425.
79. Woodward, *Origins of the New South*, pp. 249–50; C. Vann Woodward, *Tom Watson: Agrarian Rebel* (London: Oxford University Press, 1938), pp. 220, 129; Du Bois, *Black Reconstruction*, p. 353; Sheldon Hackney, *Populism to Progressivism in Alabama* (Princeton: Princeton University Press, 1969). For a more recent, critical overview, see Robert C. McMath, *American Populism* (New York: Hill and Wang, 1993).
80. J. Morgan Kousser, *The Shaping of Southern Politics* (New Haven: Yale University Press, 1974), p. 28.
81. Woodward, *Tom Watson*, p. 372; Key, *Southern Politics*, p. 9; Ira Katznelson, *Black Men, White Cities* (London: Oxford University Press, 1973), p. 106.
82. Kousser, *Shaping of Southern Politics*, pp. 36–7. See also Cobb, *Most Southern Place*, p. 85.
83. Constitutional Convention of Louisiana, *Proceedings*, p. 374.
84. Kousser, *Shaping of Southern Politics*, pp. 6, 17, 70, 156. See also Cobb, *Most Southern Place*, p. 87.
85. See Constitutional Convention of Louisiana, *Proceedings*, p. 375; Constitutional Convention of Mississippi, *Proceedings*, p. 38.
86. Hackney, *Populism to Progressivism*, p. 208.
87. Kousser, *Shaping of Southern Politics*, p. 224.
88. Woodward, *Origins of the New South*, p. 51.
89. Saxton, *White Republic*, p. 304; David Roediger, *The Wages of Whiteness* (London: Verso, 1991), p. 167; Skowronek, *New American State*, p. 87; Woodward, *Origins of the New South*, p. 266.
90. Du Bois, *Black Reconstruction*, p. 103.
91. Greenberg, *Race and State*, pp. 110, 234.
92. See J. William Harris, *Plain Folk and Gentry in a Slave Society* (Middletown, Conn.: Wesleyan University Press, 1985), p. 95.
93. I am here suggesting a middle course between the class-conflict focus of Woodward and the class-consensus argument of Hackney, as suggested

in J. Morgan Kousser, *The Shaping of Southern Politics* (New Haven: Yale University Press 1974), p. xiv, n. 2.

94. Woodward, *Strange Career of Jim Crow*, p. 65.

95. William Julius Wilson, *Power, Racism and Privilege* (New York: Free Press, 1973), pp. 96, 107; William Julius Wilson, *The Declining Significance of Race* (Chicago: University of Chicago Press, 1978), p. 48, Susan Olzak, *The Dynamics of Ethnic Competition and Conflict* (Stanford: Stanford University Press, 1992), ch. 5; Roediger, *Wages of Whiteness*, pp. 146–7.

96. Philip S. Foner, *Organized Labor and the Black Worker, 1619–1973* (New York: Praeger, 1974), pp. 48, 62, 66, 75. See also Woodward, *Origins of the New South*, p. 361.

97. Michael Dawson, *Behind the Mule* (Princeton: Princeton University Press, 1994), p. 54.

98. Roediger, *Wages of Whiteness*, p. 97.

99. Wilson, *Declining Significance of Race*, p. 110.

100. Fredrickson, *Black Image*, p. 52; F. James Davis, *Who Is Black?: One Nation's Definition* (University Park: Pennsylvania State University Press, 1991), p. 51.

101. Constitutional Convention of Mississippi, *Proceedings*, p. 10.

102. Constitutional Convention of Louisiana, *Proceedings*, p. 9.

103. Ibid., p. 380; Constitutional Convention of Mississippi, *Proceedings*, p. 700.

104. Fredrickson, *White Supremacy*, p. 197; Woodward, *Origins of the New South*, pp. 331–6. For a discussion of these strategies of exclusion, see Key, *Southern Politics*; Myrdal, *American Dilemma*, pp. 480–1; Cobb, *Most Southern Place*, p. 89.

105. Kousser, *Shaping of Southern Politics*, p. 121; Woodward, *Strange Career of Jim Crow*, p. 68.

106. Douglas S. Massey and Nancy A. Denton, *American Apartheid* (Cambridge, Mass.: Harvard University Press, 1993), pp. 10, 30, 41, 48.

107. *Plessy* v. *Ferguson*, 163 United States Supreme Court, 537 (1896), p. 544.

108. Woodward, *Strange Career of Jim Crow*, p. 87; Lawrence Wright, "One Drop of Blood," *The New Yorker* (25 July 1994), p. 47; Myrdal, *American Dilemma*, p. 606.

109. George M. Fredrickson, *The Arrogance of Race* (Middletown, Conn.: Wesleyan University Press, 1988), p. 227.

110. Constitutional Convention of Louisiana, *Proceedings*, p. 113.

111. Woodward, *Strange Career of Jim Crow*, p. 93; Myrdal, *American Dilemma*, p. 523.

112. Woodward, *Origins of the New South*, p. 351; Marable, *Race, Reform*, p. 9; Woodward, *Strange Career of Jim Crow*, p. 25; Redky, *Black Exodus*, p. 171; Williamson, *Crucible of Race*, pp. 183–9; Cobb, *Most Southern Place*, p. 114. Early lynching victims were white, according to Myrdal, *American Dilemma*, p. 560. And by the early twentieth century, when racial domination had been firmly established, lynching gradually di-

minished in frequency, as described by Davis, *Who is Black?*, p. 53; Myrdal, *American Dilemma*, p. 191.

113. Foner, *Nothing But Freedom*, p. 55; Yehudi Webster, *The Racialization of America* (New York: St Martin's Press, 1992), p. 110; Cobb, *Most Southern Place* ch. 4. Tocqueville had anticipated this outcome, as discussed in his *Democracy in America*, p. 343.

114. Cell, *Highest Stage*, pp. 104, 134; Winthrop D. Jordan, *White Over Black* (New York: Norton, 1968), p. 415; Wilson, *Declining Significance*, p. 39.

115. Massey and Denton, *American Apartheid*, pp. 30, 36.

116. Constitutional Convention of Louisiana, *Proceedings*, p. 32.

117. Cell, *Highest Stage*, p. 3; Kluger, *Simple Justice*, p. 90.

118. Williamson, *Crucible of Race*, p. 507.

119. Key, *Southern Politics*, p. 15; Roediger, *Wages of Whiteness*, p. 140; Woodward, *Reunion and Reaction*, p. 237; Lewinson, *Race, Class and Party*, pp. 46, 61.

120. Woodward, *Origins of the New South*, p. 266.

121. Williamson, *Crucible of Race*, p. 319.

122. W. E. B. Du Bois, "The Negro and Communism," *Crisis* (September 1931), pp. 315–20.

123. *Congressional Record* (51st Congress, First Session, 1892), pp. 6538–51.

124. Hackney, *Populism to Progressivism*, p. 163.

125. Wilson, *Power*, p. 56.

126. Kluger, *Simple Justice*, p. 84; Woodward, *Strange Career of Jim Crow*, p. 55; Wilson, *Power, Racism*, p. 105; Reginald Horsman, *Race and Manifest Destiny* (Cambridge, Mass.: Harvard University Press, 1981).

127. Woodward, *Origins of the New South*, p. 480; Kousser, *Shaping of Southern Politics*, p. 228.

128. Rogers M. Smith, "Beyond Tocqueville, Myrdal and Hartz: The Multiple Traditions in America," *American Political Science Review* 87.3 (September 1993), p. 561. Smith is quoting Charles Francis Adams, Jr., from 1908.

129. Myrdal, *American Dilemma*, p. 211; Ira Katznelson, Kim Geiger, and Daniel Kryder, "Limiting Liberalism: The Southern Veto in Congress, 1933–50," *Political Science Quarterly* 108.2 (Summer 1993), p. 292.

130. Nancy J. Weiss, *Farewell to the Party of Lincoln* (Princeton: Princeton University Press, 1983), pp. 15, 211, 298; Wilson, *Declining Significance*, p. 141; Myrdal, *American Dilemma*, pp. 359, 463–4; Martin Carnoy, *Faded Dreams* (Cambridge: Cambridge University Press, 1994), p. 202.

131. Weiss, *Farewell to the Party*, pp. 55, 106–7, 119, 157, 166; Robert C. Lieberman, *Race and the American Welfare State* (Cambridge, Mass.: Harvard University Press, 1998).

132. Kenneth B. Clark, "Introduction," in Talcott Parsons and Kenneth B. Clark, eds., *The Negro American* (Boston: Beacon Press, 1965), p. xiii.

133. Bureau of U.S. Department of Commerce, *The Social and Economic Status of the Black Population* (Washington, D.C.: Government Printing

Office, 1979), p. 15; John T. Donahue III and James Heckman, "Continuous versus Episodic Change: The Impact of Civil Rights Policy on the Economic Status of Blacks," *Journal of Economic Literature* 29 (December 1991), p. 1607; John R. Forund and Jay R. Williams, "Internal-External Control and Black Militancy," *Journal of Social Issues* 26.1 (Winter 1970), p. 122; Thomas Byrne Edsall and Mary D. Edsall, *Chain Reaction* (New York: Norton, 1991), p. 33; Nicholas Lemann, *The Promised Land* (New York: Random House, 1991), p. 6; Doug McAdam, *Political Process and the Development of Black Insurgency, 1930–1970* (Chicago: University of Chicago Press, 1982), p. 73.

134. Oliver Cromwell Cox, *Caste, Class and Race* (Garden City: Doubleday, 1948); Michael Reich, *Racial Inequality* (Princeton: Princeton University Press, 1981). See also Michael Omi and Howard Winant, *Racial Formation in the United States* (New York: Routledge, 1986), p. 31.

135. Olzak, *Dynamics*, p. 107; Wilson, *Power*, pp. 124, 128; Foner, *Organized Labor*, pp. 205, 215, 312.

136. Interview with Congressman Charles B. Rangel, New York, 8 April 1994.

137. See Myrdal, *American Dilemma*, p. 1016; George M. Fredrickson, "Black–White Relations Since Emancipation," in Kees Gispen, ed., *What Made the South Different?* (Jackson: University Press of Mississippi, 1990), p. 134; Cell, *Highest Stage*, pp. 5, 8; Charles V. Hamilton, *Adam Clayton Powell, Jr.* (New York: Macmillan, 1991), p. 225; Rupert Emerson and Martin Kilson, "The American Dilemma in a Changing World: The Rise of Africa and the Negro American," in Talcott Parsons and Kenneth B. Clark, eds., *The Negro American* (Boston: Beacon, 1965), pp. 626–58; Derrick A. Bell, Jr., "Comment," *Harvard Law Review* 93 (1979–80), pp. 518–33.

138. *Brown* v. *Board of Education of Topeka*, Supreme Court of the United States 347 U.S. 483 (1954).

139. Alan B. Anderson and George W. Pickering, *Confronting the Color Line* (Athens: University of Georgia Press, 1986), p. 71; Virginia Foster Durr, *Outside the Magic Circle: The Autobiography of Virginia Foster Durr* (Tuscaloosa: University of Alabama Press, 1985), p. 274.

140. Interview with Congressman John Lewis, Washington, D.C., 5 May 1993; Robert H. Brisbane, *Black Activism: Racial Revolution in the United States, 1954–70* (Valley Forge, Pa.: Judson Press, 1974), p. 31; Kluger, *Simple Justice*, p. 651; Hamilton, *Adam Clayton Powell*, pp. 200, 204; Aldon D. Morris, *The Origins of the Civil Rights Movement* (New York: Free Press, 1984), p. 28.

141. Doug McAdam, *Freedom Summer* (New York: Oxford University Press, 1988), p. 30; Taylor Branch, *Parting the Waters* (New York: Simon and Schuster, 1988), p. 224; Harris L. Wofford, *Of Kennedys and Kings* (New York: Farrar, Straus and Giroux, 1980), p. 107.

142. Wofford, *Of Kennedys and Kings*, p. 467.

143. Ibid., pp. 15, 128; interview with James Farmer, 6 May 1993. See also

John Dittmer, *Local People* (Urbana: University of Illinois Press, 1994), pp. 94, 156.

144. Wofford, *Of Kennedys and Kings*, pp. 141, 144, 157; Kenneth O'Reilly, *Racial Matters* (New York: Free Press, 1989), p. 67; James Farmer, *Lay Bare the Heart* (New York: Arbor House, 1985), p. 219.

145. Wofford, *Of Kennedys and Kings*, p. 167.

146. John F. Kennedy, Press Conference, 11 April 1962. See also Burke Marshall, "The Protest Movement and the Law," *Virginia Law Review* 51 (1965), pp. 785–803.

147. Interview with Burke Marshall, New Haven, 23 March 1994. The most notable instance of an attack on a federal official by Southern white mobs was that on Attorney General Robert Kennedy's representative, John Seigenthaler, in Montgomery in 1961. See Wofford, *Of Kennedys and Kings*, p. 154.

148. Hugh Davis Graham, *The Civil Rights Era* (New York: Oxford University Press, 1990), p. 74. See also Wofford, *Of Kennedys and Kings*, p. 176; Burke Marshall, *Federalism and Civil Rights* (New York: Columbia University Press, 1964), p. 83.

149. Branch, *Parting the Waters*, pp. 659–60.

150. Wofford, *Of Kennedys and Kings*, p. 21. See also Branch, *Parting the Waters*, p. 791. In 1961, President Kennedy's concern for the nation's image abroad led him to urge civil rights activists to refrain from protest, as discussed in Wofford, *Of Kennedys and Kings*, p. 125.

151. James Forman, *The Making of Black Revolutionaries* (New York: Macmillan, 1972), p. 108.

152. John F. Kennedy, "Address to the Nation," 11 June 1963, in Clayborne Carson, et al., eds., *The Eyes on the Prize* (New York: Penguin, 1991), p. 161.

153. Stephan Lesher, *George Wallace: American Populist* (Reading: Addison-Wesley, 1994), p. 328. See also Dittmer, *Local People*, p. 286; Cobb, *Most Southern Place*, p. 233.

154. Lyndon B. Johnson, "Foreword," in Talcott Parsons and Kenneth B. Clark, eds., *The Negro American* (Boston: Beacon Press, 1965), p. v.

155. Lesher, *Wallace*, p. 333.

156. Interview with Burke Marshall, New Haven, 23 March 1994. See also Marshall, *Federalism and Civil Rights*; McAdam, *Freedom Summer*, p. 67; Stokely Carmichael and Charles V. Hamilton, *Black Power* (New York: Random House, 1967), p. 9.

157. Nicholas Lemann, *The Promised Land* (New York: Random House, 1991), p. 352. See also Nancy J. Weiss, *Whitney M. Young, Jr. and the Struggle for Civil Rights* (Princeton: Princeton University Press, 1989), p. 143.

158. Forman, *Black Revolutionaries*, p. 265.

159. Interview with George Wallace, Montgomery, 14 March 1994. See also Jack Bass, *Taming the Storm* (New York: Doubleday, 1993), pp. 193–4.

160. Interview with Joseph Lowery, Atlanta, 29 April 1993.

161. Lesher, *George Wallace*, pp. 270, 287. See also Branch, *Parting the Waters*, p. 822.
162. Graham, *Civil Rights Era*, p. 463.
163. Lemann, *Promised Land*, p. 201; Graham, *Civil Rights Era*, p. 61. This increase of federal employment for blacks was later replicated in local-government hiring during the 1970s, supported by federal grants, as discussed in Peter Eisinger, *Black Employment in City Government, 1973–1980* (Washington: Joint Center for Political Studies, 1983).
164. Associate Control, Research and Analysis, Inc. (ACRA), *Black Opinion Survey* vol. 1, (Washington: ACRA, 1977), pp. 46–7.
165. Richard B. Freeman, *Black Elite* (New York: McGraw-Hill, 1976), p. 122.
166. Wilson, *Declining Significance*, p. 126; Freeman, *Black Elite*, p. 151; Carrell Peterson Horton and Jessie Carney Smiths, eds., *Statistical Record of Black America* (Detroit: Gale Research, 1990), p. 285; Congressional Budget Office, *Income Disparities Between Black and White Americans* (Washington, D.C.: Government Printing Office, 1977), p. 7; Manning Marable, "Black Nationalism in the 1970s: Through the Prism of Race and Class," *Socialist Review* 10. 2/3 (March/June 1980), p. 81.
167. Wilson, *Declining Significance*; Michael Hout, "Occupational Mobility of Black Men, 1962–1973," *American Sociological Review* 49 (June 1984), pp. 308–22; Sharon M. Collins, "The Making of the Black Middle Class," *Social Problems* 30.4 (April 1983), pp. 369–81; Bart Landry, *The New Black Middle Class* (Berkeley: University of California Press, 1987).
168. Daniel P. Moynihan, *Maximum Feasible Misunderstanding* (New York: Free Press, 1969), pp. 129, 149.
169. Bureau of the Census, *Social and Economic Status of the Black Population*, pp. 13–15, 145.
170. Interview with Wayne Greenhaw, Montgomery, 26 April 1993.
171. Interview with James Farmer, 6 May 1993.
172. Thomas Byrne Edsall and Mary D. Edsall, *Chain Reaction* (New York: Norton, 1991), pp. 37, 60, 66; Graham, *Civil Rights Era*, p. 163.
173. Gianfranco Poggi, *The State* (Stanford, Calif.: Stanford University Press, 1990), p. 110. This estimate includes government growth up to 1979, but most of this was achieved by the mid-1960s owing to the combined effects of the New Deal, the Second World War, and the Great Society.
174. Myrdal, *American Dilemma*, pp. 466, 1011.
175. Gavin Wright, *Old South, New South: Revolutions in the Southern Economy Since the Civil War* (New York: Basic Books, 1986), pp. 3, 42, 44, 53, 61, 170, 216, 260. See also Woodward, *Origins of the New South*, pp. 112–13, 120, 128, 301; Greenberg, *Race and State*, p. 211; Cobb, *Most Southern Place*, pp. 184, 196, 198.
176. Katznelson, Geiger, and Kryder, "Limiting Liberalism," p. 298. See also Greenberg, *Race and State*, p. 218.
177. Wright, *Old South, New South*, p. 240; Bureau of the Census, U.S. De-

partment of Commerce, *Historical Statistics of the United States* (Washington, D.C.: Government Printing Office, 1975), Series F-297–348, pp. 243–5, 295.

Chapter 7. *"Order and Progress"*

1. Carlos Hasenbalg, "Race Relations in Post-Abolition Brazil: The Smooth Preservation of Racial Inequalities," Ph.D. dissertation, University of California, Berkeley (1978), p. 258; Bolivar Lamounier, "Ideologia Conservadora e Mudanças Estruturais," *Dados* 5 (1968), Rio de Janeiro, pp. 5–21.
2. A comparable argument is presented by Karen Barkey, *Bandits and Bureaucrats: The Ottoman Route to State Centralization* (Ithaca, N.Y.: Cornell University Press, 1994).
3. Melissa Nobles, "Responding with Good Sense: The Politics of Race and Census in Contemporary Brazil," Ph.D. dissertation, Yale University, New Haven (1995), p. 15.
4. Thomas E. Skidmore, *Black into White* (New York: Oxford University Press, 1974), p. 43.
5. Donald Pierson, *Negroes in Brazil* (Chicago: University of Chicago Press, 1942), p. 346.
6. Pierre-Michel Fontaine, "Transnational Relations and Racial Mobilization," in John F. Stack, Jr., ed., *Ethnic Identities in a Transnational World* (Westport, Conn.: Greenwood, 1981), p. 144; Pierson, *Negroes in Brazil*, pp. 331, 335.
7. Florestan Fernandes, *Significado do Protesto Negro* (São Paulo: Autores Associados, 1989), p. 31; Emilia Viotta da Costa, *The Brazilian Empire* (Chicago: University of Chicago Press, 1985), pp. 202–9.
8. Robert Brent Toplin, *The Abolition of Slavery in Brazil* (New York: Atheneum, 1972), p. 256; Thomas E. Skidmore, *Politics in Brazil, 1930–64* (New York: Oxford University Press, 1967), p. 6; E. Bradford Burns, *Nationalism in Brazil* (New York: Praeger, 1968), p. 49.
9. Costa, *Brazilian Empire*, p. 233.
10. Boris Fausto, "Society and Politics," in Leslie Bethell, ed., *Brazil: Empire and Republic, 1822–1930* (Cambridge: Cambridge University Press, 1989), p. 270; Gilberto Freyre, *Brazil: An Interpretation* (New York: Knopf, 1945), p. 76.
11. Karl Lowenstein, *Brazil Under Vargas* (New York: Macmillan, 1944), p. 9.
12. A. J. R. Russell-Wood, *The Black Man in Slavery and Freedom in Colonial Brazil* (London: Macmillan, 1982), p. 198; Robert Conrad, *The Destruction of Brazilian Slavery*, (Berkeley: University of California Press, 1972), p. 157; Rebecca J. Scott, "Exploring the Meaning of Freedom: Postemancipation Societies in Comparative Perspective," *Hispanic American Historical Review* 68.3 (1988), p. 413.

13. Florestan Fernandes, *The Negro in Brazilian Society* (New York: Columbia University Press, 1969), p. 141.
14. Michael Trochim, "The Brazilian Black Guard: Racial Conflict in Post-Abolition Brazil," *The Americas* 44.3 (January 1988), pp. 286–90; Célia Maria Marinho de Azevedo, "Batismo da Liberdade: Os Abolicionistas e o Destino do Negro," *História: Questões e Debates* 9.16 (January 1988), pp. 38–63.
15. Fernandes, *Negro*, p. 28; Elide Rugai Bastos, "A Questão Racial e a Revolução Burguesa," in Maria Angela D'Incas, ed., *O Saber Militante* (Rio de Janeiro: Paz e Terra, 1987), p. 156; Robert Brent Toplin, "Abolition and the Issue of Black Freedmen's Future," in Robert Brent Toplin, ed., *Slavery and Race Relations in Latin America* (Westport, Conn.: Greenwood, 1974), p. 271.
16. Toplin, "Abolition," p. 255; Florestan Fernandes, "The Weight of the Past," in John Hope Franklin, ed., *Color and Race* (Boston: Houghton Mifflin, 1968), p. 284; Warren Dean, "Economy," in Leslie Bethell, ed., *Brazil: Empire and Republic, 1822–1930*, pp. 236–7; Célia Maria Marinho de Azevedo, *Onda Negra, Medo Branco: O Negro no Imaginario das Elites – Século XIX* (Rio de Janeiro: Paz e Terra, 1987), p. 25.
17. Skidmore, *Black into White*, pp. 138–9; Célia Maria Marinho de Azevedo, "Sinal Fechado para os Negros na Rua da Liberdade," *Humanidades* 5.17 (1988), p. 10; Azevedo, *Onda Negra*, pp. 134–7, 163.
18. Florestan Fernandes, "Luta de Raças e de Classes," *Teoria e Debate* 2 (March 1988), p. 7; Emilia Viotti da Costa, "1870–1889," in Leslie Bethell, ed., *Brazil: Empire and Republic, 1822–1930* p. 199; Freyre, *Brazil: An Interpretation*, p. 107.
19. Arthur F. Corwin, "Afro-Brazilians," in Robert Brent Toplin, ed., *Slavery and Race Relations in Latin America* (Westport, Conn.: Greenwood, 1974), p. 396; Hasenbalg, "Race Relations in Post-Abolition Brazil," pp. 155–7; Carlos Hasenbalg, "Desigualidades Raciais no Brasil," *Dados* 14 (1977), pp. 18–19; Nelson do Valle Silva and Carlos Hasenbalg, *Relações Raciais no Brasil Contemporâneo* (Rio de Janeiro: Fundo Editora, 1992), p. 106.
20. Azevedo, "Sinal Fechado," p. 10; E. Franklin Frazier, *On Race Relations* (Chicago: University of Chicago Press, 1968), p. 100. The counterargument, that immigrants' racial attitudes were instead shaped by Brazil's, is presented in Anani Dzidzienyo, *The Position of Blacks in Brazilian Society* (London: Minority Rights Group, 1971), p. 16.
21. Laura Foner and Eugene D. Genovese, eds., *Slavery in the New World* (Englewood Cliffs, N.J.: Prentice-Hall, 1969), p. 242; Eugene D. Genovese, *The World the Slaveholders Made* (New York: Pantheon, 1969), p. 14.
22. Abdias do Nascimento, *Brazil: Mixture or Massacre?* (Dover: Majority Press, 1979), p. 75; Thomas E. Skidmore, "Toward a Comparative Analysis of Race Relations since Abolition in Brazil and the United States," *Latin American Studies* 4.1 (1972), p. 8; Skidmore, *Black into White*, pp.

137, 193, 196–8; Thomas E. Skidmore, "Racial Ideas and Social Policy in Brazil, 1870–1940," in Richard Graham, ed., *The Idea of Race in Latin America* (Austin: University of Texas Press, 1990), pp. 23–5; Azevedo, *Onda Negra*, pp. 44, 166.

23. Do Nascimento, *Brazil*, p. 60
24. Azevedo, *Onda Negra*, pp. 37, 82.
25. Skidmore, "Toward a Comparative Analysis," p. 4. The "mulatto" population fell from 41.4 percent in 1890 to 21 percent in 1940. See Hasenbalg, "Race Relations in Post-Abolition Brazil," p. 142; Charles H. Wood and Jose Alberto Magno de Carvalho, *The Demography of Inequality in Brazil* (Cambridge: Cambridge University Press, 1988), p. 142.
26. E. Bradford Burns, *A History of Brazil* (New York: Columbia University Press, 1970), p. 363; Skidmore, *Black into White*, pp. 48–52.
27. Skidmore, *Black into White*, p. 77. See also Carlos Hasenbalg, "Race Relations in Modern Brazil," working paper no.87131, Latin American Institute, University of New Mexico, Alberquerque (1987), p. 9; Burns, *History of Brazil*, p. 368.
28. Skidmore, *Black into White*, p. 64.
29. Charles Wood, "Categorias Censitárias e Classificações Subjetivas de Raça no Brasil," in Peggy A. Lovell, ed., *Desigualdade Racial no Brasil Contemporâneo* (Belo Horizonte: MGSP Editores, 1991). See Nobles, "Responding with Good Sense," p. 10.
30. George Reid Andrews, *Blacks and Whites in São Paulo, Brazil, 1888–1988* (Madison: University of Wisconsin Press, 1991), p. 252.
31. Michael Hanchard, *Black Orpheus* (Princeton: Princeton University Press, 1994); Howard Winant, "Rethinking Race in Brazil," *Journal of Latin American Studies* 24 (1992), p. 177; Corwin, "Afro-Brazilians," p. 407.
32. Theodore Roosevelt, "Brazil and the Negro," *The Outlook* 106 (21 February 1914), pp. 409–11. Fifteen years later another American president, Herbert Hoover, made similar remarks about Brazil, as quoted in "A Fórmula Igualitária para Resolver a Questão Racial Americana," *Progresso* 1.9 (24 February 1929).
33. Freyre, *Brazil*, p. 120.
34. Marvin Harris, *Patterns of Race in the Americas* (Westport, Conn.: Greenwood, 1964), p. 54; Wood and Carvalho, *Demography of Inequality*, p. 137.
35. See Nobles, "Responding with Good Sense"; Andrews, *Blacks and Whites*, p. 249; Marvin Harris et al., "Who Are the Whites?: Imposed Census Categories and Racial Demography of Brazil," *Social Forces* 72.2 (December 1993), p. 452; Peggy A. Lovell, "Race, Gender and Development in Brazil," *Latin American Research Review* 29.3 (1994), p. 12.
36. Winant, "Rethinking Race in Brazil," p. 183.
37. Roberto da Matta, *Relativizando* (Petrópolis: Vozes, 1984), p. 78; Skidmore, "Toward a Comparative Analysis," p. 8.
38. Skidmore, "Racial Ideas and Social Policy in Brazil," p. 24.
39. Fernandes, *Negro in Brazilian Society*, pp. 50, 134; George M. Fredrick-

son, *The Arrogance of Race* (Middletown, Conn.: Wesleyan University Press, 1988), p. 190.

40. See David Hellwig, ed., *African-American Reflections on Brazil's Racial Paradise* (Philadelphia: Temple University Press, 1992).
41. Charles H. Wagley, ed., *Race and Class in Rural Brazil* (Paris: UNESCO, 1952), p. 151; Hasenbalg, "Race Relations in Modern Brazil," p. 9.
42. Alma Guillermoprieto, *Samba* (New York: Random House, 1990), p. 8; Jim Wafer, *The Taste of Blood: Spirit Possession in Brazilian Condomble* (Philadelphia: University of Pennsylvania Press, 1991), p. 56.
43. Davis, *Problem of Slavery*, p. 243, n. 26; Clóvis Moura, *História do Negro Brasileiro* (São Paulo: Atica, 1989), p. 31; Silva and Hasenbalg, *Relações Raciais*, p. 157; Lélia Gonzalez and Carlos Hasenbalg, *Lugar de Negro* (Rio de Janeiro: Ed. Marco Zero Limitada, 1982), p. 27.
44. Carlos Hasenbalg, "Race and Socio Economic Inequality in Brazil," Instituto Universitário de Pesquisas do Rio de Janeiro (March 1983).
45. Da Matta, *Relativizando*, p. 70; Pierre-Michel Fontaine, "Transnational Relations and Racial Mobilization," in John F. Stack, Jr., ed., *Ethnic Identities in a Transnational World* (Westport: Conn.: Greenwood, 1981), p. 144.
46. Silva and Hasenbalg, *Relações Raciais*, p. 155. See also Ambassador Rubens Ricúpero, "Racial Harmony in Brazil," *Washington Post* (30 August 1993), Letter to the Editor, as quoted in Nobles, "Responding with Good Sense," pp. 13–15.
47. Richard M. Morse, "The Heritage of Latin America," in Louis Hartz, ed., *The Founding of New Societies* (New York: Harcourt Brace and World, 1964), p. 124; Thomas E. Skidmore, "Brazilian Intellectuals and the Problem of Race, 1870–1930," Vanderbilt University, Nashville, Occasional Papers Series no. 6, p. 5. Brazilian nationalism was further reinforced by the unifying effect of the war effort during the First World War, in which blacks played a significant role in the armed forces, as discussed in Skidmore, *Black into White*, pp. 155, 188.
48. Pierre-Michel Fontaine, "Introduction," in Pierre-Michel Fontaine, ed., *Race, Class and Power in Brazil* (Center for Afro-American Studies, University of California, Los Angeles, 1985), p. 6; Silva and Hasenbalg, *Relações Raciais*, pp. 9, 154.
49. Fontaine, "Transnational Relations," p. 142.
50. Thomas E. Skidmore, "Fact and Myth: An Overview of Afro-Brazilian Studies in Brazil," Kellogg Center Working Paper no. 1, University of Notre Dame (February 1992), p. 5; Nobles, "Responding with Good Sense," p. 87. Brazil's occasional exclusion of race from the census was pursued even further in Venezuela, where since 1854 there was no census question on race or color, according to Nobles, "Responding with Good Sense," p. 48.
51. The result of this policy is indicated by a review of scholarship on race issues, in which studies of current inequality remain few. See Luiz Claudio Barcelos, Olivia Maria Gomes da Cunha, and Tereza Cristina Nas-

cimento Araujo, *Escravidadão e Relações Raciais no Brasil* (Rio de Janeiro: Centro de Estudos Afro-Asiaticos, 1991).

52. Da Matta, *Relativizando*, pp. 70, 79; Michael Hanchard, *Orpheus and Power* (Princeton: Princeton University Press, 1994).

53. Pierson, *Negroes in Brazil*, p. 225; Corwin, "Afro-Brazilians," p. 389; Hasenbalg and Huntington, "Brazilian Racial Democracy," pp. 131–5.

54. Hasenbalg, "Race and Socio Economic Inequality in Brazil," pp. 7–10; Gerald F. Bender, *Angola Under the Portuguese: The Myth and the Reality* (Berkeley: University of California Press, 1978), p. 41; Fontaine, "Introduction," p. 7.

55. Corwin, "Afro-Brazilians," p. 390.

56. Do Nascimento, *Brazil*, p. 46.

57. Robert M. Levine, *The Vargas Regime* (New York: Columbia University Press, 1970), pp. 15, 123, 151, 157; Lowenstein, *Brazil Under Vargas*, pp. 28, 63, 71; Skidmore, *Politics in Brazil*, pp. 23, 34.

58. Levine, *Vargas Regime*, p. 13; Freyre, *Brazil*, p. 78; Mauricio A. Font, *Coffee, Contention and Change* (Cambridge: Blackwell, 1990), p. 6.

59. Skidmore, *Politics in Brazil*, pp. 29, 38.

60. Lowenstein, *Brazil Under Vargas*, p. 37.

61. Directoria Geral de Estatística, *Anuário Estatístico do Brasil* (Rio de Janeiro: Typographia de Estatística, 1916), vol. 1, p. 169; (1939–40, Ano IV), pp. 816, 1409.

62. Levine, *Vargas Regime*, p. 13; Skidmore, *Politics in Brazil*, p. 35; Margaret Keck, *The Workers' Party and Democratization in Brazil* (New Haven: Yale University Press, 1992), p. 31.

63. See Philippe Schmitter, "Still the Century of Corporatism," in Frederick B. Pike and Thomas Stritch, eds., *The New Corporatism* (Notre Dame, Ind.: University of Notre Dame Press, 1974), pp. 93–4.

64. Burns, *History of Brazil*, p. 415; Keck, *Workers' Party*, p. 62; Octavio Ianni, *Crisis in Brazil* (New York: Columbia University Press, 1970), p. 50.

65. Biorn Maybury-Lewis, "The Politics of the Possible: The Growth and Political Development of the Brazilian Rural Workers' Trade Union Movement, 1964–1985," Ph.D. dissertation, Columbia University, New York (1993).

66. Skidmore, *Politics in Brazil*, pp. 50–6.

67. Gonzalez and Hasenbalg, *Lugar de Negro*, p. 23; Allison Raphael, "Samba and Social Control," Ph.D. dissertation, Columbia University, New York (1980), pp. 90–8; Diana DeG. Brown, *Umbanda: Religion and Politics in Urban Brazil* (Ann Arbor: UMI Research Press, 1986), pp. 145–7; interview with Luiz Felipe Alencastro, São Paulo, 9 July 1993. An exception to Vargas's racial tolerance was the 1934 ban on mixed marriages.

68. Interview with Januário Garcia, Rio de Janeiro, 21 July 1993. See also Michael Mitchell, "Racial Consciousness and the Political Attitudes and Behavior of Blacks in São Paulo, Brazil," Ph.D. dissertation, Indiana University, Bloomington (1977), p. 130.

69. Peggy Ann Lovell, "Racial Inequality and the Brazilian Labor Market," Ph.D. dissertation, University of Florida, Gainesville (1989), p. 12; Maria Helena Moreira Alves, *State and Opposition in Military Brazil* (Austin: University of Texas Press, 1985); Thomas E. Skidmore, *The Politics of Military Rule in Brazil, 1964–85* (New York: Oxford University Press, 1988), p. 11; Youssef Cohen, *The Manipulation of Consent* (Pittsburgh: University of Pittsburgh Press, 1989); Wood and Carvalho, *Demography of Inequality*, p. 108.

70. Skidmore, *Politics in Brazil*, pp. 181, 228.

71. Skidmore, *Politics in Brazil*, p. 248.

72. Keck, *Workers' Party*, p. 21.

73. "In Chile or Argentina . . . the military killed more than one hundred times more people per capita than in Brazil. . . . On a per capita basis, for every person who disappeared or died in official custody in Brazil, ten died in Uruguay, and over three hundred died in Argentina." Alfred Stepan, *Rethinking Military Politics: Brazil and the Southern Cone* (Princeton: Princeton University Press, 1988), pp. 64, 69.

74. Nelson do Valle Silva, "Black–White Income Differentials: Brazil, 1960," Ph.D. dissertation, University of Michigan, Ann Arbor (1978), pp. 99, 131.

75. Interview with João Jorge Santos Rodrigues, Salvador, Bahia, 15 June 1993.

76. See Howard Winant, "Rethinking Race in Brazil," *Journal of Latin American Studies*, 24 (1992), pp. 174–6.

77. Carlos Hasenbalg, "Desigualdades Raciais no Brasil," *Dados* 14 (1977), p. 11; Hasenbalg, "Race Relations in Post-Abolition Brazil," pp. 186, 189, 197.

78. Degler, *Neither Black nor White*, p. 147. Whites also living in the favelas were similarly affected.

79. Fontaine, *Race, Class and Power*, p. ix.

80. Winant, "Rethinking Race in Brazil," p. 187.

81. Jan Fiola, "Race Relations in Brazil: A Reassessment of the Racial Democracy Thesis," Program in Latin American Studies, Occasional Paper Series no. 24, University of Massachusetts, Amherst (1990), p. 17; do Nascimento, *Brazil*, p. xi; James H. Kennedy, "Political Liberalization, Black Consciousness and Recent Afro-Brazilian Literature," *Phylon* 47.3 (1986), pp. 199–209; Lovell, "Racial Inequality," pp. 13–14.

82. See Keck, *Workers' Party*, p. 1; Guillermo O'Donnell, "Challenges to Democratization in Brazil," *World Policy Journal* 5.2 (Spring 1988), pp. 281–300.

83. Adam Przeworski, *Democracy and the Market* (Cambridge: Cambridge University Press, 1991), pp. 60, 74; Frances Hagopian, "The Compromised Consolidation: The Political Class in the Brazilian Transition," in Scott Mainwaring et al., eds., *Issues in Democratic Consolidation* (Notre Dame, Ind.: University of Notre Dame Press, 1992), p. 264.

84. Keck, *Workers' Party*, p. 25; Guillermo O'Donnell and Philippe C.

Schmitter, *Transitions from Authoritarian Rule: Tentative Conclusions about Uncertain Democracies* (Baltimore: Johns Hopkins University Press, 1986), pp. 38, 47; Sonia E. Alvarez, *Engendering Democracy in Brazil* (Princeton: Princeton University Press, 1990), p. 14; Johannes Rantete and Hermann Giliomee, "Transition to Democracy Through Transaction?" *African Affairs* 91 (1992), p. 524; Samuel P. Huntington, "Reform and Stability in South Africa," *International Security* 6.4 (Spring 1982).

85. "Momento Político," *Força Negra* 1.0 (May 1979).
86. O'Donnell and Schmitter, *Transitions*, p. 11.
87. Keck, *Workers' Party*, pp. 7, 64, 66, 78, 170; Przeworski, *Democracy and the Market*, p. 122, n. 46; Alfred Stepan, ed., *Democratizing Brazil* (New York: Oxford University Press, 1989); Gay Seidman, "Fighting for the Rights to be Happy," *Work in Progress* 67 (June 1990); Gay Seidman, *Manufacturing Militance: Workers' Movements in Brazil and South Africa, 1970–1985* (Berkeley: University of California Press, 1994); Alvarez, *Engendering Democracy*, p. 110.
88. Przeworksi, *Democracy and the Market*, p. 59, n. 12; Stepan, *Rethinking Military Politics*, pp. 32–3; Scott Mainwaring, "Urban Popular Movements, Identity, and Democracy in Brazil," *Comparative Political Studies* 20.2 (July 1987), pp. 131–59.
89. Keck, *Workers' Party*, p. 38; Alvarez, *Engendering Democracy*, p. 36; Przeworski, *Democracy and the Market*, p. 91, n. 68; O'Donnell and Schmitter, *Transitions*, p. 54; Scott Mainwaring and Edward Viola, "New Social Movements, Political Culture and Democracy," *Telos* 61 (Fall 1984), p. 25.
90. Ben Ross Schneider, *Politics Within the State: Elite Bureaucrats and Industrial Policy in Authoritarian Brazil* (Pittsburgh: University of Pittsburgh Press, 1991), p. 247.
91. Harris, *Patterns of Race in the Americas*, pp. 96–8.
92. Herbert S. Klein, *Social Change in Brazil, 1945–1985: The Incomplete Transition* (Albuquerque: University of New Mexico Press, 1989), p. 1.
93. Carl Degler, *Neither Black nor White* (New York: Macmillan, 1971), p. 99.
94. Carlos Hasenbalg and Nelson do Valle Silva, "Industrialization, Employment and Stratification in Brazil," in John D. Wirth, ed., *State and Society in Brazil* (Boulder: Westview, 1987), pp. 77–8.
95. Pierre Van den Berghe, *Race and Racism* (New York: Wiley, 1967), p. 70.
96. Youssef Cohen, *The Manipulation of Consent* (Pittsburgh: University of Pittsburgh Press, 1989).
97. Anani Dzidzienyo, "Brazil," in Jay A. Sigler, ed., *International Handbook on Race and Race Relations* (New York: Greenwood, 1987), pp. 26, 33; Hasenbalg, "Race Relations in Post-Abolition Brazil," p. 236.
98. Skidmore, "Fact and Myth," p. 11; Dzidzienyo, "Brazil," p. 33; "O Mal Secreto," *Jornal do Brasil* (21 April 1993).
99. "Less than 2 percent of federal civil service employees were blacks, and

most of them were in lower echelons," according to Gerald J. Bender, *Angola Under the Portuguese* (Berkeley: University of California Press, 1978), p. 42. See also Degler, *Neither Black nor White*, p. 148; Jean-Claude Garcia-Zamor, "Social Mobility of Negroes in Brazil," *Journal of Inter-American Studies and World Affairs* 12.2 (April 1970), p. 251.

Comparative Racial Domination: An Overview

1. See John W. Cell, *The Highest Stage of White Supremacy* (Cambridge: Cambridge University Press, 1982), p. 104; William Julius Wilson, *Power, Racism and Privilege* (New York: Free Press, 1973), pp. 41, 42, 73, 76, 93; William Julius Wilson, *The Declining Significance of Race* (Chicago: University of Chicago Press, 1978), p. 46; C. Vann Woodward, *The Strange Career of Jim Crow* (New York: Oxford University Press, 1957); Pierre Van den Berghe, *Race and Racism* (New York: Wiley, 1967), pp. 27–30; Susan Olzak, *The Dynamics of Ethnic Competition and Conflict* (Stanford, Calif.: Stanford University Press, 1992), p. 209.
2. Olzak, *Dynamics*, p. 108. See also John Rex, *Race Relations in Sociological Theory* (London: Routledge and Kegan Paul, 1970), p. 191.
3. Daniel Patrick Moynihan, "Employment, Income, and the Ordeal of the Black Family," in Talcott Parsons and Kenneth B. Clark, eds., *The Negro American* (Boston: Beacon, 1965), p. 137; Doug McAdam, *Political Process and the Development of Black Insurgency, 1930–1970* (Chicago: University of Chicago Press, 1982), p. 88.
4. See Edna Bonacich, "A Theory of Ethnic Antagonism: The Split Labor Market," *American Sociological Review* 37 (October 1972), pp. 547–59; Edna Bonacich, "Capitalism and Race Relations in South Africa: A Split Labor Market Analysis," in Maurice Zeitlin, ed., *Political Power and Social Theory* (Greenwich: JAI Press, 1981), vol. 2, pp. 241, 249; Wilson, *Power, Racism and Privilege*, p. 53; Michael Reich, *Racial Inequality* (Princeton: Princeton University Press, 1981).
5. See Florestan Fernandes, *The Negro in Brazilian Society* (New York: Columbia University Press, 1969).
6. See Harold Wolpe, "Capitalism and Cheap Labour Power in South Africa," *Economy and Society* 1.4 (November 1972); Deborah Posel, *The Making of Apartheid* (Oxford: Clarendon Press, 1991), pp. 9–19.
7. See Martin Legassick, "South Africa: Forced Labor, Industrialization and Racial Differentiation," in Richard Harris, ed., *The Political Economy of Africa* (New York: Wiley, 1975); Wolpe, "Capitalism and Cheap Labour Power"; Frederick Johnstone, *Race, State and Class* (London: Routledge, 1976); Posel, *Making of Apartheid*, pp. 9–19; Merle Lipton, *Capitalism and Apartheid* (London: Wildwood, 1985); Stanley Greenberg, *Race and State in Capitalist Development* (New Haven: Yale University Press, 1980), pp. 177, 184.
8. See James McPherson, *The Struggle for Equality* (Princeton: Princeton University Press, 1964), pp. 41, 381.

9. Greenberg, *Race and State*, pp. 129, 141.
10. H. Hoetink, *Slavery and Race Relations in Latin America* (New York: Harper and Row, 1973), pp. 21, 33; Greenberg, *Race and State*, p. 276. See also Gunnar Myrdal, *An American Dilemma* (New York: Harper and Row, 1944), p. 391.
11. C. Vann Woodward, *Origins of the New South* (Baton Rouge: Louisiana State University Press, 1951), p. 257. See also Wilson, *Declining Significance*, pp. 58–9; Rogers M. Smith, "Beyond Tocqueville, Myrdal and Hartz: The Multiple Traditions in America," *American Political Science Review* 87.3 (September 1993), p. 551.
12. See E. P. Thompson, *The Making of the English Working Class* (New York: Knopf, 1966).
13. Joel Williamson, *A Rage for Order* (New York: Oxford University Press, 1986), p. viii. See also Michael Omi and Howard Winant, *Racial Formation in the United States* (London: Routledge and Kegan Paul, 1985), p. 65.
14. Greenberg, *Race and State*, p. 406.
15. Karl Polanyi, *The Great Transformation* (Beacon: Boston, 1944), ch. 1.
16. Adam Przeworski, *Capitalism and Social Democracy* (Cambridge: Cambridge University Press, 1985), p. 136.
17. Ibid., pp. 136–48. See also Ralph Miliband, *The State in Capitalist Development* (London: Weidenfeld and Nicolson, 1969).
18. Antonio Gramsci, *Selections from the Prison Notebooks*, ed. Quinton Hoare and Geoffrey Nowell Smith, (New York: International Publishers, 1971), p. 182.
19. Przeworski, *Capitalism*, p. 197.
20. Kimberlie Williams Crenshaw, "Race, Reform and Retrenchment: Transformation and Legitimation in Antidiscrimination Law," *Harvard Law Review* 101.7 (May 1988), p. 1336. See also David Roediger, *The Wages of Whiteness* (London: Verso, 1991), p. 7.
21. Przeworski, *Capitalism*, pp. 143, 201; Karl Marx, *Capital* (New York: International Publishers, 1967), p. 283; N. Poulantzas, *Political Power and Social Classes* (London: New Left Books, 1973).
22. Przeworski, *Capitalism*, p. 202.
23. Ibid., pp. 140, 164–5.
24. Greenberg, *Race and State*, pp. 26–7.
25. Rex, *Race Relations*, p. 94.
26. See Michael Burawoy, "The Capitalist State in South Africa," in Maurice Zeitlin, ed., *Political Power and Social History* (Greenwich: JAI, 1981), vol. 2, pp. 279–335.
27. Peter Evans, *Embedded Autonomy* (Princeton: Princeton University Press, 1995), p. 12; Omi and Winant, *Racial Formation*, p. 79. For more general discussions of state-class interests, see Miliband, *State in Capitalist Development*; Poulantzas, *Political Power*; Claus Offe, *Disorganized Capitalism* (Cambridge: MIT Press, 1985).

Part Three. Race Making from Below

Chapter 8. "We Are a Rock"

1. Jeff Guy, *The Destruction of the Zulu Kingdom* (London: Longmans, 1979); James O. Gump, *The Dust Rose Like Smoke* (Lincoln: University of Nebraska Press, 1994). Gump offers a fascinating comparison of early Zulu and Native American resistance.
2. Andre Odendaal, *Vukani Bantu!: The Beginnings of Black Protest Politics in South Africa to 1912* (Cape Town: David Philip, 1984), pp. 7–12. See also George M. Fredrickson, *Black Liberation* (New York: Oxford University Press, 1995), p. 42.
3. Fredrickson, *Black Liberation*, pp. 58, 77, 80.
4. South African Native Affairs Commission, *Report of the Commission* (Cape Town: Government Printer, 1905), pp. 63–7. See also Odendaal, *Vukani Bantu!*, pp. 23–7; Fredrickson, *Black Liberation*, ch. 2.
5. See T. R. H. Davenport, *South Africa: A Modern History* (Toronto: University of Toronto Press, 1977), Part 1; Leroy Vail, ed., *The Creation of Tribalism in Southern Africa* (Berkeley: University of California Press, 1991); Gump, *Dust Rose*, p. 78.
6. Peter Walshe, *The Rise of African Nationalism in South Africa* (Berkeley: University of California Press, 1971), p. 6.
7. Odendaal, *Vukani Bantu!*, p. 8.
8. See Walshe, *Rise of African Nationalism*, pp. 20, 23–4; D. D. T. Jabavu, "Native Unrest," (July 1920), in Thomas Karis and Gwendolen M. Carter, eds., *From Protest to Challenge* (Stanford, Calif.: Hoover Institution Press, 1972), vol. 1, pp. 122, 221.
9. Gavin Lewis, *Between the Wire and the Wall* (Johannesburg: David Philip, 1987), p. 64; J. D. T. Jabavu, "Native Unrest," p. 120.
10. Walshe, *Rise of African Nationalism*, p. 34. Walshe is quoting from Seme's founding speech of 8 January 1912.
11. Pixley ka Isaka Seme, "Native Union," (24 October 1911), in Karis and Carter, eds., *From Protest to Challenge*, vol. 1, p. 72.
12. Walshe, *Rise of African Nationalism*, p. 38; Odendaal, *Vukani Bantu!*, pp. 97–9.
13. Pixley ka Isaka Seme, "The Regeneration of Africa," in Karis and Carter, eds., *From Protest to Challenge*, vol. 1, p. 71.
14. Nelson Mandela, *Long Walk to Freedom* (Boston: Little, Brown, 1994), p. 67. For a provocative counterargument stressing continued official ethnic division, see Mahmood Mamdani, *Citizen and Subject* (Princeton: Princeton University Press, 1996).
15. South African Native National Congress, "Petition to King George V" (20 July 1914), in Karis and Carter, eds., *From Protest to Challenge*, vol. 1, p. 125.
16. South African Native National Congress, "Petition to King George V"

(16 December 1918), in Karis and Carter, eds., *From Protest to Challenge*, vol. 1, p. 140.

17. "All African Convention Proceedings and Resolutions," (15–18 December 1935), in Karis and Carter, eds., *From Protest to Challenge*, vol. 2, p. 32.

18. J. D. T. Jabavu, "Native Unrest," (July 1920), in Karis and Carter, eds., *From Protest to Challenge*, vol. 1, p. 120.

19. Lewis, *Between the Wire and the Wall*, pp. 93, 105, 107; Shula Marks and Stanley Trapido, eds., *The Politics of Race, Class, and Nationalism in Twentieth Century South Africa* (London: Longman, 1987), p. 211.

20. "Report on Proceedings and Resolutions of the Annual Conference of the ANC" (4–5 June 1926), in Karis and Carter, eds., *From Protest to Challenge*, vol. 1, p. 301; Leonard Thompson, *A History of South Africa* (New Haven: Yale University Press, 1990), p. 176.

21. See W. A. de Klerk, *The Puritans of Africa* (Harmondsworth: Penguin, 1975), p. 200; Fredrickson, *Black Liberation*, p. 229.

22. Karis and Carter, eds., *From Protest to Challenge*, vol. 2, pp. 79, 8.

23. Thompson, *History of South Africa*, p. 181; Tom Lodge, *Black Politics in South Africa since 1945* (Johannesburg: Ravan, 1983), p. 9.

24. "Constitution of the ANC Youth League" (1944), in Karis and Carter, eds., *From Protest to Challenge*, vol. 2, pp. 310; "Congress Youth League Manifesto" (March 1944), in Karis and Carter, eds., *From Protest to Challenge*, vol. 2, p. 300.

25. See Mandela, *Long Walk*, pp. 97, 125.

26. Lodge, *Black Politics*, pp. 26–33; Mandela, *Long Walk*, pp. 99, 121.

27. Mandela, *Long Walk*, p. 106.

28. An alliance had been initially forged with "the Doctors' Pact" between the ANC and Indian Congresses in 1947, as described in Mandela, *Long Walk*, p. 95. This alliance was later folded into the broader "Congress Alliance."

29. Ibid., pp. 165, 104. See also Fredrickson, *Black Liberation*, p. 245.

30. Commission for the Socio-Economic Development of the Bantu Areas within the Union of South Africa (Tomlinson Commission), *Summary of the Report* (Pretoria: Government Printer, 1955), p. 104.

31. Lodge, *Black Politics*, p. 234; interview with Zwelakhe Sisulu, Johannesburg, 15 August 1986. For a more general discussion of the influence of the Communist Party, see Heribert Adam and Kogila Moodley, *The Opening of the Apartheid Mind* (Berkeley: University of California Press, 1993), p. 95.

32. See quotes from Cyril Ramaphosa in *New Era* 2.2 (June 1987), p. 1.

33. For example, see the disparaging comments about the PAC in Mandela, *Long Walk*, pp. 206, 253, 258, 293.

34. Central Statistical Services, *South African Statistics, 1988* (Pretoria: Government Printer, 1988), Tables 5.11, 7.5. See also N. E. Wiehahn, *The Complete Wiehahn Report* (Johannesburg: Lex Patria, 1982), p. xxiii; Commission of Inquiry into Legislation Affecting the Utilization of Man-

power (Reikert Commission), *Report* (Pretoria: Government Printer, 1979), p. 167.

35. Steve Biko, *I Write What I Like*, ed. Aelred Stubbs (San Francisco: Harper and Row, 1978), pp. 27, 25.

36. Commission of Inquiry into Matters Relating to the Coloured Population Group (Theron Commission), *Report* (Pretoria: Government Printer, 1976), p. 449.

37. Interview with Manas Buthelezi, Johannesburg, February 1988. For general overviews, see Anthony W. Marx, *Lessons of Struggle: South African Internal Opposition, 1960–1990* (New York: Oxford University Press, 1992), ch. 2; Gail M. Gerhart, *Black Power in South Africa* (Berkeley: University of California Press, 1978).

38. Interview with Fanyana Mazibukwe, Johannesburg, April 1988.

39. Interview with Jay Naidoo, Johannesburg, March 1988. See Marx, *Lessons of Struggle*, chs. 3–5.

40. Jeffrey Herbst, "Prospects for Revolution in South Africa," *Political Science Quarterly* 103.4 (1988), p. 668; "South Africa," *The Economist* (20 March 1993), p. 4.

41. David Yudelman, *The Emergence of Modern South Africa* (Westport, Conn.: Greenwood, 1983), pp. 3, 269. The turning point in rising black labor activism was marked by the 1973 wildcat strikes in Durban, as discussed in Wiehahn, *Wiehahn Report*, p. 30. See also Marx, *Lessons of Struggle*, ch. 6.

42. See Robert Price, *The Apartheid State in Crisis* (New York: Oxford University Press, 1991).

43. Interview with Helen Suzman, Johannesburg, 11 May 1994.

44. See Cynthia Enloe, *Ethnic Conflict and Political Development* (Boston: Little, Brown, 1973), pp. 216–58. See also Cynthia Enloe, *Ethnic Soldiers* (Middlesex: Penguin, 1980); D. E. H. Russell, *Rebellion, Revolution and Armed Force* (New York: Academic Press, 1974), pp. 78–9.

45. Interview with P. J. de Lange, Johannesburg, 2 May 1994; interview with Beyers Naude, Johannesburg, 29 April 1994.

46. See Gerhard Mare and George Hamilton, *An Appetite for Power: Buthelezi's Inkatha and South Africa* (Johannesburg: Ravan, 1987); Mzala, *Gatsha Buthelezi: Chief with a Double Agenda* (London: Zed, 1988); Adam and Moodley, *Opening of the Apartheid Mind*, ch. 6; Marks and Trapido, eds., *Politics of Race, Class and Nationalism*, p. 54.

47. Interview with Gerrit Viljoen, Pretoria, 28 April 1994.

48. Interview with Oliver Tambo, Washington, D.C., 27 January 1987.

49. Interview with Fred Rundle of AWB, Johannesburg, May 1994.

50. Interview with Jaap Marais, Pretoria, 4 May 1994.

51. Ibid.

52. Ibid.

53. Interview with Pieter Mulder, Pretoria, 4 May 1994.

54. Mandela, *Long Walk*, p. 435.

55. Interview with Gerrit Viljoen, Pretoria, 28 April 1994.

56. Ibid. See also F. W. de Klerk, "Address by State President" (2 February 1990), in Robert Schrire, *Adapt or Die: The End of White Politics in South Africa* (New York: Ford Foundation/Foreign Policy Association, 1991), p. 161; Adam and Moodley, *Opening of the Apartheid Mind*, p. 166; Johannes Rantete and Hermann Giliomee, "Transition to Democracy through Transaction?" *African Affairs* 91 (1992), p. 519.

57. Tomlinson Commission, *Report*, p. 104.

58. Anthony W. Marx, "International Intervention in South Africa," *Journal of International Affairs* 46.1 (Summer 1992), pp. 175–6; Timothy D. Sisk, *Democratization in South Africa* (Princeton: Princeton University Press, 1995), p. 82.

59. F. W. de Klerk, "Address by the State President," in Schrire, *Adapt or Die*, p. 171; Allister Sparks, "Transition in South Africa," *Program of African Studies News and Events*, Northwestern University, Evanston (Winter 1993), manuscript.

60. Mandela, *Long Walk*, p. 503.

61. Interview with Allan Boesak, Johannesburg, 7 April 1988.

62. Schrire, *Adapt or Die*, p. 25.

63. Interview with Walter Sisulu, Johannesburg, 2 May 1994,

64. Interview with Neville Alexander, Johannesburg, 5 May 1994.

65. Interview with Fatima Meer, Durban, 4 July 1986.

66. Mandela, *Long Walk*, p. 506.

67. "Interview with Oliver Tambo," *Cape Times* (4 November 1985). See also Raymond Suttner and Jeremy Cronin, *Thirty Years of the Freedom Charter* (Johannesburg: Ravan, 1986), p. 129.

68. Interview with Cyril Ramaphosa, June 1988; Joe Slovo, "The Negotiations Victory," *The African Communist* (Fourth Quarter 1993), pp. 6–13.

69. Interview with Gerrit Viljoen, Pretoria, 28 April 1994.

70. Craig Charney, "Voices of a New Democracy: African Expectations in the New South Africa," Research Report no. 38, Johannesburg: Centre for Policy Studies, January 1995.

71. Interview with P. J. de Lange, Johannesburg, 2 May 1994.

72. Interview with Helen Suzman, Johannesburg, 11 May 1994. See also Allister Sparks, *Tomorrow is Another Country* (Sandton: Struik, 1995).

73. Interview with Gerrit Viljoen, Pretoria, 28 April 1994.

74. Interview with Neville Alexander, Johannesburg, 5 May 1994.

75. Interview with Gerrit Viljoen, Pretoria, 28 April 1994.

76. See Hennie Kotze, "Toward an Elite Settlement," *Indicator South Africa* 10.2 (Autumn 1993), p. 5. I am here contesting the argument made in Samuel P. Huntington, "Reform and Stability in South Africa," *International Security* 6.4 (Spring 1982).

77. See Ian Shapiro, "Democratic Innovation: South Africa in Economic Perspective," *World Politics* 46.1 (October 1993); Sisk, *Democratization in South Africa*, pp. 88, 115, 120.

78. For a prior insightful discussion of such constitutional arrangements, see

Donald L. Horowitz, *A Democratic South Africa?* (Berkeley: University of California Press, 1991).

79. Sam C. Nolutshungu, "Reflections on National Unity in South Africa," *Third World Quarterly* 13.4 (1993), p. 11.

80. Estelle Randall and Chris Louw, "Cabinet Orders Report on Secret Land Deal," *Weekly Mail and Guardian* (27 May 1994), p. 6

81. Interview with Beyers Naude, Johannesburg, 29 April 1994.

82. African National Congress, *The Reconstruction and Development Programme* (Johannesburg: Umanyano, 1994), p. 6.

83. Dennis Beckett, "Drawing a Line at Deception," *The Star* (May 20, 1994), p. 12.

84. See Courtney Jung and Ian Shapiro, "South Africa's Negotiated Transition," *Politics and Society* 23.3 (1993). In 1996, the National Party left the Government of National Unity to form such an opposition.

85. Interview with Gerrit Viljoen, Pretoria, 28 April 1994. See also Sisk, *Democratization in South Africa*, p. 136.

86. See Joe Slovo, "The Working Class and Nation-Building," in Maria van Diepen, ed., *The National Question in South Africa* (London: Zed, 1988), p. 149.

87. Interview with Neville Alexander, Johannesburg, 5 May 1994.

88. Interview with Helen Suzman, Johannesburg, 11 May 1994.

89. Interview with Beyers Naude, Johannesburg, 29 April 1994.

90. Interview with Neville Alexander, Johannesburg, 5 May 1994; interview with Breyten Breytenbach, Johannesburg, 25 April 1994.

91. Interview with Pieter Mulder, Pretoria, 4 May 1994; interview with Fred Rundle, Johannesburg, 3 May 1994.

92. Interview with Neville Alexander, Johannesburg, 5 May 1994.

93. Bill Keller, "The Revolution Won, Workers are Still Unhappy," *New York Times* (23 July 1994), p. 2; Bill Keller, "A Post-Apartheid Nightmare: Hospitals Swamped," *New York Times* (29 August 1994), p. A4; Bill Keller, "Corporate Foe of Apartheid Finds Rewards Elusive," *New York Times* (9 December 1994), p. A4; Reg Rumney, "Perks in the RDP Firing Line," *Weekly Mail and Guardian* (23 September 1994), p. B1.

94. Interview with Nat Ramokgopa, Johannesburg, April 1988.

95. Frank Chothia, "Mistakes and Omissions Cost the ANC the Natal Vote," *Weekly Mail and Guardian* (13 May 1994), p. 15; Mondi waka Makhanya, "In the Coloured Cape Flats, Mandela's Just a Kaffir," *Weekly Mail and Guardian* (25 March 1994), p. 16.

96. Interview with Mamphela Ramphele, Johannesburg, 18 August 1986.

97. Amy Waldman, "Apartheid's Reminders Quickly Fade," *New York Times* (15 June 1994), p. A10; *Weekly Mail and Guardian* (16 April 1993), p. 2.

98. Interview with P. J. de Lange, Johannesburg, 2 May 1994.

99. Interview with Neville Alexander, Johannesburg, 5 May 1994. See also Ernesto Laclau, *Reflections on the Revolution of our Time* (London: Verso, 1990), p. 156.

Chapter 9. Burying Jim Crow

1. Vincent Harding, *There Is a River* (New York: Harcourt Brace Jovanovich, 1981), pp. 71, 95.
2. Ibid., pp. 121, 146, 158.
3. Barbara Fields, "Slavery, Race and Ideology in the United States of America," *New Left Review* 181, (1990), p. 115.
4. See J. Morgan Kousser, *The Shaping of Southern Politics* (New Haven: Yale University Press, 1974), p. 250.
5. Ibid., p. 212.
6. See Wilson Jeremiah Moses, *The Golden Age of Black Nationalism: 1850–1925* (New York: Oxford University Press, 1978), pp. 53–4; George M. Fredrickson, *Black Liberation* (New York: Oxford University Press, 1995), p. 28; Edwin S. Redky, *Black Exodus* (New Haven: Yale University Press, 1969), pp. 18–23; Sperling Stuckey, *Ideological Origins of Black Nationalism* (Boston: Beacon, 1972), p. 199; Eric Foner, *Reconstruction* (New York: Harper and Row, 1988), pp. 288, 598–9; Victor Ullman, *Martin Delany* (Boston: Beacon, 1971); E. U. Essien-Udom, *Black Nationalism* (Chicago: University of Chicago Press, 1962), p. 19; Robert H. Brisbane, *Black Activism* (Valley Forge, Pa.: Judson Press, 1974), p. 11.
7. William Julius Wilson, *Power, Racism and Privilege* (New York: Free Press, 1973), p. 56.
8. W. E. B. Du Bois, *The Souls of Black Folks* in *Three Negro Classics* (New York: Avon, 1965), p. 245; Floyd Barbour, ed., *The Black Power Revolt* (Toronto: Macmillan, 1968), pp. 36–7; Richard Kluger, *Simple Justice* (New York: Knopf, 1980), p. 37; W. E. B. Du Bois, *Black Reconstruction in America* (New York: Atheneum, 1992), p. 14; Gunnar Myrdal, *An American Dilemma* (New York: Harper and Row, 1944), p. 737. See also William S. McFeely, *Frederick Douglass* (New York: Norton, 1991).
9. Moses, *Golden Age*, pp. 84, 96; Derrick A. Bell, Jr., *Faces at the Bottom of the Well* (New York: Basic Books, 1992), p. 40; Redky, *Black Exodus*, p. 32; Eric Foner, *Free Soil, Free Labor, Free Men* (London: Oxford University Press, 1970), p. 299; Judith N. Shklar, *American Citizenship* (Cambridge, Mass.: Harvard University Press, 1991), p. 52.
10. Frederick Douglass, "Our Elevation as a race . . ." (1847), reprinted in John H. Bracey, August Meier, and Elliott Rudwick, eds., *Black Nationalism in America* (Indianapolis: Bobbs-Merrill, 1970), p. 58.
11. Joel Williamson, *The Crucible of Race* (New York: Oxford University Press, 1984), p. 70.
12. Raymond L. Hall, ed., *Black Separatism and Social Reality* (New York: Pergamon, 1977), p. 5.
13. Charles V. Hamilton, *The Black Experience in American Politics* (New York: Putnam, 1973), p. 28.
14. Myrdal, *American Dilemma*, p. 65. Washington's accommodationism remained unshaken, even when he was beaten by hoodlums immediately

after his most famously conciliatory speech at the 1895 Atlanta Exposition. See Bart Landry, *The New Black Middle Class* (Berkeley: University of California Press, 1987), p. 18.

15. See Myrdal, *American Dilemma*, p. 739; Shklar, *American Citizenship*, p. 20; C. Vann Woodward, *Origins of the New South* (Baton Rouge: Louisiana State University Press, 1951), pp. 337, 360; Fredrickson, *Black Liberation*, p. 36.

16. See W. E. B. Du Bois, "The Negro Problem," in Philip S. Foner, ed., *W. E. B. Du Bois Speaks* (New York: Pathfinder, 1970), p. 223; David Levering Lewis, *W. E. B. Du Bois – Biography of a Race* (New York: Holt, 1993); Mark D. Higbee, "W. E. B. Du Bois and the Politics of Liberation, 1917–1963," Ph.D. dissertation, Columbia University, New York (1995), p. 40; Charles V. Hamilton, "The Welfare of Black Americans," *Political Science Quarterly* 101.2 (1986); Moses, *Golden Age*, p. 133.

17. Du Bois, "Loyalty," *Crisis* (May 1917), p. 8; Higbee, "Du Bois," pp. 71, 85, 94; Michael Dawson, *Behind the Mule* (Princeton: Princeton University Press, 1994), pp. 31, 102.

18. Du Bois, *Souls of Black Folks*, in *Three Negro Classics*, p. 215.

19. W. E. B. Du Bois, "The Conservation of the Races," in Foner, ed., *W. E. B. Du Bois Speaks*, p. 81; Higbee, "Du Bois," pp. 251, 256.

20. Du Bois, "Conservation of the Races," pp. 73–7.

21. See ibid., p. 79; Myrdal, *American Dilemma*, pp. 683, 698. For further discussion of Du Bois's views on race, see Kwame Anthony Appiah, *In My Father's House* (London: Methuen, 1992), ch. 2.

22. W. E. B. Du Bois, "Dear Reader," *Crisis* (April 1919), p. 299. See also Fredrickson, *Black Liberation*, p. 109.

23. W. E. B. Du Bois, *Dusk at Dawn* (New York: Harcourt, Brace, 1940), p. 275. The Communist Party had enjoyed considerable black support, especially after its efforts in defense of the Scottsboro boys. See Manning Marable, *Race, Reform and Rebellion* (Jackson: University Press of Mississippi, 1991), p. 20; Fredrickson, *Black Liberation* ch. 5.

24. Interview with Gloster Current, New York, 3 March 1993.

25. See Lewis M. Killian, *The Impossible Revolution? Black Power and the American Dream* (New York: Random House, 1968), p. 94; William H. Chafe, *Civilities and Civil Rights* (New York: Oxford University Press, 1980), p. 117.

26. Doug McAdam, *Political Process and the Development of Black Insurgency, 1930–1970* (Chicago: University of Chicago Press, 1982), p. 134.

27. Hamilton, *Black Experience in American Politics*, p. 45; Myrdal, *American Dilemma*, p. 746; Marcus Garvey, "Philosophy and Opinions, 1923," in Floyd Barbour, ed., *Black Power Revolt* (Toronto: Macmillan, 1969), p. 57.

28. Du Bois, *Souls of Black Folks* in *Three Negro Classics*, p. 347.

29. Thomas Byrne Edsall and Mary D. Edsall, *Chain Reaction* (New York: Norton, 1991), p. 117; Wilson, *Power*, pp. 146–7. See also Richard B. Freeman, *Black Elite* (New York: McGraw Hill, 1976), p. 5; Landry, *New*

Black Middle Class; Daniel Patrick Moynihan, "Employment, Income, and the Ordeal of the Negro Family," in Talcott Parsons and Kenneth B. Clark, eds., *The Negro American* (Boston: Beacon, 1965), pp. 134–59; Marable, *Race*, pp. 16–7; Hall, *Black Separatism*, p. 72.

30. See Hubert M. Blalock, Jr., *Black–White Relations in the 1980s* (New York: Praeger, 1979), p. 6; Michael Hughes and Bradley R. Hertel, "The Significance of Color Remains," *Social Forces* 69.1 (1990). For an example of how earlier black middle-class activists distanced themselves from the black poor, see Moses, *Golden Age*, p. 107.

31. Gerald L. Dillingham, "The Emerging Black Middle Class: Class Consciousness or Race Consciousness?" *Ethnic and Racial Studies* 4.4 (October 1981), p. 433; Gary T. Marx, *Protest and Prejudice* (New York: Harper and Row, 1969), p. 56. See also Manning Marable, *Black American Politics* (London: Verso, 1985), p. 165.

32. Stokely Carmichael and Charles V. Hamilton, *Black Power* (New York: Random House, 1967), p. 50; Landry, *New Black Middle Class*, p. 72.

33. Interview with Charles Rangel, New York, 8 April 1993; Douglas S. Massey and Nancy A. Denton, *American Apartheid* (Cambridge, Mass.: Harvard University Press, 1993), pp. 77, 85.

34. Interview with Virginia Foster Durr, Montgomery, 26 April 1993.

35. Carmichael and Hamilton, *Black Power*, p. 54. See also William Julius Wilson, *The Declining Significance of Race* (Chicago: University of Chicago Press, 1978), p. 164.

36. E. Franklin Frazier, *Black Bourgeoisie* (New York: Free Press, 1957). See also Wilson, *Power*, p. 11; Massey and Denton, *American Apartheid*, p. 216.

37. Wilson, *Declining Significance*, p. 135.

38. Interview with Kwame Ture (aka Stokely Carmichael), New York, 19 March 1993. See also Dennis Chong, *Collective Action and the Civil Rights Movement* (Chicago: University of Chicago Press, 1991); Chafe, *Civilities*, pp. 132–4.

39. See Myrdal, *American Dilemma*, pp. 863, 873, 876, 935; Fredrickson, *Black Liberation*, p. 93; John Dittmer, *Local People* (Urbana: University of Illinois Press, 1994), pp. 75–6. The best general discussion of this theme is provided by Aldon Morris, *The Origins of the Civil Rights Movement* (New York: Free Press, 1984). The role of white support for indigenous organizations is discussed in J. Craig Jenkins and Craig M. Eckert, "Channeling Black Insurgency," *American Sociological Review* 51 (December 1986), p. 821.

40. Interview with Andrew Young, Atlanta, 14 March 1994.

41. Interview with George Houser, 19 February 1993. See McAdam, *Political Process*, p. 152, for a quantitative study of the preponderance of the South in "movement initiated action, 1955–65."

42. Patricia Gurin and Edgar Epps, *Black Consciousness, Identity and Achievement* (New York: Wiley, 1975), p. 278; Edsall and Edsall, *Chain Reaction*, p. 8; Interview with Kwame Ture, New York, 19 March 1993.

43. Interview with James Farmer, 6 May 1994.
44. Interview with Percy Sutton, New York, 24 February 1993. See also James Forman, *The Making of Black Revolutionaries* (New York: Macmillan, 1972), p. 93; Myrdal, *American Dilemma*, pp. 1004, 1008.
45. Fred R. Harris and Roger Wilkins, eds., *Quiet Riots* (New York: Pantheon, 1988), p. 7.
46. Clayborne Carson, *In Struggle* (Cambridge, Mass.: Harvard University Press, 1981), p. 54.
47. Brisbane, *Black Activism*, p. 22; Kenneth O'Reilly, *Racial Matters* (New York: Free Press, 1989), p. 51. See also Myrdal, *American Dilemma*, p. xxxvi; Chafe, *Civilities*, pp. 65–6; Dittmer, *Local People*, pp. 41–5, 68.
48. Taylor Branch, *Parting the Waters* (New York: Simon and Schuster, 1988), p. 150; David J. Garrow, *Bearing the Cross* (New York: Random House, 1986), p. 85.
49. Interview with Julian Bond, Washington, D.C., 5 May 1993. See also Morris, *Origins of the Civil Rights Movement*, p. 4; Harris Wofford, *Of Kennedys and Kings* (New York: Farrar, Straus and Giroux, 1980), p. 112.
50. Interview with Andrew Young, Atlanta, 14 March 1993.
51. Virginia Foster Durr, *Outside the Magic Circle* (Tuscaloosa: University of Alabama Press, 1985), p. 284.
52. Garrow, *Bearing the Cross*, p. 27; Morris, *Origins of the Civil Rights Movement*, p. 17; Branch, *Parting the Waters*, p. 140.
53. Interview with Fred Grey, Tuskegee, 7 April 1993; interview with Andrew Young, Atlanta, 14 March 1994.
54. Durr, *Outside the Magic Circle*, p. 278. See also Rosa Parks, *Rosa Parks: My Story* (New York: Dial Books, 1992). Parks was further encouraged and protected by her employers, Virginia and Clifford Durr, leading white Montgomery liberals.
55. Interview with James Farmer, 6 May 1993.
56. Ibid.
57. Ibid.
58. Garrow, *Bearing the Cross*, p. 513; Branch, *Parting the Waters*, p. 780; Julius Lester, *Revolutionary Notes* (New York: Baron, 1969), p. 85. Ironically, King's movement could not be lambasted by Southerners for trying to overthrow the government, for such an aim would have resonated with Southern pride in the region's efforts to do just that a century earlier, as humorously described in Durr, *Magic Circle*, p. 266.
59. Hugh Davis Graham, *The Civil Rights Era* (New York: Oxford University Press, 1990), p. 164; Garrow, *Bearing the Cross*, pp. 484, 488.
60. Interview with Marvin Rich, New York, 3 March 1992.
61. Interview with Burke Marshall, New Haven, 23 March 1994. See also Dittmer, *Local People*, p. 149.
62. Interview with Bob Mants, Montgomery, 26 April 1993. See also Dittmer, *Local People*, pp. 56–8; James C. Cobb, *The Most Southern Place on Earth* (New York: Oxford University Press, 1992), p. 218.
63. Interview with Wayne Greenhaw, Montgomery, 26 April 1994.

64. Interview with James Farmer, 6 May 1993.
65. See Carson, *In Struggle*, p. 11; Gurin and Epps, *Black Consciousness*, p. 193; Chafe, *Civilities*, p. 136; Dittmer, *Local People*, p. 87.
66. See Minutes of SNCC Staff Conference, 11 May 1966, from the Archive of the Martin Luther King Center for Nonviolence. See also B. J. Miles, "SNCC Summary of Cash Receipts," 1 January – 31 December 1964, King Center Archive; Letter to Ralph Abernathy from John Lewis, 19 August 1965, King Center Archive; Forman, *Making of Black Revolutionaries*, p. 221; Meier et al., *Black Protest*, p. 144.
67. Interview with Kwame Ture, New York, 19 March 1993;
68. Interview with Bob Mants, Montgomery, 26 April 1993. While the civil rights organizations remained formally committed to nonviolence, they did occasionally enjoy the protection of armed groups, such as the Deacons of Defense.
69. Forman, *Making of Black Revolutionaries*, p. 265.
70. "SNCC Staff Conference Minutes," May 11, 1966, from the King Center Archive.
71. Graham, *Civil Rights Era*, p. 147; Interview with Andrew Young, Atlanta, 14 March 1993. See also McAdam, *Political Process*, p. 177; Carson, *In Struggle*, p. 62.
    King's deputy, Rev. Wyatt T. Walker, also understood this dynamic, welcoming the repression in Birmingham with elation: "We had some police brutality. They brought out the dogs . . . We've got a movement!" as cited in Forman, *Making of Black Revolutionaries*, p. 312.
72. Interview with James Farmer, 6 May 1993. See also Steven E. Barkan, "Legal Control of the Southern Civil Rights Movement," *American Sociological Review* 49 (1984), pp. 556–9.
73. Quoted in Alan B. Anderson and George W. Pickering, *Confronting the Color Line* (Athens: University of Georgia Press, 1986), p. 183.
74. Carmichael and Hamilton, *Black Power*, p. 70; interview with Joseph Lowery, Atlanta, 29 April 1993; interview with Willie Ricks, Atlanta, 28 April 1993.
75. Interview with Hosea Williams, Atlanta, 29 April 1993. See also Garrow, *Bearing the Cross*, pp. 369, 577.
76. Interview with George Houser, New York, 19 February 1993; James Farmer, *Lay Bare the Heart* (New York: Arbor House, 1985), p. 213.
77. Durr, *Outside the Magic Circle*, p. 298.
78. August Meier and Elliott Rudwick, *CORE: A Study in the Civil Rights Movement* (Urbana: University of Illinois Press, 1975), pp. 173, 259; Howard Zinn, *SNCC: The New Abolitionists* (Boston: Beacon, 1964), p. 58.
79. John F. Kennedy, "Nationally Televised Speech," 11 June 1963, in Carson et al., *Eyes on the Prize*, p. 161.
80. John Lewis, "Text of Speech to be Delivered at the Lincoln Memorial," 28 August 1963, in Carson et al., *Eyes on the Prize*, p. 164.

81. Lyndon Johnson, "Forward," in Talcott Parsons and Kenneth B. Clark, eds., *The Negro American* (Boston: Beacon, 1965), p. v.
82. See Garrow, *Bearing the Cross*, p. 400; Marable, *Race*, p. 82. Debates about the Selma march are discussed in the letter from John Lewis to Martin Luther King, 7 March 1965, in the King Archive.
83. Interview with Willie Ricks, Atlanta, 28 April 1993.
84. Interview with Andrew Young, Atlanta, 14 March 1993.
85. Lyndon Johnson, "Address to Joint Session of Congress," 15 March 1965.
86. Interview with Barbara Omalade, New York, 22 March 1993.
87. Interview with Jamil Abdullah Al-Amin (aka H. Rap Brown), Atlanta, 27 April 1993. See also Harris and Wilkins, *Quiet Riots*, p. 84; Hamilton, *Adam Clayton Powell, Jr.*, p. 361.
88. Interview with Kwame Ture (aka Stokely Carmichael), 19 March 1993.
89. Interview with Kathleen Cleaver, New York, 5 May 1993. See also Peter Goldman, *The Death and Life of Malcolm X* (Urbana: University of Illinois Press, 1979), p. 186; Stokely Carmichael, "Power and Racism," in Barbour, ed., *Black Power Revolt*, p. 63; Sidney Tarrow, *Power in Movement* (Cambridge: Cambridge University Press, 1994), p. 46.
90. Bureau of the Census, U.S. Department of Commerce, *Historical Statistics of the United States, Colonial Times to 1970* (Washington, D.C.: Government Printing Office, 1975), Part One, p. 95. See also Nicholas Lemann, *The Promised Land* (New York: Random House, 1991), p. 6.
91. Interview with Barbara Omalade, New York, 22 March 1993.
92. Interview with James Farmer, 6 May 1993.
93. Interview with John Lewis, Washington, D.C., 5 May 1993; Doug McAdam, *Freedom Summer* (New York: Oxford University Press, 1988), p. 121. See also Carson, *In Struggle*, p. 127; Wofford, *Of Kennedys and Kings*, p. 181; Dittmer, *Local People* ch. 12; Cobb, *Most Southern Place*, p. 234. It is worth noting that activists' disillusionment with Johnson did not preclude 95% of blacks from voting for him in 1964, as reported in William Brink and Louis Harris, *Black and White* (New York: Simon and Schuster, 1966), p. 75.
94. See Edward G. Carmines and James A. Stimson, *Issue Evolution: Race and Transformation of American Politics* (Princeton: Princeton University Press, 1989), pp. 47, 63, 71.
95. Interview with Marvin Rich, New York, 3 March 1992.
96. Farmer, *Lay Bare the Heart*, p. 258.
97. Interview with Hosea Williams, Atlanta, 29 April 1993.
98. Quoted in Goldman, *Death and Life*, p. 51.
99. Massey and Denton, *American Apartheid*, p. 149.
100. Anderson and Pickering, *Confronting the Color Line*, pp. 191–2, 357. By 1968 Mayor Daley was clearly ready to use violence against agitators, in particular protestors at the Democratic National Convention in Chicago.

101. Interview with Willie Ricks, Atlanta, 28 April 1993; Anderson and Pickering, *Confronting the Color Line*, p. 260.
102. Carmichael and Hamilton, *Black Power*, p. 9.
103. See McAdam, *Political Process*, pp. 192–3. A notable departure from Johnson's reluctance to press further for civil rights was his support for "affirmative action," as described in his speech at Howard University on 4 June 1965. See Carson, et al., *Eyes on the Prize*, pp. 611–13.
104. Quoted in Anderson and Pickering, *Confronting the Color Line*, p. 150.
105. Meier and Rudwick, *CORE*, p. 428.
106. See O'Reilly, *Racial Matters*; Brink and Harris, *Black and White*, p. 134; Zinn, *SNCC*, p. 74; Dittmer, *Local People*, pp. 238, 304. For a discussion of the implicit trade-off between social programs and Vietnam, see Daniel Patrick Moynihan, *Maximum Feasible Misunderstanding* (New York: Free Press, 1969), pp. 5, 155; Garrow, *Bearing the Cross*, p. 470; Anderson and Pickering, *Confronting the Color Line*, p. 319; Wofford, *Of Kennedys and Kings*, p. 332.
107. Stokely Carmichael, "Dear Friends" letter, no date, King Center Archives.
108. See the following items from the King Center Archive: SNCC Staff Meeting Minutes, 11 May 1966; Letter from John Lewis to A. Philip Randolph, 14 December 1965; Western Union telegram from Martin Luther King et al to Stokely Carmichael, 4 August 1966. See also Hamilton, *Black American Experience*, pp. 206–10.
109. SNCC Staff Conference, 11 May 1966, pp. 2, 6, King Center Archive.
110. Durr, *Outside the Magic Circle*, pp. 301, 318; Carmines and Stimson, *Issue Evolution*, p. 49.
111. Interview with Percy Sutton, New York, 24 February 1993.
112. Interview with Hosea Williams, Atlanta, 29 April 1993.
113. Brink and Harris, *Black and White*, p. 16; Robert M. Fogelson, *Violence as Protest* (Garden City, N.Y.: Doubleday, 1971), p. 3; Harris and Wilkins, *Quiet Riots*, pp. 10–11; Brisbane, *Black Activism*, p. 175.
114. Meier et al., *Black Protest in the Sixties*, p. 15; Manus I. Midlarsky, "Analyzing Diffusion and Contagion Effects: The Urban Disorders of the 1960s," *American Political Science Review* 72.3 (September 1978), pp. 996–1010; Thomas F. Pettigrew, *Racially Separate or Together?* (New York: McGraw-Hill, 1971), p. 160; Doug McAdam, "Tactical Innovation and the Pace of Insurgency," *American Sociological Review* 48 (December 1983), pp. 735–54.
115. See Otto Kerner, *Supplemental Studies for the National Advisory Commission on Civil Disorders* (Washington, D.C.: Government Printing Office, 1968), pp. 48, 223, 236; Fogelson, *Violence as Protest*, ch. 2; David O. Sears and John B. McConahay, "Participation in the Los Angles Riot," *Social Problems* 17.1 (1969), pp. 3–20; Seymour Spilerman, "The Causes of Racial Disturbances," *American Sociological Review* 35.4 (August 1970), p. 628; Gary T. Marx, "Civil Disorders and the Agents of Social Control," *Journal of Social Issues* 26.1 (Winter 1970), pp. 31–46;

Brisbane, *Black Activism*, p. 149; Nathan Coplan, "The New Ghetto Man," *Journal of Social Issues* 26.1 (Winter 1970), p. 71.

116. Interview with Roger Wilkins, Washington, D.C., 5 May 1993.

117. Roger Wilkins, *A Man's Life* (New York: Simon and Schuster, 1982), p. 143.

118. See Coplan, "New Ghetto Man," p. 64; Aldon Morris, Shirley J. Hachett, and Ronald E. Brown, "The Civil Rights Movement and Black Political Socialization," in B. S. Sigwel, ed., *Political Learning in Adulthood* (Chicago: University of Chicago Press, 1989), p. 289; Seymour Spilerman, "Structural Characteristics of Cities and the Severity of Racial Disorders," *American Sociological Review* 41.5 (October 1976), pp. 771–92; William R. Kelly and David Snyder, "Racial Violence and Socioeconomic Changes Among Blacks in the United States," *Social Forces* 58.3 (March 1980), pp. 739–60.

119. Interview with Bob Mants, Montgomery, 26 April 1993.

120. See Jeffrey M. Paige, "Political Orientation and Riot Participation," *American Sociological Review* 36 (October 1971), pp. 810–20.

121. Quoted in Anderson and Pickering, *Confronting the Color Line*, p. 266.

122. Robert J. Samuelson, "Riots," *Science* 157 (August 1967), pp. 663–5.

123. Kerner, *Supplemental Studies*, pp. 8–9, 47; Fogelson, *Violence as Protest*, p. 17; Bob Blauner, *Black Lives, White Lives* (Berkeley: University of California Press, 1989), p. 15; James W. Button, *Black Violence: The Political Impact of the 1960s Riots* (Princeton: Princeton University Press, 1978), p. 175.

124. Interview with Roger Wilkins, Washington, D.C., 5 May 1993. See also Hubert Blalock, Jr., *Black–White Relations in the 1980s* (New York: Praeger, 1979), p. 8; Kenneth O'Reilly, *Racial Matters* (New York: Free Press, 1989), p. 231; Button, *Black Violence*, p. 9; David O. Sears, "Black Attitudes toward the Political System in the Aftermath of the Watts Insurrection," *Midwest Journal of Political Science* 8.4 (November 1969), p. 526; Sanford F. Schram and J. Patrick Turbett, "Civil Disorder and the Welfare Explosion," *American Sociological Review* 48 (1983), pp. 408–14.

125. Graham, *Civil Rights Era*, p. 304.

126. See Edsall and Edsall, *Chain Reaction*, pp. 81, 83; Martin Carnoy, *Faded Dreams* (Cambridge: Cambridge University Press, 1994), p. 212. Cuts in implementation of civil rights had predated Nixon, as discussed in Graham, *Civil Rights Era*, p. 239; John T. McCartney, *Black Power Ideologies* (Philadelphia: Temple University Press, 1992), p. 129.

127. Button, *Black Violence*, pp. 108–42; Edsall and Edsall, *Chain Reaction*, pp. 72, 81, 97; Tarrow, *Power in Movement*, p. 113.

128. Anderson and Pickering, *Confronting the Color Line*, pp. 376–7; Manning Marable, "Black Nationalism in the 1970s," *Socialist Review* 10.2/3 (March/June 1980), p. 71; Edsall and Edsall, *Chain Reaction*, p. 86.

129. Quoted in O'Reilly, *Racial Matters*, p. 120. See also Carmichael and Hamilton, *Black Power*, pp. 5, 9, 56; Black United Front, "A Black Man-

ifesto," 24 June 1968, King Center Archive; Gurr and Epps, *Black Consciousness*, p. 210. See also Hamilton, *Black Experience*, p. 206.

130. Albert O. Hirschman, *Exit, Voice and Loyalty* (Cambridge, Mass.: Harvard University Press, 1970), p. 112.

131. McAdam, *Political Process*, p. 190.

132. Interview with Bob Mants, Montgomery, 26 April 1993. See Carson, *In Struggle*, pp. 52, 101, 162, 209, 278; Garrow, *Bearing the Cross*, p. 482; Forman, *Making of Black Revolutionaries*, p. 457; Killian, *Impossible Revolution*, p. 141; Lemann, *Promised Land*, p. 159; Brink and Harris, *Black and White*, pp. 263–6; Chafe, *Civilities*, pp. 244–58.

133. Interview with James Farmer, 6 May 1993. See also Lemann, *Promised Land*, p. 201; Garrow, *Bearing the Cross*, p. 540; Debra Friedman and Doug McAdam, "Collective Identity and Activism," in Aldon Morris and Carol Mueller, eds., *Frontiers in Social Movement Theory* (New Haven: Yale University Press, 1992), pp. 169–70.

134. Stokely Carmichael, "On Black Power," SNCC, Washington, D.C., leaflet, no date, King Center Archive. Class divisions within the civil rights movement are discussed in Dittmer, *Local People*, p. 347.

135. Carmichael and Hamilton, *Black Power*, p. 35. See also Lester, *Revolutionary Notes*, p. 104.

136. Interview with Roger Wilkins, Washington, D.C., 5 May 1993. See also Hamilton, *Black Experience*, pp. 112, 146; William L. Van Deburg, *New Day in Babylon* (Chicago: University of Chicago Press, 1992); Maulana Ron Karenga, "From the Quotable Karenga," in Barbour, ed., *Black Power Revolt* pp. 190–200; Theodore Draper, *Rediscovery of Black Nationalism* (New York: Viking, 1969), p. 149; Marable, "Black Nationalism," p. 89; Kerner, *Supplemental Studies*, p. 6; Harold Cruse, *The Crisis of the Negro Intellectual* (New York: Morrow, 1967); Michael Omi and Howard Winant, *Racial Formation in the United States* (New York: Routledge, 1986), p. 42.

137. Robert L. Allen, *A Guide to Black Power* (London: Victor Gollanz, 1979), p. 154; Floyd McKissick, "Programs for Black Power," in Barbour, ed., *Black Power Revolt* p. 211.

138. Carmichael and Hamilton, *Black Power*, pp. 44, 49. Whitney Young explicitly put forward a pluralist interpretation of Black Power, as discussed in Nancy J. Weiss, *Whitney M. Young, Jr., and the Struggle for Civil Rights* (Princeton: Princeton University Press, 1989), p. 182.

139. Carmichael and Hamilton, *Black Power*, p. 53; Stokely Carmichael, "Power and Racism," in Barbour, ed., *Black Power Revolt* p. 69.

140. Carmichael and Hamilton, *Black Power*, p. 46. See also Blalock, *Black–White Relations*, p. 168; Carson, *In Struggle*, p. 138.

141. Howard Schuman and Shirley Hackett, *Black Racial Attitudes* (Ann Arbor: University of Michigan Press, 1974), p. 6. See also Robert F. Williams, *Negroes with Guns* (New York: Marzani and Munsell, 1962).

142. Interview with Willie Ricks, Atlanta, 28 April 1993.

143. Interview with Daniel Patrick Moynihan, Washington, D.C., March 1993.
144. Interview with Kwame Ture, New York, 19 March 1993; interview with Marvin Rich, New York, 3 March 1993.
145. Brink and Harris, *Black and White*, p. 54; J. D. Aberbach and J. L. Walker, "The Meaning of Black Power," *American Political Science Review* 64.2 (June 1970), p. 368. For even higher estimates of support for Black Power or black pride, see Blauner, *Black Lives*, p. 12; Kerner, *Supplemental Studies*, p. 19.
146. Carson, *In Struggle*, p. 223. See also Garrow, *Bearing the Cross*, pp. 497, 533; Marable, *Race*, p. 95.
147. Carson, *In Struggle*, p. 151.
148. Stokely Carmichael, "Speech in Havana Cuba," August 1967, King Center Archive; Stokely Carmichael, "Report from the Chairman," SNCC Staff Meeting, 5 May 1967, King Center Archive; Carson, *In Struggle*, pp. 154, 227. By 1966, SNCC was also questioning its commitment to nonviolence, as discussed in James Forman, *Sammy Younge, Jr.* (Washington, D.C.: Open Hand, 1986).
149. Interview with Bill Epton, New York, 9 March 1993. See the following items from the King Center Archive: SNCC, "Semi-Introspective," 1964 discussion paper; SNCC, "Central Committee Report," May 1967; SNCC Staff Meeting Minutes, May 1967. See also Lemann, *Promised Land*, p. 162; Dittmer, *Local People*, p. 332.
150. Meier and Rudwick, *CORE*, pp. 290, 341, 387; Farmer, *Lay Bare the Heart*, p. 307.
151. Less well-known black separatist organizations included the League of Revolutionary Black Workers, the Revolutionary Action Movement (RAM), and groups formed by LeRoi Jones and Robert F. Williams, the latter a former U.S. marine. See Marable, *Race*, p. 116; Leroi Jones, "The Need for a Cultural Base," in Barbour, ed., *Black Power Revolt*; Robert F. Williams, "Is Violence Necessary to Combat Injustice?" in Carson et al., *Eyes on the Prize*, pp. 110–2.
152. Sam E. Anderson, "Black Students," *Black Scholar* (January/February 1977); Harlem Branch of the Black Panther Party, "Unity, Black Power, Self-Determination," no date, King Center Archive. SNCC assistance in founding the Panthers led to the merger of the two in 1968.
153. Hamilton, *Black Experience*, p. 227; Black Panther Party, "Order from the Black Panther Party National Central Committee: Outline of Responsibility by Rank and File," no date, King Center Archive. That the Panthers did not support armed insurrection at the time is indicated by their efforts to quell a riot in the Bay area after King's assassination, as discussed in Brisbane, *Black Activism*, p. 212.
154. Van Deburg, *New Day*, p. 159. See also Black Panther Party, "Memo from the Central Committee to the National Advisory Cabinet," "Projects and Programs," 1968, King Center Archive.

155. Marable, *Race*, p. 110. By 1969, the Panthers had a circulation of 10,000 for their newsletter, according to Brisbane, *Black Activism*, p. 218.

156. For the classic discussion of the Nation of Islam, see Essien-Udom, *Black Nationalism*.

157. See Malcolm X (with Alex Haley), *The Autobiography of Malcolm X* (New York: Random House, 1964), p. 280.

158. Goldman, *Death and Life*, p. 395. See Bracey et al., *Black Nationalism*, p. 417; Herbert H. Haines, *Black Radicals and the Civil Rights Mainstream, 1954–1970* (Knoxville: University of Tennessee Press, 1988); Weiss, *Whitney Young Junior*, p. 123.

159. See James H. Cone, *Martin and Malcolm and America* (Maryknoll: Orbis, 1991).

160. Interview with Kwame Ture, New York, 19 March 1993; letter from James Shabazz, Secretary, The Muslim Mosque, Inc., to John Lewis, SNCC, 15 May 1964, King Center Archive. See also Malcolm X, *Autobiography*, p. 397.

   For a parallel effort to unify opposition in South Africa launched by Steve Biko, see Anthony W. Marx, *Lessons of Struggle* (New York: Oxford University Press, 1992), pp. 82–3.

161. Landry, *New Black Middle Class*, p. 2. See also Christopher Jencks, "Affirmative Action for Blacks," *American Behavioral Scientist* 28.6 (July/August 1985), pp. 746–51; John J. Donohue III and James Heckman, "Continuous versus Episodic Change," *Journal of Economic Literature* 29 (December 1991), p. 1630; Jonathan S. Leonard, "Splitting Blacks?" National Bureau of Economic Research, Working Paper Series no. 1327 (1984); William Julius Wilson, *The Truly Disadvantaged* (Chicago: University of Chicago Press, 1987), pp. 30, 110–11; Freeman, *Black Elite*; Marable, *Race*, pp. 97–105; Hall, *Black Separatism*, p. 72; Michael Hout, "Occupational Mobility of Black Men, 1962–73," *American Sociological Review* 49 (June 1984), pp. 308–22; Cornell Paterson Horton and Jessie Carney Smith, *Statistical Record of Black America* (Detroit: Gale Research, 1990), pp. 264, 285, 292, 419; Dawson, *Behind the Mule*, pp. 9, 20, 30.

162. See Andrew Hacker, *Two Nations* (New York: Scribner's, 1992), p. 97; Blauner, *Black Lives*, pp. 166–7, 242; Elijah Anderson, *Streetwise* (Chicago: University of Chicago Press, 1990), p. 2; Landry, *New Black Middle Class*, p. 148; Melvin L. Oliver and Thomas M. Shapiro, *Black Wealth/White Wealth* (New York: Routledge, 1995).

163. Interview with Gloster Current, New York, 3 March 1993; Derrick A. Bell, Jr., *Faces at the Bottom of the Well* (New York: Basic Books, 1992), p. 26.

164. See Dawson, *Behind the Mule*, pp. 45, 88, 121; Jennifer Hochschild, *Facing Up to the American Dream: Race, Class and the Soul of the Nation* (Princeton: Princeton University Press, 1995); Massey and Denton, *American Apartheid*.

165. See United States Department of Education, *Digest of Educational Sta-*

tistics (Washington, D.C.: Government Printing Office, 1988), p. 26. See also Bell, *Faces at the Bottom*; Wilson, *Truly Disadvantaged*; Carnoy, *Faded Dreams*, pp. 14, 23, 162.

166. Interview with Bob Mants, Montgomery, 26 April 1993.

167. Dawson, *Behind the Mule*, pp. 23, 29; Massey and Denton, *American Apartheid*; Oliver and Shapiro, *Black Wealth/White Wealth*; Steven Shulman and William Darity, Jr., *The Question of Discrimination* (Middletown, Conn.: Wesleyan University Press, 1989).

168. Bureau of the Census, U.S. Department of Commerce, *The Social and Economic Status of the Black Population* (Washington, D.C.: Government Printing Office, 1979), pp. 145-6. By 1990, there were more than 7,000 black elected officials. The Congressional Black Caucus was formed in 1971.

169. See Carmichael and Hamilton, *Black Power*, p. 16; Massey and Denton, *American Apartheid*, p. 155.

170. The rising enthusiasm for black electoral participation as an alternative to protests is described in Associate Control, Research and Analysis, *ACRA Black Opinion Survey* (Washington, D.C.: ACRA, 1977), pp. 5, 65. The highpoint of the convergence between black nationalism and electoral participation came with the 1972 Gary convention, as discussed in Marable, *Black American Politics*, p. 187; Carson et al., *Eyes on the Prize*, p. 239. By 1973, even former Panther Huey Newton was also running for office, after having secured a $4 million Model City federal grant for Oakland, as discussed in Hall, *Black Separatism*, p. 77. See also Forman, *Making Black Revolutionaries*, p. 443; McCartney, *Black Political Ideologies*, p. 178. In 1990, former Black Panther member Bobby Rush was elected to Congress.

Interest in electoral politics was arguably enhanced by the rise of black municipal employment and the election of blacks to local office, as discussed by Peter K. Eisinger, *Black Employment in City Government, 1973-1980* (Washington: Joint Center for Political Studies, 1983).

171. Goldman, *Death and Life*, p. 224. The sense of integration via participation was encouraged by instances in which whites voted for black representatives, as discussed in Hacker, *Two Nations*, p. 207.

172. Dawson, *Behind the Mule*, pp. 101, 108.

173. Interview with Hosea Williams, Atlanta, 29 April 1993.

174. See Ira Katznelson, *City Trenches* (New York: Pantheon, 1981), p. 95.

175. See Adolph L. Reed, Jr., *The Jesse Jackson Phenomenon* (New Haven: Yale University Press, 1986); Jesse L. Jackson, *Straight from the Heart* (Philadelphia: Fortress Press, 1987).

176. Edsall and Edsall, *Chain Reaction*, pp. 163, 187, 231; Carnoy, *Faded Dreams*, p. 216; Michael Omi and Howard Winant, *Racial Formation in the United States* (New York: Routledge, 1986), ch. 7.

177. Interview with Joseph Lowery, Atlanta, 29 April 1993.

178. Interview with Charles Rangel, New York, 8 April 1993. See also David Bradley, "Malcolm's Mythmaking," *Transition* 56 (1992), pp. 20-59.

179. See Henry Louis Gates, Jr., "Radical Rappers," *New York Times* (16 December 1990), p. 32.

180. F. James Davis, *Who is Black?* (University Park: Pennsylvania State University Press, 1991), p. 134; Lawrence Wright, "One Drop of Blood," *New Yorker* (25 July 1994), p. 55; Interview with Virginia Durr, Montgomery, 25 April 1993.

181. Kimberlie Williams Crenshaw, "Race, Reform and Retrenchment: Transformation and Legitimation in Antidiscrimination Law," *Harvard Law Review* 101.7 (May 1988), p. 1331.

182. Hochschild, *Facing Up to the American Dream*.

183. Crenshaw, "Race, Reform and Retrenchment," p. 1336.

184. Interview with Joseph Lowery, Atlanta, 29 April 1993.

185. Interview with Burke Marshall, New Haven, 23 March 1994.

Chapter 10. Breaching Brazil's Pact of Silence

1. See Carvalho Franco, *Homens Livres na Ordem Escravocrata* (São Paulo: Kairós, 1983). For general background, see Michael Hanchard, *Orpheus and Power* (Princeton: Princeton University Press, 1995).

2. Charles Wagley, *Race and Class in Rural Brazil* (Paris: UNESCO, 1952), p. 7. See also Carl N. Degler, *Neither Black nor White* (New York: Macmillan, 1971), p. 95.

3. Anani Dzidzienyo, *The Position of Blacks in Brazilian Society* (London: Minority Rights Group, 1971), p. 14. See also Howard Winant, "Rethinking Race in Brazil," *Journal of Latin American Studies* 24 (1992).

4. Abdias do Nascimento, *Brazil: Mixture or Massacre?* (Dover: Majority Press, 1979), p. 2.

5. Interview with Luis Alberto, Salvador, 15 June 1993. See also Carlos Hasenbalg, "Race Relations in Post-Abolition Brazil," Ph.D. dissertation, University of California, Berkeley (1978), p. 210.

6. Florestan Fernandes, *The Negro in Brazilian Society* (New York: Columbia University Press, 1969), p. 389.

7. Interview with Clóvis Moura, São Paulo, 8 July 1993.

8. Melissa Nobles, "Responding with Good Sense: The Politics of Race and Census in Contemporary Brazil," Ph.D. dissertation, Yale University, New Haven (1995), pp. 58, 65, 77.

9. Ibid., p. 119; George Reid Andrews, *Blacks and Whites in São Paulo Brazil, 1888–1988* (Madison: University of Wisconsin Press, 1991), pp. 249–55; Charles Wood, "Categorias Censitárias e Classificações Subjetivas de Raça no Brasil," in Peggy Lovell, ed., *Desigualdade Racial no Brasil Contemporâneo* (Belo Horizonte: UFM, 1991); Peggy Lovell, "Race, Gender and Development in Brazil," *Latin American Research Review* 29.3 (1994); Marvin Harris et al., "Who Are the Whites?" *Social Forces* 72.2 (December 1993); Jan Fiola, "Race Relations in Brazil," Program in Latin American Studies, Occasional Paper Series no. 24, University of Massachusetts, Amherst, (1990), p. 19.

10. Roger Bastide, "The Development of Race Relations in Brazil," in Guy Hunter, ed., *Industrialization and Race Relations* (London: Oxford University Press, 1965), pp. 16, 20; Wagley, *Race and Class*, p. 77; Fernandes, *Negro in Brazilian Society*, p. 420.

11. Interview with Gerson Martinez, Rio de Janeiro, 21 July 1993; interview with Januário Garcia, Rio de Janeiro, 21 July 1993. See also Wagley, *Race and Class*, p. 59.

12. Interview with Januário Garcia, Rio de Janeiro, 21 July 1993; Fiola, "Race Relations in Brazil," p. 11.

13. Anani Dzidzienyo, "Afro-Brasileiros no Contexto Nacional e Internacional," Lovell, ed., in *Desigualdade Racial* p. 58; Fernandes, *Negro in Brazilian Society*, p. 230; Arthur F. Corwin, "Afro-Brazilians," in Robert Brent Toplin, ed., *Slavery and Race Relations in Latin America* (Westport, Conn.: Greenwood, 1974), p. 393; Donald Pierson, *Negroes in Brazil* (Chicago: University of Chicago Press, 1942), p. 225.

14. See David J. Hellwig, ed., *African-American Reflections on Brazil's Racial Paradise* (Philadelphia: Temple University Press, 1992), p. 98; Florestan Fernandes, *Significado do Protesto Negro* (São Paulo: Autores Associados, 1989), p. 68.

15. See Charles H. Wood and Jose Alberto Magno de Carvalho, *The Demography of Inequality in Brazil* (Cambridge: Cambridge University Press, 1988), pp. 3, 76, 139; Thomas E. Skidmore, "Fact and Myth: An Overview of Afro-Brazilian Studies in Brazil," Kellogg Institute Working Paper no. 1, University of Notre Dame, Notre Dame, Ind. (1992), p. 9; Carlos Hasenbalg and Suellen Huntington, "Brazilian Racial Democracy: Reality or Myth?" *Humboldt Journal of Social Relations* 10.1 (Fall/Winter 1982–3), p. 136; Nelson do Valle Silva and Carlos Hasenbalg, *Relações Raciais no Brasil Contemporâneo* (Rio de Janeiro: Rio Fundo Editora, 1992), p. 152; Clóvis Moura, "Estratégia do Imobilismo Social Contra o Negro no Mercado de Trabalho," *São Paulo em Perspectiva* 2.2 (April/June 1988), p. 46; Fiola, "Race Relations in Brazil," p. 29; Edward E. Telles, "Residential Segregation by Skin Color in Brazil," *American Sociological Review* 57 (April 1992), p. 186.

16. For differences in occupational status and wage levels, see Silva and Hasenbalg, *Relações Raciais*, pp. 14, 114; Peggy Ann Lovell, "Racial Inequality and the Brazilian Labor Market," Ph.D. dissertation, University of Florida, Gainesville (1989); I. K. Sundiata, "Late Twentieth Century Patterns of Race Relations in Brazil and the United States," *Phylon* 48.1 (1987), p. 69.
    For differences of wage levels by race in each occupational category, see Luis Felipe de Alencastro, *Veja* (11 May 1988), p. 22.

17. Moura, "Estratagia," p. 45; Waldir José de Quadros, "O Milagre Brasileiro e a Expansão da Nova Classe Média" (Campinas: Instituto de Economia da Universidade Estadual de Campinas, 1991), pp. 132–3. See Lovell, "Racial Inequality," p. 45.

18. See Nelson do Valle Silva, "Black–White Income Differentials: Brazil, 1960," Ph.D. dissertation, University of Michigan, Ann Arbor (1978).
19. See Fiola, "Race Relations in Brazil," p. 23; Wood and Carvalho, *Demography of Inequality*, p. 144; Telles, "Residential Segregation," p. 188; Ney dos Santos Oliveira, "Favelas and Ghettos," Ph.D. dissertation, Columbia University, New York (1996).
20. For differences of literacy and education, see Silva and Hasenbalg, *Relações*, pp. 81, 83, 152; Carlos Hasenbalg, "Race and Socio Economic Inequality in Brazil," in Pierre-Michel Fontaine, ed., *Race, Class and Power in Brazil* (Los Angeles: University of California, Center for Afro-American Studies, 1985), pp. 30, 37; Hasenbalg and Huntington, "Brazilian Racial Democracy," p. 136; Hasenbalg, "Race Relations in Post-Abolition Brazil," pp. 186, 189, 192.

    For differences of literacy levels, see Silva and Hasenbalg, *Relações*, p. 152; Fiola, "Race Relations in Brazil," p. 23; Robert M. Levine, "Turning on the Lights," *Latin American Research Review* 24.2 (1989), pp. 201–7.

    For differences of education levels, see Hasenbalg and Huntington, "Brazilian Racial Democracy," p. 136. These differences are exacerbated by the generally low quality of public primary education on which poor blacks depend, as compared with the higher quality of private primary schools that whites can afford. Whites are then better prepared and are more likely to be able to gain entrance to public universities, exacerbating educational inequalities further. As a result, income disparities increase at higher levels of educational attainment, as discussed in Thomas E. Skidmore, "Fact and Myth," p. 12.
21. See Hasenbalg and Huntington, "Brazilian Racial Democracy," p. 138; Wood and Carvalho, *Demography of Inequality*, p. 139. For a lower estimate on the effect of discrimination, see Lovell, "Race, Gender and Development," p. 29.
22. Wagley, *Race and Class*, p. 70.
23. See Fernandes, *Negro in Brazilian Society*, p. 246; Mitchell, "Black Consciousness," p. 210.
24. Interview with Carlos Alberto Medeiros, 14 July 1993; Anani Dzidzienyo, "Brazil," in Jay A. Sigler, ed., *International Handbook on Race and Race Relations* (New York: Greenwood, 1987), p. 28.
25. Interview with Carlos Alberto Medeiros, Rio de Janeiro, 14 July 1993.
26. Nobles, "Responding with Good Sense," p. 182.
27. Interview with Januário Garcia, Rio de Janeiro, 21 July 1993.
28. See Franklin W. Knight, *The African Dimension in Latin American Societies* (New York: Macmillan, 1974), p. 90.
29. Interview with Clóvis Moura, São Paulo, 8 July 1993.
30. Interview with Carlos Alberto Medeiros, Rio de Janeiro, 14 July 1993. See also Carlos Hasenbalg and Nelson do Valle Silva, "Notas sobre Desigualdade Racial e Política no Brasil," Conference on Racial Politics in Contemporary Brazil, Austin, Tex. (8–10 April 1993), p. 21.

31. See Hasenbalg, "Race Relations in Post-Abolition Brazil," p. 291.
32. Quoting Florestan Fernandes, in Maria Ercília do Nascimento, "A Estratégia da Desigualdade: O Movimento Negro dos Anos 70," M.A. thesis, Pontifícia Universidade Católica de São Paulo (1989), p. 63.
33. See Fernandes, *Negro in Brazilian Society*, pp. 211–33; Fernandes, "Brazil," p. 20.
34. Mitchell, "Racial Consciousness," pp. 40, 131; George Reid Andrews, *Blacks and Whites in São Paulo, Brazil, 1988–1988* (Madison: University of Wisconsin Press, 1991), p. 149. See also *A Voz da Raça* (25 March 1933); Clóvis Moura, "Organizações Negras," in Paul Singer and Vinícius Caldeira Brant, eds., *São Paulo: O Povo em Movimento* (Petrópolis: Vozes, 1980), pp.154–6. The Frente failed to establish a chapter among the poorer but more densely black populated region of Bahia, as discussed in Pierson, *Negroes in Brazil*, p. 343.
35. *A Voz da Raça* (July 1937); *A Voz da Raça* (18 March 1933).
36. Interview with Abdias do Nascimento, Rio de Janeiro, 28 July 1993; Clóvis Moura, *História do Negro Brasileiro* (São Paulo: Atica, 1989), p. 72; *A Voz da Raça* (29 April 1933; 6 May 1933, 10 June 1933, 24 June 1933). Considerable disagreement within the Frente produced at least six major factional disputes in seven years, according to Mitchell, "Racial Consciousness," p. 137.
37. Célia Maria Marinho de Azevedo, "Sinal Fechado para os Negros na Rua da Liberdade," *Humanidades* 5.17 (1988), p. 12. As further indication of the currency of Freyre's image of "racial democracy" at this time, in 1934 Freyre himself helped to organize the first Afro-Brazilian Congress in Recife, as discussed in A. J. R. Russell-Wood, *The Black Man in Slavery and Freedom in Colonial Brazil* (London: Macmillan, 1982), p. 7.
38. Do Nascimento, *Brazil*, p. 45; Clóvis Moura, *Brasil: Raízes do Protesto Negro* (São Paulo: Global, 1983), pp. 103–4. See also Moura, "Organizações Negras," p. 157.
39. Interview with Abdias do Nascimento, Rio de Janeiro, 28 July 1993.
40. Pierre-Michel Fontaine, "Transnational Relations and Racial Mobilization: Emerging Black Movements in Brazil," in John F. Stack, Jr., ed., *Ethnic Identities in a Transnational World* (Westport, Conn.: Greenwood, 1981), p. 148; Moura, *História*, p. 76; Dzidzienyo, "Afro-Brasileiros no Contexto Nacional," p. 58. Abdias do Nascimento's efforts were later informed by frequent analogies with the United States, where he was in exile during Brazil's military regime.
41. Moura, *Brasil*, pp. 62–6; Moura, "Organizações Negras," pp. 159–66; Edward E. Telles, "Afro-Brazilian Identity, Mobilization and Segregation," Conference in Racial Politics in Brazil, Austin, Tex., (10 April 1993), p. 5; Diana DeG. Brown, *Umbanda: Religion and Politics in Urban Brazil* (Ann Arbor: University of Michigan Research Press, 1986), pp. 5, 146.
42. Allison Raphael, "Samba and Social Control," Ph.D. dissertation, Columbia University, New York (1980), pp. 90–182. For a comparison of

Brazilian *carnaval* and New Orleans Mardi Gras, see Roberto da Matta, *Carnivals, Rogues and Heroes: An Interpretation of the Brazilian Dilemma* (Notre Dame, Ind.: University of Notre Dame Press, 1991).

43. See Brown, *Umbanda*, pp. 170, 178, 198.
44. See Michael Mitchell, "Blacks and the Abertura Democratica," in Fontaine, ed., *Race, Class and Power in Brazil*, p. 108. For an alternative view of Black Soul, as more threatening to the social order, see Winant, "Rethinking Race in Brazil," p. 189.
45. See Moura, *Brasil*, pp. 170-4; Lélia Gonzalez and Carlos Hasenbalg, *Lugar de Negro* (Rio de Janeiro: Marco Zero Limitada, 1982), pp. 30, 50.
46. Interview with Carlos Alberto Medeiros, Rio de Janeiro, 14 July 1993. See also Winant, "Rethinking Race in Brazil," p. 183. The culturalist component of the MNU was coordinated by the IPCN, an organization that excluded whites, "founded with international contact by an elite of doctors, psychologists, artists, lawyers and professors," according to an interview with Armoury Mendes Pereira, Rio de Janeiro, 25 June 1993. See also Gonzalez and Hasenbalg, *Lugar de Negro*, p. 37.
47. Interview with Januário Garcia, Rio de Janeiro, 21 July 1993; *MNU Journal* 16 (June–August 1989), pp. 1, 10; Gonzalez and Hasenbalg, *Lugar de Negro*, p. 43; Moura, *Brasil*, p. 167.
48. Interview with Joel Rufino dos Santos, Rio de Janeiro, 27 July 1993; Interview with Hamilton Cordoso, São Paulo, 7 July 1993.
49. Interview with Benedita da Silva, Rio de Janeiro, 20 July 1993. See Santos, "O Movimento," p. 298; Gonzalez and Hasenbalg, *Lugar de Negro*, p. 52; Gregory Freeland, "The Changing Black Political Movement in Brazil," paper presented at the Latin American Studies Association, Los Angeles, (24-7 September 1992), p. 20; Silva and Hasenbalg, *Relações*, p. 159.
50. Santos, "O Movimento," p. 293; Interview with Carlos Alberto Medeiros, Rio de Janeiro, 14 July 1993.
51. Interview with Clóvis Moura, São Paulo, 8 July 1993.
52. Elza Berquó and Luiz Felipe de Alencastro, "A Emergência do Voto Negro," *Novos Estudos* 33 (July 1992), p. 77.
53. Clóvis Luis Pereira Oliveira, "O Negro Sobe ao Palanque," Centro de Recursos Humanos, paper no. 5, Universidade Federal da Bahia (July 1992), pp. 2, 12.
54. See "Por Quê Negro Não Vota em Negro?" *Voz do Negro* 4.17 (November 1987); Ana Lucia E. F. Valente, *Política e Relações Raciais* (São Paulo: FFLCH-USP, 1986); Gonzalez and Hasenbalg, *Lugar de Negro*, p. 55.
55. Interview with Abdias do Nascimento, Rio de Janeiro, 28 July 1993.
56. Interview with Benedita da Silva, Rio de Janeiro, 20 July 1993. See also Interview with Benedita da Silva, "A Primera Deputada Negra do Brasil," *Nêgo* 13 (1987). Da Silva remains committed to addressing issues of race from the Senate, as described in Benedita da Silva, *Zumbi* (Brasília, 1996).
57. Interview with Luis Alberto, Salvador, 15 June 1993.

58. Interview with Francisco Weffort, São Paulo, 9 July 1993; Interview with Abdias do Nascimento, Rio de Janeiro, 28 July 1993.
59. Interview with Benedita da Silva, Rio de Janeiro, 20 July 1993.
60. Interview with Hamilton Cordoso, São Paulo, 7 July 1993. See also Thomas E. Skidmore, "Race and Class in Brazil," in Fontaine, ed., *Race, Class and Power*, p. 17; Skidmore, "Fact and Myth," p. 10; Silva and Hasenbalg, *Relações*, p. 160.
61. "MNU e as Ideologias Brancas," *MNU Journal* 18 (January–March 1991), p. 11.
62. Interview with Wânia Santanna, São Paulo, 20 July 1993. See also Rebecca Reichmann, "Equal Opportunity and Identity Politics: Race, and Gender and Denial in Brazil," manuscript, January 1995.
63. Nobles, "Responding with Good Sense," pp. 22, 25. See also Winant, "Rethinking Race in Brazil."
64. Nobles, "Responding with Good Sense," p. 133. See also Peter Fry, "Why Brazil is Different," *Times Literary Supplement* (8 December 1995), p. 7.
65. Nobles, "Responding with Good Sense," p. 152.
66. Interview with João Jorge Santos Rodrigues, Salvador, 15 June 1993; Interview with Abdias do Nascimento, Rio de Janeiro, 28 July 1993..
67. Interview with João Jorge Santos Rodrigues, Salvador, 15 June 1993.
68. See Fiola, "Race Relations in Brazil," p. 1; Andrews, *Blacks and Whites*, p. 219; Hanchard, *Orpheus and Power*.
69. Interview with Joel Rufino dos Santos, Rio de Janeiro, 27 July 1993.
70. Fernando Henrique Cardoso, "Discurso," International Seminar on "Multiculturalism and Racism," Brasília, 2 July 1996.
71. See Sérgio Buarque de Holanda, *Raízes do Brasil* (Rio de Janeiro: José Olympio, 1983); da Matta, *Carnivals, Rogues and Heroes*, pp. 139–81.
72. Moura, "Organizações Negras," p. 145.
73. Frances Hagopian, "The Compromised Consolidation: The Political Class in the Brazilian Transition," in Scott Mainwaring, Guillermo O'Donnell, and J. Samuel Valenzuela, eds., *Issues in Democratic Consolidation* (Notre Dame, Ind.: University of Notre Dame Press, 1992), p. 281.
74. Carlos Hasenbalg, "Race Relations in Modern Brazil," working paper no. 87131, Latin American Institute, University of New Mexico, Albuquerque (1987), p. 10.
75. For evidence of the high level of violence, see Carlos Veríssimo, "Genocide in Brazil," *Global Affairs* 2.2 (April–May 1991); Freeland, "Changing Black Political Movement," p. 9; Milton Barbosa, "Violência Political em São Paulo," *MNU Journal* 17 (September–November 1989), p. 7.
76. Interview with Januário Garcia, Rio de Janeiro, 21 July 1993.
77. Ibid.
78. Interview with Wânia Santanna, São Paulo, 20 July 1993.
79. Interview with Jorge da Silva, Rio de Janeiro, 28 July 1993.

Chapter 11. Conclusion

1. Joseph Schumpteter, *Capitalism, Socialism and Democracy* (New York: Harper, 1947), pp. 12–13.
2. See E. E. Schattschneider, *The Semisovereign People* (Hinsdale, Ill.: Dryden Press, 1960). This argument might also help to explain the greater salience of class and class conflict in Western Europe, where class differentiation tends to be more rigid and often legally enforced.
3. See Schumpeter, *Capitalism, Socialism and Democracy*, pp. 244–5.

Bibliography

Aberbach, J. D., and J. L. Walker. "The Meaning of Black Power." *American Political Science Review* 64.2 (June 1970).

Adam, Heribert, and Hermann Giliomee. *Ethnic Power Mobilized: Can South Africa Survive?* New Haven: Yale University Press, 1979.

Adam, Heribert, and Kogila Moodley. *The Opening of the Apartheid Mind.* Berkeley: University of California Press, 1993.

Adams, Julia. "Trading States, Trading Places." *Comparative Studies in Society and History* 36.2 (April 1994).

African National Congress. *Documents of the Second National Consultative Conference of the ANC.* 16–23 June 1985.

The Reconstruction and Development Programme. Johannesburg: Umanyano, 1994.

Akenson, Donald Harman. *God's People.* Montreal: McGill and Queen's University Press, 1991.

Alencastro, Luiz Felipe de. "Being Black in Brazil." *World Press Review.* July 1988.

"Prefácio: Sob o Trópico de Capricórnio." *O Negro e o Ouro.* Edited by Anthony Sampson. São Paulo: Companhia das Letras, 1987.

"Proletarios e Escravos." *CEBRAP–Novos Estudos* 21 (July 1988).

"Qui parle de democratie raciale?" *Bresil* 44 (November 1982).

Alexander, Neville. *Sow the Wind.* Braamfontein: Skotaville, 1985.

Allen, Robert L. *A Guide to Black Power.* London: Victor Gollanz, 1979.

Alvarez, Sonia E. *Engendering Democracy in Brazil.* Princeton: Princeton University Press, 1990.

Alves, Maria Helena Moreira. *State and Opposition in Military Brazil.* Austin: University of Texas Press, 1985.

Anderson, Alan B., and George W. Pickering. *Confronting the Color Line.* Athens: University of Georgia Press, 1986.

Anderson, Benedict. *Imagined Communities.* London: Verso, 1983.

Anderson, Elijah. *Streetwise: Race, Class and Change in Urban Communities.* Chicago: University of Chicago Press, 1990.

Anderson, Perry. *Lineages of the Absolutist State*. London: Verso, 1974.
"Portugal and the End of Ultra-Colonialism 2." *New Left Review* 16 (July–August 1962).
Anderson, Sam E. "Black Students." *Black Scholar* (January–February 1977).
Andrews, George Reid. *Blacks and Whites in São Paulo, Brazil, 1888–1988*. Madison: University of Wisconsin Press, 1991.
"Comparing the Comparers: White Supremacy in the United States and South Africa." *Journal of Social History* 20 (1987).
"Race and the State in Colonial Brazil." *Latin American Research Review* 19.3 (1984).
Appiah, Kwame Anthony. *In My Father's House*. London: Methuen, 1992.
Apter, David E. *The Politics of Modernization*. Chicago: University of Chicago Press, 1967.
Arendt, Hannah. *The Origins of Totalitarianism*. New York: Harcourt Brace Jovanovich, 1951.
Ashforth, Adam. *The Politics of Official Discourse in Twentieth Century South Africa*. Oxford: Clarendon Press, 1990.
Associate Control, Research and Analysis, Inc. (ACRA). *Black Opinion Survey*, vol. 1. Washington: ACRA, 1977.
Azevedo, Célia Maria Marinho de. "Batismo da Liberdade: Os Abolicionistas e o Destino do Negro." *História: Questões e Debates* 9.16 (January 1988).
Onda Negra, Medo Branco: O Negro no Imáginario das Elites–Seculo XIX. Rio de Janeiro: Paz e Terra, 1987.
"Sinal Fechado para os Negros na Rua da Liberdade." *Humanidades* 5.17 (1988).
Badie, Bertrand, and Pierre Birnbaum. *The Sociology of the State*. Chicago: University of Chicago Press, 1983.
Baldwin, James. *Notes of a Native Son*. Boston: Beacon, 1955.
Balibar, Etienne, and Immanuel Wallerstein. *Race, Nation, Class: Ambiguous Identities*. London: Verso, 1991.
Banton, Michael. *Race Relations*. London: Tavistock, 1967.
Barbosa, Milton. "Violência Political em São Paulo." *MNU Journal* 17 (September–November 1989).
Barbour, Floyd, ed. *The Black Power Revolt*. Toronto: Macmillan, 1968.
Barcelos, Luiz Claudio, Olivia Maria Gomes da Cunha, and Tereza Cristina Nascimento Araujo. *Escravidão e Relações Raciais no Brasil*. Rio de Janeiro: Centro de Estudos Afro-Asiáticos, 1991.
Barkan, Stephen E. "Legal Control of the Southern Civil Rights Movement." *American Sociological Review* 49 (1984).
Barkey, Karen. *Bandits and Bureaucrats: The Ottoman Route to State Centralization* Ithaca, N.Y.: Cornell University Press, 1994.
Barzun, Jacques. *Race: A Study in Superstition*. New York: Harper, 1937.
Bass, Jack. *Taming the Storm*. New York: Doubleday, 1993.

Bastide, Roger. *The African Religions of Brazil.* Baltimore: Johns Hopkins University Press, 1978.

"The Development of Race Relations in Brazil." *Industrialization and Race Relations.* Edited by Guy Hunter. London: Oxford University Press, 1965.

Bastos, Elide Rugai. "A Questão Racial e a Revolução Burguesa." *O Saber Militante.* Edited by Maria Angela D'Incas. Rio de Janeiro: Paz e Terra, 1987.

Beard, Charles A., and Mary Beard. *The Rise of American Civilization.* New York: Macmillan, 1927.

Bell, Derrick A., Jr. "Comment." *Harvard Law Review* 93 (1979–80).

Faces at the Bottom of the Well. New York: Basic Books, 1992.

Bender, Gerald F. *Angola Under the Portuguese: The Myth and the Reality.* Berkeley: University of California Press, 1978.

Bendix, Reinhard. *Nation-Building and Citizenship.* New York: Wiley, 1964.

Bennett, Lerone, Jr. *Black Power USA.* Chicago: Johnson, 1967.

Bensel, Richard F. *Yankee Leviathan: The Origins of Central State Authority in America, 1859–1877.* Cambridge: Cambridge University Press, 1990.

Berqúo, Elza, and Luiz Felipe de Alencastro. "A Emergência do Voto Negro." *Novo Estudos* 33 (July 1992).

Bethell, Leslie. "The Independence of Brazil." *Brazil: Empire and Republic, 1822–1930.* Edited by Leslie Bethell. Cambridge: Cambridge University Press, 1989.

Biddiss, Michael D. *The Father of Racist Ideology.* New York: Weybright and Talley, 1970.

Biddiss, Michael D., ed. *Gobineau: Selected Political Writings.* New York: Harper and Row, 1970.

Biko, Steve. *I Write What I Like.* Edited by Aelerd Stubbs. San Francisco: Harper and Row, 1986.

Birnbaum, Pierre. *States and Collective Action.* Cambridge: Cambridge University Press, 1988.

Blalok, Hubert M., Jr. *Black–White Relations in the 1980s.* New York: Praeger, 1979.

Blauner, Bob. *Black Lives, White Lives.* Berkeley: University of California Press, 1989.

Boesak, Allan. *Black and Reformed.* Braamfontein: Skotaville, 1984.

Bonacich, Edna. "Capitalism and Race Relations in South Africa: A Split Labor Market Analysis." *Political Power and Social Theory.* Edited by Maurice Zeitlin. Greenwich: JAI Press, 1981.

"A Theory of Ethnic Antagonism: The Split Labor Market." *American Sociological Review* 37 (October 1972).

Boxer, C. R. *Four Centuries of Portuguese Expansion, 1415–1825.* Berkeley: University of California Press, 1969.

The Golden Age of Brazil, 1695–1750. Berkeley: University of California Press, 1962.

Bracey, John H., August Meier, and Elliott Rudwick, eds. *Black Nationalism in America*. Indianapolis: Bobbs-Merrill, 1970.

Bradley, David. "Malcolm's Mythmaking." *Transition* 56 (1992), pp. 20–59.

Branch, Taylor. *Parting the Waters*. New York: Simon and Schuster, 1988.

Breuilly, John. *Nationalism and the State*. Chicago: University of Chicago Press, 1982.

Bright, Charles, and Susan Harding, eds. *Statemaking and Social Movements*. Ann Arbor: University of Michigan, 1984.

Brink, William, and Louis Harris. *Black and White*. New York: Simon and Schuster, 1966.

Brisbane, Robert H. *Black Activism: Racial Revolution in the United States, 1954–70*. Valley Forge, Pa.: Judson Press, 1974.

Brooks, Alan, and Jeremy Brickhill. *Whirlwind Before the Storm*. London: International Defense and Aid Fund for Southern Africa, 1980.

Brown, Diana DeG. *Umbanda: Religion and Politics in Urban Brazil*. Ann Arbor: UMI Research Press, 1986.

Brown, Diana DeG., and Mario Bick. "Religion, Class and Context: Continuities and Discontinuities in Brazilian Umbanda." *American Ethnologist* 14.1 (February 1987).

Brubaker, Rogers. *Citizenship and Nationhood in France and Germany*. Cambridge: Harvard University Press, 1992.

Bundy, Colin. *The Rise and Fall of the South African Peasantry*. Berkeley: University of California Press, 1979.

Burawoy, Michael. "The Capitalist State in South Africa: Marxist and Sociological Perspectives on Race and Class." *Political Power and Social Theory*. Edited by Maurice Zeitlin. Greenwich: JAI Press, 1981.

Bureau of the Census, U.S. Department of Commerce. *Historical Statistics of the United States, Colonial Times to 1970*. Washington, D.C.: Government Printing Office, 1975.

The Social and Economic Status of the Black Population. Washington, D.C.: Government Printing Office, 1979.

Burns, E. Bradford. *A History of Brazil*. New York: Columbia University Press, 1970.

Nationalism in Brazil. New York: Praeger, 1968.

Perspectives on Brazilian History. New York: Columbia University, 1967.

Button, James W. *Black Violence: The Political Impact of the 1960's Riots*. Princeton: Princeton University Press, 1978.

Calhoun, Craig. *Social Theory and the Politics of Identity*. Cambridge: Blackwell, 1994.

Canny, Nicholas, and Anthony Pagden. *Colonial Identity in the Atlantic World, 1500–1800*. Princeton: Princeton University Press, 1987.

Cardoso, Fernando Henrique. "Discurso." International Seminar on Multiculturalism and Racism, Brasilia, (2 July 1996).

Carmichael, Stokely. "Power and Racism." *The Black Power Revolt*. Edited by Floyd Barber. New York: Harper and Row, 1973.

Carmichael, Stokely, and Charles V. Hamilton. *Black Power: The Politics of Liberation in America*. New York: Random House, 1967.

Carmines, Edward G., and James A. Stimson. *Issue Evolution: Race and the Transformation of American Politics*. Princeton: Princeton University Press, 1989.

Carnoy, Martin. *Faded Dreams*. Cambridge: Cambridge University Press, 1994.

Carson, Clayborne. *In Struggle*. Cambridge: Harvard University Press. 1981.

Carson, Clayborne, et al., eds. *The Eyes on the Prize Reader*. New York: Penguin. 1991.

Cell, John W. *The Highest Stage of White Supremacy*. Cambridge: Cambridge University Press, 1982.

Central Statistical Services. *South African Statistics, 1986*. Pretoria: Government Printer, 1986.

South African Statistics, 1988. Pretoria: Government Printer, 1988.

Chafe, William H. *Civilities and Civil Rights*. New York: Oxford University Press, 1980.

Charney, Craig. "Voices of a New South Africa." Research Report no. 38, Centre for Policy Studies, Johannesburg, (January 1995).

Chong, Dennis. *Collective Action and the Civil Rights Movement*. Chicago: University of Chicago Press, 1991.

Clark, Kenneth B. "Introduction." *The Negro American*. Edited by Talcott Parsons and Kenneth B. Clark. Boston: Beacon Press, 1965.

Cobb, James C. *The Most Southern Place on Earth*. New York: Oxford University Press, 1992.

Cohen, Jean. "Strategy or Identity." *Social Research* 52.4 (Winter 1985).

Cohen, Youssef. *The Manipulation of Consent*. Pittsburgh: University of Pittsburgh Press, 1989.

Cole, Leonard A. *Blacks in Power*. Princeton: Princeton University Press, 1976.

Collins, Sharon M. "The Making of the Black Middle Class." *Social Problems* 30.4 (April 1983).

Comaroff, John, and Jean Comaroff. *Ethnography and the Historical Imagination*. Boulder: Westview, 1992.

Commission of Inquiry into Legislation Affecting the Utilization of Manpower (Riekert Commission). *Report*. Pretoria: Government Printer, 1979.

Commission of Inquiry into Matters Relating to the Coloured Population Group (Theron Commission). *Report*. Pretoria: Government Printer, 1976.

Commission for the Socio-Economic Development of the Bantu Areas within the Union of South Africa (Tomlinson Commission). *Summary of the Report*. Pretoria: Government Printer, 1955.

Cone, James. *Martin and Malcolm and America*. Maryknoll, N.Y.: Orbis, 1991.

Congressional Budget Office. *Income Disparities Between Black and White Americans*. Washington, D.C.: Government Printing Office, 1977.

Connor, Walker. *Ethnonationalism*. Princeton: Princeton University Press, 1994.

Conrad, Robert. *Children of God's Fire*. Princeton: Princeton University Press, 1983.

The Destruction of Brazilian Slavery. Berkeley: University of California Press, 1972.

"Neither Slave nor Free: The Emancipados of Brazil, 1818–1868." *Hispanic American Historical Review* 53.1 (February 1973).

"Nineteenth Century Brazilian Slavery." *Slavery and Race Relations in Latin America*. Edited by Robert Brent Toplin. Westport, Conn.: Greenwood, 1974.

Constitutional Convention of the State of Louisiana. *Official Journal of the Proceedings*. New Orleans: H. J. Hearsey, 1898.

Constitutional Convention of the State of Mississippi. *Journal of the Proceedings*. Jackson: E. L. Martin, 1890.

Coplan, Nathan. "The New Ghetto Man." *Journal of Social Issues* 26.1 (Winter 1970).

Cornevin, Marianne. *Apartheid: Power and Historical Falsification*. Paris: UNESCO, 1980.

Corwin, Arthur F. "Afro-Brazilians." *Slavery and Race Relations in Latin America*. Edited by Robert Brent Toplin. Westport, Conn.: Greenwood, 1974.

Costa, Emilia Viotti da. "1870–1889." *Brazil: Empire and Republic, 1822–1930*. Edited by Leslie Bethell. Cambridge: Cambridge University Press, 1989.

The Brazilian Empire. Chicago: University of Chicago Press, 1985.

Cox, Oliver Cromwell. *Caste, Class and Race*. Garden City, N.Y.: Doubleday, 1948.

Crenshaw, Kimberlie Williams. "Race, Reform and Retrenchment: Transformation and Legitimation in Antidiscrimination Law." *Harvard Law Review* 101.7 (May 1988).

Cruse, Harold. *The Crisis of the Negro Intellectual*. New York: William Morrow, 1967.

Dahrendorf, Ralf. *Class and Class Conflict in Industrial Society*. Stanford, Calif.: Stanford University Press, 1959.

Dalton, Russell J., and Manfred Kuechler. *Challenging the Political Order*. New York: Oxford University Press, 1990.

da Matta, Roberto. *Carnivals, Rogues and Heroes*. Notre Dame, Ind.: University of Notre Dame Press, 1991.

Relativizando. Petrópolis: Vozes, 1984.

Darity, William, Jr. *The Question of Discrimination*. Middletown, Conn.: Wesleyan University Press, 1989.

Darwin, Charles. *The Descent of Man*. London: J. Murray, 1871.

da Silva, Benedita. "A Primera Deputada Negra do Brasil." *Nego* 13 (1987). *Zumbi*. Brasilia, 1996.

Davenport, T. R. H. *South Africa: A Modern History*. Toronto: University of Toronto Press, 1977.

Davies, Robert, et al. "Class Struggle and the Periodization of the State in South Africa." *Review of African Political Economy* 7 (September–December 1976).

Davis, David Brion. *The Problem of Slavery in Western Culture*. New York: Oxford University Press, 1966.

"The Triumph of the Country." *New York Review of Books* 12 (May 1994).

Davis, F. James. *Who is Black?: One Nation's Definition*. University Park: Pennsylvania State University Press, 1991.

Dawson, Michael. *Behind the Mule*. Princeton: Princeton University Press, 1994.

Dean, Warren. "Economy." *Brazil: Empire and Republic, 1822–1930*. Edited by Leslie Bethell. Cambridge: Cambridge University Press, 1989.

Degler, Carl N. *Neither Black nor White*. New York: Macmillan, 1971.

The Other South. Boston: Northeastern University Press, 1982.

De Kiewiet, C. W. *A History of South Africa*. London: Oxford University Press, 1941.

The Imperial Factor in South Africa. Cambridge: Cambridge University Press, 1937.

de Klerk, W. A. *The Puritans in Africa: A History of Afrikanerdom*. Harmondsworth: Penguin, 1975.

The Second (R)evolution. Johannesburg: Jonathan Ball, 1984.

Denoon, Donald. *A Grand Illusion*. London: Longman, 1973.

Settler Capitalism. Oxford: Clarendon Press, 1983.

DeSantis, Vincent P. *Republicans Face the Southern Question*. New York: Greenwood, 1959.

"Rutherford B. Hayes and the Removal of the Troops." *Region, Race and Reconstruction*. Edited by J. Morgan Kousser and James M. McPherson. New York: Oxford University Press, 1982.

de Villiers, Rene. "Afrikaner Nationalism." *The Oxford History of South Africa*. Vol 2. Edited by Monica Wilson and Leonard Thompson. Oxford: Clarendon Press, 1971.

Dillingham, Gerald L. "The Emerging Black Middle Class: Class Consciousness or Race Consciousness?" *Ethnic and Racial Studies* 44 (October 1981).

Directoria Geral de Estatística. *Anuário Estatístico do Brasil*. Rio de Janeiro: Typographia de Estatística, 1916.

Dittmer, John. *Local People*. Urbana: University of Illinois Press, 1994.

Dominguez, Virginia R. *White by Definition*. New Brunswick, N.J.: Rutgers University Press, 1986.

Donahue, John T., III, and James Heckman. "Continuous versus Episodic

Change: The Impact of Civil Rights Policy on the Economic Status of Blacks." *Journal of Economic Literature* 29 (December 1991).

do Nascimento, Abdias. *Brazil: Mixture or Massacre?* Dover: Majority Press, 1979.

"Sedepron." *Nova Etapa de auma Antiga Luta*. São Paulo, 1991.

do Nascimento, Maria Ercilia. "A Estratégia da Desigualdade: O Movimento Negro dos Anos 70." M.A. thesis, Pontifícia Universidade Catolica de São Paulo, 1989.

Draper, Theodore. *The Rediscovery of Black Nationalism*. New York: Viking, 1969.

Drescher, Seymour. "Brazilian Abolition in Comparative Perspective." *Hispanic American Historical Review* 68.3 (1988).

Du Bois, W. E. B. *Black Reconstruction in America*. New York: Atheneum, 1992.

"Conservation of the Races." *W. E. B. Du Bois Speaks*. Edited by Philip S. Foner. New York: Pathfinder, 1970.

"Dear Reader." *Crisis* (April 1919).

Dusk at Dawn. New York: Harcourt Brace, 1940.

"Loyalty." *Crisis* (May 1917).

"The Negro and Communism." *Crisis*. (September 1931).

The Souls of Black Folks. New York: Penguin, 1989. Also reprinted in *Three Negro Classics*. New York: Avon, 1965.

Dubow, Saul. *Racial Segregation and the Origins of Apartheid in South Africa, 1919–36*. London: Macmillan, 1989.

Dumond, Dwight Lowell. *Anti-Slavery*. Ann Arbor: University of Michigan Press, 1961.

Durr, Virginia Foster. *Outside the Magic Circle: The Autobiography of Virginia Foster Durr*. Tuscaloosa: University of Alabama Press, 1985.

du Toit, Andre. "No Chosen People." *American Historical Review* 88.4 (October 1983).

Dzidzienyo, Anani. "Afro-Brasileiros no Contexto Nactional e Internacional." *Desigualdade Racial no Brasil Contemporâneo*. Edited by Peggy A. Lovell. Belo Horizonte: UFM, 1991.

"Brazil." *International Handbook on Race and Race Relations*. Edited by Jay A. Sigler. New York: Greenwood, 1987.

The Position of Blacks in Brazilian Society. London: Minority Rights Group, 1971.

Edsall, Thomas Byrne, and Mary D. Edsall. *Chain Reaction*. New York: Norton, 1991.

Eisinger, Peter. *Black Employment in City Government, 1973–1980*. Washington: Joint Center for Political Studies, 1983.

Elkins, Stanley. *Slavery*. Chicago: University of Chicago Press, 1959.

Elster, Jon. *Nuts and Bolts for the Social Sciences*. Cambridge: Cambridge University Press, 1989.

Emerson, Rupert, and Martin Kilson. "The American Dilemma in a Changing World: The Rise of Africa and the Negro American." *The*

Negro American. Edited by Talcott Parsons and Kenneth B. Clark. Boston: Beacon, 1965.

Enloe, Cynthia. *Ethnic Conflict and Political Development.* Boston: Little, Brown, 1973.

Ethnic Soldiers. Middlesex: Penguin, 1980.

Escobar, Arturo, and Sonia Alvarez. *The Making of Social Movements in Latin America.* Boulder: Westview, 1992.

Essien-Udom, E. U. *Black Nationalism.* Chicago: University of Chicago Press, 1962.

Evans, Peter. *Embedded Autonomy.* Princeton: Princeton University Press. 1995.

Evans, Peter, Dietrich Rueschmeyer, and Theda Skocpol. *Bringing the State Back In.* Cambridge: Cambridge University Press, 1985.

Fanon, Frantz. *Black Skin, White Masks.* New York: Grove Press, 1967.

The Wretched of the Earth. New York: Grove Press, 1968.

Farmer, James. *Lay Bare the Heart.* New York: Arbor House, 1985.

Fausto, Boris. "Society and Politics." *Brazil: Empire and Republic, 1822–1930.* Edited by Leslie Bethell. Cambridge: Cambridge University Press, 1989.

Fernandes, Florestan. "Beyond Poverty." *Slavery and Race Relations in Latin America.* Edited by Robert Brent Toplin. Westport: Greenwood, 1974.

"Luta de Raças e de Classes." *Teoria e Debate* 2 (March 1988).

The Negro in Brazilian Society. New York: Columbia University Press, 1969.

Significado do Protesto Negro. São Paulo: Autores Associados, 1989.

"The Weight of the Past." *Color and Race.* Edited by John Hope Franklin. Boston: Houghton Mifflin, 1968.

Fields, Barbara J. "Ideology and Race in American History." *Region, Race, and Reconstruction.* Edited by J. Morgan Kousser and James M. McPherson. New York: Oxford University Press, 1982.

"Slavery, Race and Ideology in the United States of America." *New Left Review* 181 (1990).

Fiola, Jan. "Race Relations in Brazil: A Reassessment of the Racial Democracy Thesis." Program in Latin American Studies, Occasional Paper Series no. 24. Amherst: University of Massachusetts, 1990.

Flory, Thomas. "Race and Social Control in Independent Brazil." *Journal of Latin American Studies* 9.2 (1977).

Fogel, Robert William, and Stanley L. Engerman. *Time on the Cross.* Boston: Little, Brown, 1974.

Fogelson, Robert M. *Violence as Protest.* Garden City, N.Y.: Doubleday, 1971.

Foner, Eric. *Free Soil, Free Labor, Free Men.* London: Oxford University Press, 1970.

Nothing But Freedom. Baton Rouge: Louisiana State University Press, 1983.

Reconstruction. New York: Harper and Row, 1988.

359

Foner, Laura, and Eugene D. Genovese, eds. *Slavery in the New World*. Englewood Cliffs, N.J.: Prentice-Hall, 1969.

Foner, Philip S. *Organized Labor and the Black Worker, 1619–1973*. New York: Praeger, 1974.

Foner, Philip S., ed. *W. E. B. Du Bois Speaks*. New York: Pathfinder, 1970.

Font, Mauricio A. *Coffee, Contention and Change*. Cambridge: Blackwell, 1990.

Fontaine, Pierre-Michel. "Introduction." *Race, Class and Power in Brazil*. Edited by Pierre-Michel Fontaine. Center for Afro-American Studies, Los Angeles: University of California Press, 1985.

"Transnational Relations and Racial Mobilization." *Ethnic Identities in a Transnational World*. Edited by John F. Stack. Jr. Westport, Conn.: Greenwood, 1981.

Foote, Shelby. *The Civil War*. New York: Vintage Books, 1986.

Forman, James. *The Making of Black Revolutionaries*. New York: Macmillan, 1972.

Sammy Younge, Jr. Washington: Open Hand, 1986.

Forund, John R., and Jay R. Williams. "Internal-External Control and Black Militancy." *Journal of Social Issues* 26.1 (Winter 1970).

Foucault, Michel. *Power/Knowledge*. Edited by Colin Gordon. New York: Pantheon, 1972.

Franco, Carvalho. *Homens Livres na Ordem Escravocrata*. São Paulo: Kairós, 1983.

Franklin, John Hope. *Reconstruction After the Civil War*. Chicago: University of Chicago Press, 1961.

Frazier, E. Franklin. *Black Bourgeoisie*. New York: Collier Macmillan, 1957.
On Race Relations. Chicago: University of Chicago Press, 1968.
"Some Aspects of Race Relations in Brazil." *Phylon* 33 (1942).

Fredrickson, George M. *The Arrogance of Race*. Middletown, Conn.: Wesleyan University Press, 1988.

The Black Image in the White Mind. Middletown Conn.: Wesleyan University Press, 1971.

Black Liberation: A Comparative History of Black Ideologies in the United States and South Africa. New York: Oxford University Press, 1995.

"Black–White Relations Since Emancipation: The Search for a Comparative Perspective." *What Made the South Different?* Edited by Kees Gispen. Jackson: University Press of Mississippi, 1990.

"Demonizing the American Dilemma." *New York Review of Books* 19 (October 1995).

"From Exceptionalism to Variability." *Journal of American History* (September 1995).

The Inner Civil War. Urbana: University of Illinois Press, 1965.

"Reflections on the Comparative History and Sociology of Racism." Manuscript, 1994.

White Supremacy. Oxford: Oxford University Press, 1981.

Freeland, Gregory. "The Changing Black Political Movement in Brazil."

Paper presented at the Latin American Studies Association, Los Angeles, 24–7 September 1992.

Freeman, Richard B. *Black Elite*. New York: McGraw-Hill, 1976.

Freyre, Gilberto. *Brazil: An Interpretation*. New York: Knopf, 1945.

The Mansions and the Shanties. Berkeley: University of California Press, 1986.

The Masters and the Slaves. Berkeley: University of California Press, 1986.

Friedman, Debra, and Doug McAdam. "Collective Identity and Activism." *Frontiers in Social Movement Theory*. Edited by Aldon Morris and Carol Mueller. New Haven: Yale University Press, 1992.

Friedman, Steven. *Building Tomorrow Today: African Workers in Trade Unions, 1970–1984*. Johannesburg: Ravan, 1987.

Fry, Peter. *Para Inglês Ver*. Rio de Janerio: Zahar Editores, 1982.

"Why Brazil is Different." *Times Literary Supplement*, (8 December 1995).

Furtado, Celso. *The Economic Growth of Brazil*. Berkeley: University of California Press, 1971.

Garcia-Zamor, Jean-Claude. "Social Mobility of Negroes in Brazil." *Journal of Inter-American Studies and World Affairs* 12.2 (April 1970).

Garrow, David J. *Bearing the Cross*. New York: Vintage, 1986.

Garvey, Marcus. "Philosophy and Opinions, 1923." *The Black Power Revolt*. Edited by Floyd Barbour. Toronto: Macmillan, 1969.

Gates, Henry Louis, Jr. "Radical Rappers." *New York Times* (16 December 1990).

Geertz, Clifford. "The Integrative Revolution." *Old Societies and New States*. New York: Free Press, 1963.

Gellner, Ernest. *Nations and Nationalism*. Ithaca, N.Y.: Cornell University Press, 1983.

Genovese, Eugene D. *From Rebellion to Revolution: Afro-American Slave Revolts in the Making of the Modern World*. Baton Rouge: Louisiana State University Press, 1979.

Roll, Jordan, Roll. New York: Random House, 1972.

The World the Slaveholders Made. New York: Pantheon, 1969.

Gerhart, Gail M. *Black Power in South Africa*. Berkeley: University of California Press, 1978.

Gerstner, Jonathan Neil. *The Thousand Generation Covenant*. Leiden: E. J. Brill, 1991.

Giliomee, Hermann. "The Beginnings of Afrikaner Ethnic Consciousness, 1850–1915." *The Creation of Tribalism in Southern Africa*. Edited by Leroy Vail. Berkeley: University of California Press, 1989.

Giliomee, Hermann, and Lawrence Schlemmer. *From Apartheid to Nation-Building*. Cape Town: Oxford University Press, 1989.

Gilroy, Paul. "One Nation under a Groove." *Anatomy of Racism*. Edited by David Theo Goldberg, Minneapolis: University of Minnesota Press, 1990.

Goldin, Claudia Dale. *Urban Slavery in the American South, 1820–1860*. Chicago: University of Chicago Press, 1976.

Goldin, Ian. *Making Race*. Cape Town: Maskew Miller Longman, 1987.

Goldman, Peter. *The Death and Life of Malcolm X*. Urbana: University of Illinois Press, 1973.

Gonzalez, Lélia, and Carlos Hasenbalg. *Lugar de Negro*. Rio de Janeiro: Marco Zero Limitada, 1982.

Graham, Hugh Davis. *The Civil Rights Era*. New York: Oxford University Press, 1990.

Graham, Richard. "Economics or Culture?" *What Made the South Different?* Edited by Kees Gispen. Jackson: University Press of Mississippi, 1990.

"1850–1870." *Brazil: Empire and Republic, 1822–1930*. Edited by Leslie Bethell. Cambridge: Cambridge University Press, 1989.

"Slavery and Economic Development." *Comparative Studies in History and Society* 23.4 (October 1981).

Gramsci, Antonio. *Selections from the Prison Notebooks*. Edited by Quinton Hoare and Geoffrey Nowell Smith. New York: International Publishers, 1971.

Greenberg, Stanley. *Race and State in Capitalist Development*. New Haven: Yale University Press, 1980.

Guillermoprieto, Alma. *Samba*. New York: Random House, 1990.

Gump, James O. *The Dust Rose Like Smoke*. Lincoln: University of Nebraska Press, 1994.

Gurin, Patricia, and Edgar Epps. *Black Consciousness, Identity and Achievement*. New York: Wiley, 1975.

Gurr, Ted Robert. *Why Men Rebel*. Princeton: Princeton University Press, 1970.

Guy, Jeff. *The Destruction of the Zulu Kingdom*. London: Longmans, 1979.

Haberly, David T. *Three Sad Races: Racial Identity and National Consciousness in Brazilian Literature*. Cambridge: Cambridge University Press, 1983.

Hacker, Andrew. *Two Nations*. New York: Scribner's, 1992.

Hackney, Sheldon. *Populism to Progressivism in Alabama*. Princeton: Princeton University Press, 1969.

Hagopian, Frances. "The Compromised Consolidation: The Political Class in the Brazilian Transition." *Issues in Democratic Consolidation*. Edited by Scott Mainwaring, Guillermo O'Donnell, and J. Samuel Valenzuela. Notre Dame, Ind.: University of Notre Dam Press, 1992.

Haines, Herbert H. *Black Radicals and the Civil Rights Mainstream, 1954–1970*. Knoxville: University of Tennessee Press, 1988.

Hall, Raymond L., ed. *Black Separatism and Social Reality*. New York: Pergamon, 1977.

Hall, Stuart. "New Ethnicities." *Race, Culture and Difference*. Edited by James Donald and Ali Rottansi. Newbury Park, Calif: Sage, 1992.

"Race, Articulation and Societies Structured in Dominance." *Sociological*

Theories: Race and Colonialism. Edited by M. O'Callaghan. Paris: UNESCO.

Hamilton, Charles V. *Adam Clayton Powell, Jr.* New York: Macmillan, 1991.

The Black Experience in American Politics. New York: Putnam, 1973.

"The Welfare of Black Americans." *Political Science Quarterly* 101.2 (1986).

Hanchard, Michael George. *Orpheus and Power.* Princeton: Princeton University Press, 1994.

Hardin, Russell. *Collective Action.* Baltimore: Johns Hopkins University Press, 1982.

Harding, Vincent. *There Is a River.* New York: Harcourt Brace Jovanovich, 1981.

Harris, Fred R., and Roger W. Wilkins. *Quiet Riots.* New York: Pantheon, 1988.

Harris, J. William. *Plain Folk and Gentry in a Slave Society.* Middletown, Conn.: Wesleyan University Press. 1985.

Harris, Marvin. *Patterns of Race in the Americas.* Westport, Conn.: Greenwood, 1964.

Harris, Marvin, et al. "Who Are the Whites?" *Social Forces* 72.2 (1993).

Harrison, David. *The White Tribe of Africa.* Berkeley: University of California Press, 1981.

Hartz, Louis. *The Founding of New Societies.* New York: Harcourt Brace and World, 1964.

Hasenbalg, Carlos. "Desigualdades Raciais no Brasil." *Dados* 14 (1977).

"Race and Socio Economic Inequality in Brazil." Instituto Universitário de Pesquisas do Rio de Janeiro, March 1983.

"Race Relations in Modern Brazil." Working paper no. 87131. Latin American Institute, University of New Mexico, Albuquerque (1987).

"Race Relations in Post-Abolition Brazil: The Smooth Preservation of Racial Inequalities." Ph.D. dissertation, University of California, Berkeley, 1978.

Hasenbalg, Carlos, and Suellen Huntington. "Brazilian Racial Democracy: Reality or Myth?" *Humboldt Journal of Social Relations* 10.1 (Fall/Winter 1982–3).

Hasenbalg, Carlos, and Nelson do Valle Silva. "Industrialization, Employment and Stratification in Brazil." *State and Society in Brazil.* Edited by John D. Wirth. Boulder: Westview, 1987.

"Notas Sobre Desigualdade Racial e Política no Brasil." Conference on Racial Politics in Contemporary Brazil, Austin, Tex. (8–10 April 1993).

Hellwig, David, ed. *African-American Reflections on Brazil's Racial Paradise.* Philadelphia: Temple University Press, 1992.

Herbst, Jeffrey. "Prospects for Revolution in South Africa." *Political Science Quarterly* 103.4 (1988).

Higbee, Mark D. "W. E. B. Du Bois and the Politics of Liberation, 1917–1963." Ph.D. dissertation, Columbia University, New York, 1995.

Higginbotham, A. Leon, Jr. "Racism in American and South African Courts: Similarities and Differences." *New York University Law Review* 65.3 (June 1990).

Hirschman, Albert O. *Exit, Voice and Loyalty.* Cambridge: Harvard University Press, 1970.

Hobsbawm, Eric. "Some Reflections on 'The Break-up of Britain.' " *New Left Review* 105 (1977).

Hobson, J. A. *The War in South Africa.* New York: Howard Fertig, 1969.

Hochschild, Jennifer. *Facing Up to the American Dream.* Princeton: Princeton University Press, 1995.

The New American Dilemma. New Haven: Yale University Press, 1984.

Hoetink, H. *Slavery and Race Relations in Latin America.* New York: Harper and Row, 1973.

The Two Variants in Caribbean Race Relations. London: Oxford University Press, 1967.

Holanda, Sérgio Buarque de. *Raízes do Brasil.* Rio de Janeiro: Jose Olympio, 1983.

Holzer, Harold, ed. *The Lincoln–Douglas Debates.* New York: Harper-Collins, 1993.

Hoover, Herbert. "A Fórmula Igualitária para Resolver a Questão Racial Americana." *Progresso* 1.9 (24 February 1929).

Horowitz, Donald L. *A Democratic South Africa?* Berkeley: University of California Press, 1991.

Ethnic Groups in Conflict. Berkeley: University of California Press, 1985.

Horowitz, Ralph. *The Political Economy of South Africa.* New York: Praeger, 1967.

Horsman, Reginald. *Race and Manifest Destiny.* Cambridge: Harvard University Press, 1981.

Horton, Carrell Peterson, and Jessie Carney Smiths, eds. *Statistical Record of Black America.* Detroit: Gale Research, 1990.

Hout, Michael. "Occupational Mobility of Black Men, 1962–1973." *American Sociological Review* 49 (June 1984).

Howarth, David. "Reflection on Ernesto Laclau's *New Reflections on the Revolution of our Time*." *Politikon* 19.1 (December 1991).

Hughes, Michael, and Bradley R. Hertel. "The Significance of Color Remains." *Social Forces* 69.1 (1990).

Huntington, Samuel P. "Reform and Stability in South Africa." *International Security* 6.4 (Spring 1982).

Ianni, Octávio. *Crisis in Brazil.* New York: Columbia University Press, 1970.

Jackson, Jesse L. *Straight from the Heart.* Philadelphia: Fortress Press, 1987.

Jackson, Richard L. "The Color Crisis in Latin America." *Black World* 24 (July 1975).

Jaguaribe, Helio. *Economic and Political Development: A Theoretical Approach and a Brazilian Case Study*. Cambridge: Harvard University Press, 1968.

James, C. L. R. *The Black Jacobins*. New York: Random House, 1963.

Jencks, Christopher. "Affirmative Action for Blacks." *American Behavioral Scientist* 28.6 (July–August 1985).

Jenkins, J. Craig, and Craig M. Eckert. "Channeling Black Insurgency."*American Sociological Review* 51 (December 1986).

Johnson, Lyndon Baines. "Foreword." *The Negro American*. Edited by Talcott Parsons and Kenneth B. Clark. Boston: Beacon Press, 1965.

Johnstone, Fredrick A. *Class, Race and Gold*. London: Routledge, 1976.

Jones, Leroi. "The Need for a Cultural Base." *Black Power Revolt*. Edited by Floyd B. Barbour. Boston: Collier, 1968.

Jordan, Winthrop D. *White Over Black*. New York: Norton, 1968.

Jung, Courtney, and Ian Shapiro. "South Africa's Negotiated Transition." *Politics and Society* 23.3 (1993).

Karenga, Maulana Ron. "From the Quotable Karenga." *Black Power Revolt*. Edited by Floyd B. Barbour. Boston: Collier, 1968.

Karis, Thomas. "South Africa." *Five African States*. Edited by Gwendolen Carter. Ithaca, N.Y.: Cornell University Press, 1963.

Karis, Thomas, and Gwendolen M. Carter, eds. *From Protest to Challenge*. Stanford, Calif.: Hoover Institution Press, 1973.

Kasfir, Nelson. "Explaining Ethnic Participation." *World Politics* 31.3 (April 1979).

Katznelson, Ira. *Black Men, White Cities*. London: Oxford University Press, 1973.

City Trenches. New York: Pantheon Books, 1981.

Liberalism's Crooked Circle. Princeton: Princeton University Press, 1996.

"Power in the Reformulation of Race Research." *Race, Change, and Urban Society*. Edited by Orleans and Ellis. Beverly Hills, Calif., 1971.

"The State to the Rescue?" *Social Research* 59.4 (Winter 1992).

Katznelson, Ira, Kim Geiger, and Daniel Kryder. "Limiting Liberalism: The Southern Veto in Congress, 1933–50." *Political Science Quarterly* 108.2 (Summer 1993).

Keck, Margaret. *The Workers' Party and Democratization in Brazil*. New Haven: Yale University Press, 1992.

Kedourie, Elie. *Nationalism*. Oxford: Blackwell, 1960.

Keith, Verna M., and Cedric Herring. "Skin Tone and Stratification in the Black Community." *American Journal of Sociology* 97.3 (November 1991).

Kelley, Robin D. G. *Race Rebels*. New York: Free Press, 1994.

Kelley, William R., and David Snyder. "Racial Violence and Socioeconomic Changes among Blacks in the United States." *Social Forces* 58.3 (March 1980).

Kennedy, James H. "Political Liberalization, Black Consciousness and Recent Afro-Brazilian Literature." *Phylon* 47.3 (1986).

Kennedy, John F. "Address to the Nation," 11 June 1963. *The Eyes on the*

Prize Reader. Edited by Clayborne Carson et al. New York: Penguin, 1991.

Kenney, Henry. *Architect of Apartheid: H. F. Verwoerd.* Johannesburg: Jonathan Ball, 1980.

Kerner, Otto, chair. *Report of the National Advisory Commission on Civil Disorders.* New York: Bantam, 1968
Supplemental Studies for the National Advisory Commission on Civil Disorders. Washington, D.C.: Government Printing Office, 1968.

Kestel, J. D., and D. E. van Velden. *The Peace Negotiations.* London: Richard Clay and Sons, 1912.

Key, V. O., Jr. *Southern Politics in State and Nation.* New York: Knopf, 1949.

Killian, Lewis M. *The Impossible Revolution? Black Power and the American Dream.* New York: Random House, 1968.

King, Gary, Robert O. Keohane, and Sidney Verba. *Designing Social Inquiry.* Princeton: Princeton University Press, 1994.

Klein, Herbert S. *African Slavery in Latin America and the Caribbean.* New York: Oxford University Press, 1986.
The Middle Passage. Princeton: Princeton University Press, 1978.
Social Change in Brazil, 1945–1985: The Incomplete Transition. Albuquerque: University of New Mexico Press, 1989.

Kluger, Richard. *Simple Justice.* New York: Knopf, 1976.

Knight, Franklin W. *The African Dimension in Latin American Societies.* New York: Macmillan, 1974.

Kotze, Hennie. "Toward an Elite Settlement." *Indicator South Africa* 10.2 (Autumn 1993).

Kousser, J. Morgan. *The Shaping of Southern Politics.* New Haven: Yale University Press, 1974.

Kuper, Leo. "African Nationalism in South Africa." *The Oxford History of South Africa,* vol. 2. Edited by Monica Wilson and Leonard Thompson. Oxford: Clarendon Press, 1971.

Kurian, George Thomas. *The New Book of World Rankings.* New York: Facts on File, 1991.

Laclau, Ernesto. *New Reflections on the Revolution of our Time.* London: Verso, 1990.

Laclau, Ernesto, and Chantal Mouffe. *Hegemony and Socialist Strategy.* London: Verso, 1985.

Laitin, David. "Hegemony and Religious Conflict." *Bringing the State Back In.* Edited by Peter B. Evans, Dietrich Rueschemeyer, and Theda Skocpol. Cambridge: Cambridge University Press, 1985.

Lamar, Howard, and Leonard Thompson. *The Frontier in History.* New Haven: Yale University Press, 1981.

Lamounier, Bolivar. "Ideologia Conservadora e Mudanças Estruturais." *Dados* 5 (1968).

Landry, Bart. *The New Black Middle Class.* Berkeley: University of California Press, 1987.

Lang, James. *Conquest and Commerce*. New York: Academic Press, 1975.
　Portuguese Brazil: The King's Plantation. New York: Academic Press, 1979.
Lasswell, Harold. *Who Gets What, When and How?* New York: McGraw-Hill, 1936.
Legassick, Martin. "The Frontier Tradition in South African Historiography." *Economy and Society in Pre-Industrial South Africa*. Edited by Shula Marks and Anthony Atmore. London: Longmans, 1980.
　"South Africa: Forced Labor, Industrialization, and Racial Differentiation." *The Political Economy of Africa*. Edited by Richard Harris. New York: Wiley, 1975.
Legassick, Martin, and Harold Wolpe. "The Bantustans and Capital Accumulation in South Africa." *Review of African Political Economy* 7 (September–December 1976).
Lemann, Nicholas. *The Promised Land*. New York: Random House, 1991.
LeMay, G. H. L. *British Supremacy in South Africa, 1899–1907*. Oxford: Clarendon Press, 1965.
Leonard, Jonathan S. "Splitting Blacks?" National Bureau of Economic Research. Working Paper no. 1327 (1984).
Lesher, Stephan. *George Wallace: American Populist*. Reading: Addison-Wesley, 1994.
Lester, Julius. *Revolutionary Notes*. New York: Baron, 1969.
Levine, Robert M. "Turning on the Lights." *Latin American Research Review* 24.2 (1989).
　The Vargas Regime. New York: Columbia University Press, 1970.
Lewin, Julius. *The Struggle for Racial Equality*. London: Longmans, 1967.
Lewinson, Paul. *Race, Class and Party*. New York: Grosset and Dunlap, 1932.
Lewis, David Levering. *W. E. B. Du Bois–Biography of a Race*. New York: Holt, 1993.
Lewis, Gavin. *Between the Wire and the Wall*. Cape Town: David Philip, 1987.
Lewis, Stephen. *The Economics of Apartheid*. New York: Council on Foreign Relations, 1990.
Lieberman, Robert C. *Race and the American Welfare State*. Cambridge, Mass.: Harvard University Press, 1998.
　"Race and the Organization of Welfare Policy." Manuscript.
　"Race, Institutions and the Administration of Social Policy." Manuscript.
Lipset, Seymour Martin. *The First New Nation*. New York: Norton, 1979.
Lipsky, Michael. "Protest as Political Resource." *American Political Science Review* 62 (1968), pp. 1144–58.
Lipton, Merle. *Capitalism and Apartheid*. London: Wildwood, 1985.
Lodge, Tom. *Black Politics in South Africa since 1945*. Johannesburg: Ravan, 1983.

Lodge, Tom, and Bill Nasson. *All, Here and Now*. New York: Ford Foundation, 1991.

Lovell, Peggy Ann. "Race, Gender and Development in Brazil." *Latin American Research Review* 29.3 (1994).

"Racial Inequality and the Brazilian Labor Market." Ph.D. dissertation, University of Florida, Gainesville, 1989.

Lowenstein, Karl. *Brazil Under Vargas*. New York: Macmillan, 1944.

Lustick, Ian. "History, Historiography, and Political Science." *American Political Science Review* 90.3 (September 1996), pp. 1144–58.

MacCrone, I. D. *Race Attitudes in South Africa*. Johannesburg: University of the Witwatersrand Press, 1937.

Mainwaring, Scott. "Urban Popular Movements, Identity, and Democracy in Brazil." *Comparative Political Studies* 20.2 (July 1987).

Mainwaring, Scott, and Edward Viola. "New Social Movements, Political Culture and Democracy." *Telos* 61 (Fall 1984).

Malcolm X and Alex Haley. *The Autobiography of Malcolm X*. Harmondsworth: Penguin, 1965.

Mamdani, Mahmood. *Citizen and Subject*. Princeton: Princeton University Press, 1996.

Mandela, Nelson. *Long Walk to Freedom*. Boston: Little, Brown, 1994.

Mann, Michael. "The Autonomous Power of the State." *Archives Européenes de Sociologie* 25 (1984).

Marable, Manning. *Black American Politics*, London: Verso, 1985.

"Black Nationalism in the 1970's: Through the Prism of Race and Class." *Socialist Review* 10.2/3 (March/June 1980).

Race, Reform, and Rebellion. Jackson: University Press of Mississippi, 1991.

March, James G., and John P. Olsen. *Rediscovering Institutions*. New York: Free Press, 1989.

Mare, Gerhard, and George Hamilton. *An Appetite for Power: Buthelezi's Inkatha and South Africa*. Johannesburg: Ravan, 1987.

Marks, Shula. "Review Article: Scrambling for South Africa." *Journal of African History*, 23 (1982).

Marks, Shula, and Stanley Trapido. "Lord Milner and the South African State." *History Workshop* 8 (Autumn 1979).

Marks, Shula, and Stanley Trapido, eds. *The Politics of Race, Class and Nationalism in Twentieth Century South Africa*. London: Longman, 1987.

Marshall, Burke. *Federalism and Civil Rights*, New York: Columbia University Press, 1964.

"The Protest Movement and the Law." *Virginia Law Review* 51 (1965).

Marshall, T. H. *Citizenship and Social Class*. London: Pluto, 1992.

Marx, Anthony W. "International Intervention in South Africa." *Journal of International Affairs* 46.1 (Summer 1992).

Lessons of Struggle: South African Internal Opposition, 1960–1990. New York: Oxford University Press, 1992.

Marx, Gary T. "Civil Disorders and the Agents of Social Control." *Journal of Social Issues* 26.1 (Winter 1970).

Protest and Prejudice. New York: Harper and Row, 1967.

Marx, Karl. *Capital.* New York: International Publishers, 1967.

"The Poverty of Philosophy." *Karl Marx: Selected Writings.* Edited by David McLellan. Oxford: Oxford University Press, 1977.

Marx, Karl, and Friedrich Engels. "The Communist Manifesto." *Karl Marx: Selected Writings.* Edited by David McLellan. Oxford: Oxford University Press, 1977.

Massey, Douglas S., and Nancy A. Denton. *American Apartheid.* Cambridge, Mass: Harvard University Press, 1993.

Mattoso, Katia de Queirós. "Slave, Free and Freed Family Structures in Nineteenth Century Salvador, Bahia." *Luso-Brazilian Review* 25.1 (1988).

Maxwell, Kenneth R. *Conflicts and Conspiracies: Brazil and Portugal, 1750–1808.* Cambridge: Cambridge University Press, 1973.

Maybury-Lewis, Biorn. "The Politics of the Possible: The Growth and Political Development of the Brazilian Rural Workers' Trade Union Movement, 1964–1985." Ph.D. dissertation, Columbia University, New York, 1993.

McAdam, Doug. *Freedom Summer,* New York: Oxford University Press, 1988.

Political Process and the Development of Black Insurgency, 1930–1970. Chicago: University of Chicago Press, 1982.

"Tactical Innovation and the Pace of Insurgency." *American Sociological Review* 48 (December 1983).

McAdam, Doug, John D. McCarthy, and Mayer N. Zald. "Social Movements." *The Handbook of Sociology.* Edited by Neil J. Smelser. Newbury Park, Calif.: Sage, 1988.

McCarthy, John D., and Mayer N. Zald. "Resource Mobilization and Social Movements." *American Journal of Sociology* 82.6 (May 1977).

McCartney, John T. *Black Power Ideologies.* Philadelphia: Temple University Press, 1992.

McFeely, William S. *Frederick Douglass.* New York: Norton, 1991.

McKissick, Floyd. "Programs for Black Power." *Black Power Revolt.* Edited by Floyd B. Barbour. Boston: Collier, 1968.

McMath, Robert. *American Populism.* New York: Hill and Wang, 1993.

McPherson, James M. *Battle Cry of Freedom.* New York: Oxford University Press, 1988.

The Struggle for Equality. Princeton: Princeton University Press, 1964.

Meier, August, and Elliott Rudwick. *CORE.* Urbana: University of Illinois Press, 1975.

Meier, August, Elliott Rudwick, and Frances L. Broderick, eds. *Black Protest Thought in the Twentieth Century.* New York: Macmillan, 1971.

Midlarsky, Manus I. "Analyzing Diffusion and Contagion Effects: The

Urban Disorders of the 1960s." *American Political Science Review* 72.3 (September 1978).

Miles, Robert. *Racism.* London: Routledge, 1989.

Miliband, Ralph. *The State in Capitalist Development.* London: Weidenfeld and Nicolson, 1969.

Mitchell, Michael. "Blacks and the *Abertura Democrática.*" *Race, Class and Power in Brazil.* Edited by Pierre-Michel Fontaine. Los Angeles: Center for Afro-American Studies, University of California at Los Angeles, 1985.

"Racial Consciousness and the Political Attitudes and Behavior of Blacks in São Paulo, Brazil." Ph.D. dissertation, Indiana University, Bloomington, 1977.

Montagu, Ashley. *Man's Most Dangerous Myth: The Fallacy of Race.* New York: Oxford University Press, 1974.

Montgomery, David. *Beyond Equality.* New York: Knopf, 1967.

Moodie, T. Dunbar. *The Rise of Afrikanerdom.* Berkeley: University of California Press, 1975.

Moog, Vianna. *Bandierantes and Pioneers.* New York: Braziller, 1964.

Moore, Barrington, Jr. *Social Origins of Dictatorship and Democracy.* Boston: Beacon, 1966.

Morgan, Edmund S. *American Slavery/American Freedom.* New York: Norton, 1975.

Morris, Aldon. *The Origins of the Civil Rights Movement.* New York: Free Press, 1984.

Morris, Aldon, Shirley J. Hachett, and Ronald E. Brown. "The Civil Rights Movement and Black Political Socialization." *Political Learning in Adulthood.* Edited by B. S. Sigwel. Chicago: University of Chicago Press, 1989.

Morris, Aldon, and Carol McLurg Mueller, eds. *Frontiers in Social Movement Theory.* New Haven: Yale University Press, 1992.

Morse, Richard M. "The Heritage of Latin America." *The Founding of New Societies.* Edited by Louis Hartz. New York: Harcourt Brace and World, 1964.

Moses, Wilson Jeremiah. *The Golden Age of Black Nationalism, 1850–1925.* New York: Oxford University Press, 1978.

Moura, Clóvis. *Brasil: Raízes do Protesto Negro.* São Paulo: Global, 1983.

"Estratégia do Imobilismo Social Contra o Negro no Mercado de Trabalho." *São Paulo em Perspectiva* 2.2 (April–June 1988).

História do Negro Brasileiro. São Paulo: Atica, 1989.

"Organizações Negras." *São Paulo: O Povo em Movimento.* Edited by Paul Singer and V. Caldeira Brant. Petrópolis: Vozes, 1980.

Rebeliões da Senzala. São Paulo: Livraria Editora Ciências Humanas, 1981.

Moynihan, Daniel P. "Employment, Income, and the Ordeal of the Black Family." *The Negro American.* Edited by Talcott Parsons and Kenneth B. Clark. Boston: Beacon, 1965.

Maximum Feasible Misunderstanding. New York: Free Press, 1969.

Muller, Edward N., and Karl-Dieter Opp. "Rational Choice and Rebellious Collective Action." *American Political Science Review* 80.2 (June 1986).

Mullins, Elizabeth, and Paul Sites. "The Origins of Contemporary Eminent Black Americans." *American Sociological Review* 49 (October 1984).

Myrdal, Gunnar. *An American Dilemma.* New York: Harper and Row, 1944.

"An American Dilemma." *Race* 4.1 (November 1962).

Mzala. *Gatsha Buthelezi: Chief with a Double Agenda.* London: Zed, 1988.

Nabuco, Joaquim. *O. Abolicionismo.* São Paulo, 1938.

Nobles, Melissa. "Responding with Good Sense: The Politics of Race and Census in Contemporary Brazil." Ph.D. dissertation, Yale University, New Haven, 1995.

Nolutshungu, Sam C. *Changing South Africa.* Cape Town: David Philip, 1982.

"Reflections on National Unity in South Africa." *Third World Quarterly* 13.4 (1993).

North, Douglass C. *Institutions, Institutional Change and Economic Performance.* Cambridge: Cambridge University Press, 1990.

Oberschall, Anthony. "Theories of Social Conflict." *Annual Review of Sociology* 41 (1978).

Odendaal, Andre. *Vukani Bantu! The Beginnings of Black Protest Politics in South Africa to 1912.* Cape Town: David Philip. 1984.

O'Donnell, Guillermo. "Challenges to Democratization in Brazil." *World Policy Journal* 5.2 (Spring 1988).

O'Donnell, Guillermo, and Philippe C. Schmitter. *Transitions from Authoritarian Rule: Tentative Conclusions about Uncertain Democracies.* Baltimore: Johns Hopkins University Press, 1986.

Offe, Claus. *Disorganized Capitalism.* Cambridge: MIT Press, 1985.

Oliveira, Clóvis Luis Pereira. "O Negro Sobe ao Palanque." Centro de Recursos Humanos, paper no. 5, Universidade Federal da Bahia, July 1992.

Oliveira, Ney dos Santos. "Favelas and Ghettos." Ph.D. dissertation, Columbia University, New York, 1996.

Oliver, Melvin L., and Thomas M. Shapiro. *Black Wealth/White Wealth.* New York: Routledge, 1995.

Oliver, Pamela, et al. "A Theory of Critical Mass." *American Journal of Sociology* 91.3 (November 1985).

Olzak, Susan. *The Dynamics of Ethnic Competition and Conflict.* Stanford, Calif.: Stanford University Press, 1992.

O'Meara, Dan. *Volkskapitalisme.* Johannesburg: Ravan, 1983.

Omi, Michael, and Howard Winant. *Racial Formation in the United States.* New York: Routledge, 1986.

O'Reilly, Kenneth. *Racial Matters.* New York: Free Press, 1989.

Paige, Jeffrey M. "Political Orientation and Riot Participation." *American Sociological Review* 36 (October 1971).

Pakenham, Thomas. *The Boer War*. New York: Random House, 1979.

Parkin, Frank. *Marxism and Class Theory: A Bourgeois Critique*. New York: Columbia University Press, 1979.

Max Weber. Chichester: Ellis Horwood, 1982.

Parks, Rosa. *Rosa Parks: My Story*. New York: Dial Books, 1992.

Patterson, Orlando. *Slavery and Social Death*. Cambridge, Mass.: Harvard University Press, 1982.

Patterson, Sheila. *Colour and Culture in South Africa*. London: Routledge and Kegan Paul, 1953.

Pettigrew, Thomas F. *Racially Separate or Together?* New York: McGraw-Hill, 1971.

Phillips, Ulrick Bonnell. *The Course of the South to Secession*. New York: Hill and Wang, 1939.

Life and Labor in the Old South. Boston: Little, Brown, 1951.

Pierson, Donald. *Negroes in Brazil*. Chicago: University of Chicago Press, 1942.

Pierson, Paul. "When Effect Becomes Cause." *World Politics* 45 (July 1993).

Poggi, Gianfranco. *The State*. Stanford, Calif.: Stanford University Press, 1990.

Polanyi, Karl. *The Great Transformation*. Beacon: Boston, 1944.

Poliakov, Leon. *The Aryan Myth: A History of Racist and Nationalist Ideas in Europe*. New York: Basic Books, 1971.

Posel, Deborah. *The Making of Apartheid, 1948–1961*. Oxford: Clarendon Press, 1991.

"Rethinking the Race–Class Debate in South African Historiography." *Social Dynamics* 9.1 (1983).

Poulantzas, N. *Political Power and Social Classes*. London: New Left Books, 1973.

Powell, Walter W., and Paul DiMaggio. *The New Institutionalism in Organizational Analysis*. Chicago: University of Chicago Press, 1991.

Prado, Caio, Jr. *The Colonial Background of Modern Brazil*. Berkeley: University of California Press, 1969.

Price, Robert M. *The Apartheid State in Crisis*. New York: Oxford University Press, 1991.

Prucha, Francis Paul. *The Great Father*. Lincoln: University of Nebraska Press, 1984.

Przeworski, Adam. *Capitalism and Social Democracy*. Cambridge: Cambridge University Press, 1985.

Democracy and the Market, Cambridge: Cambridge University Press, 1991.

Quadros, Waldir José de. "O Milagre Brasileiro e a Expansão da Nova Classe Média." Campinas: Instituto de Economia da Universidade Estadual de Campinas, 1991.

Rantete, Johannes, and Hermann Giliomee. "Transition to Democracy Through Transaction?" *African Affairs* 91 (1992).

Raphael, Allison. "Samba and Social Control." Ph.D. dissertation, Columbia University, New York, 1980.

Redkey, Edwin S. *Black Exodus*. New Haven: Yale University Press, 1969.

Reed, Adolph L., Jr. *The Jesse Jackson Phenomenon*. New Haven: Yale University Press, 1986.

Reed, Adolph L., Jr., ed. *Race, Politics and Culture*. New York: Greenwood, 1984.

Reich, Michael. *Racial Inequality*. Princeton: Princeton University Press, 1981.

Reichmann, Rebecca. "Brazil's Denial of Race." *NACLA Report on the Americas* 27.6 (May/June 1995).

Rex, John. "The Plural Society: The South African Case." *Race* 12.4 (1971).

Race Relations in Sociological Theory. London: Routledge and Kegan Paul, 1970.

Rodrigues, Nina. *Os Africanos no Brasil*. São Paulo: Cia Ed. Nacional, 1977.

Roediger, David R. *The Wages of Whiteness*. London: Verso, 1991.

Roett, Riordan. *Brazil: Politics in a Patrimonial Society*. New York: Praeger, 1984.

Rokkan, Stein. "Dimensions of State Formation and Nation-Building." *The Formation of National States in Western Europe*. Edited by Charles Tilly. Princeton: Princeton University Press, 1975.

Roosevelt, Theodore. "Brazil and the Negro." *The Outlook* 106 (21 February 1914).

Rotberg, Robert M. *The Founder*. New York: Oxford University Press, 1988.

Rout, Leslie B., Jr. "The African in Colonial Brazil." *The African Diaspora*. Edited by Martin L. Kilson and Robert I. Rotberg. Cambridge, Mass.: Harvard University Press, 1976.

Russell, D. E. H. *Rebellion, Revolution and Armed Force*. New York: Academic Press, 1974.

Russell-Wood, A. J. R. *The Black Man in Slavery and Freedom in Colonial Brazil*. London: Macmillan, 1982.

"Colonial Brazil." *Neither Slave Nor Free*. Edited by David W. Cohen and Jack P. Greene. Baltimore: Johns Hopkins University Press, 1972.

Said, Edward. *Orientalism*. New York: Random House, 1978.

Samuelson, Robert J. "Riots." *Science* 157 (August 1967), pp. 663–5.

Savage, Michael. "Costs of Enforcing Apartheid and Problems of Change." *African Affairs* 76:304 (1977).

Saxton, Alexander. *The Rise and Fall of the White Republic*. London: Verso, 1990.

Schama, Simon. *The Embarrassment of Riches*. Berkeley: University of California Press, 1988.

Schattschneider, E. E. *Politics, Pressures and Tariffs*. New York: Prentice-Hall, 1935.

The Semisovereign People. Hinsdale, Ill.: Dryden Press, 1960.

Schlesinger, Arthur, Jr. *The Disuniting of America*. New York: Norton, 1992.

Schmitter, Philippe. "Still the Century of Corporatism." *The New Corporatism*. Edited by Frederick B. Pike and Thomas Stritch. Notre Dame, Ind.: University of Notre Dame Press, 1974.

Schneider, Anne, and Helen Ingram. "Social Construction of Target Populations: Implications for Politics and Policy." *American Political Science Review* 87.2 (June 1993).

Schneider, Ben Ross. *Politics Within the State: Elite Bureaucrats and Industrial Policy in Authoritarian Brazil*. Pittsburgh: University of Pittsburgh Press, 1991.

Schram, Sanford F., and J. Patrick Turbett. "Civil Disorder and the Welfare Explosion." *American Sociological Review* 48 (1983).

Schrire, Robert. *Adapt or Die: The End of White Politics in South Africa*. New York: Ford Foundation/Foreign Policy Association, 1991.

Schuman, Howard, and Shirley Hackett. *Black Racial Attitudes*. Ann Arbor: University of Michigan Press, 1974.

Schumpeter, Joseph. *Capitalism, Socialism and Democracy*. New York: Harper, 1947.

Schwartz, Michael. *Radical Protest and Social Structure*. New York: Academic Press, 1976.

Schwartz, Stuart B. "Patterns of Slaveholding in the Americas." *American Historical Review* 87.1 (February 1982).

Slaves, Peasants and Rebels. Urbana: University of Illinois Press, 1992.

Scott, James C. *Weapons of the Weak*. New Haven: Yale University Press, 1985.

Scott, Rebecca J. "Defining the Boundaries of Freedom in the World of Cane." *American Historical Review* (February 1994).

"Exploring the Meaning of Freedom: Postemancipation Societies in Comparative Perspective." *Hispanic American Historical Review* 68.3 (1988).

Sears, David O. "Black Attitudes toward the Political System in the Aftermath of the Watts Insurrection." *Midwest Journal of Political Science* 8.4 (November 1969).

Sears, David O., and John B. McConahay. "Participation in the Los Angeles Riot." *Social Problems* 17.1 (1969).

See, Katherine O'Sullivan, and William Julius Wilson. "Race and Ethnicity." *The Handbook of Sociology*. Edited by Neil J. Smelser. Newbury Park, Calif.: Sage, 1988.

Seidman, Gay. "Fighting for the Rights to be Happy." *Work in Progress* 67 (June 1990).

Manufacturing Militance: Workers' Movements in Brazil and South Africa, 1970–1985. Berkeley: University of California Press, 1994.

Shapiro, Ian. "Democratic Innovation: South Africa in Economic Perspective." *World Politics* 46.1 (October 1993).

Shefter, Martin. "Trade Unions and Political Machines." *Working Class Formation*. Edited by Ira Katznelson and Aristide Zolberg. Princeton: Princeton University Press, 1986.

Shell, Robert. *Children of Bondage*. Hanover, N.H.: University Press of New England, 1994.

Shklar, Judith N. *American Citizenship: The Quest for Inclusion*. Cambridge, Mass.: Harvard University Press, 1991.

Silva, Nelson do Valle. "Black–White Income Differentials: Brazil, 1960." Ph.D. dissertation, University of Michigan, Ann Arbor, 1978.

"Updating the Cost of Not Being White in Brazil." *Race, Class, and Power in Brazil*. Edited by Pierre-Michel Fontaine. Los Angeles: Center for Afro-American Studies, University of California, 1985.

Silva, Nelson do Valle, and Carlos Hasenbalg. *Relações Raciais no Brasil Contemporâneo*. Rio de Janeiro: Rio Fundo Editora, 1992.

Sisk, Timothy D. *Democratization in South Africa*. Princeton: Princeton University Press, 1995.

Skidmore, Thomas E. "Bi-Racial U.S. versus Multi-Racial Brazil: Is the Contrast still Valid?" Conference on Racism and Race Relations in the Countries of the African Diaspora, Rio de Janeiro (June 1992).

Black into White: Race and Nationality in Brazilian Thought. New York: Oxford University Press, 1974.

"Brazilian Intellectuals and the Problem of Race, 1870–1930." Vanderbilt University, Nashville, Occasional Papers Series no. 6 (1969).

"Fact and Myth: An Overview of Afro-Brazilian Studies in Brazil." Kellogg Center Working Paper no. 1, University of Notre Dame (February 1992).

Politics in Brazil, 1930–64, New York: Oxford University Press, 1967.

The Politics of Military Rule in Brazil, 1964–85. New York: Oxford University Press, 1988.

"Race and Class in Brazil." *Race, Class and Power in Brazil*. Edited by Pierre-Michel Fontaine. Los Angeles: Center for Afro-American Studies, University of California, 1985.

"Racial Ideas and Social Policy in Brazil, 1870–1940." *The Idea of Race in Latin America*. Edited by Richard Graham. Austin: University of Texas Press, 1990.

"Toward a Comparative Analysis of Race Relations since Abolition in Brazil and the United States." *Latin American Studies* 4.1 (1972).

Skocpol, Theda. "Bringing the State Back In." *Bringing the State Back In*. Edited by Peter Evans, Dietrich Reuschmeyer, and Theda Skocpol. Cambridge: Cambridge University Press, 1985.

Protecting Soldiers and Mothers. Cambridge, Mass.: Harvard University Press, 1992.

Skocpol, Theda, and Margaret Somers. "The Uses of Comparative History in Macrosocial Inquiry." *Comparative Studies in Society and History* 22.2 (1980).

Skowronek, Stephen. *Building a New American State*. Cambridge: Cambridge University Press, 1982.

Slovo, Joe. "The Negotiations Victory." *African Communist* (Fourth Quarter, 1993).

"The Working Class and Nation-Building." *The National Question in South Africa*. Edited by Maria van Diepen. London: Zed, 1988.

Smith, Iain R. *The Origins of the South African War, 1899–1902*. London: Longman, 1996.

Smith, Rogers M. "Beyond Tocqueville, Myrdal and Hartz: The Multiple Traditions in America." *American Political Science Review* 87.3 (September 1993).

Smuts, Jan. *Greater South Africa*. Johannesburg: Truth Legion, 1940.

Solaun, Mauricio, and Sidney Kronus. *Discrimination with Violence*. New York: Wiley, 1973.

Somers, Margaret R. "Citizenship and the Place of the Public Sphere." *American Sociological Review* 58 (October 1993).

Sommer, Doris. *Foundational Fictions*. Berkeley: University of California Press, 1991.

South African Council of Churches. *Emergency Convocation of Churches*. Johannesburg, 1988.

South African Native Affairs Commission. *Report of the Commission*. Cape Town: Government Printer, 1905.

Sparks, Allister. *Tomorrow is Another Country*. Sandton: Struik, 1995.

"Transition in South Africa." *Program of African Studies News and Events*. Northwestern University, Evanston, Ill. (Winter 1993).

Spilerman, Seymour. "The Causes of Racial Disturbances." *American Sociological Review* 35.4 (August 1970).

"Structural Characteristics of Cities and the Severity of Racial Disorders." *American Sociological Review* 41.5 (October 1976).

Stampp, Kenneth M. *The Causes of the Civil War*. New York: Simon and Schuster, 1959.

The Era of Reconstruction. New York: Random House, 1965.

Starr, Paul. "Social Categories and Claims in the Liberal State." *How Classification Works*. Edited by Mary Douglas and David Hull. Edinburgh: Edinburgh University Press, 1992.

Steinmo, Sven, Kathleen Thielen, and Frank Longstreth. *Structuring Politics*. Cambridge: Cambridge University Press, 1992.

Stepan, Alfred. *Rethinking Military Politics: Brazil and the Southern Cone*. Princeton: Princeton University Press, 1988.

Stepan, Alfred, ed. *Democratizing Brazil*. New York: Oxford University Press, 1989.

Stepan, Nancy. *The Idea of Race in Science: Great Britain 1800–1960*. London: Macmillan, 1982.

Stinchcombe, Arthur. "Social Structure and Politics." *Handbook of Political Science*, vol. 3. Edited by Nelson W. Polsby and Fred Greenstein. Reading: Addison-Wesley, 1975.

Stoller, Ann L. "Making Empire Respectable." *American Ethnologist* 16.4 (November 1989).

Stuckey, Sperling. *Ideological Origins of Black Nationalism*. Boston: Beacon, 1972.

Sundiata, I. K. "Late Twentieth Century Patterns of Race Relations in Brazil and the United States." *Phylon* 48.1 (1987).

Suttner, Raymond, and Jeremy Cronin. *Thirty Years of the Freedom Charter*. Johannesburg: Ravan, 1986.

Tannenbaum, Frank. *Slave and Citizen*. New York: Knopf, 1946.

Tarrow, Sidney. *Power in Movement*. Cambridge: Cambridge University Press, 1994.

"Struggling to Reform." Western Societies Working Paper no. 15 (1983), Cornell University, Ithaca, N.Y.

Taylor, Charles Lewis, and David A. Jodice. *World Handbook of Political and Social Indicators*. New Haven: Yale University Press, 1983.

Taylor, Rupert. "Racial Terminology and the Question of Race in South Africa." Manuscript, 1994.

Teles dos Santos, Jocélio. "Ex-Escrava Porprietária de Escrava." Programa de Estudo do Negro na Bahia. Salvador: Federal University of Bahia, 1991.

Telles, Edward E. "Afro-Brazilian Identity, Mobilization and Segregation." Conference on Racial Politics in Brazil, Austin, Tex. (10 April 1993).

"Residential Segregation by Skin Color in Brazil." *American Sociological Review* 57 (April 1992).

Thompson, E. P. *The Making of the English Working Class*. New York: Knopf, 1966.

Thompson, Leonard. "The Compromise of Union." *The Oxford History of South Africa*, vol. 2. Edited by Monica Wilson and Leonard Thompson. Oxford: Clarendon Press, 1971.

"Cooperation and Conflict: The High Veld." *The Oxford History of South Africa*, vol. 1. Edited by Monica Wilson and Leonard Thompson. New York: Oxford University Press, 1969.

"Great Britain and the Afrikaner Republics." *The Oxford History of South Africa*, vol. 2. Edited by Monica Wilson and Leonard Thompson. Oxford: Clarendon Press, 1971.

A History of South Africa. New Haven: Yale University Press, 1990.

"The South African Dilemma." *The Founding of New Societies*. Edited by Louis Hartz. New York: Harcourt, 1964.

Unification of South Africa. Oxford: Clarendon Press, 1960.

Tilly, Charles. *Coercion, Capital, and European States, AD 990–1992*. Cambridge: Blackwell, 1990.

"How to Detect, Describe and Explain Repertoires of Contention." Center for the Study of Social Change, New School for Social Research, New York. Working paper no. 150 (October 1992).

"Models and Realities of Popular Collective Action." *Social Research* 52.4 (Winter 1985).

Popular Contention in Great Britain, 1758–1834. Cambridge: Harvard University Press, 1995.

"Reflections on the History of European Statemaking." *The Formation of National States in Western Europe.* Edited by Charles Tilly. Princeton: Princeton University Press, 1975.

"To Explain Historical Processes." Center for the Study of Social Change, New School for Social Research, New York. Working Paper no. 168 (July 1993).

Tocqueville, Alexis de. *Democracy in America*, Garden City, N.Y.: Anchor/ Doubleday, 1969.

Toplin, Robert Brent. "Abolition and the Issue of Black Freedmen's Future." *Slavery and Race Relations in Latin America.* Edited by Robert Brent Toplin. Westport, Conn.: Greenwood, 1974.

The Abolition of Slavery in Brazil. New York: Atheneum, 1972.

Trochim, Michael. "The Brazilian Black Guard: Racial Conflict in Post-Abolition Brazil." *The Americas* 44.3 (January 1988).

Ullman, Victor. *Martin Delaney.* Boston: Beacon, 1971.

UNESCO. *Statements on Race and Race Prejudice.* Paris: UNESCO, 1950, 1951, 1964, 1967.

United States Department of Education. *Digest of Educational Statistics.* Washington, D.C.: Government Printing Office, 1988.

United States Supreme Court. *Brown v. Board of Education* 347 (1954).

United States Supreme Court. *Plessy v. Ferguson* 163 (1896).

Vail, Leroy, ed. *The Creation of Tribalism in Southern Africa.* Berkeley: University of California Press, 1989.

Valelly, Richard M. "Party, Coercion, and Inclusion: The Two Reconstructions of the South's Electoral Politics." *Politics and Society* 21.1 (March 1993).

Valente, Lúcia E. F. *Política e Relações Raciais.* São Paulo: FFLCH-USP, 1986.

Van Deburg, William L. *New Day in Babylon.* Chicago: University of Chicago Press, 1992.

Van den Berghe, Pierre. *Race and Racism.* New York: Wiley, 1967.

van den Heever, C. M. *General J. B. M. Hertzog.* Johannesburg: APB Bookstore, 1946.

Verba, Sidney, B. Ahmed, and A. Bhatt. *Caste, Race and Politics.* Beverly Hills: Sage, 1971.

Veríssimo, Carlos. "Genocide in Brazil." *Global Affairs* 2.2 (April–May 1991).

Von Martius, Karl Friedrich Philipp. "Como Se Deve Escrever a História do Brasil." *Revista do Instituto Histórico e Geográfico Brasileiro* 6 (1844).

Wade, Peter. *Blackness and Race Mixing*. Baltimore: Johns Hopkins University Press, 1993.

Wafer, Jim. *The Taste of Blood: Spirit Possession in Brazilian Condomble*. Philadelphia: University of Pennsylvania Press, 1991.

Wagley, Charles. *Race and Class in Rural Brazil*. Paris: UNESCO, 1952.

Wallerstein, Immanuel. *The Modern World-System II*. New York: Academic Press, 1980.

Walshe, Peter. *The Rise of African Nationalism in South Africa*. Berkeley: University of California Press, 1971.

Weber, Max. "Class, Status, Power." *From Max Weber*. Edited by H. H. Gerth and C. Wright Mills. New York: Oxford University Press, 1946.

Webster, Yehudi. *The Racialization of America*. New York: St. Martin's Press, 1992.

Weingast, Barry R. "Institutions and Political Commitment: A New Political Economy of the American Civil War." Manuscript, November 1994.

Weiss, Nancy J. *Farewell to the Party of Lincoln*. Princeton: Princeton University Press, 1983.

   Whitney M. Young, Jr. and the Struggle for Civil Rights. Princeton: Princeton University Press, 1989.

Wiehahn, N. E. *The Complete Wiehahn Report*. Johannesburg: Lex Patria. 1982.

Wilkins, Ivor, and Hans Strydom. *The Super Afrikaners*. Johannesburg: J. Ball, 1978.

Wilkins, Roger M. *A Man's Life*. New York: Simon and Schuster, 1982.

Williams, Basil, ed. *The Shelborne Memorandum*. London: Oxford University Press, 1925.

Williams, Robert F. "Is Violence Necessary to Combat Injustice?" *Eyes on the Prize Reader*. Edited by Clayborne Carson et al. New York: Penguin, 1991.

   Negroes with Guns. New York: Marzani and Munsell, 1962.

Williamson, Joel. *The Crucible of Race*. New York: Oxford University Press, 1984.

   New People. New York: New York University Press, 1984.

   A Rage for Order. New York: Oxford University Press, 1986.

Wills, Garry. *Lincoln at Gettysburg*. New York: Simon and Schuster, 1992.

Wilson, Francis. *Labour in the South African Gold Mines, 1911–1969*. Cambridge: Cambridge University Press, 1972.

Wilson, Monica. "Cooperation and Conflict." *The Oxford History of South Africa*, vol. 1. Edited by Monica Wilson and Leonard Thompson. New York: Oxford University Press, 1969.

Wilson, William Julius. *The Declining Significance of Race*. Chicago: University of Chicago Press, 1978.

   Power, Racism and Privilege. New York: Free Press, 1973.

The Truly Disadvantaged. Chicago: University of Chicago Press, 1987.

Winant, Howard. "Rethinking Race in Brazil." *Journal of Latin American Studies* 24 (1992).

Wofford, Harris L. *Of Kennedys and Kings*. New York: Farrar, Straus and Giroux, 1980.

Wolpe, Harold. "Capitalism and Cheap Labour Power in South Africa." *Economy and Society* 1.4 (November 1972).

Wood, Charles. "Categorias Censitárias e Classificações Subjetivas de Raça no Brasil." *Desigualdade Racial no Brasil Contemporâneo*. Edited by Peggy A. Lovell. Belo Horizonte: MGSP Editores, 1991

Wood, Charles H., and Jose Alberto Magno de Carvalho. *The Demography of Inequality in Brazil*. Cambridge: Cambridge University Press, 1988.

Woodward, C. Vann. "Editor's Introduction." James M. McPherson, *Battle Cry of Freedom*. New York: Oxford University Press, 1988.

Origins of the New South. Baton Rouge: Louisiana State University Press, 1951.

Reunion and Reaction. Boston: Little, Brown, 1951.

The Strange Career of Jim Crow. New York: Oxford University Press, 1957.

Tom Watson: Agrarian Rebel. London: Oxford University Press, 1938.

World Bank, The. *World Tables*. Baltimore: Johns Hopkins University Press, 1989–90.

Wright, Gavin. *Old South, New South: Revolutions in the Southern Economy Since the Civil War*. New York: Basic Books, 1986.

Wright, Lawrence. "One Drop of Blood." *The New Yorker* (25 July 1994).

Wright, Winthrop R. *Café con Leche*. Austin: University of Texas Press, 1990.

Young, Crawford. *The Politics of Cultural Pluralism*. Madison: University of Wisconsin Press, 1976.

Yudelman, David. *The Emergence of Modern South Africa*. Westport, Conn.: Greenwood, 1983.

"Industrialization, Race Relations and Change in South Africa." *African Affairs* 74. 294 (January 1975).

Zimmerman, Ben. "Race Relations." *Race and Class in Rural Brazil*. Edited by Charles Wagley. Paris: UNESCO, 1952.

Zinn, Howard. *SNCC: The New Abolitionists*. Boston: Beacon, 1964.

Zolberg, Aristide. "Moments of Madness." *Politics and Society* 2 (1978).

Index